CITY OF HOPE

JERUSALEM FROM BIBLICAL TO MODERN TIMES

The Memorial Foundation for Jewish Culture

CITY OF HOPE

JERUSALEM FROM BIBLICAL TO MODERN TIMES

MORDECAI NAOR

YAD IZHAK BEN-ZVI   YEDIOTH AHRONOTH   CHEMED BOOKS

Translation - Ethel Broido, Lila M. Korn
Epilogue - Edward Levin
Text Editor - Lila M. Korn
Copy Editor - Michael Glatzer
Visuals Editor - Eyal Ben-Eliahu
Art Advisor - Dr. Shalom Sabar
Editor English language publications - Yohai Goell
Book and Cover Design - Studio Mira Kedar
Artwork - Revital (Tirosh) Viner
Printing - Hamakor Press, Jerusalem

© Copyright by Yad Izhak Ben-Zvi
   Yedioth Ahronoth - Chemed Books

Printed in Israel, 1996

ISBN 965-217-130-1

Contents

Preface

City of Hope originally appeared in Hebrew in June 1995 under the title, "Yerushalayim, Ir Va'am" (Jerusalem, City and People). In Israel it was the first major publication to mark the inauguration of "Jerusalem 3,000" commemorations and was presented to President Ezer Weizman in June 1995. It met with great success, going through several printings totalling tens of thousands of volumes.

The inspiration for City of Hope: Jerusalem from Biblical to Modern Times came from The Memorial Foundation for Jewish Culture and its dedicated Executive Vice President, Dr. Jerry Hochbaum. The guidelines for the book's conception emerged from a conversation between Dr. Hochbaum and Dr. Zvi Zameret, the Director of Yad Izhak Ben-Zvi.

During its decades of work rebuilding and nurturing Jewish culture after the Holocaust, the Memorial Foundation has underwritten works of scholarship and supported young scholars and potential communal leaders. It has supplied Jewish communities worldwide with basic works to bolster proud and informed Jewish identity.

To accomplish the task of assembling the history of Jerusalem, the Memorial Foundation turned to Yad Ben-Zvi, Israel's principle scholarly institute documenting the history of the land of Israel and the history of Jerusalem. Yad Ben-Zvi fosters cross-fertilization of the work of eminent historians, archeologists, philosophers, economists, geographers, and many others. This volume is a digest of this multidisciplinary approach.

A number of fine scholars, whose names appear in the Editorial Board listing, are owed a debt of thanks for their careful oversight and guidance of the progress of the Hebrew volume. In addition, various chapters benefitted from the contributions of Dr. Dan Bahat, Dr. Meir Bar-Asher, Prof. Yehoshua Ben-Arieh, Dr. Gideon Biger, Prof. Amnon Cohen, Dr. Avraham David, Dr. Yosef Drori, Prof. Mordechai Eliav, Hillel Geva, Prof. Moshe Gil, Dr. Menahem Hirshman, Dr. Oded Ir-Shai, Rami Israeli, Prof. B.Z. Kedar, Prof. Aharon Oppenheimer, Prof. Miriam Rosen-Ayalon, Dr. Rehav Rubin, Prof. Zev Safrai, and Dr. Margalit Shiloh.

Advisors who were of inestimable help in preparing the English edition were: Dr. Reuven Amitai-Preiss, Dr. Mordechai Bar-On, Prof. Zev Harvey, Dr. Menahem Hirshman, Dr. Oded Ir-Shai and Prof. Daniel Schwartz.

City of Hope features a scholarly epilogue written by Prof. Menachem Elon, former Deputy President of the Israel Supreme Court and President of the World Congress of Jewish Studies. His article deals with the status of Jerusalem as capital of the Jewish people in Jewish thought and tradition, in periods of independence and of dispersion; and the status of the Temple Mount and united Jerusalem as the capital of the State of Israel in Israeli law and the decisions of the Supreme Court.

A number of dedicated employees of Yad Ben-Zvi made a great contribution to the Hebrew volume. They are Deputy Director Chana Biderman, Eyal Ben-Eliahu, Shlomit Meshulam, Hananel Goldberg, Hava Lion, Ruth Peleg and Sarit Hoch. Recognition is owed to Mira Kedar and Revital (Tirosh) Viner of Mira Kedar Graphic Design Studio, who gave the volume its special 'look,' and worked with great dedication to see this project through.

Introduction

The very mention of Jerusalem evokes a rich brocade of ideas and images in the mind of the western reader. Jerusalem is a place, a symbol, a concept. It is a focus of dreams, prayers and hopes.

Jerusalem plays a powerful role for the three major monotheistic faiths. The challenge of setting down its history is daunting indeed, for account must be made of the passionate emotions it evokes, and as great a task is presented by gaps in the historical record brought about by repeated invasions Jerusalem endured over the centuries, which saw the murder and exile of its inhabitants, the looting of the city and burning of its study halls.

In Israel, Jerusalem's history is being painstakingly documented by scholars with a breathtaking range of expertise. From those who study the city's ancient physical remains, to others steeped in the immense corpus of Jewish literature relating to Jerusalem, and still others who study the writings of the early church fathers and records of the Muslim religious court, the historical record has been enriched in recent decades by a growing body of works which shed light on both the Earthly and Heavenly Jerusalem.

"City of Hope: Jerusalem from Biblical to Modern Times" is the first attempt to bring the fruits of this broad scholarship to a general readership. It offers a multi-faceted account of the city, tracing sequence of events and famous personalities, the course of the city walls and population estimates through the centuries, archeological finds, architectural features, and spiritual and intellectual trends. We hope this volume will be a treat for the eye and mind of the reader, and stimulate a lifetime of interest in Jerusalem.

THE FIRST TEMPLE PERIOD

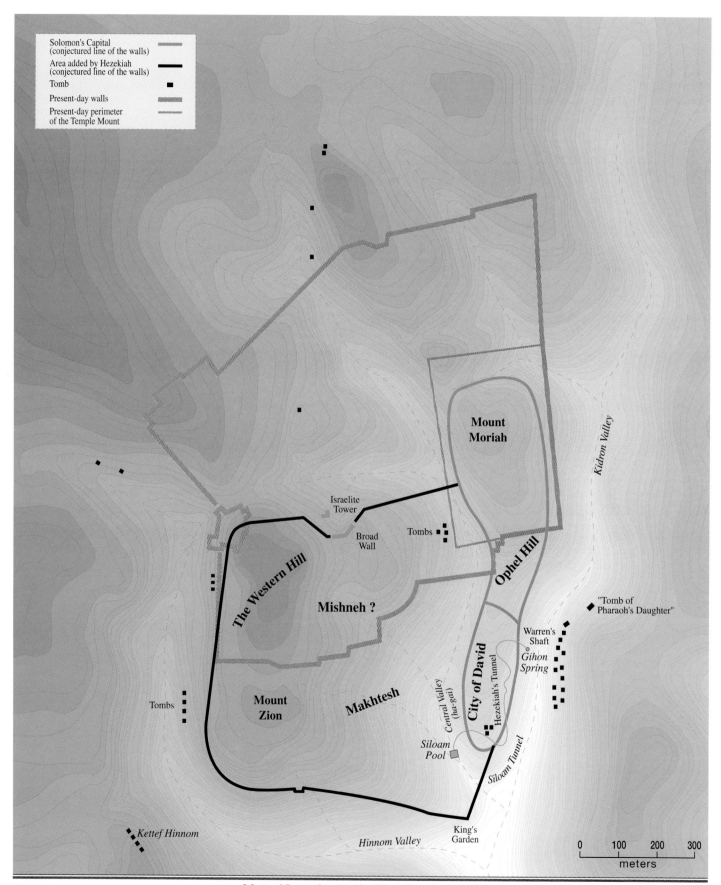

Solomon's Capital
(conjectured line of the walls)

Area added by Hezekiah
(conjectured line of the walls)

Tomb

Present-day walls

Present-day perimeter
of the Temple Mount

Mount
Moriah

Kidron Valley

Israelite
Tower

Broad
Wall

Tombs

Ophel Hill

The Western Hill

Mishneh ?

"Tomb of
Pharaoh's Daughter"

Warren's
Shaft

Gihon
Spring

City of David

Hezekiah's Tunnel

Tombs

Mount
Zion

Makhtesh

Central Valley
(ha-gai)

Siloam Tunnel

Siloam
Pool

Kettef Hinnom

Hinnom Valley

King's
Garden

0   100   200   300

meters

Map of Jerusalem in the First Temple period

Artistic rendering of Jerusalem in its glory in the days of King Solomon. At right the Holy Temple rises above government complex and royal palace. At left City of David and below it entry cave to Gihon Spring.
View from Mt. of Olives looking northwest

The city of Jerusalem is not only the political capital of Israel, it is also and perhaps primarily, a holy city. It has been linked with sanctity and the hallowing of God's name through the ages. Earlier and later Jewish sources – the Bible, legal codes, legends of the Jews and their prayerbook, all reinforce and amplify Jerusalem's sanctity. The city is held sacred by Christianity and Islam as well. In those two religions Jerusalem plays an important role, though in each, cities other than Jerusalem have equal or greater sacred status. For the Jewish people Jerusalem is singular in status, the foremost holy city.

About three thousand years ago David king of Israel made Jerusalem the capital of his kingdom. The city remained both the political and religious capital of the people for many hundreds of years. After a short period of destruction and exile it resumed its position as their capital with the rebuilding of the Temple, and hundreds of years later suffered destruction once more. During subsequent millennia Jerusalem was often conquered. Byzantines, Arabs, Turks, the British and others controlled it. Sometimes it was designated a political capital, while for long periods it was eclipsed politically by other centers. For the Jewish people Jerusalem remained their spiritual capital. In their daily prayer, studies and ceremonies, Jews through the generations reinforced their identification with Jerusalem, accepting the Psalmist's oath, "If I forget you, O Jerusalem, let my right hand forget its cunning, let my tongue stick to my palate if I cease to think of you, if I do not keep Jerusalem in memory even at my happiest hour" (Psalms 137:6).

The process by which Jerusalem became sacred can be traced through the biblical narrative to actions taken by King David. Prior to his reign there is no evidence in the biblical narrative to indicate Jerusalem's sacredness. The Israelites worshiped the Lord in Shechem, Bethel and Hebron among other sites, and Jerusalem was an alien enclave called Jebus, set between the tribal

Remains of Canaanite city wall, near Siloam Pool

territories of Judah and Benjamin. The biblical book of Judges, which describes events prior to David's era, tells of a Levite traveller on the road to Mt. Ephraim who "travelled as far as the vicinity of Jebus – that is, Jerusalem...Towards evening his servant suggested, 'Let us turn aside to this town of the Jebusites and spend the night in it.' The Levite responded, 'We will not turn aside to a town of aliens who are not of Israel, but will continue to Gibeah'" (Judges 19:11).

Many years after that episode, David conquered Jerusalem from the Jebusites and turned it into his capital. His intent to establish the holy character of the city can be seen in two episodes. The first, recounted in II Samuel 6:12-18, was his command that the sacred Ark of the Covenant be brought up to Jerusalem, though at that point there was no permanent home for it. (His son Solomon would later fulfill this aspect of David's

mission.) The second episode concerns the account in II Samuel 24 of the purchase of the threshing floor of Araunah the Jebusite, just outside the north wall of Jerusalem. This would become the site of the Holy Temple, one of whose central functions was to house the Ark. The tale of the purchase indicates the special character of the site. The narrative recounts David's efforts to deliver the Israelites from a plague which had claimed some seventy-seven thousand victims from Dan to Beersheba. David arrested the pestilence – just as the avenging angel reached Araunah's threshing floor – by purchasing the threshing-floor and two oxen from Araunah, and sacrificing the oxen to the glory of God as an act of repentance. Thereupon the plague ceased.

The narrative of David's purchase of the threshing floor closely parallels the biblical account of the Patriarch Abraham's purchase of the Cave of Machpelah in Hebron, and clearly has political significance. David, at that point king of all he surveyed, still insisted on purchasing in a straightforward legal transaction the site on which the Holy Temple would be built.

The hill on which the threshing floor stood was incorporated within the walls of Jerusalem, and the Holy Temple was built upon it by David's son and heir, Solomon. The resplendant building, site of a daily cycle of ritual and sacrificial services, was dedicated in an impressive ceremony. The Temple imparted the ultimate validity to the holiness of Jerusalem, which David had done much to establish as a political capital. Under Solomon, the city also became a thriving economic center. After Solomon's death, the rebel Jeroboam son of Nebat understood the significance of the focus upon Jerusalem. His rebellion culminated in the division of the kingdom. He immediately set up rival ritualist centers in Bethel and Dan in order to draw the attention of the northern inhabitants away from Jerusalem. The choice of Bethel and Dan was hardly accidental; it served to recall earlier times, prior to David's conquest of Jerusalem, when Israelite religious practices were carried out in a decentralized manner at these two sites among others. The biblical narrative makes it clear that many northern inhabitants accepted the refocusing of religious attention away from Jerusalem, however in Judah, the city's central sanctity endured, and the view developed that Jerusalem's sanctity could be traced back to the days of Abraham the Patriarch.

An echo of the connection between Jerusalem and Abraham may be found in two episodes in the book of Genesis. The first tells of the meeting with Melchizedek king of Salem (traditionally identified as Jerusalem). Abraham appears as a hero, and Melchizedek blesses him: "Blessed be Abram of God most high, Creator of heaven and earth. And blessed be God Most High, Who had delivered your foes into your hand" (Gen.14:19-20). The account of Melchizedek's blessing suggests the basis for setting the sanctity of Jerusalem before Jewish settlement, in that it indicates the Lord was worshiped in Salem in Abraham's time.

The second story is the well-known tale of the binding of Isaac. The account in Genesis 17 locates the site of God's testing of Abraham on a mountain in the land of Moriah. The name Moriah appears in II Chronicles 2:1. There the Temple Mount is identified with Mt. Moriah.

The common identity established in Chronicles between the Temple Mount and Mt. Moriah brings together the two elements concerning the sanctification of Jerusalem: the one of King David's time and the other linked to Abraham.

Jerusalem Becomes the Capital

David first assumed the monarchy in Hebron in approximately 1010 B.C.E. The biblical narrative lends itself to the following modern political analysis. David wanted to establish an entirely new capital, as not a few rulers did elsewhere in the ancient Near East. Like them, David wanted his capital to be linked with his own name and dynasty, and wanted to further solidify control by establishing in the city a permanent temple to his God. An ancient Israelite concept held that the Lord does not choose a single family to rule over his people and does not choose one site as His permanent dwelling place. David therefore needed religious legitimacy for his dynasty, and this was provided by the prophet Nathan's

'The Binding of Isaac' on Mount Moriah. Illumination from the Breslau Mahzor (festival prayer book) early fourteenth century

5

David strums his harp. Illuminated initial word panel for the Book of Psalms. Rothschild Miscellany, Italy ca. 1470

vision in which the Lord promises David that he will rule the kingdom forever.

Further political analysis cites David's ascension to the throne after a bitter conflict with the House of Saul. King Saul had chosen a capital on a nearby hill within the tribal portion of Benjamin. Jerusalem, located just south of Saul's capital in an area which did not belong to any one tribe, was both geographically central and suited to David's political purpose of healing and unification. It could physically reinforce the unifying character of his kingdom and moderate the former organizational pattern along tribal lines.

If Jerusalem's political advantage was apparent, its natural assets as a capital were distinctly less than ideal. Scholars cite four criteria for the success of an ancient urban settlement: favorable defense conditions, ample water supply, an approximately one mile radius of arable land, and location on major trade crossroads. Jerusalem

The southeastern hill upon which the City of David stood. At right, the Kidron Valley. At left, the Central Valley which later in the First Temple period divided the City of David hill from the Western Hill

'Yachin and Boaz,' the two pillars at the entrance to the Holy Temple, depicted in embroidery on an ark cover. Germany 1783

was well, but not ideally, suited for defense in time of war. Its location in rocky, hilly terrain and its proximity to the desert caused it to fall short of the criteria for fertile land. It was not located on a trade crossroads, but stood at a distance from the major north-south and east-west trade routes. Finally, its water resources were not abundant. The city was built on the saddle of a hill above the Gihon Spring, the only truly proximate source of water. The Gihon flowed abundantly throughout the year and could supply the needs of a small community. Another spring, En-rogel, was at a greater distance from the town, which rendered it of some use in agriculture but useless in wartime. Whenever in history Jerusalem thrived, it did so despite, not because of its geographical characteristics. Beginning with David and Solomon, Jerusalem in its prime moments was supported by all the inhabitants of the land, and often by many who lived well beyond its borders.

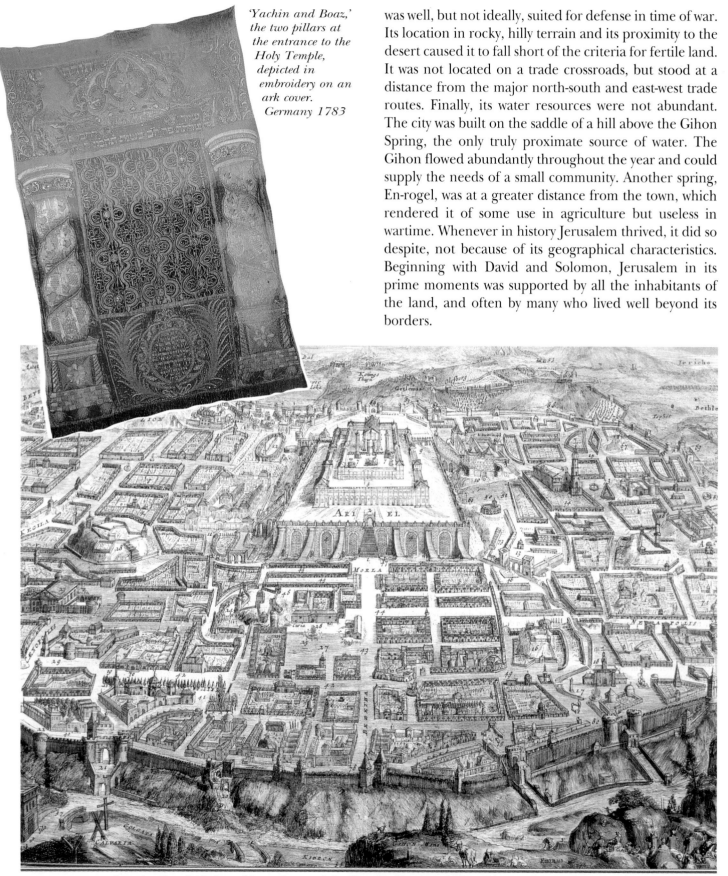

Imaginative depiction of Jerusalem and the Temple. Romeyn de Hoogh map, Amsterdam 1715

David's Jerusalem covered some ten acres in the area known today as The City of David. It was on an elongated hill atop the source of the Gihon Spring, just south of today's Old City wall. Scholars are of the opinion that Jerusalem had about a thousand inhabitants in David's time.

The Temple

Jerusalem underwent great change during the reign of David's son, Solomon. He cultivated the city's regal image as well as its role as a religious and national center. Buildings, chief among them a new royal palace, were constructed in the area just north of the former city boundary, and the city expanded northward to include the hill of Araunah's threshing floor, designated as the Temple Mount. The two hills and a fill area between them, were encompassed by city walls.

The crowning achievement of Solomon's great construction enterprise was the Holy Temple. The Temple was a place for sacrificial worship, prayer, and rites of thanksgiving. From the biblical books of Kings and Chronicles, a glimpse emerges of the beauty of the Temple's large hewn stones, carved gilded beams and luxurious imported wood. The Bible recounts details of the construction, and the crews of masons and thousands of laborers who worked for

Thumbsize ivory pomegranate bears the carved inscription, 'Belonging to the Tem(ple of the Lor)d, holy to the priests.' This artifact may come from Solomon's Temple. Israel Museum, Jerusalem

seven years to complete the structure. The building was divided into three sections: the *ulam*, Portico or Great Hall; the *heikhal*, an enclosure for ritual service; and the *dvir* (alt. *kodesh kodashim*) the Holy of Holies or Shrine in which the Ark of the Covenant stood, concealed from view. There were also storage areas and a treasury. At the buildings outer entrance were two columns, Yachin and Boaz. The scent of incense pervaded the interior, rising from two altars. A small altar of cedarwood coated with gold stood before the Holy of Holies, while the main sacrificial altar stood outside, in the Temple courtyard.

Construction of the Temple took thirteen years. Its dedication was celebrated with great solemnity in the presence of a massive audience. Solomon summoned the elders of Israel, the heads of the tribes, to escort the priests bringing up the Ark of the Covenant (I Kings, 8:1-2) to its place "beneath the wings of the cherubim, in the Shrine of the House, in the Holy of Holies." King Solomon and all the guests walked before the Ark. As the narrative describes the scene, a cloud filled the House, and the priests had to leave. The cloud represented the presence of God. Solomon declared, (I Kings 8:12-13) "The Lord has chosen to abide in a thick cloud; I have now built for You a stately House, a place where You may dwell forever."

In his prayer, Solomon went on to review the sacred history that led to the great day: the covenantal relationship between the invisible, law-giving God and the people of Israel, God's promise to perpetuate the Davidic line in association with Jerusalem and the Temple, and the role of the Temple as a place to beseech God, who is asked to "give heed and pardon" (Kings 8:30). This is an indication of the religious and national value of the Temple – the place where the Israelites would pray to God whenever a nationwide catastrophe would affect them (famine, plague, or danger from an enemy). Solomon's prayer also expressed the hope that the Temple would serve as a place of prayer for all nations, an idea that would be repeated by the prophet: "For My House shall be called a house of prayer for all peoples" (Isaiah 56:7).

Royal City, Sacred City

The biblical narrative lends itself to a modern analysis of Solomon's reign as the time when the ideology of Chosen Dynasty and Chosen House (of worship) came to be linked. This linkage, already seen in ancient Sumerian literature, is found in records of the Mesopotamian royal courts as well. It appears in biblical literature in eloquent form in several books of the Prophets and in the Psalms.

Among the common themes with other ancient ideologies are the image of the sacred city to which nations and kings flock to bring gifts and obeisance, the temple city atop the hill, and the temple city as the center of the world. One biblical example of these themes can be seen in the text of Isaiah: "In the days to come, the Mount of the Lord's House shall stand firm above the mountains...and all the nations shall gaze on it with joy. And the many peoples shall go and say: 'Come, let us go up to the Mount of the Lord...'" (Isaiah 2:2).

Ancient Israelite prophecy linked some unique concepts with Jerusalem and the Holy Temple. One example is the connection between the holy city and the hope for peace. One instance of many is found in Isaiah 33:20: "When you gaze upon Zion, our city of assembly, your eyes shall behold Jerusalem as a secure homestead, a tent not to be transported, whose pegs shall never be pulled up..."

Another unique concept of Jerusalem is that which links the city with faith in the One God and the rejection of idolatry: "O Lord, my strength and my stronghold, my refuge in day of trouble. To you nations shall come from the ends of the earth and say: Our fathers inherited utter delusions, things that are futile and worthless. Can a man make gods for himself?" (Jeremiah 16:19-20)

The ancient city of Jerusalem so movingly alluded to in religious metaphor, had an everyday material life and appearance. It covered an area of about thirty acres during Solomon's reign, and is thought to have held some three thousand inhabitants. On the southern end of the Temple Mount, outside the Temple enclosure, stood the center of government. It consisted of a number of impressive buildings: the Hall of Columns, probably the antechamber to the royal court; the Throne Room where the king sat in judgment over his people; the Lebanese Forest House where the royal treasure was kept, and the Royal Palace (I Kings, chapters 8-9).

Jerusalem served as the capital of a large country in Solomon's day. Solomon had statesmanlike acumen and forged significant diplomatic contacts, making pacts with a series of kings. He married Gentile women and through these unions strengthened his bonds with foreign countries. His foremost diplomatic marriage was to the daughter of the pharoah of Egypt. Pharoahs did not ordinarily offer their daughters to foreign royalty. In Jerusalem, Pharoah's daughter was given her own palace.

Solomon was on particularly good terms with King Hiram of Tyre, who supplied the cedars of Lebanon used in the Temple's construction and sent professional builders to help with that monumental project. Jerusalem received many royal visitors. The brief biblical account of the Queen of Sheba's visit has been augmented over time by legendary material. The biblical text is indicative of the Solomonic kingdom's widespread economic contacts.

The Divided Kingdom

The biblical narrative links the people of Israel's security within their boundaries with faithfulness to God and loyalty to David and Solomon, His servants. A modernist's understanding of the politics and security of the kingdom dwells more upon evidence of political conditions of the ancient Near East. In this view, the growth of the Davidic and Solomonic kingdom was made possible by the absence of strong powers in the area. Egypt was riven by internal strife; Assyria was still contained within its borders and the Aramean kingdoms in Syria had been defeated by David. Towards the end of Solomon's reign there was a change in the balance of power: in Egypt King Shishak began to extend his sovereignty in the direction of Palestine; Aram-Damascus rebelled; and on the horizon, Assyria began to display interest in Syria-Palestine. This was the threshold of a period of invasions and pacts with various political powers, particularly Mesopotamia and Egypt.

With the division of the kingdom at the beginning of the reign of Solomon's son Rehoboam (ca. 928 B.C.E.) Jerusalem's glory was somewhat reduced. The northern tribes rebelled over the issue of the preferential status accorded to the tribe of Judah. Two states arose where once Solomon's united kingdom had stood – the northern Kingdom of Israel and the southern Kingdom of Judah. For the next three hundred and fifty years Jerusalem was capital of the southern kingdom, which consisted mainly of the tribal territories of Judah and Simon. Jerusalem's status was undermined when, as mentioned earlier, the rebel Jeroboam set up two rival ritual centers in Bethel and Dan. These centers competed with Jerusalem, which had only been the capital for two generations prior to the division of the kingdom. Simultaneously, the kingdom of Judah became involved in wars which depleted its resources. The biblical narrative recounts instances when Temple treasures were given to various foreign rulers.

During the period of the divided kingdom several kings of Judah fortified Jerusalem, enlarged the Temple and took steps to advance its central status. With the destruction by Assyria of the northern kingdom and the rival cultic centers, Jerusalem became the religious and national focus of the entire Israelite nation. The daily Temple services were augmented by grand ceremonials during the pilgrimage festivals, when many additional worshipers came up to the city. Echoes of the exalted mood of these occasions appear in the book of Psalms: "Our feet stood inside your gates, O Jerusalem, Jerusalem built up, a city knit together, to which tribes would make pilgrimage... to praise the name of the Lord. There the thrones of judgment stood, thrones of the house of David. Pray for the well-being of Jerusalem; May those who love you be at peace..." (Psalms 122).

"A song of ascent to David. I was happy when they said, let us go to the House of God."
Modern depiction of Jews ascending to Jerusalem during a pilgrimage festival. Artist, Shalom of Safed

Until 1967 the question of Jerusalem's physical proportions during the First Temple period divided biblical archeologists. One group of scholars, 'the minimalists,' postulated that the city walls encompassed only the Eastern Hill, including the City of David and the Temple Mount. According to this view the city would have encompassed approximately sixty acres. The other school of archeologists, 'the maximalists,' claimed that Jerusalem in the late First Temple period included the aforementioned areas and had expanded to include the area near the Pool of Siloam and the *Mishneh* and *Makhtesh* quarters on the Western Hill. This would have put the city's area at about one hundred and fifty acres, a more suitable size for a capital city. Archeological excavations carried out after the Six-Day War of June 1967 revealed remnants of First Temple era city walls and defense towers on the Western Hill, thus substantiating the view of 'the maximalists.' The ancient city had indeed outgrown the original ridge on which it was founded.

Above: Siloam Pool and Tunnel entrance
Below: The Siloam Inscription, late eighth century B.C.E.
was discovered fixed to the tunnel wall, and is now in the
Archeological Museum, Istanbul, Turkey

The Reign of Hezekiah

During the reign of King Hezekiah of Judah, the kingdom of Israel came to an end and the territory was incorporated into the Assyrian provincial system. Jerusalem became the one remaining spiritual and national center in the land. Hezekiah tried to extend protection and influence over the inhabitants who had not been exiled. He invited the survivors to come on pilgrimage to Jerusalem and participate in the Passover festival. During his reign Hezekiah expended great effort to purify the country of practices which might lead to syncretism, such as revering the image of a copper snake (see II Kings 18:3-4). Hezekiah was committed to strengthening the nation's attachment to the Davidic dynasty, Jerusalem, and the Temple. He abolished the 'high places', sites outside Jerusalem which were the inappropriate scenes of sacrifices to the God of Israel. Hezekiah was influenced by the great classical prophet Isaiah, who prophesied in Jerusalem during his reign, passionately advocating social justice, extolling the role of the Davidic dynasty (Isaiah 11:1) and the Temple in Jerusalem, where, in the End of Days, "instruction shall come forth from Zion, the word of the Lord from Jerusalem." According to Proverbs 25:1, during Hezekiah's reign a significant effort was undertaken to record the literary-cultural heritage of the people. The Proverbs of Solomon were copied down by Hezekiah's scribes.

Another of Hezekiah's achievements was the strengthening of Jerusalem's fortifications and repair of its walls, as well as the addition of another wall, which connected the Western Hill (the *Mishneh*) with the Eastern Hill. In modern day Israel Hezekiah's name is perhaps best known for one of his achievements, the water project he commissioned in order to render the waters of the Gihon Spring accessible to Jeruslemites in wartime, while hiding them from the enemy. The water tunnel was discovered in the nineteenth century, and today a walk through its waters provides a living encounter with the Bible.

Hezekiah's effort regarding the tunnel is depicted briefly in the Bible: "The other events of Hezekiah's reign, and all his exploits, and how he made the pool and the conduit and brought water into the city, are recorded in the Annals of the Kings of Judah" (II Kings 20:20).

An ancient Hebrew inscription was found in the tunnel, whose text describes the meeting of two teams of tunnelers who had begun their work at opposite ends of the tunnel's course. Their marvel at their feat of meeting one another is understandable in view of the engineering techniques available at the time. The inscription seems to indicate that the diggers followed a natural, water-created fissure in the rock, and in this manner managed to meet one another. The inscription further states that the length of the tunnel was 1200 cubits, that is, more than 1,800 feet, and that the tunnel lay more than 150 feet beneath the surface.

The fortified area of Jerusalem during Hezekiah's reign covered some one hundred and fifty acres, encompassing the entire Western Hill. Its population is estimated at fifteen to twenty thousand inhabitants, and it was the prime city in the Kingdom of Judah. Jerusalem's economy was based on its spiritual and political singularity and on a thriving agricultural hinterland. It enjoyed an appreciable prosperity which declined towards the end of the eighth and beginning of the seventh centuries B.C.E, when Sennacherib king of Assyria besieged it.

Sennacherib's Siege and its Surprising End

In 722-720 B.C.E. Assyria conquered the northern Kingdom of Israel and exiled its inhabitants. This cataclysm has been preserved in Jewish national memory as the exile and wandering of the Ten Lost Tribes. Actually, a considerable number apparently escaped southward to the neighboring kingdom of Judah. Some scholars attribute the growth of Jerusalem towards the end of the eighth century B.C.E. to an influx of these refugees.

King Hezekiah of Judah had long tried to avoid a conflict with the Assyrians, but changed his mind in 705 B.C.E. after hearing that Assyria had experienced a series of upheavals including the death in battle of its king, Sargon, and the rebellion of the Chaldean ruler of Babylonia in the eastern area of the Assyrian empire. Hezekiah allied himself with kings of lands in the western reaches of the Assyrian empire. Two of his allies were Sidqa of Ashkelon and Luli of Sidon. The text of II Kings

20:12 indicates that Hezekiah may have coordinated the rebellion with the Chaldean king of Babylonia. Sennacherib, the new Assyrian king, suppressed the uprising in Babylonia and turned westward in 701 B.C.E. first attacking Hezekiah's allies. The Phoenician coastal cities surrendered and their ruler fled to Cyprus. Sidqa king of Ashkelon was captured. An Egyptian army came to the rebels' aid and a decisive battle was fought in the plain of Eltekeh near present-day Yavne. The Assyrians emerged victorious. Now it was the turn of the Kingdom of Judah, and prospects were not good. Sennacherib's chronicler tells how Assyrian forces plundered 46 Judean cities, and deporting the inhabitants.

Sennacherib's prism inscription contains an account of his campaign in Judah and siege of Jerusalem

A Roman period stone quarry at the southern end of the City of David hill. In it were discovered caves believed, in the early twentieth century, to be the burial sites of the royal house of David

The Assyrian army laid siege to Jerusalem and demanded its surrender. The prophet Isaiah urged King Hezekiah not to submit: "Assuredly, thus said the Lord concerning the king of Assyria: He shall not enter this city: He shall not shoot an arrow at it, or advance upon it with a shield, or pile up a siege mound against it. He shall go back by the way he came..." (II Kings 19:32). Sennacherib did not take Jerusalem. The biblical account tells how an angel of the Lord slew one hundred eighty thousand Assyrian soldiers in one night. In the Sennacherib inscriptions it is recorded that the king returned to his country after receiving heavy tribute from Hezekiah and taking his cities. From most of the sources, including both biblical and Assyrian, two facts emerge: Jerusalem was not captured by Sennacherib, but Hezekiah capitulated to the king of Assyria, who imposed

a heavy tax on him. In order to pay the tax, Hezekiah took all the gold and silver from the royal treasures as well as from the Temple and even removed the silver-plating from its doors. The blow suffered by Judah and Jerusalem as a result of Sennacherib's campaign was a lasting one, felt until the Babylonian conquest a hundred years later. However, the fact that Jerusalem was not captured enhanced its special aura and led many to the mistaken belief that the city was invincible.

The Reign of Josiah

The increasing spiritual and national importance of Jerusalem which began in Hezekiah's time became more evident during the reign of Josiah, whose era was the last glorious epoch of the kingdom of Judah. Josiah's rule began after a difficult period, both politically and religiously. Judah was a vassal state of the Assyrian empire. Josiah began his rule at the tender age of eight and decided in his eighteenth regnal year to "cleanse the land and the Temple" of idolatry. By his order the Temple was renovated and in the course of the work a dramatic discovery was made, "a scroll of the Lord's Teaching" (II Chron. 34:14). Most scholars agree that the scroll was the biblical book of Deuteronomy, an often eloquent work structured in the form of a covenant. It stresses the absolute prohibition of the worship of God anywhere except in the place chosen by God. Josiah read the scroll aloud to his people, and proceeded with the elimination of idolatrous practices from his kingdom. All altars and small temples in Judah were destroyed and the priests of the 'high places' were brought to Jerusalem and not permitted to conduct sacrificial ritual. People in the provincial areas were left with no choice but to go to

Jerusalem on pilgrimage. Josiah's greatest achievement was centralizing the site of the sacrificial rituals, turning Jerusalem into the people's sole ritual and spiritual focus.

The crowning glory of Josiah's reform was the covenant made with God "to follow the Lord and observe His commandments, His injunctions and His laws... to fulfill all the terms of the covenant written in this scroll" (II Chronicles 34:31). In this context there was a particularly heartfelt celebration of the Passover festival, with masses of people descending upon Jerusalem in pilgrimage. "Since the time of the prophet Samuel, no Passover like that one had ever been kept in Israel; none of the kings... had kept a Passover like the one kept by Josiah and the priests and Levites and all Judah and Israel there present, and the inhabitants of Jerusalem" (II Chronicles 35:18).

Josiah's reforms had profound religious significance. From that time forward, monotheism as practiced by the people of Israel was understood to mean not only

Nebuchadnezzar besieges and conquers Jerusalem. From the Augustin Calmet map, 1711

Illuminated manuscript of the biblical Scroll of Lamentations. Nebuchadnezzar riding a lion approaches Jerusalem. Kalonymus Bible, southern Germany, 1238 C.E.

adherence to a grand abstract concept, but performance of law and ritual as well, with emphasis on ritual as practiced in the Temple in Jerusalem.

After Josiah's death in 609 B.C.E., conditions in the kingdom of Judah began to deteriorate. Far away, Babylonia overtook Assyria as the next great Mesopotamian empire. Babylonia adopted Assyrian policy towards Jerusalem.

The Destruction of Jerusalem

The last kings of Judah did not quite understand the political developments of their time, and made a number of unwise alliances. In response to the rebellion of Judah's King Jehoiakim, Nebuchadnezzar king of Babylonia sent a punitive force against Judah in 598 B.C.E. and laid siege to Jerusalem. King Jehoiachin, who

ruled Judah for only three months, surrendered and was deported to Babylon together with his kingdom's social elite and its political and military leadership.

The Babylonian king chose Zedekiah, Jehoiachin's uncle, to rule over the already weakened kingdom of Judah. The next ten years were the last of the Davidic dynasty's role in Jerusalem, and they were marked by poor leadership. The expulsion of Judah's social, political and military elite led to decline. King Zedekiah, weak and hesitant, was essentially a regent appointed by the Babylonians, yet he decided to defy his master and thus brought catastrophe on his kingdom. The exhortations of the prophet Jeremiah, who warned him not to take up arms against Babylonia, were to no avail. Zedekiah rose up against the king of Babylonia, relying on promises of support from Egypt. In 588 B.C.E. Babylonian armies once again invaded Judah. Though Zedekiah's Egyptian ally sent help, it was to no avail. Nebuchadnezzar mounted a campaign of destruction against the fortified cities of Judah and then proceeded to Jerusalem. Archeological research has unearthed evidence of the destruction of Judah's fortified cities. A group of ostraca (notes written on pottery sherds) known as the Lachish letters, describe the last days of the fortress cities Lachish and Azekah during this era.

The true end of the kingdom of Judah came with the destruction of Jerusalem and the Holy Temple. Babylonian soldiers surrounded Jerusalem for a protracted siege, building ramparts and moving up siege machines to the city walls. In spite of the fearsome effect that must have been created by all this military preparation, it appears that the famine endured by Jerusalem's besieged inhabitants was the most effective means of achieving their submission. The Babylonian assault eventually came from the north, a side of Jerusalem difficult to defend owing to its level topography. In the summer of 586 B.C.E. Jerusalem's walls were breached. King Zedekiah tried to flee, was caught and taken as a prisoner to Babylonia. Babylonian soldiers ran amok in Jerusalem, killing and plundering. A month later, between the seventh and the tenth days of the month of Av, they laid waste to the city, set fire to the walls and demolished the Holy Temple. The king's treasury and the Temple were sacked, and many precious objects from the Temple were brought to Babylon as a victory display. Jerusalem of the Davidic dynasty, which had stood on its hill since David made the city his capital, was a ruin.

The fate of the survivors is described in several biblical works. It is a tale of wandering in the countryside, flight from wild beasts (the walled cities having been destroyed) and death by plague. Most of the surviving inhabitants of Jerusalem and Judah were exiled to Babylon "where they were servants to him [Nebuchadnezzar] and his sons until the reign of the kingdom of Persia" (II Chron. 36:20). Only poor Judeans were left behind to farm. These gloomy descriptions serve as the background to the Scroll of Lamentations which mourns the destruction of the city that was "full of people... great among the nations," and which now stood lonely and destroyed, stripped of its Temple, bereft of its worshippers on festivals and Sabbath.

Jerusalem in the Visions of the Prophets and in the Psalms

The Book of Lamentations voices the hope of a return to God, His embrace of His people, and the restoration of Jerusalem. Jerusalem became the central symbol of the Jewish people's spiritual and physical salvation, and of their independence. The books of Isaiah and Micah have as central motifs visions of the Redemption and the End of Days in which Jerusalem plays an important part ("For instruction shall come forth from Zion, the word of the Lord from Jerusalem," Micah 4:2). In the prophetic literature Jerusalem also plays a part in the downfall of nations who threaten to destroy the people of Israel. In Zachariah 12:2 Jerusalem is described as "a bowl of reeling for the peoples all around." The Mt. of Olives will be the scene of a critical battle after which survivors from among the enemy nations will come peacefully to Jerusalem to celebrate the Sukkot (Tabernacles) festival. The tranquil presence of elderly people on the streets of Jerusalem is a prophetic image symbolizing the Redemption.

Jerusalem appears prominently in the Book of Psalms. The city serves as a central focal point and endless praises are sung to it. It is "the joy of the whole earth" (Psalms 48:2) and a place of exceptional beauty. The blessing, "May the Lord bless you from Zion; may you share the prosperity of Jerusalem all the days of your life, and live

to see your children's children. May all be well with Israel," (Psalms 128:5) has long been the benediction of choice for Jews on a day of great happiness. Numerous citations of Jerusalem from the Psalms were eventually incorporated into the prayerbook of the Jews, which absorbed the conception of the city as predominant symbol of the people's hopes and yearning for salvation.

Jerusalem also resounds through Christian liturgy, owing to the patterning of that liturgy on Jewish sources, in particular Psalms.

Archeological Finds

Archeological excavations carried out in Jerusalem from the mid-nineteenth century onward have unearthed many finds of the First Temple period and earlier. Intense archeological excavation since 1967 has revealed several large sections of the ancient city. These discoveries provide a fresh perspective on Jerusalem of the First Temple period, distinct from the biblical focus on the religious and moral development of the people. They offer a glimpse of the material culture of ancient Jerusalemites, their everyday tools, needs and activities. Finds include fortifications, water-works, palaces and other dwellings, tools for daily use and for ritual purposes, inscriptions, seals and weights, and cosmetic accessories.

The prophet Jeremiah laments the destruction of Jerusalem, as depicted by the sixteenth century Dutch master Rembrandt van Rijn

Water supply was an important issue in ancient Jerusalem. Remains of waterworks have been found, the best known of which is the Siloam Tunnel, mentioned earlier in this chapter. A tower was found opposite the Gihon spring, attached to the ancient wall, through which people evidently went down to draw water from the spring. The biblical Book of Nehemiah mentions a certain "Gate of the Fountain" in the wall, and modern scholars think this tower served a similar function to the one mentioned by Nehemiah.

A more sophisticated ancient engineering enterprise is Warren's Shaft, named for Captain Charles Warren, the British archaeologist who discovered the shaft, or vertical tunnel, which was reached via a long stepped tunnel whose entrance was within the ancient city. The shaft descended into the mountain, to the Gihon Spring. This carved shaft made it possible for First Temple Jerusalemites to draw water from the spring unobserved by an enemy outside the city.

In recent years the City of David archeological site has provided a wealth of material remains of life during and prior to the First Temple period. Above the Gihon Spring, remains of city walls from the Canaanite period (the eighteenth century B.C.E.) have been found. Sections of walls have been revealed dating from the age of the Israelite monarchy. Completion of the walls is credited in the biblical account to Solomon, who "finished building his palace, and the House of the Lord, and the walls around Jerusalem" (I Kings 3:1). Excavations have also revealed residential buildings built against the walls and into corner tower fortifications of the city from the final days of the kingdom of Judah.

At the City of David archeological sites, there have been major finds from the seventh and sixth centuries

Descent toward Warren's Shaft is by steps carved into the bedrock

B.C.E. which include corroborating evidence of the biblical account of the destruction of Jerusalem by the Babylonians. Fire clearly destroyed buildings and buried their rich interior furnishings and other items in layers of ash. Innumerable arrowheads were found, confirming that battles took place on the walls. At one site, forty-nine clay bulae (signature seal-impressions used to seal papyrus documents) were found. Some of the bulae bear the titles of highly-placed officials of the latter days of the Kingdom of Judah, such as "the king's son" and "(the one) in charge of the palace."

At the City of David site, other finds include ostraca, whole pottery objects, and hundreds of figurines, mostly of women and animals. The figurines are evidence of pagan-influenced ritual which was practiced in Jerusalem within sight of the Temple Mount. This is corroboration of a situation decried many times in the biblical narrative.

At quite a distance from the City of David site, in the Jewish Quarter of modern Jerusalem's Old City, large structural finds dating to the late First Temple period were unearthed. A section of a broad wall and a defense tower were built during King Hezekiah's reign to

Bulae (clay seal-impressions) found in the City of David archeological excavations

*The Broad Wall, late First Temple period, as it appeared when it was uncovered in 1968. Its discovery resolved
a long-standing question concerning the area encompassed by late First Temple period Jerusalem*

Rolled silver scroll from First Temple period, with the Bible's priestly blessing engraved on it, found in a burial cave overlooking the Hinnom Valley

strengthen the defenses of his upper city, the *Mishneh,* against Assyrian attack. As was mentioned earlier, these finds proved that Jerusalem of the First Temple period had grown dramatically in size and population. The course of the Broad Wall clearly took precedence over pre-existing housing, lending support to the biblical account of Hezekiah's rushed effort to strengthen his city.

A third area in which remnants of First Temple residential structures have been found lies beyond today's Zion Gate, near the Dormition Abbey. This indicates the extent to which the Western Hill was inhabited.

Ancient burial caves provide information about the beliefs and cultural practices of First Temple period Jerusalemites. The location

of these caves also provides evidence of the size of Jerusalem at different stages of the First Temple period. Since the dead could not be laid to rest within the city, burial caves were located just outside the city limits, thus enabling scholars to roughly outline the city boundaries. There are early burial caves on the slopes of the Kidron Valley to ancient Jerusalem's east, and the Hinnom Valley to its south and west. After the city's expansion to the Western Hill, burial had to be stopped in that area, and was extended northward beyond today's Damascus Gate. First Temple period burial caves were usually subject to plunder over many centuries. In spite of this, archeologists have good reason to continue investigating them. One of the most important finds in biblical archeology was made in a burial cave: a small, rolled silver scroll on which was inscribed the oldest known text of a biblical verse. Its inscription is perhaps an appropriate close to this chapter, whose historical account closes by detailing Jerusalem's destruction and the hope for better days: "The Lord Bless you and protect you! The Lord deal kindly and graciously with you! The Lord bestow His favor upon you and grant you peace" (Numbers 26:24-26).

Area G archeological site, City of David hill. At center is a First Temple period dwelling dubbed 'The House of Ahiel.' This site has yielded finds from the Canaanite, First Temple and Second Temple periods

THE EARLY SECOND TEMPLE PERIOD

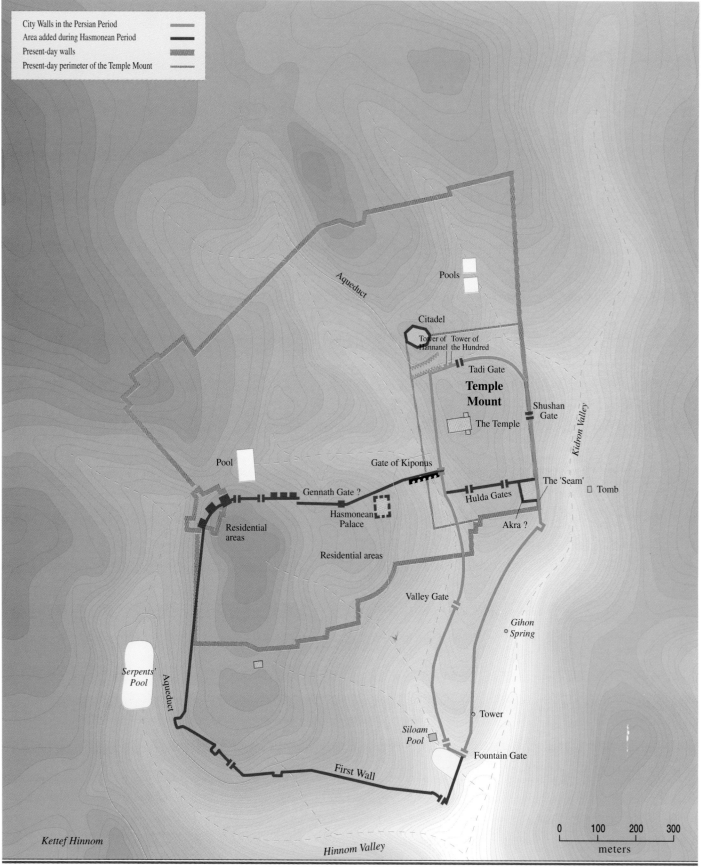

City Walls in the Persian Period
Area added during Hasmonean Period
Present-day walls
Present-day perimeter of the Temple Mount

Aqueduct

Pools

Citadel

Tower of Tower of
Hannanel the Hundred

Tadi Gate

**Temple
Mount**

Shushan
Gate

The Temple

Kidron Valley

Pool

Gate of Kiponus

The 'Seam'

Gennath Gate ?

Tomb

Hasmonean
Palace

Hulda Gates

Residential
areas

Akra ?

Residential areas

Valley Gate

Gihon
Spring

Serpents'
Pool

Aqueduct

Tower

Siloam
Pool

Fountain Gate

First Wall

0   100   200   300

Kettef Hinnom

meters

Hinnom Valley

Jerusalem from the days of the Return to Zion through the Hasmonean period

"By the rivers of Babylon, there we sat, sat and wept, as we remembered Zion." Psalm 137 in micrographic art expresses the vision of the Return to Zion. Artist: Shmuel Shulman, Safed (1843-1900)

The dedication ceremony of the Second Temple took place in 515 B.C.E., some seventy years after the destruction of the First Temple. Its construction took more than a decade. The return of the exiles and reconstruction of the Temple inaugurated the Second Temple period, which was destined to span six hundred years, from the encounter between the Jews and the eastern empires of Babylonia and Persia, to their encounters with the civilizations of Greece and Rome. Simultaneously, this period would witness significant religious and intellectual developments that would mold the Jewish faith. During the first centuries of this era, the

canonization of the Holy Writ marked the end of the biblical period. In terms of religious practice, the returnees had solidly rejected idolatrous ritual, and observed Judaism largely as it has become familiar since. They formed a nation united in belief in a single God, devoted to the worship of this one Divinity and observance of His laws. They were guided by the last of their prophets, their elders and sages.

Before the Return to Zion, Jerusalem stood ruined for nearly fifty years. The devastation incurred by the Babylonians was immense: the Temple and city were destroyed and all but a few inhabitants exiled. Our knowledge is scanty of the life left behind in Judah after the destruction. From biblical accounts and surviving written sources it seems that the nearby Edomites, having participated in Jerusalem's destruction, penetrated into southern Judah and controlled areas that had been depopulated (See Psalms 137:7). Unlike the Assyrians, who conquered the Kingdom of Israel and forced an exchange of populations, the Babylonians did not settle alien peoples in Jerusalem or Judah; they remained desolate.

The exiled Jews in Babylonia maintained a patriarchal framework. Many lived in agricultural settlements and cherished the idea of return to their country of origin. Among them was the prophet Ezekiel, who foretold his people's return to their homeland. In the Vision of the Dry Bones (Ezekiel 37) the Lord promises to breathe life into the people's dry bones and return them to their land. Ezekiel's words in chapters 47-48 describe the Jews' eventual re-settlement in Judah according to tribal organization, with some changes in the locations of tribal portions compared to their locations in prior biblical accounts. The tribal portion of Judah remains at the center in Ezekiel's account, and Jerusalem retains its central position and overriding importance. Ezekiel prophesies the rebuilding of the Holy Temple around which the priests and Levites will reside, for their designated life-task is to serve in the Temple and conduct the rituals. He foretells that representatives from every tribe will reside in Jerusalem, but the city will not belong to any one tribe.

The Edict of Cyrus and the Return to Zion

The exiled Jews in Babylonia were given the chance to return to Zion because of a far-reaching political re-alignment in the Fertile Crescent. In 539 B.C.E., fifty years into the exile, the city of Babylon, center of a large empire, was conquered without a fight by Cyrus king of Persia. He pursued a policy of restoration of peoples to their lands and a return of their looted gods to their temples. This can be seen in the text of the Cyrus Cylinder. Cyrus' policy toward the Jews is recorded in the biblical Book of Ezra. Known as the Cyrus Edict, it states: "Thus said King Cyrus of Persia: The Lord God of

Heaven has given me all the kingdoms of the earth and has charged me with building Him a house in Jerusalem, which is in Judah. Anyone of you of all His people... let him go up to Jerusalem that is in Judah and build the

The Cyrus Cylinder, sixth century B.C.E., declares Cyrus' policy towards various peoples in his kingdom, allowing them to return to their homelands

House of the Lord God of Israel..." (Ezra 1:2-3). In Ezra chapter 6 there is a second version of the Edict, in the Aramaic language, the vernacular of Babylonia-Persia. It was probably for the use of the royal chancellery. This version contains the physical proportions of the Temple and Cyrus' obligation to finance its reconstruction from the royal treasury. In an unprecedented move, Cyrus permitted the transfer of money from Babylonia to Jerusalem to build the Temple, and he returned the silver and gold vessels taken by the Babylonians during the conquest in 586 B.C.E.

The Cyrus Edict aroused an enthusiastic response among the exiles, and in a short time a first caravan of returners to Zion was organized and on its way. As recalled in Ezra chapter 2, it consisted of 42,360 souls. Historians assume that this number includes people who came to Judah during subsequent decades. Added to these were more than seven thousand slaves and hand-maidens, as well as two hundred male and female singers. Despite these impressive figures, those who returned to Zion were only a small proportion of the Jewish exiles in Babylonia. Others, perhaps the majority, preferred to remain. Many returnees went back to their original settlements in Judah. Only a few set out for the ruined Jerusalem, mainly those directly responsible for religious rites, such as priests, Levites and others who filled auxiliary functions in the Temple.

Jerusalem – Temple City

In 538 B.C.E. the first wave of returnees was led by the 'the prince of Judah,' Sheshbazzar, whom Cyrus appointed governor of the province of Judah in order to rebuild the Holy Temple. He was given the holy vessels to return to the Holy Temple in Jerusalem. Some years later a second group of immigrants arrived, led by Zerubbabel son of Shealtiel, who like Sheshbazzar was given the title of governor. Both Sheshbazzar and Zerubbabel were descendants of the House of David. Their periods of leadership seem to mark the last active rule by David's descendants.

Arriving in Jerusalem, the returnees found a city in rubble, its walls toppled in many places and its Temple a ruin. Under the leadership of Zerubbabel and Joshua the son of Jozadak, the high priest, the returnees erected an altar as the first step towards rebuilding the Temple. Construction continued for years, with frequent lengthy interruptions. One cause of the interruptions was interference by "the people of the land," or Samarians, inhabitants of the province of Samaria, in which the Assyrians forcibly settled foreigners after the destruction of the kingdom of Israel. The Samarians wanted to take part in the rebuilding, it being understood that this was a claim to worship in the finished structure with the Jews. When they were rejected, the Samarians addressed the Persian authorities, accusing the Jews of treasonous intent in rebuilding and fortifying Jerusalem. A period of investigation and appeals delayed work on the Temple. The Jews were eventually vindicated.

A second cause for delay was the economic distress of the returnees, which led them to neglect public and ritual matters. This provoked an admonishment from the prophet Haggai: "Is it a time for you to dwell in your paneled houses, while this House is lying in ruins?... Go up to the hills and get timber,

Ezra the Scribe wearing phylacteries, praying near books of the Bible. Illumination from the Amiatinus Bible, a Latin manuscript of the nine century C.E., now in Florence, Italy

and rebuild the House; then will I look on it with favor and I will be be glorified, said the Lord" (Haggai 1:4,8).

The prophet's exhortation inspired a response among the people and their leaders, who took up the task of rebuilding in the second regnal year of the reign of Darius king of Persia (520 B.C.E.). The Second Temple was dedicated in 515 B.C.E. in the presence of the entire community and with the approval of the Persian authorities. The new building seems to have been a humble structure by comparison with the First Temple, built by Solomon at great expense. Those who remembered Solomon's temple or had been told of its splendor wept in disappointment. However, they were consoled by the prophet Haggai: "The glory of this latter

Bust of the Persian ruler Darius I in characteristic style of the earlier Assyrian empire

house shall be higher than of the former one, said the Lord of Hosts: and in this place I will grant prosperity..." (Haggai 2:9).

Ezra and Nehemiah

The historical record is sparce concerning Judah and Jerusalem in the decades between the dedication of the Temple in 515 B.C.E. and the arrival of Ezra the Scribe with a wave of immigrants in the mid-fifth century. We know that Jerusalem was essentially an unwalled city, mostly in ruin and sparsely inhabited. We hear of no further activity of leaders of Davidic lineage. Ezra was not of Davidic descent, but belonged to a highborn priestly family. He was expert in the Teaching of Moses and had apparently held an official position at the court of Artaxerxes I, perhaps as secretary or advisor on Jewish matters.

Some five thousand people accompanied Ezra when he went up to Jerusalem, after having obtained approval from the Persian king to strengthen the weak Jewish population in Judah. The Persian regime afforded Ezra extensive authority. He could take with him people, silver and gold, organize life in Judah according to the laws of the Torah, and exempt from taxes all who dealt with sacred matters. Among his first acts were the appointment of judges who would adjudicate according to Torah law.

Ezra made the canonical Torah (in effect the constitution of the Jewish faith) into the law of the province of Judah. Its study and public recital became an integral part of Jewish ritual. It was the central substance of the Sabbath and festival rites, and a significant feature of what would emerge as the synagogue service.

Several months after his arrival, Ezra gathered the people in Jerusalem in the autumn month of Tishri and began the work of forming a distinct Jewish national entity. He distinguished between the returnees and the inhabitants who had not gone into exile and who had culturally blended with the surrounding peoples. He forbade intermarriage with foreign women and

Repairing the walls of Jerusalem in Nehemiah's day. Illumination from the Bible of the Duke of Alba, a fifteenth century C.E. manuscript translated from Hebrew to Castilian by Moshe Argel

demanded that the people, and particularly heads of leading families, priests and Levites, divorce foreign women to whom they were already married.

Ezra's activities were complemented by Nehemiah son of Hacaliah, who was cupbearer to the Persian king, a position of the highest court rank. Nehemiah had received reports of Jerusalem's desolation and obtained royal permission to restore it. He was appointed governor of Judah and arrived in 445 B.C.E. Three days after his arrival he made a nighttime inspection of Jerusalem's walls. The sight of them led to his forceful call: "Come, let us rebuild the walls of Jerusalem and suffer no more disgrace" (Nehemiah 2:17). The task was made difficult by surrounding rulers, who worked to prevent the refortification of Jerusalem.

Nehemiah, unlike Ezra, was experienced in military matters and fully aware of the authority extended to him by the Persian king. He armed his civilian builders and organized them into teams to rebuild the walls by sections, while also defending themselves. "The basket-carriers were burdened, doing work with one hand while the other held a weapon... the builders each had his sword girded at his side as he was building... And so we worked on, while half were holding lances, from the break of day until the stars appeared" (Nehemiah 4:10). Work was completed in just fifty two days. There followed an inauguration ceremony during which two processions circumscribed the rebuilt city walls, one headed by Nehemiah and the other by Ezra the Scribe.

Scholars are divided on the question of the course of Nehemiah's walls. Most archeologists maintain that Jerusalem in Nehemiah's time was much smaller than it had been prior to the Babylonian conquest. It consisted mainly of the City of David hill and adjoining Temple Mount, an area of some thirty acres, no more than one fourth the city's size on the eve of its destruction. The account in the book of Nehemiah indicates that the population of Jerusalem had decreased as well. When the walls were finally reconstructed, Nehemiah ordered a relocation of Levites to Jerusalem. As this did not suffice, he ordered that lots be drawn to re-settle one tenth of the rural population in Jerusalem.

Nehemiah introduced social and religious reforms, urging the prosperous inhabitants of Judah to return fields and houses taken in payment of debts and to cancel the debts of the poor. He guaranteed the Temple's income by placing a tithe on all the inhabitants of the province, and saw to it that the privileged priestly families were prevented from monopolizing the flow of money into Temple coffers.

Together, Ezra and Nehemiah worked to shape Jerusalem's Jewish character. The city gates were closed on Sabbath eve to make sure there were no commercial dealings or hauling of cargo. Nehemiah like Ezra, called on those who had married foreign women to divorce them. The peak of their combined effort was the grand public Pledge undertaken by masses of the people gathered in Jerusalem on the holidays marking the beginning of the year. Priests, leaders and common folk swore their loyalty to God, to be expressed by observing His commandments (Nehemiah 10:29). They promised strict adherence to the Sabbath laws, to the rules governing the seventh (Sabbatical) year including cancellation of debts, to payment of a third of a shekel for the Temple's needs and to the prohibition of marriage with the non-Jewish 'People of the Land.' This public Pledge to adhere to the practical expressions of Judaism played a critical part in the creation of a distinctive Jewish identity for the land and society of Judah and the capital, Jerusalem.

Jerusalem – Temple City, Capital of Yehud

Jerusalem's high status in the early Second Temple period was attributable to several factors. It was a Temple city with special privileges, the capital of the province of Judah (*Yehud* in Aramaic) and the seat of the provincial governor, whose power

Obverse and reverse of coin of the province of Yehud. On one side the word YHD appears, on the other a lily, apparently a well-known Jewish symbol

derived from the king of Persia. A military force was at his disposal. He and his high officials were responsible for provincial administration and the collection of taxes. The governor was the highest official of the central government while the high priest represented the Jewish population before the authorities. The Persian authorities' support of the Temple was demonstrated by donations and tax exemptions for those who served there. From this period onward it was customary in the Temple to bring sacrifices for the well-being of the king. This type of prayer was retained during the hellenistic and Roman periods and thereafter.

Jerusalem had concentric spheres of influence: the nearest was made up of Jews of the province of Judah, which stretched from Beth-zur in the Hebron hills to Bethel in the hills of Benjamin, from Jericho in the east to the Ono valley in the west. Within this area, the population was directly subordinate to the administration in Jerusalem. The second sphere included parts of Palestine outside these boundaries, for which Jerusalem was a national and spiritual center. Finally Jerusalem exerted its influence on Diaspora communities from Persia to Egypt, all of which acknowledged the centrality of the city and Holy Temple.

Archeological Finds from the Persian Period

Archeologists believe that a city gate discovered on the western side of the City of David hill is the Valley Gate mentioned in the book of Nehemiah. There are few pottery finds from the Persian period in Jerusalem, all of them discovered on the Western Hill. Material evidence shows that a cemetery known to have been used at the end of the First Temple period resumed this function after the Return to Zion. It is located on the slope of the Hinnom Valley known as Ketef Hinnom.

The right to mint coins testified to the respected political status of a Persian province; Judah enjoyed this right. Most coins and the seals from this period belong to the last decades of Persian rule. A number of coins were found in Jerusalem and its vicinity on which the name *Yehud* appears; it also appears on seal impressions on jar handles. Names of Judean rulers such as Yehoezer, Ahzai, Hananiah and Yehezkiyahu appear on other coins and seals. These names are not known from any other source. On one coin, the name Yehohanan the Priest is found.

Certain artifacts are distinctive by virtue of their absence. The small cultic figurines so common in earlier periods have not been found among the material finds of the province of Judah. This absence is in keeping with the biblical account which emphasizes the exclusiveness of monotheistic belief among the returning exiles.

The limited material finds of the early Second Temple period cause scholars to rely on contemporary written sources for information on this period. From letters found in Elephantine, in southern Egypt, it emerges that there were connections between Jerusalem and the Jewish military colony there. Instructions were found regarding Passover observance, and it is assumed that these came from Jerusalem. In another letter addressed to the governor of Judah, the people of Elephantine recall their application to the governor of Samaria and to Yohanan the High Priest in Jerusalem to plead their cause with the Persian authorities. These letters are evidence that the Jews of Elephantine felt themselves closely bound to Jerusalem.

The Early Hellenistic Period

Two centuries of Persian rule over Judah ended in 332 B.C.E. when the area (with the exception of Gaza) submitted peacefully to the Macedonian conqueror Alexander the Great, marking a new era – the hellenistic period. A Talmudic legend tells of a brief, friendly exchange between Alexander and the High Priest. Josephus Flavius elaborates on this meeting (Antiquities II) describing an agreement whereby the Jews would be able to observe their religion freely and alien gods would not be introduced into the land or its capital, Jerusalem. These accounts reflect reality, in that the province of Judah, hellenized in name to Judea, submitted peacefully

The Passover letter, instructions to the Jews of Elephantine (Yeb) Egypt on the proper observance of the festival

to Alexander and its cultural autonomy remained intact. The cordiality of the early relationship did not last through the hellenistic period. Eventually a tense and painful encounter developed between two great civilizations of the ancient world – Greek and Jewish.

Jerusalem under the Ptolemaic Dynasty

Alexander died prematurely and his empire was divided among his generals. The two whose histories would affect Judea were Ptolemy and Seleucus. During the years 301-200 B.C.E. Judea was ruled by Ptolemaic Egypt, while the other great Macedonian dynasty of the region, Seleucid Syria, also laid claim to the area of southern Syria-Phoenicia, which included Judea. Initially the chief change wrought by hellenistic rule was the arrival of Macedonian and Greek settlers, whose settlements were organized along different plans than had been known in the area until then. Greek military colonies were established, and ancient cities changed under the influence of hellenism, reorganizing themselves along the patterns of the Greek *polis* (city-state). The advanced Greek trading system and agricultural methods brought economic progress to Judea, which lay in an area that became an important link in the trade patterns of the Ptolemaic kingdom.

Hellenistic culture gradually infiltrated Judea, however Jerusalem was for a long time resistant to change because of its sacred Jewish character, the presence of the Temple within its precincts, and its mountain location at a time when hellenization was occuring much more rapidly in towns along the Mediterranean coast and in Trans-Jordan.

Aramaic inscription on Second Temple era burial stone: "Here were transferred the bones of Uzziah King of Israel. Do not open." Scholars surmise that the biblical king's remains were moved to a new site because Jerusalem had grown to encompass the original site

The Jews and their feelings towards Jerusalem made a distinct impression in the Greek world. The second century B.C.E. Greek historian Polybius described the inhabitants of Judea as "a people who lived around a temple called Jerusalem." The Letter of Aristeas, written by an Alexandrian Jew of that period, described Jerusalem similarly. "The city sits at the hub of the entire land of the Jews... on a high and exalted mountain, at the top of which a glorious temple has been constructed." On the beauties of the Temple he added, "the view is so pleasant that it is difficult to part from it."

The high priest continued to head the Jewish populace of Judea, fulfilling both religious and political leadership roles. He was the Judeans' representative at the royal court, and was responsible for collecting taxes due the Ptolemaic treasury. Hecataeus, a Greek historian of the beginning of the hellenistic period observed: "The Jews have no king at all. The leadership of the nation is regularly entrusted to a priest regarded as superior to his colleagues in wisdom and virtue, whom they call the High Priest." There was also a Council of Elders, or

Mosaic depiction of Alexander the Great, Pompeii, Italy

Gerousia, which functioned as a combined legislature and high court, guided by the laws of the Torah. It was composed of priests and representatives of the provincial towns of Judea.

Under Ptolemaic rule Jerusalem's size and population increased. Hecataeus estimated that in Jerusalem there were a hundred and twenty thousand souls. This is probably an overestimate, but indicates that Jerusalem was a large city for those times.

The priests were the highest class within Judean society, in particular those who were closely associated with the family of the high priest. Other priests lived in country towns and villages and went to Jerusalem to serve in the Temple when the turn of their watch came, as well as for the three pilgrimage festivals. Eventually the wealthiest priestly clans became hellenized, along with prosperous non-priestly families, and wealthy Jewish families in Trans-Jordan such as the family of the

Tobiads. Thus, a small, hellenized social element began to form in Jerusalem, however most Jerusalemites, along with Jews living in towns, villages and agricultural settlements were barely touched by Greek cultural influences.

Ptolemaic respect for the uniqueness of Judaism and Judean culture changed towards the end of the third century B.C.E., when Judea was caught between the warring empires, Ptolemaic Egypt to the southwest and Seleucid Syria to the northeast. The Third Book of Maccabees contains an account of an attempt by Ptolemy IV to enter the Holy of Holies of the Temple of Jerusalem, thereby provoking a passionate public outcry which threatened his safety. The story supports evidence of the overwhelming place of the Temple in the hearts of the Jews. In addition, it testifies to the preservation of Jewish religious and social autonomy even in the absence of a king. The story abounds in irony, as it recounts the

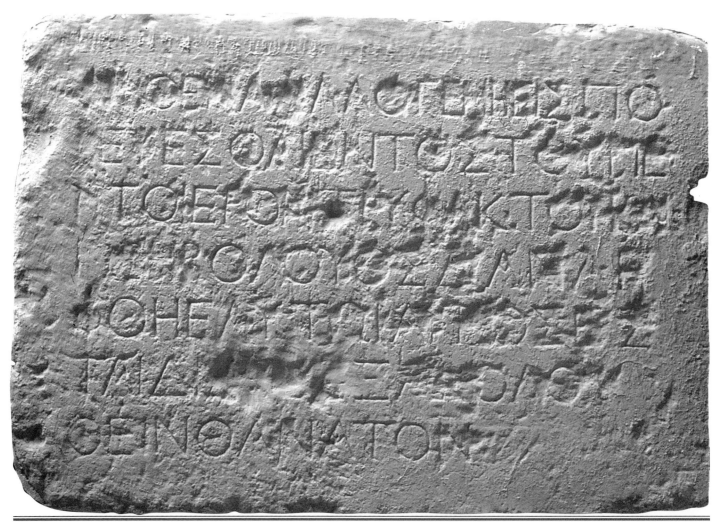

Stone-carved Greek inscription forbids non-Jews to enter the area of the Temple. Scholars surmise the inscription was on the 'soreg' or balustrade surrounding the Temple. The inscription, which dates to the Herodion period, reflects a prohibition that long preceded Herod's time

subservience to Jewish law even of the ruler by whose grace the Jews had their autonomy. A carved inscription in Greek found on a stone of the Temple and dating to the late Second Temple period confirms the continuation of the prohibition on Gentiles entering the sacred precincts of the Temple of Jerusalem. (see p.30)

Under Seleucid Rule

In 200 B.C.E. Judea came under Seleucid rule, which began in a benign enough manner. The Seleucid monarch Antiochus III ordered the restoration of Judea and Jerusalem, which had suffered the ravages of battle. In a comprehensive agreement, the Jews of Judea were promised continued religious and national autonomy and permitted a system of government in keeping with the law of their forefathers. High political and religious functionaries (priests, members of the Gerousia, scribes, and psalm-singers of the Temple) were exempted from government taxes. Non-Jews would continue to be barred from the Temple precincts.

Within a few decades there were far-reaching changes in the Seleucid attitude, owing to political and financial crises in the empire. The Seleucid kings were forced to raise money and naturally turned to treasures kept in the ancient temples of the lands they controlled. In this context they saw the Temple in Jerusalem as a worthy objective. In addition, they needed to draft men for their armies, and saw the total hellenization of regions as a necessary step toward this end. Neither of these trends boded well for the Jews of Judea and their faith. There were additional, internal threats to their religious and

The seam on the southeastern corner of the Temple Mount marks the meeting of hellenistic and Herodian stonework. Some scholars suggest hellenistic stones are remnants of the Akra fortress

Handles of wine jugs (amphorae) originally from Rhodes, bear Greek inscriptions. They were found in the Lower City (Ophel Hill) of Jerusalem

cultural integrity posed by the wealthy, hellenized ranks of Jewish society. One of them, attempting to curry favor with the Seleucid king, invited him to investigate the extent of moneys kept in the Temple Treasury in Jerusalem. The king's delegate arrived and investigated, but was diverted and persuaded not to take any funds. Although there is no evidence that the king intended to harm the Temple or impinge upon Judean religious autonomy, this event aroused public outrage and can be viewed as the first clash between the Seleucids and the Jews. That the delegate's arrival occurred at the instigation of a hellenized priest boded ill for the former unified character of Jewish life in Judea.

The penetration of hellenism occurred on a number of societal levels. Some Judeans, attracted to the outer trappings of Greek culture, spoke Greek and adopted Greek names. Others went further by introducing Greek customs into their daily lives in architecture, dress, culinary habits and entertainment. Yet others

Judah Maccabee leading his forces into Jerusalem. From a crusader manuscript illuminated in Acre, late thirteenth century

variance with Jewish culture. The Greek gymnasium was the chief educational institution which instilled Greek knowledge, sports and warfare skills in the youthful generation, and produced worthy citizens for the polis. In every polis the gymnasium was a major social gathering place, and was profoundly rooted in Greek paganism. Jason's effort to turn Jerusalem into the *polis* Antiochia meant nullification of a rich assemblage of Jewish laws concerning Jerusalem, and cancellation of the heritage and values of generations of Jews. His moves, and the changes in Jerusalem's lifestyle, antagonized many of the city's residents. Most were not radical hellenizers and were distraught by the turn of events. After some years, Jason was deposed and the high priesthood was taken over by Menelaus, whose Grecophilism was even more radical than Jason's. In a gross deviation from Jewish law, Menelaus ascended to the high priesthood without being a member of the priestly line. He simply bribed the Seleucids with a larger sum than his predecessor.

The hellenistic character of Jerusalem-Antiochia was further advanced by the stationing of a foreign garrison in town to support the Grecophiles against the general Jewish population. This garrison was stationed in a citadel known as the Akra. Scholars infer from the description in the Second Book of Maccabees that the Akra stood at the southern end of the Temple Mount and overlooked the sacred Temple compound. Thus hostile foreigners could view the proceedings on the Mount. Antiochus IV sent a foreign populace to Jerusalem, and these together with the Grecophiles, changed the character of the city. Many of Jerusalem's Jewish inhabitants moved to the desert and outlying settlements. Further events which scandalized them were the robbery of the Temple Treasury, and Antiochus' looting of Temple implements such as the Golden Altar, Eternal Lamp and other items made of precious metals. When a false rumor spread that the king had died, disorder ensued.

The Hasmonean Rebellion and Rededication of the Temple

With the wholehearted encouragement of the radical hellenists among the Jews, perhaps even on their initiative, Antiochus IV Epiphanes imposed harsh

internalized Greek culture and values, and were prepared to forego the basic substance of Judaism. In the first half of the second century B.C.E., the latter Grecophiles, also known as radical hellenizers, were responsible for efforts to hellenize Jerusalem's character.

In 174 B.C.E., the radical hellenist priest Joshua, who had adopted the Greek name Jason, set out to radically alter the Jewish character of Jerusalem. His two major changes, supported by the Seleucid king Antiochus IV, were the building of a gymnasium in Jerusalem and the city's transformation into a hellenistic *polis* called Antiochia. The standard Greek *polis* (city-state) functioned according to rules and mores at considerable

At the foot of Jerusalem's Old City wall just south of the Citadel, a remnant of the Hasmonean First Wall protrudes

decrees on the Jews in 167 B.C.E. in order to restore order in Judea and achieve the final hellenization of the province. The people were not permitted to carry out essential Jewish laws. They could not study the Torah, circumcise their sons or adopt traditional names. They were forced to eat forbidden foods and participate in pagan rituals. The Temple was desecrated: sacrifices to the Lord were forbidden and the Temple became the site of worship of Zeus.

The decrees of Antiochus and their effect on the masses of Judean Jews who were faithful to Judaism, changed the course of Jewish history. Many Jews were prepared for martyrdom, and this era in Judea marks the first time the world saw mass martyrdom for the sake of religious belief. This became an example for Jews and non-Jews in future ages.

The Jews rose up against the Seleucid regime, initially in the rural areas of northern Judea and the Plain of Lydda. The leadership of the revolt emerged in the town of Modi'in some twenty miles north-west of the capital. Mattathias (Matityahu) a respected priest of the Hasmon clan, together with his sons and the inhabitants of the Modi'in region, inspired the people of Judea to rebellion. Their aim was to bring about the abrogation of the harsh Seleucid decrees, purify the Temple, and restore Jerusalem to its Jewish character.

The strategy of the Jewish forces under Judah son of Mattathias (who had the nickname 'Maccabee,' possibly meaning hammer) was to prevent reinforcements from reaching Jerusalem. They engaged in well planned hit-and-run attacks. After three years of conflict, Judah Maccabee entered Jerusalem at the head of his men, cleansed the Temple of all evidence of pagan ritual and resupplied it with materials necessary for performance of traditional Jewish observances. The Temple was rededicated on the 25th of the month of Kislev in 164 B.C.E., and the festival of Hanukkah (Rededication) has been celebrated in Jewish tradition ever since. This episode in Jerusalem's history is looked upon as the world's first struggle for religious freedom. In Jewish tradition it is commemorated in prayer: "(God) in Your great mercy... delivered the strong into the hands of the weak, the many into the hands of the few, the impure into the hands of the pure, the wicked into the hands of the righteous, and the wanton into the hands of the students of your Torah... Your children came to the Holy of Holies of Your House, cleansed your Temple... and kindled lights in the Courtyards of your Sanctuary..." Jewish tradition links the rededication with a miracle whereby an amount of ritually pure oil sufficient for only one day's use lasted eight days, thus the celebration of eight days of Hanukkah.

It seems that Judaism had never been so threatened by extinction as it was during the persecution of Antiochus Ephiphanes. Most of the Jewish nation lived under Seleucid rule, in Judea and elsewhere. Though there were Jews in Egypt, Asia Minor and other areas outside Seleucid control, it is highly doubtful whether they would have been able to keep the nation and religion alive if Jerusalem and Judea had been destroyed or thoroughly hellenized. The continuation of the Jewish people was secured by the success of the Hasmoneans.

The fighting continued for a number of years, and Judah was killed. His brothers Jonathan and then Simon succeeded him. During Jonathan's rule Jerusalem was partly under Seleucid domination (the Akra fortress) and partly under Hasmonean rule. A series of military and political moves and the decline of the Seleucid empire resulted in Jonathan's strengthening his hold over Judea and extending its borders. After his death in 143 B.C.E. his brother Simon conquered the Akra and destroyed it. Hasmonean supremacy in Jerusalem was complete, and a new period began in Judea and Jerusalem.

A Period of Political Independence: The Hasmonean Dynasty

In 140 B.C.E. a Great Assembly met in Jerusalem and chose Simon as ethnarch (*Nasi*). Simon also assumed the positions of high priest and commander of the army. Thus civil, religious and military functions were bestowed upon one man. The decision of the Great Assembly declared these offices hereditary 'until a true prophet shall arise' (I Maccabees 14:27). The decision set several precedents: the office of high priest became the province of the Hasmonean priestly clan alone; and political, religious and military authority rested on one individual, a situation anomalous in Jewish history. This decision affected the entire development of the Jewish state under Hasmonean rule. Simon ruled until 135 B.C.E., when he was assassinated by his son-in-law Ptolemy (Talmai). His son John (Yohanan) Hyrcanus I succeeded him. The Seleucid sovereign, Antiochus VII, was not pleased with the growing extension of the Judean borders, which began under John Hyrcanus I's leadership, and sent armies to fight Judea, besieging Jerusalem for over a year. The city's defenders repelled the Seleucid attack but the Seleucids eventually gained the upper hand and John Hyrcanus I succumbed. He was forced to witness the destruction of the walls of Jerusalem. In addition, he was obliged to return the port of Jaffa, Gezer and other cities to the Seleucids.

The disintegration of the Seleucid empire beginning with the death of Antiochus VII just a few years later, made possible the restoration of Judea's independence and the extension of its borders. For some seventy years, the Hasmoneans conquered areas on both sides of the Jordan. Since David and Solomon's time, no independent country of the size of Hasmonean Judea had existed in the immediate region. Jerusalem, which until then had been the capital of the province of Judea, became the capital of a large country.

Finds and Mysteries

In the course of their years in power, the Hasmoneans fortified and restored Jerusalem. The first to do so was Judah Maccabee, and his brothers followed suit. They broadened the built-up area of the city in the direction of the southwest hilltop and built a new, elegant quarter on its western ridge subsequently called the Upper City. Beginning in the days of Simon's rule a wall went up which ringed this southwest hill. It is known as the First Wall. Its remains dating to Hasmonean times were first discovered in the mid-nineteenth century. Today scholarly opinion is divided regarding the course of the Hasmonean walls, and hence the size of the city they enclosed. Some scholars maintain that sections of Hasmonean wall are to be found in the present-day area of Jaffa Gate and the Tower of David. Others limit the course of the Hasmonean wall to the perimeter of today's Jewish Quarter. Other sites have been suggested as well.

In archeological excavations in the Jewish Quarter of the Old City, remains of Hasmonean buildings and ritual baths have been discovered, however Hasmonean finds are not extensive. The assumption is that their relative paucity in an area known to have been developed by the Hasmoneans, is the result of site clearance and over-building during later periods, especially King Herod's (the late Second Temple period). From what has been found, scholars note that Hasmonean buildings show a simplicity of style compared with buildings of the later period. Hellenistic influence in building style can be seen, and a similar influence has been noted on tombs from this period. Several prominent Hasmonean sites have yet to be discovered. The Hasmonean palace

Wine-jug (amphora) handle with five-pointed design and the word 'Jerusalem'

and the capital's citadel still offer a challenge to future archeologists, and while it is known that the Akra fortress was destroyed, the question of where it stood is still unanswered.

Material Culture

Finds relating to everyday life of the Hasmonean period reflect the functioning of Judea as an economic center whose ships plied Mediterranean ports and traded in material goods. Pottery bowls, amphorae for oil and wine, and lamps have been found, along with many seals on jug handles originating in the eastern Greek isles. Another find is a particularly interesting collection of seals bearing the five-pointed insignia (Solomon's shield) and the word 'Yrslm' (Jerusalem). In Jerusalem and elsewhere, coins struck by Hasmonean rulers have been found, among them those of John Hyrcanus and Alexander Jannai. These coins bear evidence of the uniqueness of the Hasmonean state of Judea. There is a marked absence of rulers' portraits, or depictions of gods and animals, common features of Seleucid coins of the time. This may be understood as a reflection of strict observance of the third commandment of the Decalogue. Instead, there is an abundance of inscriptions, cornucopia, fruit, palm leaves, anchors, and the lily flower, a common Jewish symbol at the time.

Jerusalem during the Hasmonean period reached a new peak in its development. The Temple was again the center of Jewish life; pilgrims came from all over Eretz Israel as well as from the Diaspora – from Egypt and Asia Minor, Babylonia and Persia – and even from Europe. The ascent (*aliyah*) to Jerusalem for the three pilgrimage festivals (Passover, the Feast of Weeks and the Feast of Booths) was an act of religious dedication, and had economic significance as well. Pilgrims made various donations above and beyond the half shekel which all Jews were obliged to send annually for the Temple's upkeep.

The Last of the Hasmoneans

John Hyrcanus' authority over Jerusalem lasted more than thirty years, until 104 B.C.E. His successor Judah

Aristobulus ruled for only a year and a half, and his most noteworthy gesture was his adoption of the title of king rather than ethnarch. Alexander Jannai took the reins of power in 103 B.C.E., retained the title of king and was high priest and commander-in-chief of the army as well. In the course of his twenty-seven year reign Judea witnessed frequent warfare as a result of his continued expansionist policy, and internally, there was a period of social discord and persecution in which Jannai ordered the deaths of many Pharisaic scholars and their supporters. In 76 B.C.E. Jannai was succeeded by his wife Salome Alexandra (Shlomzion) who sought to calm the social discord wrought by her husband, and favored the Pharisee religious and social leadership (see below) over the rival Sadducees, who had been favored by her husband. Upon Salome Alexandra's death, a fraternal conflict broke out between her two sons. The resultant period of confusion provided an opening for Roman intervention in Judea. This in turn resulted in the end of the Hasmonean dynasty during the reign of Salome's grandson, Mattathias Antigonus.

Pharisees and Sadduccees

Two significant social groupings emerged during the Hasmonean period, Sadducees and Pharisees. They differed from one another on a host of social, economic and religious issues. The Sadduccees were mainly of the upper classes: the priestly aristocracy in Jerusalem, wealthy merchants, and the senior ranks of the army. By Hasmonean times a few priestly clans in Jerusalem were garnering more than their share of the people's donations, and were also actively involved in the hellenist trading system – thus accumulating real wealth. They formed the core of the Sadducees, a distinctly non-populist social group.

Coin of King Alexander Jannai displays unique characteristics of Hasmonean coinage. Left, horns of plenty with Greek inscription 'Jonathan the King.' Right, 'Jonathan the High Priest and the Council of the Jews.' Note the absence of human or animal forms

The Torah scholars became the *de facto* representatives of the common people and were known as Pharisees, (*prushim*) a word which can suggest the meaning 'interpreters' (of Torah law) or 'separatists.' The Pharisaic scholars asserted a continuity in the Oral Tradition (the bulk of which concerns methods of interpreting Torah law) that went back to Sinai. By contrast, the Sadducees took a literalist stance on interpetation of Torah, thus eliminating the need to turn to the Pharisaic rabbis for guidance. On the whole, the masses of the people were drawn to the Pharisees.

In the early period of their reign, the Hasmonean family heeded the sages, for the Hasmonean cause had been animated by deep religious considerations. However, the Hasmonean rulers gradually succumbed to hellenistic influences, and tensions arose between them and the rabbinic leadership. Hasmonean decisions regarding the conquest of territories and forging of various foreign alliances seemed clearly animated by a hellenistic outlook. A related cause of the disaffection was the adoption by Hasmonean leaders of the powers, and eventually the title of king. Insofar as the Hasmoneans were all of priestly descent, they could never, according to Jewish law, be kings. The Hasmoneans' disregard of sacred tradition was one of many breaches that accomplished the alienation of the common people and Pharisaic sages. The Sadducee aristocracy on the other hand, favored the Hasmonean royal house, and derived economic and social privilege from it.

Pharisee interpretation gained the upper hand in Judean society. In the coming period a tense relationship continued between Pharisees and Sadducees, and contributed to Jerusalem's downfall in 70 C.E.

The politicization of the sacred Temple service, the tense situation in the holy city of Jerusalem and the internal divisions within the Jewish population led some religious purists to form sectarian groupings. Their goal was to live a purely Jewish life uncontaminated by hellenistic influences. These groups are known by the collective term Essenes, although much about their nature and relationship to one another remains to be discovered. The Essene sect (or sects) endured until the Roman defeat of the Jews in 70 C.E.

Jerusalem in the late Hasmonean period was home to a great variety of Jews and a number of non-Jews as well.

At the same time, it was the sacred capital of all the Jews of a far-flung Diaspora. The link of Diaspora Jews with Jerusalem, their tithing of income to support it, and their pilgrimage visits, helped Jews living afar to preserve their connection with the Jewish people, and left the Roman world with a distinctive impression of Jerusalem.

Jerusalem Falls to the Romans

During the years in which the Hasmonean rulers gradually built up their kingdom, imperial Rome was busy extending its sovereignty. Early Hasmonean leaders considered Rome a friend, while later kings in effect invited Rome to take over Judea. The Hasmonean brothers Hyrcanus II and Aristobulus II hastened the fall of Judea to Rome by involving the country in civil war. The affair culminated in a three month Roman siege of Jerusalem followed by Pompey's conquest of the city. Pompey entered the Holy of Holies – an act which scandalized the people, and which they were powerless to respond to. Roman soldiers destroyed sections of Jerusalem and slaughtered resisters in the Temple compound, however the Temple was left standing. The Hasmonean-built city walls of Jerusalem, symbol of the pride and power of the Hasmonean dynasty, were destroyed. After eighty years as an independent unit, Pompey declared Judea a Roman province and greatly reduced its size, severing it from the coastal plain, part of Idumea, Samaria and the Trans-Jordanian string of hellenized cities known as the Decapolis.

Difficult days lay ahead for Judea and Jerusalem under Roman domination, yet in certain ways the coming period, known as the late Second Temple period, was one of the greatest in the city's history.

Hasmonean tower uncovered in Jerusalem's Upper City, today's Jewish Quarter

THE LATE SECOND TEMPLE PERIOD

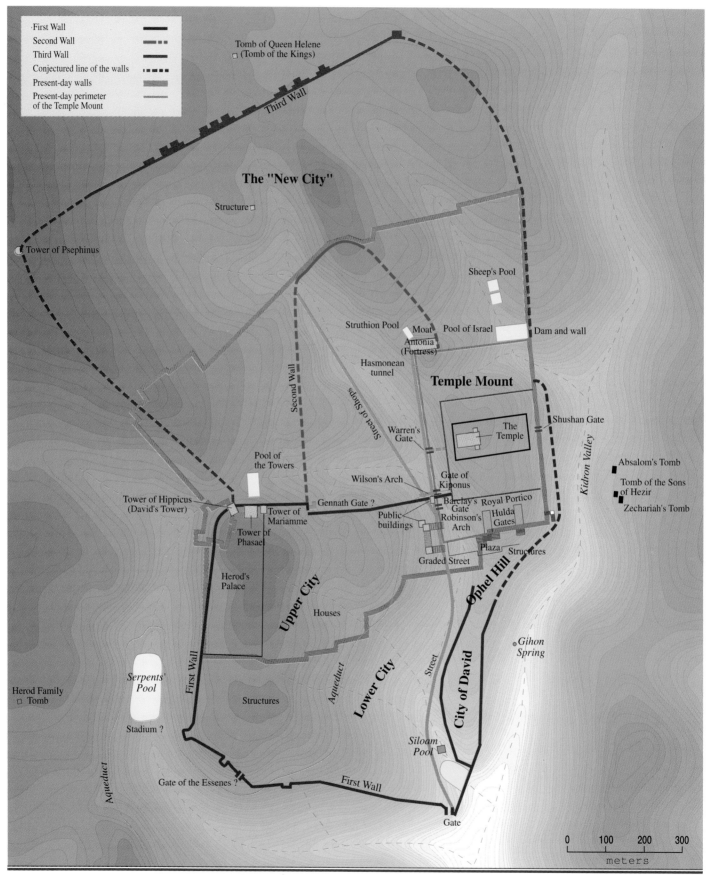

Legend:
- First Wall
- Second Wall
- Third Wall
- Conjectured line of the walls
- Present-day walls
- Present-day perimeter of the Temple Mount

Tomb of Queen Helene
(Tomb of the Kings)

Third Wall

The "New City"

Structure

Tower of Psephinus

Sheep's Pool

Struthion Pool
Moat
Antonia
(Fortress)
Pool of Israel
Dam and wall

Hasmonean
tunnel

Temple Mount

Street of Shops

Shushan Gate

The
Temple

Second Wall

Warren's
Gate

Kidron Valley

Pool of
the Towers

Wilson's Arch

Gate of
Kiponus

Absalom's Tomb

Tomb of the Sons
of Hezir

Zechariah's Tomb

Gennath Gate ?

Barclay's
Gate
Robinson's
Arch

Royal Portico

Tower of Hippicus
(David's Tower)

Tower of
Mariamme

Public
buildings

Hulda
Gates

Tower of
Phasael

Plaza
Structures

Graded Street

Herod's
Palace

Upper City

Ophel Hill

Houses

First Wall

City of David

Gihon
Spring

Serpents'
Pool

Aqueduct

Lower City

Street

Herod Family
Tomb

Structures

Stadium ?

Siloam
Pool

Aqueduct

Gate of the Essenes ?

First Wall

Gate

0   100   200   300
meters

Jerusalem in the late Second Temple period

Reconstruction of the Temple Mount viewed from the southwest. The grand Herodian flight of stairs leads from the street to the Royal Portico. The overpass known today as Robinson's Arch bridges a pedestrian walkway

The Roman conquest of Jerusalem in 37 B.C.E. marked the end of Jewish political sovereignty, however its inhabitants retained a great degree of autonomy over their internal affairs. The Romans placed no restrictions on Jerusalem's expansion or internal development, and for more than one hundred years the city saw great physical development and intermittent periods of civil calm and strife, until 70 C.E. when the Romans destroyed Jerusalem and with it the Second Temple, which had stood for more than six centuries.

Capital of the Jewish Nation

Jerusalem during the late Second Temple period continued to be the geographical and political center of Judea and the focal point of Jewish ritual concentrated in the Temple. It was capital of the Jewish people in Judea and the Diaspora, a city aptly described by Philo, the first century C.E. Alexandrian Jewish philosopher as "the metropolis not only for Judea but for many lands, because of its colonies," i.e. Diaspora communities.

The most important social and administrative institutions of the Jews were located in Jerusalem. Kings ruled from there, and after the monarchy was discontinued several Hasmonean descendants who administered different areas of the country under the aegis of Rome maintained homes in Jerusalem. The high priest and priestly aristocracy resided in the city. The Great Sanhedrin also met in Jerusalem, in offices located in the Temple complex, a fact which enhanced its already considerable prestige. In the administrative sphere the Sanhedrin's authority extended only over Judea, however in matters of religion and interpretation of Jewish law its authority extended to Jewish communities throughout the Diaspora. Jerusalem was home to the greatest sages of the Jews and was commonly accepted as the central place for study of the Torah.

Holy City

As 'the holy city' Jerusalem accrued a host of laudatory descriptions in Jewish tradition. Several sources describe it as the navel of the world, or standing at the center of the world, a worthy dwelling place for the prophetic spirit. In the heart of Jerusalem stood the Temple, to which was attributed the highest level of holiness. In the Mishnah, Jerusalem's sanctity is depicted at the apex of an ascending scale of holiness. "There are ten measures of holiness: the land of Israel is the holiest of all countries...the towns near the walls of Jerusalem derive

sanctity from her... the area within the walls (of Jerusalem) is more sacred than (the towns outside)... the Temple Mount is yet more sacred..." (Mishnah, Tractate Kelim 1:7-8) The sanctity of Jerusalem had implications in the halakhah (Jewish law). The closer an individual planned to come to the most sacred precincts of the Temple compound, the more stringent were the requirements for entry. Entry onto the Temple Mount was barred to ritually impure Jews; up to a certain point, Gentiles and Jewish men and women could proceed; beyond that point only Jews, and so forth.

In this period a number of laws tacitly expressed the idea that aspects of the Temple's sanctity devolved upon the city as a whole. For instance, it was permissible to eat the sacrificial lamb of the Passover meal in every part of the city. Members of the Essene sect regarded Jerusalem's sanctity as a central religious value, and their laws demanded an especially stringent standard of ritual purity for the city, above and beyond what the Pharisaic scholars required. As a result, the Essenes objected to

Steps (partially restored) fronting the Hulda Gates served pilgrims ascending to the Temple. Large stones afforded steps a look of grandeur

many activities that went on in the city and particularly in the Temple. They eventually departed radically from the conduct of the rest of the people, eschewing entry into the Temple confines out of deference for the holiness of the place, or perhaps because they thought it had become defiled.

In the literature of the Dead Sea Sect a new conceptualization of Jerusalem appears, the notion of the heavenly Jerusalem, which would replace the terrestrial city. Evidence of this idea of Jerusalem is found in rabbinic literature as well as in early Christian literature.

A considerable portion of Jewish law concerns itself with worship of the Lord in the Holy Temple. Special offerings were made on holidays; those who had made vows and those who wanted to be ritually purified came to the Temple to make the proper sacrifices; offerings were brought by individuals seeking atonement for sins. The sins of the entire Community of Israel were atoned in the Temple on the Day of Atonement in a ritual involving a series of actions by the high priest, among them the dispatching of the scapegoat to Azazel in the wilderness, and the high priest's entry into the Holy of Holies to burn incense and ask atonement for the sins of all the Jewish people.

Above: The handle of a stone jar inscribed with the word 'korban' (sacrifice) and two upside-down birds. Below: reconstruction of the inscription and design

Apart from the inhabitants of Jerusalem, Jews came to the Temple from all over Palestine and the Diaspora to fulfill the commandment of pilgrimage. Various sources indicate that towards the end of the Second Temple period the thrice yearly pilgrimage to Jerusalem took on the aspect of a mass movement. Myriads of pilgrims together with Jerusalem's native inhabitants congregated and worshipped together in the broad plazas of the Temple. In addition there were recent converts to Judaism who were obliged to make special sacrifices, and God-fearing non-Jews who were interested in Judaism.

Masses of visitors took up temporary residence in the city and its environs; lodging was provided gratis, and tents and booths were erected around the walls. Special laws regarding hospitality to pilgrims clarify the Mishnah's observation that "No man ever said 'The place is too confined for me to lodge in Jerusalem.'" (Tractate Avot 5:5). It was customary not to charge for accomodation, for Jerusalem belonged to the whole Jewish people.

The religious regulations governing hospitality to pilgrims did not prevent Jerusalem and its residents from prospering as a result of the massive pilgrimages. Moreover, the pilgrims brought donations and other funds which they had set aside in accordance with halakhah, to be turned over or spent in Jerusalem. In addition, every Jew in the country and the Diaspora contributed a half shekel annually for sacrifices in the Temple, for covering judges' salaries, grants to scribes, and other expenses of the Temple and the city. From the Mishnah we learn that the streets of Jerusalem, its walls and water delivery system were maintained by funds from the half-shekel donation. This was the tangible expression of the attachment of the Jewish people to Jerusalem and the Temple. Josephus Flavius cites an imperial Roman decree which stated that Jews, wherever they were traditionally in habit of doing so, were permitted to collect and transmit funds dedicated to Jerusalem, and were not to be interfered with in this activity.

The affiliation of the entire people with Jerusalem and the Temple was further reinforced by the various delegations of Jews who arrived in Jerusalem everyday to stand beside the priests as they engaged in the divine service. The priests were organized in twenty-four workshifts, each lasting two weeks. There were twenty-four parallel (*ma'amadot*) groups from among the people. Those people who did not take part in the sacrificial ritual would gather in study and prayer in the Temple and throughout the country.

Jews who came from the far corners of the Diaspora, speaking various languages and exhibiting various cultural influences, were united in Jerusalem where a common identification with the Jewish people enveloped them all.

The Reign of King Herod

Although it deprived Judea of sovereignty, Rome nevertheless acknowledged the descendants of the Hasmonean dynasty as religious leaders. Hyrcanus the son of Alexander Jannai was appointed ethnarch or custodian of the people, and also functioned as high priest. Antipater, an astute politician and friend of Rome whose roots were in Idumea, Judea's southern neighbor, was appointed procurator (governor) of Judea. Antipater's father had been converted to Judaism during the proselytizing campaign of the Hasmonean king John Hyrcanus, a bit of family history which would later plague his son Herod. Antipater had his elder son, Phasael, appointed governor of Jerusalem while his younger son, Herod, became governor of Galilee.

In about 40 B.C.E. an effort was made in Judea to overthrow Roman rule and restore the Hasmonean royal house to complete sovereignty. Conditions seemed ripe for this plan as Rome was beset by internal squabbles and there was disarray in the empire's eastern provinces because of a Parthian invasion – which reached Jerusalem itself. The Hasmonean kingdom was briefly restored, however the Romans soon put their house in order and set out to dominate Judea once again. During this period of struggle, Herod the son of Antipater followed a vigorously pro-Roman policy. He survived the uprising (his brother Phasael did not) and escaped to Rome, where he had access to high politicial personages.

Hasmonean coin with an early depiction of the Candelabrum of the Temple, struck by the last Hasmonean king, Mattathias Antigonus

Herod persuaded the Senate to rely on him to carry out imperial policy. He was crowned king of Judea and granted the title, 'Ally and Friend of the Roman People.' Herod returned to Jerusalem at the head of an army of mercenaries to defeat Mattathias Antigonus, the Hasmonean. The city's inhabitants resisted Herod, and Jerusalem was besieged and forced to surrender. Herod's entry into the city was accompanied by a slaughter of his opponents, the adherents of Mattathias Antigonus. The way was clear for Herod to assume the royal role, however throughout his reign he had to contend with the bitter resentment of a good portion of the people of Judea and the sages, for having done Rome's bidding in ending Hasmonean rule and for his thoroughly Roman orientation.

Herod is a towering and controversial historical figure. He occupied the throne in Jerusalem for thirty-three years, from 37–4 B.C.E. He brought the country economic prosperity and introduced the most modern building and engineering technology, accomplishing projects which brought Judea and Jerusalem to the attention of the entire Roman world. At the same time he was a single-minded autocrat whose political machinations kept the ruling elite in a constant state of tension. He freely ordered the murders of his enemies and was fixed on eliminating the remaining members of the Hasmonean royal line, an objective he largely achieved, and which included the murders of his wife Mariamne and his own sons by her. In his public conduct Herod was careful not to overtly transgress the laws of the Jewish religion, yet he profoundly offended Jewish sensibilities and is known in Jewish tradition as a wicked king. Herod's political objective was to demonstrate his absolute adherence to Rome while also representing the aspirations of the Jews. He strove to strengthen hellenistic cultural elements in the country while also stressing the fact that he was a Jewish king.

An expression of the people's resentment of Herod was their discontent over his Idumean descent. This was viewed as ample reason to render him ineligible for the monarchy, for the biblical verse states, "Be sure to set as king over yourself one of your own people; you must not set a foreigner over you, one who is not your kinsman" (Deut. 17:15). In order to bolster his legitimacy and draw closer to the people, Herod made a judicious marriage to Mariamne the Hasmonean. The same motive inspired

Reconstruction of the facade of Herod's Sanctuary. This most sacred precinct was the focal point of the Temple Mount enclosure. Its dimensions were codified by halakhah and could not be changed from those established for the First Temple

Inscribed stone discovered at the level of the paved street that skirted the southwest corner of the Temple Mount. Incomplete inscription reads, "To the trumpet-call building to pr... (proclaim)." The stone may be part of the corner tower from which trumpet calls signalled the start of Sabbaths and festivals

him, throughout his reign, to spare no effort on behalf of Jerusalem.

Herod was one of the greatest builders of Jerusalem in all the city's history – if not the greatest. During his reign the city was radically transformed, becoming one of the most beautiful of the ancient world. The first century Roman historian Pliny called it "the most famous beyond comparison among eastern cities." The only other city that Pliny described in such a way was Babylon. The Roman historian Tacitus noted that the Temple in Jerusalem was renowned for its immense riches. Tacitus exclaimed as well upon the beauty of the city's towers when viewed from the distance. Contemporary Jewish sources could not conceal their admiration for the Temple. "Whoever has not seen the (Temple) building of Herod, has never seen a beautiful building in his life" (Babylonian Talmud, Baba Batra 4b).

His efforts for Jerusalem and the Temple notwithstanding, Herod was intent on disseminating Roman culture in Judea. This has been borne out by recent archeological excavations and there is literary support of it as well. The first century C.E. Jewish historian Josephus Flavius mentions that Herod built a theater, amphitheater, hippodrome and stadium in Jerusalem, structures which have not yet been discovered. Such buildings and their purposes were not to the liking of the sages nor to a portion of Jerusalem's community. Herod was mindful of the people's temperament and the need to preserve Jerusalem's

unique character. While in other cities which he built or enhanced Herod incorporated the pagan style replete with statuary and forms of living things, he refrained from doing so in Jerusalem.

Building the Temple

In the eighteenth year of his rule (19 B.C.E.) Herod commenced an enormous enterprise: the reconstruction of the Temple of Jerusalem. Herod had in mind a large-scale project; expanding the Temple Mount platfrom to accommodate his new buildings would be a gargantuan task. He knew that it would be hard to obtain even tacit support from the people for such a large and costly operation, so he called for a massive gathering in which he cited the economic prosperity he had brought to the country and revealed his intentions to commence a holier and more beautiful project than had ever been known in contemporary times. It is clear from the account in Josephus's Jewish Antiquities, (15:11,1) that the people did not share Herod's enthusiasm for the project. Its ambitious scope seemed unachievable; they feared he would destroy the existing structure and not finish the new one. The king promised not to commence construction until everything was ready for the completion of his enterprise; "So he said in advance – and did not disappoint them." This sensitivity to the people's concerns did not prevent Herod from mounting a golden eagle over the gates of the Temple, apparently in deference to Rome. This carved symbol of Roman rule was an image of a living form, understood by the Jews to contravene the second commandment of the Decalogue. Its placement on the Temple structure led to popular unrest, and a number of scholars tried to chop it down, knowing full well that this act could lead to their deaths. (Indeed, they were executed; it seems that the eagle was left off the building). Herod's effort to mount the golden eagle demonstrates how great was the cultural divide between the king and his people.

A Gigantic Project

The enlargement of the Temple Mount platform was an enormous undertaking, from the standpoint of both economics and engineering. Herod's builders constructed retaining walls around the Temple Mount which reached a height of 44 feet. The western retaining wall was 533 yards long, the eastern – 506 yards, the southern – 308 yards and the northern, 346 yards. Thus a large trapezoidal expanse was formed covering an area of 36 acres. The platform was supported in part by an enormous quantity of packed dirt and debris, (scholars estimate it at ca. 750,000 cubic yards) and in part by vaulted arches which allowed for utilization of the area below the platform as storage space and underground passageways. (One of these areas extended some 2,750 square yards and is today known as 'Solomon's Stables' – a misnomer first applied to it during the Crusades.) During the period of the Temple platform's construction, five or six underground ramps were built, to which access could be gained by flights of steps. The ramps eventually served pilgrims entering the Temple area from the street below. The platform was turned into a splendid esplanade by overlaying it with with stone slabs 16 inches thick. Similar stones were used to pave the streets to the south and west of the Temple Mount, and some of these have been unearthed.

The retaining walls supporting the esplanade were 15 feet thick and their foundations were inserted into bedrock. The builders used large stones for the retaining walls, mostly 6 feet long, but there were also much longer stones, one of them 39 feet long. They weighed from six to sixty tons. This was undoubtedly one of the largest building projects of the ancient world.

The stones of the retaining walls, visible today in the Western and Southern Walls, were distinctively chiselled and bevelled. They featured protruding facades and receding frames, a style known today as Herodian stonework. Watchtowers were built at the corners of the retaining walls, one of which served as the spot from which beginnings of festivals were heralded with a fanfare of trumpets.

Along most of the southern end of the Temple Mount Herod built a Royal Portico (stoa in Greek), a magnificent colonnaded building with a roof supported by four rows of 162 columns crowned by Corinthian capitals. "And the thickness of each column was such that it would take three men with outstretched arms touching one another to envelop it; its height was twenty-seven feet... Since there were four rows, they made three aisles

among them, under the porticoes" (Josephus' Antiquities, 15:411). This structure was meant for civil, economic and judicial functions and was a meeting place for cohorts of the political leadership. The Great Sanhedrin met beneath the stoa in the Chamber of Hewn Stone, its permanent home.

The principle access to the Temple Mount plaza was in the southern retaining wall, where the Hulda Gates led beneath the Royal Portico to steps by which visitors ascended to the Esplanade. After crossing the Esplanade a visitor would reach the *soreg* or balustrade, a barrier which surrounded the Temple on all sides, serving to bar non-Jews from entry. Trespass by anyone not permitted by halakhah to be in the Temple confines, was punishable by death. This is evident in a Greek inscription found on two excavated stones of the Temple: "A stranger may not go beyond the balustrade and

The southwest corner of the Temple compound retaining wall exhibits typical Herodian stone-bevelling

enclosure around the Temple. Anyone caught doing so will be liable for his own ensuing death" (see p. 30).

The immense stones used for the retaining walls of the Temple were hewn locally and rolled down nearby slopes toward the construction site. Others were transported by rolling them across wooden cylinders over short distances. Stones to be hauled over longer distances were transported on wagons drawn by oxen. Ramps of packed dirt were prepared at the construction site. Levers or cranes were used to lift the stones into place.

According to Josephus, preparations for construction of the Temple compound lasted eight years; thousands of laborers engaged in stonemasonry and woodwork.

Another three years passed between the beginning of construction and the Temple's dedication. The Temple's sacred sanctuary was built by priests over an eighteen month period. The project was not completed during Herod's lifetime, but only decades after his death.

The enormous budget needed for this project was funded by Herod from four major sources: the kingdoms' taxes, the half-shekel donated by every Jew in Palestine and the Diaspora, special taxes imposed on the inhabitants of the kingdom, and partly from Herod's own treasury – apparently a generous sum.

The sacred Temple precincts including the Sanctuary rose in the heart of the expansive Temple Mount compound. The Sanctuary reached some 55 yards in height, and the walls were three feet thick on average. The interior was superb, its walls overlaid with gold. The building was divided into three open spaces: the Holy of Holies or Shrine, which stood over the Foundation Stone; the *heikhal*, a central room containing various ritual objects (the Candelabrum, Golden Altar, Table etc.) and the *ulam*, Portico or Great Hall.

Sacrificial rites were conducted in the courtyard in front of the Sanctuary. The eastern edge of the courtyard, delineated by distinctive paving stones, was the Ezrat Israel (men's section). At the eastern side of this section Nicanor's Gate (a magnificent structure donated by an Alexandrian Jew) opened onto a flight of fifteen steps leading down to the Ezrat Nashim or women's section, an area where Jewish women as well as men were permitted.

Around the courtyard of the Sanctuary there were a variety of offices for different purposes. Altogether the Temple and its courtyards occupied an area of more than two and a half acres, with the entire compound surrounded by a wall 66 feet high.

Herod's Additional Building Projects

Herod devoted decades of his life to building in Jerusalem. In addition to the enormous Temple reconstruction project, he erected a large fortress called the Antonia, a royal palace, towers on the city walls, parks, paved streets, markets and many public buildings.

The Antonia fortress stood north of the Temple Mount. It was named after the Roman ruler Mark

Reconstruction of the Antonia fortress north of the Temple

Remnant of one of the Hulda Gates in the south retaining wall. These gates were the main entrance to the Temple Mount

can be inferred from the discovery of part of the foundation, which measures 143 x 363 yards. Josephus indicates that the palace had two opulent reception halls, hundreds of guest rooms and large ornamental gardens with fountains, waterfalls and dovecotes.

The palace was located near the western entrance to the walled city. There Herod erected three towers which formed part of the citadel guarding the entrance. The three – Phasael, Hippicus, and Mariamne – were impressive structures, reaching heights of 150 feet. The foundations of these towers are visible today, although archeologists are divided on the question of the exact identity of each. For instance, the foundation of today's Tower of David clearly displays trademark Herodian stonework, however opinion is divided as to whether this was Phasael or Hippicus.

Institutions and Society

Next to monotheism, the rule of the Torah was one of the most outstanding characteristics of Judaism of the Second Temple period. Differences that existed in Judean society concerning Torah focused on what the Torah intended in a given situation, not on its dominance over the life of the Jew. The rule of Torah must be understood in connection with the development of Jewish law, or halakhah, 'the path wherein Israel walks.' The halakhah (the main part of the Oral Tradition) governed all aspects of personal and public conduct: prayer, laws of ritual purity, Sabbath and festivals, marital relations, personal status, civil and criminal proceedings, tithes and other laws relating to the land, which could only be fulfilled in the land of Israel. The roots of the halakhah went back to far earlier times, but its main development began during the Second Temple period.

The Great Sanhedrin in Jerusalem was the chief arbiter of the halakhah. It was both a legislative and judicial institution in which seventy-one members conducted learned analyses and debate, interpreted and promulgated law. Its membership included priests, Levites and commoners, Jerusalem residents, people from the countryside and from Transjordan. Priests connected with the clan of the high priest formed a distinct group and held Sadducean opinions. Another

Antony, one of Herod's benefactors. According to Josephus' description, it was a quadrangular building with towers at its four corners. The southeastern tower was the tallest of the four; from it the proceedings on the Temple Mount could easily be viewed.

The king's palace was erected in the western part of the city on the site of the present-day Armenian quarter, near today's Jaffa Gate. It did not survive. Its proportions

"Theodotus son of Vetenos priest and head of the synagogue..." This inscribed stone testifies to the presence of synagogues in Jerusalem prior to the Temple's destruction. The inscription also indicates that the synagogue functioned as a hostel for Jews coming from the Diaspora

group were the Pharisee scholars, whose opinions usually dominated.

An essential role for the Sanhedrin was proclaiming the New Moon and the leap-year. These were critical responsibilities as they determined the correct dates for festivals. This information was transmitted to Jewish communities all over Judea and beyond. As far away as Babylonia, Jews received the information by means of a system of bonfires lit on the peaks of the highest hills.

The Sanhedrin was the authority overseeing the proper conduct of the Temple service. It also maintained an archive attached to the Temple in which were stored judicial documents, records of verdicts, contracts, and documents pertaining to priestly lineage.

Towards the end of the Second Temple period, synagogues may have proliferated throughout Jerusalem. A later source, the Jerusalem Talmud (Megillah 3a) mentions that there were no fewer that 480 synagogues in the city; this figure seems inflated. Synagogues were a lively aspect of the people's lifestyle, meeting places for social groups who gathered on the basis of their occupations or countries of origin. The synagogues or Houses of Gathering contained rooms for the study of Bible (The Written Law) and Mishnah (Oral Tradition) Worshippers would face in the direction of the Holy Temple during prayer.

The royal household was another of Jerusalem's central institutions. The palace, a palatial edifice in the accepted ornamental style of the East, was undoubtedly the scene of constant activity and intrigue. It employed hundreds of aides, advisors and administrators who functioned alongside members of the aristocracy, known as the 'friends' of the king. All manner of servants filled its halls. Herod surrounded himself with ministers, poets and writers who were thoroughly conversant with Greek and Roman culture. Herod's efforts to immerse himself in Roman culture extended to sending a number of his sons to Rome to be educated.

In the late Second Temple period a priestly aristocracy was at the summit of the Judean social structure. In the early Second Temple period the high priesthood was vouchsafed for the priestly clan of Zadok (from whence the term Sadducee derives), while in the Hasmonean period the office was inherited by members of the Jehoiariv priestly clan, the clan of the Hasmoneans. Later on, after Herod replaced the Hasmoneans, the office was divided among a number of priestly clans, among them the houses of Boethus, Phiabi, Hanan and Katros. Herod inspired loyalty and obligation among the priestly aristocracy through political alliances. He had a system of rotation by which he appointed to the high priesthood his chosen candidates from the different priestly clans. Included

among them were priests who did not reside in Palestine but stemmed from the Diaspora. This rotational approach, later adopted by the Romans, had a marked influence on the structure of Jerusalem society.

In the late Second Temple period a significant social role was played by two groups which had emerged during the Hasmonean period, the Pharisees and Sadducees. The elite Sadducee social stratum was composed mainly of the priestly aristocracy, and included other people of wealth. Not surpisingly, this group attached a good deal of prestige to the priesthood and service in the Temple. The Pharisees, in contrast, were not equatable with one specific socio-economic class. They were dedicated to the halakhah and stressed behavioral norms which were the obligation of every Jew; they saw themselves as representing the entire people. They educated the people toward careful observance of the halakah but did not demand adherence to strictures "that most of the community cannot cope with."

A third social grouping which endured throughout the Second Temple period was the Essene sect, or group of sects. A portion of its members lived an ascetic, communal lifestyle in Judean desert locations. They devoted themselves to study of Torah, eschatological speculation and manual labor, while strictly observing ritual purity. It appears that their move to the desert can be understood as a rejection of the everyday life of Jerusalem, and its profane tendencies. The life and thought of these sectarians continues to be a compelling interest for historians and archeologists, who base much of their research on the collection of ancient Hebrew documents known as the Dead Sea Scrolls. Josephus mentions an Essene Gate in the southwest area of Jerusalem, causing scholars to speculate upon the possible presence in the city of a community with a distinctive lifestyle.

A number of messianic groups emerged during the late Second Temple period. It was a time of intense Jewish study coupled with political, economic and social discontent. While Jewish study was focused in the main on biblical text and halakhah, another essential aspect was speculation concerning the meaning of life and the End of Days, a concept involving notions of national redemption, an end of individual suffering, and resurrection of the dead. The End of Days was connected with the idea of the coming of a royal messiah

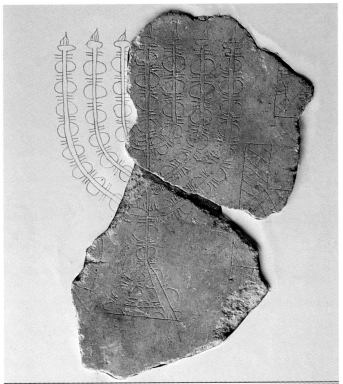

Design of a candelabrum etched in plaster discovered in a residence in the Upper City. The drawing was likely done by priests who had seen the Candelabrum of the Temple

Kidron Valley tombs of the Second Temple period. Left, tomb of Sons of Hezir. Center, monument known as Tomb of Zechariah. Right, another tomb. Above, on the slope of the Mount of Olives, a later cemetery. Upper left, Gethsemane

('annointed') of the House of David, and, as appears in the biblical book of Daniel, expectation of a time of unprecedented trouble during which the fall of the world's kingdoms would occur, followed by the resurrection of the kingdom of Israel, which would inherit their places. Messianic expectations were an active factor in political life during the late Second Temple period. In particular the era of rule by Roman procurators saw revolts motivated by messianic expectations.

The Beginnings of Christianity

Of the messianic movements in the late Second Temple period, all but one disappeared after the failures or deaths of their founders. The movement which emerged from the beliefs of the followers of Jesus of Nazareth developed into a faith of outstanding importance in the history of western civilzation.

According to Gospel accounts, Jesus was born in Judea during the rule of Herod, the rebuilder of the Temple, and grew up in Nazareth in the Galilee during the rule of Herod Antipas.

In the Gospel accounts, the connection between Jesus and Jerusalem is established when he arrives in the city shortly before the Passover festival to preach a message that `the kingdom of heaven' has already begun. His last visit in and around the city lasted about one week. The Gospel accounts place Jesus at several Jerusalem sites including Mount Zion, the area of the Temple, and the nearby Mount of Olives, where he and his followers lamented the predestined fate of the city – that is, its utter destruction. Entering Jerusalem on donkeyback (a description which conforms to a vision in the book of Zechariah 9:9), Jesus is depicted as being received with veneration by a crowd to whom he was presented as the herald of good tidings and a descendant of the house of David. The accounts describe his entry into the vicinity of the Temple with other pilgrims, where he chastised the money-changers, peddlers and hawkers of doves who were a common presence in the area. Afterwards he is depicted as arguing with priests and elders.

On Mount Zion Jesus ate a ceremonial Passover meal (*seder*) with his disciples in a spot not far from the palace of the High Priest Caiaphas. This meal is known in Christianity as the Last Supper. As the night proceeded, he went out with his companions to walk around Jerusalem and its surroundings. The company crossed the Kidron Valley and went up to the Gethsemane area at the foot of the Mount of Olives. The Gospel accounts portray Jesus' arrest as a result of a betrayal by one of his students, and his interrogation by the High Priest Caiaphas and sages during the course of that same night. The account suggests that this interrogation was conducted by the Sanhedrin, however this contradicts several stringent requirements in rabbinic literature for meetings of that body, including prohibitions on its meeting at night and on the eves of Sabbaths and festivals.

Jesus is depicted as having been handed over to the Roman procurator, Pontius Pilate, before whom he stood accused of political agitation and rebellion against Roman rule. He was tried and sentenced to death, and forced to bear a large wooden cross on his back which he carried through the streets of Jerusalem to the place of his execution. The means of execution was crucifixion, a well-known form of Roman punishment. After his death, his body was interred in a cave and a heavy stone was used to block the entrance. The Gospels recount that on the following Sunday the cave was found empty. Jesus' resurrection and ascension to heaven are essentials of Christianity. The traditionally accepted sites of Jesus' week in Jerusalem, including the site of the trial by the Romans, the street through which he bore the cross and particularly the sites of his crucifixion and burial, are venerated by Christians.

Jerusalem's symbolic and theological significance for Christianity evolved in a later period of the religion's development, though its roots are in Jewish concepts.

Authority in Jerusalem at the End of the Second Temple Period

Herod's kingdom did not last long after his death in 4 B.C.E. The Romans divided it among his sons, and Jerusalem was governed by Archelaus, who was ethnarch rather than king. He ruled for ten years which were difficult for the city's inhabitants, and was deposed by Rome, whereupon Judea became a province ruled by Roman governors, or procurators. Jerusalem's prestige began to decline in the context of the Roman world as it was no longer home to a king, and was stripped of its function as capital when Judea was converted into a Roman province and the hellenized port of Caesarea, built by Herod, was made capital.

Coin with head of Agrippa I

The inhabitants of Judea and Jerusalem were divided on the subject of Roman rule. The aristocracy generally collaborated with the authorities while the masses and the Pharisee leadership were dissatisfied, an attitude which became more marked over time owing to the policies of the Roman procurators, who destroyed much of the country's economy and drove many into poverty. The procurator Pontius Pilate, who ruled from 26-36 C.E. was known for his cruel, uncompromising character. His effort to enter Jerusalem with a company of soldiers bearing symbols of the Roman legion and depictions of Tiberius Caesar provoked the ire of Jerusalemites, numbers of whom made their way to Caesarea to protest. Angry encounters with Pilate took place in Caesarea, even though the people were courting death by opposing him. Josephus records that ultimately Pilate was impressed by their nobility in defense of Jerusalem's sanctity. Prior to the end of his term Pilate again angered Jerusalemites by appropriating funds from the Temple treasury for construction of an aqueduct.

There was usually an atmosphere of uneasy understanding between the Jews of Judea and the Roman empire, however events during the reign of the emperor Gaius Caligula (37-41 C.E.) caused an open break. Caligula ordered the placement of a statue bearing his likeness in the Temple of Jerusalem, provoking a

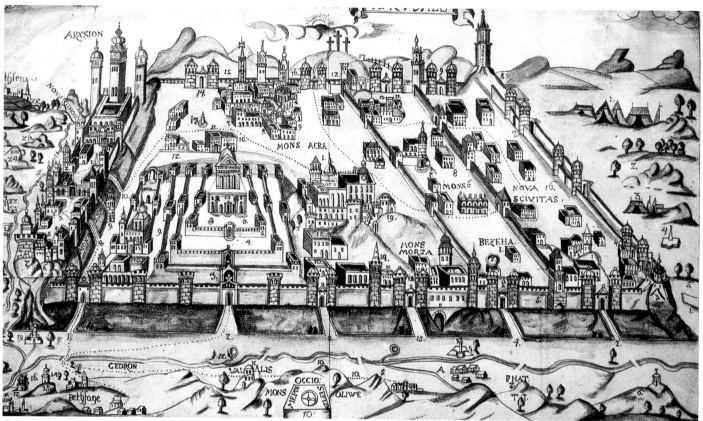

Map of Jerusalem, apparently from the 16th century, with Temple prominently featured. Jerusalem is depicted divided into three sections: central section, with the Temple to its east; southern section with Mt. Zion; northern section divided into three strips: the First, Second and Third walls

firestorm of indignation. Although this plan was not carried out, it left Jerusalem's residents with considerable bitterness toward foreign rule and dependence on a monarchy which could again be ruled by one capricious individual.

To make amends to the Jews, the Romans in 41 C.E. set Agrippa I – the grandson of Herod and Mariamne the Hasmonean, to rule over them. His reign interrupted two periods of rule by procurators. Agrippa I had already ruled parts of Palestine from the year 37 C.E. Like his grandfather Herod, he knew Rome well and was comfortable in its culture, however he was far more concerned than Herod had been with his relationship with the Jews and their faith. Towards the end of his rule he made the welfare of the Jewish nation his main concern, and identified entirely with its needs. As a result he was loved by the Jews and supported by their leadership. The Mishnah recounts that in the prayer for the Feast of Tabernacles (*Sukkot*) in the Temple, when

Agrippa read aloud the lines (Deuteronomy 17:15) prohibiting the Jews from setting a stranger as king over them, his eyes filled with tears. All those present called out encouragement, saying, "Do not fear, Agrippa, you are our brother, you are our brother!"

Agrippa I planned to strengthen Jerusalem's fortifications and build a wall around the new section of the city, a project that in the opinion of Josephus (Jewish Antiquities 19.326) would have made the city impregnable. The plan became known to the Roman procurator in Syria, who prevented its execution.

With the death of Agrippa I in 44 C.E. the second period of rule by procurators began. In twenty-two years Judea was governed by seven procurators who all pursued coarse and shortsighted policies which contributing to worsening relations between the Jews of Judea and Rome. At the same time, sectarianism and extremism became more evident in Jewish society. In certain circles in Jerusalem and other regions of the country, a rebellious atmosphere prevailed. In Jerusalem violent street encounters occurred between Roman soldiers and Jews, especially during pilgrimage festivals when the city was crowded with visitors. Events such as the desecration of a Torah scroll and one Roman soldier's display of obscene gestures towards pilgrims contributed to tensions, although the Roman authorities punished offenders. Pilgrims from distant towns shared information about discontent in other parts of the country. The procurator Florus, the last before the outbreak of the Great Revolt, attempted to confiscate funds from the Temple treasury, wheruapon the citizens of Jerusalem mocked him in the streets, crying out, "Alms, alms for Florus!"

The fabric of Jerusalem society disintigrated as clashes occurred between Jews of various sects and social groups. Extremist freedom fighters were active in the countryside and particularly in the Galilee region, and were also present in Jerusalem. Also maneuvering for mastery were members of the priestly aristocracy who hired ruffians to gain control of the city's streets. A division occurred in the priestly caste between those connected with the clans of the high priests and the rest of the priesthood. The great families sent representatives to the granaries to collect tithes and the common priests became impoverished. While all this was happening, clashes were also occurring between the various ethnic groups in Palestine – Jews, Greeks, Samaritans, and others. The Romans were determined to keep the situation in hand. Jerusalem was drawn into insurrection.

Daily Life at the End of the Second Temple Period

Under Roman rule, Jerusalem's area had grown threefold – from 162 to 450 acres, and its population at the end of the Second Temple Period is estimated to have run to many tens of thousands, perhaps even a hundred thousand inhabitants. During the Great Revolt large numbers of refugees from the north of the country and Judea's rural settlements concentrated in the city.

Jerusalem was a city of wide streets, evidence of which has been revealed by excavations at the foot of the Temple Mount and at a number of other sites in the Old City. There were street markets, shops, and public and private buildings some of which were simple structures while others were ornate buildings whose owners were intent on an ostentatious display of wealth.

Scholars consider Jerusalem to have been one of the largest cities in the Roman empire. Only Rome, Alexandria, and Antioch were larger. The masses of

The Palatial (Herodian) Mansion: elegant residence uncovered during excavation of the Upper City, Jerusalem's elite neighborhood

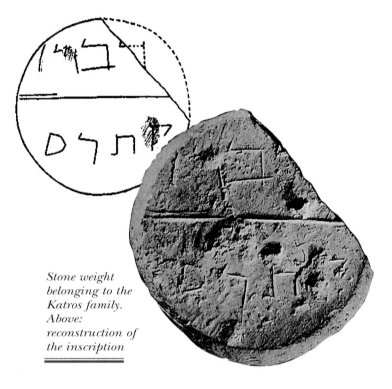

Stone weight belonging to the Katros family. Above: reconstruction of the inscription

pilgrims that came to the city three times a year undoubtedly contributed to its status.

The oldest part of town, the City of David area, lay in the east. In the late Second Temple period it contained public buildings to accommodate pilgrims planning to enter the Temple compound. In this area apparently stood the grand homes of the royal family of Adiabene, whose members had converted to Judaism and settled in Jerusalem. Also in this area were ancient water sources which had been technologically improved in order to meet the need of the large population of this period.

Another residential area stood on the western side of the Tyropaeon ('Cheesemaker's Valley'), opposite the City of David hill. It was a middle and working class neighborhood.

On the height of the the Western Hill stood the Upper City, remnants of which have been discovered in the present-day Jewish Quarter. It was the aristocratic neighborhood. Archaeological excavations have revealed handsome residences, such as the Palatial (Herodian) Mansion (*Beth ha-Middoth*) which even in its ruins reflects the the wealth of its occupants. It covered some 1800 feet and its cellars held cisterns and ritual baths - evidence of strict observance of the rites of ritual purity. The floors were decorated with mosaics and the walls covered with frescos. The large salon, probably used for receptions, was embellished by etched patterns of stylized flora and geometric designs in stucco walls. Evidently the artists refrained from portraying human and animal figures. Household objects including a table and imported glassware reveal the high economic status of the proprietors.

The Burnt House, uncovered not far from that spot, bears evidence of the great fire which took place during the destruction of the Upper City in autumn of 70 C.E. Coins were found on the floor, some from the era of the last Roman rulers and some from the time of the Great Revolt (66-70 C.E.). On a stone weight found in the house, the words "of the family of Katros" are etched. Katros is a known priestly family of the late Second Temple era, and the weight may have been used for official purposes.

Jerusalemites maintained their own systems of domestic water collection and storage. Each household had a plastered cistern. Rainwater was conducted to the cisterns from rooftops and courtyards. The municipal authorities saw to additional sources of water for use in the Temple, for the needs of the many pilgrims and the public. Pools and reservoirs were built inside the city and in ravines outside the walls. Two aqueducts dating to this period display advanced engineering techniques. They brought water from the Hebron Hills via Bethlehem to Jerusalem. The building of the aqueducts is ascribed to the Hasmoneans; their restoration and extension was the work of Herod and the Roman procurators, who initiated improvements to meet the demand for Jerusalem's growing populace.

Burial Sites around Jerusalem

According to Jewish law, it was forbidden to bury the dead within the city walls. Burial fields surrounded Jerusalem on every side, at a minimum distance of 50 cubits (ca. 300 feet). The dead were buried in the earth or in burial caves. After a year, the bones were assembled for re-interment in ossuaries (small stone coffins) which were placed in niches in burial caves. A small number of sarcophagi (large stone coffins) have also been found in Jerusalem burial sites. Ossuaries have been found bearing Hebrew, Aramaic or Greek inscriptions. These

Section of the lintel of 'Tombs of the Kings,' a series of magnificent tombs ascribed to the royal family of Adiabene

include the name and lineage of the deceased and sometimes the deceased's title and origin as well. Some are decorated with geometric and floral designs executed with varying degrees of skill. There are a group of impressive tombs in the Kidron Valley which date to the Second Temple period. Particularly worth noting are the four rock-carved tombs called the Tomb of the Sons of Hezir, Zechariah's Tomb, Jehoshaphat's Tomb, and Absalom's Tomb. The latter three, named for biblical figures, acquired their names long after the biblical period. They were built in hellenistic style with Eastern and Jewish decorative motifs. Another splendid group tomb is known as the Tombs of the Kings. In the past it was mistakenly identified as the burial place of the kings of Judah. Today, it is believed to have belonged to the royal family of Adiabene, or to an Arab tribal queen.

The Beginning of the Great Revolt

The Great Revolt of the Jews against Rome erupted in 66 C.E. Various factors contributed to its oubtreak; prime among them was the crude attitude of the procurators towards the Jewish population of Judea, and the bad relationship between the Jews and the hellenistic cities in Judea. These Greco-Syrian enclaves were favored by the procurators at the expense of the rest of the population. Friction between the Jewish majority and the favored gentiles eventually erupted into rioting in Caesarea and other cities, and massacres of Jews occurred.

Josephus Flavius blamed the more extremist Jewish groups, whom he termed Zealots, for the deterioration of life in Jerusalem to an almost anarchic state, and for

Silver shekel coin of the period of the Great Revolt bears image of three pomegranates and words "Jerusalem the holy." Other side shows goblet and inscription: Shekel of Israel Year Two

provoking Rome by suspending the routine Temple sacrifices for the well-being of the emperor. The messianic movements mentioned earlier in this chapter also prepared the way for revolt, as there was a sharp contrast between the apocalyptic Jewish expectation and the reality of subjugation to Roman rule. In addition, memory of the successful Hasmonean revolt, in which the few triumphed against the many, was perhaps a factor that spurred on the insurgents. Finally, news of rebellions in other provinces was probably an additional motivator. There is ample reason to assume that most of the Jewish population of Judea rejected the spiritual-cultural world of the Roman empire and supported the rebels, even if they did not actively participate in the Great Revolt.

In the summer of 66 C.E. riots broke out in Jerusalem, sparked by the procurator Florus' crass disregard of Jewish sensibilities. Fighting broke out between crowds and Roman army units. Prominent figures among the priesthood and leaders of the Pharisees tried to calm the atmosphere in the city. They also appealed to the procurator Florus and to King Agrippa II (who ruled in the north of the country) to send troops to the city. Jerusalem was divided between two camps: the Roman forces along with the more moderate Jerusalemites were located in the Upper City, while the rebels controlled the Lower City and the Temple. In the course of a few days the insurgents managed to take control of most of the Upper City, including the palaces and archives where the public's promissory notes were stored. In a gesture with distinct social significance, the rebels burnt the archives. After taking the royal palace the rebels were prepared to negotiate with the more moderate parties of the Jews but refused to deal with the Roman soldiers. The soldiers barricaded themselves in the towers of Mariamne, Hippicus, and Phasael, and although they would have surrendered to the rebels, they were not given the chance; Jewish fighters killed almost all of them. The rebels also killed members of the moderate Jewish leadership. Rebellion spread to other parts of the country and the uprising continued sporadically until 73 C.E.

From Rebellion to War

After the rebels killed the remnants of the Roman garrison in Jerusalem, the situation was transformed from riot to revolt, a situation with far greater political implications. The Roman procurator in Syria, Cestius Gallus, sent a large force to Jerusalem to quell the uprising. His troops attacked Jerusalem twice in one week and then retreated suddenly in the direction of the coast. Josephus Flavius had difficulty explaining this move and claimed that the city was about to fall. However it seems that Jewish resistance was stronger than Cestius Gallus had anticipated, and he hesitated to continue fighting as winter approached. For the Roman soldiers, the withdrawal from Jerusalem was a nightmare, as Jewish fighters pursued them as far as Beth Horon (the scene of a great Maccabee victory against the Syrian Greeks centuries earlier). It was as if the battles of the Maccabees were being re-fought. Thousands of Romans soliders were killed, and it was with some difficulty that Gallus managed to extract most of his army.

Jerusalem was excited by this turn of events. Many believed that Judea could overcome mighty Rome. A new

Remains of the Phasael (or Hippicus) tower in the area of the present-day Citadel

Spearhead unearthed in the Burnt House. Alongside it lay the armbone of a young girl who was evidently trying to escape the fire which destroyed the Upper City in early autumn of 70 C.E.

After Cestius Gallus' defeat a more extensive Roman attack was expected, and indeed the emperor Nero sent one of his ablest generals, Vespasian, to put down the rebellion. Vespasian was joined by his son Titus. The decision was made to quell the insurgency in the Galilee before heading on to Jerusalem. The battles in the north took place in the summer of 67 C.E. and the Romans had a number of victories, although Jewish opposition was strong. A Jewish commander in the Galilee, Joseph ben Matityahu went over to the Roman side and is known to us today as Josephus Flavius. He would eventually produce for his Roman masters the first history of the Jewish people as well as an account of the revolt, and other works. In the winter of 67-68 C.E. the country had a respite, as the Romans were not inclined to fight during the rainy season. Vespasian's advisors suggested that he go up to Jerusalem and conquer it, but the Roman commander hesitated because he believed, correctly, that internal strife in the city would weaken its ability to withstand attack. In the meantime, his armies conquered Judean and Idumean cities and gradually reduced the area in the hands of the insurgents; Jerusalem stood isolated and surrounded by enemies.

The comparatively moderate rebel government in Jerusalem lasted for more than a year, until the winter of 67-68. Meanwhile the city filled with refugees from the areas taken by Vespasian. Among the refugees was John of Giscala (*Gush Halav*) who had made his mark in the battles in the Galilee. Quarrels among the leaders of the Zealots and between the Zealots and their opponents continued without respite. Anarchy reigned and an ample number of bandits were prepared to loot and murder their opponents. The Zealots wished to seize control of the leadership in Jerusalem. Their opponents besieged them in their stronghold on the Temple Mount, where the Zealots had appointed a new high priest, a gesture which can be understood as expressing disdain for the priestly aristocracy. The siege of the Zealots in the Temple compound was lifted by a force of Idumeans who came to the Zealots' aid. Leaders who had opposed the Zealots were executed. Jerusalem was embroiled in bloody civil war. The tension in the city was not only a reflection of different ideologies but also an expression of economic and social gaps among the factions. According to Josephus, many left the city at this stage and urged Vespasian to conquer it.

leadership of decidedly rebellious spirit was established in Jerusalem, although it also included some leaders of the more moderate factions, among them the former High Priest Hanan, Joshua ben Gamla, and the Pharisee, Rabban Simeon ben Gamliel. The new government immediately went about strengthening Jerusalem, and within a comparatively short time completed the Third Wall encompassing the large built-up area in the northern part of the city. Weapons and armor were collected and fighters received training. During the war, the rebel government struck coins of the value of one shekel, half-shekel, quarter-shekel, and smaller denominations. The dates inscribed on the coins related to the war: Year One, Year Two, etc. These were issued over the course of five years (66-70 C.E.).

On the eve of the Roman attack Jerusalem was torn between various forces. John of Giscala (*Gush Halav*) and the Zealots were allied and held the Temple compound. They were opposed by the remaining moderates as well as the Idumeans, who ceased supporting the Zealots when they saw for themselves the cruelty of Zealot tactics. The forces outside the Temple compound were led by Simeon bar Giora and included groups of fighters with various aims – from respectable citizens to robbers and plunderers. They dominated parts of the Upper and Lower City consuming food supplies and equipment, committing murder and pillage, and generally adversely affecting the city's capacity to withstand siege. Civil war continued for approximately one year, until the spring of 70, when all the factions finally found a common language, and the city appointed a single commander, Simeon Bar Giora. By that point Jerusalem had been drained of resources.

The Fall of Jerusalem and Destruction of the Second Temple

In 69 C.E. Vespasian became emperor (this was the year of Nero's death, a year which witnessed four emperors in succession.) Titus, Vespasian's son, assumed command of the Roman armies in Palestine. In the spring of 70, he led more than sixty thousand soldiers to Jerusalem, and besieged the city. At the beginning of the siege some Jews were able to slip past the gates and strike at Roman soldiers. Titus managed to check these sorties and organized his forces for another attack on the walls. Prior to that, however, Titus proposed conditions for peace in the city, using Josephus Flavius as go-between. His terms were rejected. At that point, the Romans mobilized and broke through the Third Wall after fifteen days of assault, and the Second Wall after five days. Titus again proposed peace terms, which were rejected. The Jewish fighters displayed courage and ability. Many were killed by the Romans, but murderous squabbling and the lack of a central command were the undoing of the twenty-three thousand Jewish defenders. The condition of the inhabitants within the walls was grim; starvation reigned. Among those who fell were many who tried to join the Romans and were killed attempting to escape. Others who succeeded in reaching the Romans camp were tortured before being put to death.

The Romans built ramparts and batteries and thereby gained control of the Antonia fortress, which allowed them to overlook the Temple compound. This placed the defenders of the Temple in an impossible situation. In mid-summer, on the 17th of Tammuz, the daily sacrifices in the Temple ceased. Fire consumed the Royal Portico on the southern end of the Temple compound; the spirit of the fighters broke; they looked on as if paralyzed. The breakthrough into the Temple Mount evidently occurred on the 8th of Av. Fire consumed the Temple on the 9th and 10th of Av in 70 C.E., on the anniversary of the date that the First Temple was destroyed

Evidence of the fire in the Palatial (Herodian) Mansion in the Upper City. Still apparent, red-toned frescoed walls, a sign of the luxurious style of the house

Remnants of frescoed walls from homes in the Upper City.
The range of colors and designs testifies to the luxurious character of the homes

by the Babylonians. (Although the date of the Babylonian destruction is cited in II Kings, 25:18, as the 7th of Av, neither that first destruction nor this second lasted only one day, and the sages decided upon a date to mark both calamities: the 9th of Av.) The struggle in Jerusalem's streets lasted another month. In early autumn, on the 8th of Elul, the Upper City was set afire and thousands were killed. According to Josephus, the number of Jerusalemites who died during the siege was more than a million. Tacitus estimated it at six hundred thousand. These numbers may be exaggerated, but the death toll was clearly enormous. The grim fate of the survivors was described by Josephus: "... the tallest and handsomest were kept for the triumphal procession; of the rest, those over seventeen were put in irons and sent to hard labor in Egypt, while great numbers were sent by Titus to the provinces to perish in the theaters by sword or wild beasts; those under seventeen were sold." He also described the fate of the defeated city. It and the Temple were razed. The tall towers were spared. All the rest of the fortifications were so completely levelled that no visitor would believe the place had once been inhabited.

The horrors and lessons of the destruction of the Second Temple became part of the cultural legacy of the Jewish people. A fine example of what came to be their understanding of the tragedy is found in the Babylonian Talmud (Yoma 9b). "Why was the First Temple destroyed? Because of three transgressions (that violated it): because of idol worship, sexual immorality, and wanton bloodshed. But the Second Temple, (whose generation) studied Torah, observed the commandments, and engaged in charitable acts, why was it destroyed? Because of baseless hatred – which demonstrates that baseless hatred is as weighty as three transgressions: idol worship, sexual immorality and wanton bloodshed."

THE RULE OF ROME
AELIA CAPITOLINA

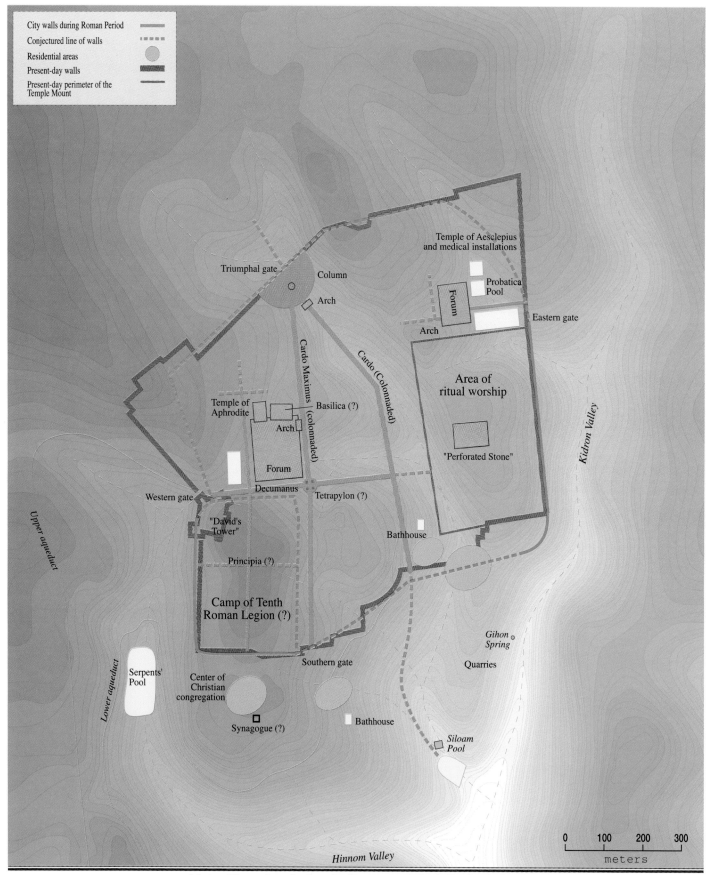

City walls during Roman Period
Conjectured line of walls
Residential areas
Present-day walls
Present-day perimeter of the
Temple Mount

Triumphal gate
Column
Arch

Temple of Aesclepius
and medical installations

Forum
Probatica
Pool

Arch
Eastern gate

Cardo Maximus

Cardo (Colonnaded)

Temple of
Aphrodite
Basilica (?)

Arch

Basilica (colonnaded)

Forum

Area of
ritual worship

"Perforated Stone"

Kidron Valley

Decumanus

Western gate
Tetrapylon (?)

"David's
Tower"

Bathhouse

Principia (?)

Upper aqueduct

Camp of Tenth
Roman Legion (?)

Gihon
Spring

Southern gate
Quarries

Serpents'
Pool

Center of
Christian
congregation

Lower aqueduct

Synagogue (?)
Bathhouse

Siloam
Pool

0   100   200   300

meters

Hinnom Valley

Map of Jerusalem during the Roman period: Aelia Capitolina

Bas-relief on the triumphal arch of Titus in Rome depicts Roman soldiers carrying off the Temple's holy objects. The arch was erected in 81 C.E. to commemorate the Roman victory over Judea

In autumn 70 C.E. the Holy Temple of Jerusalem was a mound of rubble rising above a destroyed city. Of all Jerusalem's once magnificent structures, the only ones left standing were the retaining walls of the Temple Mount, including the segment known as the Western Wall, and three defense towers near the western entrance to the city.

The Romans were adamant that Jerusalem remain desolate; even the trees in the vicinity of the city had been destroyed during the siege. The functions of regional capital had been transferred to Caesarea during the revolt, and remained there. A heavy tax burden was placed upon the Jews, a portion of which went to support Roman troops stationed in Judea to control them. The tax burden fell mainly on farmers, and there is evidence of forced labor and confiscation of beasts of burden for use in public projects such as road building and repair. A special tax was levied by Rome on every Jew of the Empire – in Judea and the Diaspora. Two drachmas were to be paid to the Roman treasury in place of the half shekel the Jews had previously contributed to the Temple. This tax was collected as a contribution to Jupiter Capitolinus, the main god of Rome, based on the notion that with the conquest, the Jews' God had become

Detail of ark curtain from a synagogue in northern Italy. Under the depiction of Jerusalem surrounded by a wall is the inscription 'Black on White in memory of the destruction.' Expressions of sorrow over the destruction of the Temple are an ever-present artisitic motif in synagogues through the centuries

subject to Jupiter. While this tax was not in itself heavy enough to be a financial burden, it was a painful humiliation.

Evidence indicates that soldiers of the Tenth Legion were stationed in Jerusalem after its destruction, and a number of them established families, as was customary practice for soldiers in distant postings. In archeological excavations in the Old City, remnants of tiles, clay pipes and a large number of round clay bricks and roof tiles were found, all bearing the hallmark of the Tenth Legion ("LXF, Legio X Fretensis") This would indicate that in and around Jerusalem, Roman soldiers were engaged in the production of building materials. Other objects were found, such as remnants of columns and tombstones, which bear inscribed names of Roman emperors, military leaders and army units of the period. In the late nineteenth century an inscription was unearthed north

of the Citadel which mentions Marcus Junius Maximus, a commander of the Tenth Legion. Additional inscriptions were discovered in the northern sector of the Old City, among them the tombstone of the soldier Tiberius Claudius Fatalis, who lived in Jerusalem with his wife at the end of the first century, some decades after the destruction of the Second Temple.

There is some question as to the site of the Roman camp. It has long been believed that this camp was located at the southern part of the city, near and perhaps including Mount Zion. However, recently it has been suggested that the camp was located in the present-day Christian quarter, near the Church of the Holy Sepulcher. Jerusalem may have had a number of Christian residents in this period. Sources suggest that Christians who had fled the city before the Great Revolt returned afterwards, settling near the Legion's camp. It is also possible that some Jews who traded with the soldiers settled near the camp.

Though they had suffered a devastating blow, the Jewish people in the land of Israel was able to recover in the decades after the destruction. Many Jews in Judea and the Diaspora who had been sold into slavery were purchased and freed by fellow Jews. Many settled in Diaspora lands, while many others returned to Judea. An agriculture-based economy was restored by the turn of the second century, and farm villages were located near Jerusalem. Yet the Jewish people were in serious difficulty politically and economically, and were suffering spiritual depression.

"If I Forget Thee O Jerusalem..."

The destruction of the city and especially the Temple, was a cataclysmic event for the Jews. From a political standpoint, their national coherence and leadership was severely threatened. For hundreds of years Jews in Judea and the Diaspora had looked to the holy city for leadership. The high priest was their symbolic leader, and was viewed by other governments as their chief representative. At the actual forefront of their leadership were the rabbinic scholars of the Great Sanhedrin of Jerusalem, of which the high priest was titular head. Communication and control between Jerusalem and the Jews of Judea and the Diaspora, was maintained through the medium of thrice yearly pilgrimages to the Temple. After the summer of 70 C.E. Jerusalem ceased to fill this role, and ceased functioning as the center of holy ritual and advanced Torah study from which Jewish identity took sustenance.

The Jews had considered Jerusalem eternal – the site where the Temple would stand forever. Its destruction seemed to them the 'end of the world.' Many were appalled that while the city and Temple were destroyed, the world went on, and the destroyers prospered. A writer of the period records his amazement: "...For thirty years now my heart is anguished, to see how You tolerate the sinners and spare the wicked while destroying Your people, and protect those who hate You... Has Babylon (Rome) behaved better than Zion?"

The Mishnah (Sotah 9:12) records perceptions that the nature of the world had changed in the wake of Jerusalem's destruction. "From the day the Temple was destroyed, there is no day without a curse, the dew has not descended for a blessing, and flavor has departed from fruits... the fatness was also removed from the fruits." Jews felt their relationship with their God had changed: "From the day of the Temple's destruction the gates of prayer have been closed... a wall of iron came down between the people of Israel and their Father in Heaven..." (Babylonian Talmud, Berakhot 32b).

Tablet reading, "Black on White in memory of the destruction," from the wall of the Italian synagogue in Jerusalem

National depression accompanied the destruction. During and after the Roman assault numbers of Jerusalemites opted to end their own lives. The Roman historian Tacitus wrote that Jews preferred death to life without their holy city. The historian Dio Cassius noted that at the time of the Roman assault upon the Temple "Jews hurled themseves upon Roman swords, others killed one another (rather than outlasting the Temple and falling into Roman hands), while still others leaped into the fires."

In the decades after the destruction, the rabbis encountered many Jews who had taken upon themselves

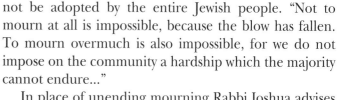
practices of self-denial; some lived in caves apart from the general community. This reality is reflected in a discussion in the Babylonian Talmud (Baba Bathra 60b). "Our Rabbis taught: When the Temple was destroyed for the second time, large numbers in Israel became ascetics, forswearing to eat meat or drink wine. Rabbi Joshua (son of Hananiah, who lived in the period immediately following the destruction) conversed with them. He said: 'My children, why do you not eat meat or drink wine?' They responded, 'Shall we eat meat which used to be brought as an offering on the altar, now that all that is come to naught? Shall we drink wine which used to be poured for libation on the altar, but now no longer?'" Later in the same account, Rabbi Joshua extends their reasoning to the point of absurdity. He says, "'If so, we ought not eat bread, for the meal offerings and Show Bread have also come to naught... and we ought not eat fruit, for the ceremony of First Fruits is likewise ended... and we ought not drink water for the Water Libation is also gone.' To this they could find no answer." Rabbi Joshua sought to convey that such ascetic conduct could

not be adopted by the entire Jewish people. "Not to mourn at all is impossible, because the blow has fallen. To mourn overmuch is also impossible, for we do not impose on the community a hardship which the majority cannot endure..."

In place of unending mourning Rabbi Joshua advises that life must go on, however the destruction ought not be forgotten, nor should mourning practices be totally dispensed with. "One who whitewashes his house leaves a portion undone; one who prepares a feast leaves one detail undone; a woman who dons her jewelry leaves some detail unattended to," all in memory of the Destruction. To this day, many traditional Jews leave a corner of wall unpainted or a detail of house renovation undone to commemorate the destruction of Jerusalem and the Temple.

For hundreds of years after the destruction, various daily customs reminded Jews of the Temple. It was common in certain congregations to decorate the heads of brides and grooms with olive wreaths, whose bitter leaves symbolized the bitterness of the Temple's loss. In other places, bridegrooms on their wedding days marked their foreheads with ashes as a sign of mourning for the Temple. Today the widespread custom of breaking a glass under the wedding canopy serves as a reminder of Jerusalem and the Temple.

The traditional Jewish prayerbook which throughout history united Jews in common worship practices, repeatedly refers to the restoration of Jerusalem and the Temple. One example of many appears in the *Amidah* the quintessential prayer of Silent Devotion: "To Jerusalem Your city may You return in compassion, and rest within it... May You rebuild it hastily in our day, an everlasting structure..." Another begins, "May our eyes behold Your return to Zion in compassion. Blessed are You Who restores His presence to Zion." Similarly the Grace After Meals expresses: "Have mercy, our God, on Your people Israel, on Jerusalem your city, on Zion the dwelling place of Your glory, on the monarchy of the house of David... and on the great and holy house which is dedicated to Your name..."

The very institution of prayer – thrice daily and four times on Sabbaths and festivals – was understood by the rabbis as a replication of the order of worship in the Temple. The adoption of many rulings

The 'four kinds' of the Sukkot festival depicted on a silver tetradrachma coin of the Bar Kokhba period.
This motif would have served to recall festival pilgrimage in the days of the Temple

which echoed the Temple service was undertaken as a means of coping with the collapse of the structure on which much of religious observance had been based. Many precepts were connected with the Temple: sacrifices, donations to priests, peace offerings, festival observances, and more. Rather than discarding these laws, the Tannaim, or rabbinic leaders of the generations immediately following the destruction, created a complex cultural reality which preserved the memory of the Temple and fulfilled many of the roles it had formerly played. A transition to a new religious attitude was urgently required, yet it should be noted that the scholars hoped the destruction was temporary, and new regulations preserved traditional practices, so they might be easily re-instituted. The granting of gifts to the priests was preserved, and Rabbi Tarfon stated that after the destruction, these donations were the equivalent of the sacrifices. The new religious attitude which emerged was based on fidelity to the halakhah, performance of good deeds and waiting for Redemption.

A mural from the ancient synagogue of Dura-Europos in Syria depicts Queen Esther (right) with a crown suggesting the piece of jewelry known as 'the City of Gold'

Rabban Johanan ben Zakkai

One rabbinic figure emerges as central to the process of re-establishing Jewish religious and communal life. He was Rabban Johanan ben Zakkai, a leading Jerusalem scholar, deputy head of the Sanhedrin, and chief Pharisee spokesman before the destruction. During the Great Revolt he warned against fanaticism, and as events progressed, may have refused to take part in the revolt. The tale of his dramatic escape from Jerusalem before the city fell, and his brief exchange with the general (soon to be emperor) Vespasian, appears in several versions in the Talmud. The upshot is that he requested passage to the coastal town of Jabneh, in order to teach his pupils. In Jabneh he established a House of Assembly which took on some of the roles of the Great Sanhedrin of Jerusalem. This gesture was in itself a bold step toward continuity, for it altered the requirement that the Sanhedrin meet and exercise its powers only in the Temple, when the sacrificial services were being conducted. The justification for usurping the Sanhedrin's powers was twofold: the need to preserve the Jewish people and faith, and the need to preserve the institution of the Sanhedrin until the time when it would be restored to its proper place in the Temple in Jerusalem.

The sages of Jabneh began hallowing New Moons and proclaiming leap years – both Sanhedrin functions – and thus preserved the Jewish calendar and its cycle of festivals. The Jabneh sages also took decisions to preserve memory of the Temple, and others to provide ways of adjusting to life without it. An instance of the former was the Jabneh decision, 'in memory of the Temple,' to allow the shofar to be blown in Jabneh even if the New Year fell on a Sabbath. This was only permitted in the Temple and its environs; elsewhere Jews were not to sound the shofar on a New Year which fell on the Sabbath. An instance of adjustment to life without the Temple is as follows: In the days when the Temple stood, only Jews who lived at a distance from Jerusalem could redeem their fourth year's crop locally, and carry the money to Jerusalem. Anyone who lived within a day's walk of the city had to bring the produce itself. Rabban Johanan ruled that even a crop planted close to the city might be redeemed.

To those who were distressed by the inability to repent of sins in the Temple Rabban Johanan taught, "Do not distress yourself, for we have another atonement that is like it... Charity: 'For charity I desire, not sacrifice.'"

In the generations following Rabban Johanan's, Jabneh's relations with Diaspora Jewish communities were enhanced, supervision of Jewish communities in the Land of Israel was fully developed and recognized by the Roman authorities, and great concern was paid to the development of Jewish law. The sages of Jabneh were able to gain control over different groups within the Jewish nation: the Sadduccee and Essene sects essentially disappeared, and moves were taken to distinguish Christianity from Judaism. There are early Christian traditions concerning the existence of Judeo-Christian sects in Eretz Israel and its vicinity during this period. They were evidently increasing missionary activities. The rabbinic leadership took steps to prevent contacts between Jews and Judeo-Christians, and during this period the separation between normative Jews and these sects became a fait accompli.

A leaf from Tractate Middot ('Measurements'). Kaufman Manuscript of the Mishnah

Jerusalem of Gold

The continued dedication of the Jews to Jerusalem is evident in records of their folk practice, legend and law. Far from losing importance, Jerusalem's significance grew. A midrash (Jewish legend) recounts the gift of the great Rabbi Akiva to his wife, Rahel – a beautiful piece of gold jewelry called a 'City of Gold,' which was worn around the neck or arm, and took the form of the silhouette or skyline of Jerusalem as it appeared in its prime. The gift, given during the degradation of Jerusalem, was a reminder of its glorious past and an expression of hope for its future.

The sages of Jabneh accumulated and preserved a record of the appearance, dimensions, laws and practices of the Temple based on the expert testimony of sages who lived during the last decades of the Second Temple's existence. The record is dispersed throughout the scholarly literature of the period. An especially rich record is found in two of the six orders of the Mishnah:

Kodashim which concerns regulations for the Temple service, ritual slaughter and permitted and fobidden foods, and *Tohorot* which deals with the laws of ritual purity. Further discussions on the Temple are included in the Tosefta, the Jerusalem and Babylonian Talmuds and the Midrash (rabbinic interpretations of Scripture). The animating factor behind this immense corpus of documentation was the hoped for national redemption and privilege of rebuilding the Temple and restoring Jerusalem.

The Heavenly Jerusalem

Along with the precise legalities recorded in the abovementioned works, there are more emotional expressions of love and longing. "Ten measures of beauty were bestowed upon the world: nine upon Jerusalem and one on the rest of the world" (Babylonian Talmud, Kiddushin 49b); "Ten measures of wisdom were

Depiction of the Temple on a wall fresco of the ancient synagogue of Dura-Europos, Syria. The Temple is depicted in the style of a hellenistic temple. In the facade of the surrounding wall are three monumental gates

Herod's temple depicted on the bottom of a gilded glass or plate. Rome, late 3rd - early 4th century

Rabbinic scholars viewed this tendency with anxiety, since it drew attention away from the rehabilitation of the people in their land. They emphasized the intrinsic connection between the physical city and the idea of Jerusalem. Specifically they stressed the view that spiritual redemption would come only after restoration of the terrestrial city and reconstruction of the Temple. Concerning this Rabbi Johanan ben Zakkai said, (Babylonian Talmud, Taanit 5a) "I will not arrive in the heavenly Jerusalem until I set foot in the earthly Jerusalem."

Pilgrimage to Jerusalem

In the wake of the destruction, the sages were divided as to whether the sanctity of the Temple site was negated or remained intact. The majority of Tanna'im and Ammora'im (scholars of the Mishnah and the Talmuds) agreed that the sanctity of the place endured in spite of the destruction. Several of their expressions relate to this issue: "There is a (type of) sanctity that is temporary and another that abides forever...;" "The holiness of the Sanctuary is enduring... for it is written, 'this is my resting place forever and ever.'" The belief in the eternal sanctity of the Temple Mount is related to the idea that the Divine Presence (*Shekhinah*) does not ever leave it. Another opinion held that the *Shekhinah* departed upon the destruction of the Temple and joined the Jewish people, as a loving mother would join her children.

The sanctity of the Temple Mount was accepted as enduring, and when pilgrims went up to Jerusalem, they scrupulously observed regulations regarding personal conduct in what had been the Temple precincts. "A person may not enter the Temple Mount with his walking stick and shoes...or with the dust of the road on his feet... I might think this held when the Temple stood, but what of the period when it does not stand? We learn (from the biblical verse) 'Observe My Sabbaths, and revere my Sanctuary,' that just as observance of the Sabbath endures forever, so does the sanctity of the Temple."

The institution of pilgrimage endured beyond the destruction of the Temple, though the experience was entirely different from pilgrimage in former times. In place of offerings, worship, and social contact with masses of fellow Jews, pilgrims after the destruction went

bestowed upon the world: nine upon Jerusalem and one on the rest of the world" (Avot d'Rabbi Nathan). "The land of Israel rests in the center of the world, and Jerusalem in the center of the land of Israel, and the Holy Temple in the center of Jerusalem, and the Sanctuary in the center of the Holy Temple, and the Ark in the center of the Sanctuary, and the Foundation Stone stands before the Ark – upon it the world was founded."

Expressions of praise and admiration depict Jerusalem before the destruction; its beauty which had no measure; its great size and population; the special wisdom of its residents and the miracles they experienced because they dwelled in Jerusalem; and of course, the city's supreme holiness. There was a tendency among poets, visionaries and thinkers to transform Jerusalem from a terrestrial city into an abstract idea. Jerusalem earned the title 'the heavenly Jerusalem' and sometimes the city as spiritual idea came to be regarded as the true Jerusalem.

up to Jerusalem to mourn, recall and lament. "If you merit the privilege of pilgrimage to Jerusalem, when you look upon it from Mount Scopus, if you are upon a donkey, dismount, and if you are shod, remove your shoes. Tear your garment and say: 'behold this sacred place has become a ruin...'"

Jews arrived in Jerusalem as individuals, in silence. They ate no meat and drank no wine on the day they beheld destroyed Jerusalem, and possibly fasted. In spite of the somber nature of the experience, pilgrimage to Jerusalem was a widespread phenomemon. We know of a Jewish donkey driver who would shepherd pilgrims on their way to Jerusalem. He inquired of the rabbis if he was obligated to tear his garment each time he came to

the city within a thirty day period. From the question it can be inferred that he accompanied visitors to Jerusalem frequently.

The sages compared the people to a dove – just as the dove never abandons its nest even when its nestlings have been taken away, 'thus Israel, even though the Temple was destroyed, did not cancel the three annual pilgrimages.' The grief served as a spur for the creation of a rich contemplative culture.

For the great Tanna, Rabbi Akiva, the sacking of Jerusalem was the very foundation of belief in the consoling vision of the prophets that the Temple would be rebuilt. To his bereft colleagues who stood with him viewing the ruins of Jerusalem Rabbi Akiva said, "Until the (sad) prophesy of Urriah was completed, I feared that the prophecy of Zechariah would not come to pass. Now that Urriah's is fulfilled, it is certain Zechariah's will be fulfilled." His colleagues responded, "Akiva you have comforted us, Akiva you have comforted us." It is noteworthy that Akiva's reasoning reflects his faith in the rebuilding of a real, material (or earthly) Jerusalem, not a spiritual or heavenly construct.

Above: A coin with portrait of Hadrian. Below: A coin commemorating the 'plowing ceremony' which determined the boundaries of a new city

Political Unrest

The period commencing in the last decades of the first century was spiritually turbulent; an apocalyptic mood gripped the land. In 115-117 C.E., under the rule of Trajan, disturbances erupted in the land of Israel, possibly an offshoot of Jewish rebellions occurring in the Diaspora at the time. The Talmud and other written sources indicate that there were gatherings of Jews on the ruined Temple Mount in Jerusalem, and that the Galilee region was turbulent. The unrest was suppressed by Roman troops, and decrees were issued against the Jewish religion. The Romans deliberately provoked the Jews by setting up an idol on the Temple Mount. In Jewish sources, elements of this period of unrest are merged with the record of the Bar Kokhba Revolt, which erupted in 132 C.E.

It seems that with the accession of Hadrian to the imperial throne in 117 C.E. a period of calm and restoration began in the eastern reaches of the Roman empire, including the land of Israel. Hadrian made efforts to restore ruined cities and rural areas, and seems to have promised the Jews that he would rebuild Jerusalem, return it to them, and allow the Temple to be rebuilt. This picture emerges from Jewish sources regarding the emperor's first visit to the land of Israel, which occurred during his first trip to the east after his rise to the throne. Beyond the promises he made, Hadrian seemed to have expressed the desire to study the Jews and their faith. Reports of the emperor's intentions spread through the Diaspora. Jews came to Jerusalem and preparations were undertaken for rebuilding the Temple.

In time, Hadrian's intentions changed. The reasons for the turnaround are unclear, but may have been motivated by reports of the emotional reaction of the Jews, and fear of the political consequences of allowing them to recover Jerusalem. His change of heart coincides with the broader picture of his having developed an abiding interest in hellenism and a distaste for 'oriental' religions. Hadrian sought to convert Jerusalem into a pagan city.

Aelia Capitolina

In 129, Hadrian apparently decided to erect a Roman city on the ruins of Jerusalem. The Jews still had the impression that he intended to rebuild the Jewish city and reconstruct the Temple. Instead, planning commenced for a city called Aelia Capitolina; Aelia after his family name (Titus Aelius Hadrianus Antonius Augustus Pius) and Capitolina after the three gods, Jupiter, Juno, and Minerva who according to Roman belief, sat on the Capitoline hill in

Silver tetradrachma coin (obverse of coin p.66) of the period of the Bar Kokhba rebellion, depicts the facade of the Temple

Rome. The first stage in building a new Roman city consisted of a plowing ceremony at which the emperor plowed the furrow which defined the city's boundaries. In Jewish tradition, this manner of plowing connoted final and utter destruction, *viz.* the stormy prophecy "...Assuredly because of you Zion shall be plowed as a field, and Jerusalem shall become heaps of ruins, and the Temple Mount a shrine in the woods" – Micah 3:12).

It is not difficult to imagine the Jewish reaction to the plowing or to the idea of establishing Jerusalem as a pagan city. Adding fuel to the fire were their raised expectations regarding the imminent reconstruction of the Jewish city they longed for, and whose rebuilding had been foretold by the prophets.

Column in memory of a Roman officer, which reads: "To Marcus Junius Maximus, commander on behalf of the caesars, of the Tenth Legion Fretensis..." The column stands in a lane in the Old City of Jerusalem

The paving of roads from Aelia Capitolina to Beth Govrin, Hebron and Lod began approximately at the time of Hadrian's visit to the country, as part of a general re-shuffling of Roman military movements at the outer limits of the Empire. The road building and preparations for building Aelia Capitolina undoubtedly increased the agitation within Jewish settlements, and with good reason, as the roads ultimately facilitated Roman suppression of the Bar Kokhba Revolt. The immediate cause of the uprising known as the Bar Kokhba Revolt is not clear, and scholars are divided on the issue. Some are

The insignia of the Tenth Legion discovered during excavations in Jerusalem

convinced that rebellion broke out because of the building of Aelia Capitolina, while others say that the rebellion predated the building of the city, and in fact provided the motivation for building a pagan city on the ruins of Jerusalem.

The Roman historian Dio Cassius wrote extensively of the Bar Kokhba Revolt, noting that the anger of the Jews had turned into revolt against the Romans: "A war neither small nor short was caused when Hadrian established in Jerusalem a city in place of that which had been destroyed, which he called Aelia Capitolina, and when he erected, on the site of the Temple of the Lord, a different temple, dedicated to Jupiter-Zeus. The Jews were shocked that foreigners were settling in the city and that pagan temples were being built there."

The uprising broke out in 132 C.E. Simon bar Kosiba became the acknowledged leader of the revolt and head of the nation. Coins were struck inscribed with the message 'Simon, Prince of Israel.' Christian sources indicate that he was referred to as Bar Kokhba ('Son of the Star') because of a belief that he was the messiah. Jewish sources indicate that the great scholar Rabbi Akiva was convinced of his messianic character.

In caves in the Judean desert a treasure trove of documents, letters and personal possessions from the time of the Bar Kokhba Revolt have been discovered. The written finds indicate that despite his appelation, "Simon Bar Kosiba, Prince of Israel," Simon did not rule as messiah or annointed monarch, but had a priest as colleague. A number of coins of the revolt bear the name of Eleazar the Priest in addition to the name of Simon Prince of Israel. Scholars assume Eleazar the Priest was Eleazar the Moda'ite, one the Jabneh scholars.

The Jews made substantial gains in the early years of the Bar Kokhba Revolt. The Tenth Legion was defeated and the Roman commander withdrew to Caesarea. The question remains of whether Bar Kokhba conquered Jerusalem during the first sweep of victories. Historians are not of one mind on this issue. Archeological finds suggest victory. Coins from the period were struck which exhibit a new standard for calendrical dating: 'Year One of the Liberation of Israel,' 'Year Two of the Freedom of Israel.' Coins have been found inscribed with the message, 'For the freedom of Jerusalem,' but with no date. Scholars are divided on whether these coins prove that the city was conquered by Bar Kokhba, or whether their message was inspirational in nature. The remarkable collection of Bar Kokhba's letters found in the area of the Dead Sea are also dated with the slogans 'Israel's Liberation' or 'The Freedom of Israel.' One letter features a damaged inscription which leads some scholars to suggest it was dispatched from Jerusalem. The writings of Appian, a second century historian from Alexandria, are also used to buttress the contention that the Jews held Jerusalem. Appian writes: "This city, Jerusalem, had been destroyed in the days of Ptolemy I of Egypt; it was afterward rebuilt, and Vespasian again destroyed it, and Hadrian did the same in our time..." The grouping of Hadrian's name with other conquerors who seized and destroyed Jerusalem could indicate that Hadrian too had to seize the city from someone, i.e. the Jews.

Even if Jerusalem was not actually conquered by Bar Kokhba, it is clear from archeological finds that its conquest was the goal of the uprising. In the final period, Roman troops pushed the insurgents towards their fortresss in Judea. Finally, the fortress of Betar, the last stronghold of the revolt, fell in 135 C.E. Jewish tradition notes that Betar fell on the ninth day of the month of Av, the date on which Jerusalem fell. In Jewish national consciousness, Bar Kokhba's uprising was a war over

Jerusalem. Its failure is associated with the city's destruction.

The Bar Kokhba Revolt was crushed and Christian sources mention the promolgatiopn of a decree forbidding jews to reside in Jerusalem and its vicinity. According to Christian sources, jews were permitted to visit only once a year, on the ninth of the month of Av, to mourn the ruins of the Temple. In the wake of the revolt, the number of dead was enormous, and many Jews were sold as slaves. Many towns and villages in Judea were razed and never rebuilt, and it was in this period that the mountainous areas in the center of the country were virtually emptied of Jews. A time of religious persecution followed the defeat; many Jews, including leading rabbinic scholars, were put to death. The Romans were particiularly intent upon preventing Jews from studying Torah or maintaining communal institutions. During this time the Jews continued the tradition of martyrdom for the sake of the faith. The medieval story of the Ten Martyrs which appears in the liturgy of the Day of Atonement is based on stories which dates to this period. Numbers of scholars fled or lived in hiding, until returning to the land several years later.

As part of a wholesale administrative and militaty reorganization of the province, and perhaps to obliterate the land's ethnic connection with the Jews, Hadrian bestowed on the territory the name Syria-Palestine.

The Mishnah and Talmuds

The issue of writing down the oral tradition became urgent, lest this catastrophic period for the Jews result in the loss of a thousands year old legal and homiletic tradition. The recording process, which had begun generations earlier, proceeded with a passion, culminating in ca. 200 C.E. in the Mishnah, the first summary and compendium of the halakhic material of the Oral Law. The Mishnah is composed of six major divisions and was edited by Rabbi Judah Hanasi ('the Prince'). The Mishnah served as the basis for further development of the Oral Law. It is the foundation for the two great Talmudic works, the Jerusalem Talmud and the Babylonian Talmud, which were developed during the Byzantine period.

A Roman Colony

After the suppression of the Bar Kokhba Revolt, the Romans set up Jerusalem as the Roman colony Aelia Capitolina. A Christian community of pagan origin began to emerge. There may have been intentional Roman suppression of Christian devotional sites. On the site of the crucifixion of Jesus, a temple to Venus-Aphrodite was erected, in all likelihood to dissociate the spot from the holiness the early Christians ascribed to it. Out of similar motive, the Romans built a temple to Asclepius, the god of healing, on the site of Jerusalem's Pool of Bethesda, where, according to Christian tradition, Jesus healed the sick and lame.

According to the Church father Jerome, the Romans placed an image of a boar on the gate of the city facing the road to Bethlehem, apparently in honor of the Tenth Legion, whose mascot was a boar.

The Romans preferred to establish Aelia Capitolina as a Roman colony rather than organize it as a polis, which was more customary throughout the empire. The motive for organizing it as a colony is still unclear. It is known that the latter designation was more prestigious. A colony's inhabitants enjoyed greater rights and privileges: they were exempt from taxation and could expect economic stability. The Romans established colonies in distant regions of the empire to support Roman rule and to help spread Roman culture. The residents were typically veterans of the army and citizens of Rome. Aelia Capitolina was settled by veterans and Greek settlers. Regarding civil administration and division of authority, it is not clear what the relationship was between the civilian inhabitants and the soldiers who were stationed in Aelia. It is also not clear which area was under army control and which belonged to the colonial administration.

Jews in Aelia Capitolina

According to the accounts of Church fathers, Jews were not permitted to live in Jerusalem or its vicinity after the revolt. A ban of this kind is not mentioned in Talmudic literature, which indicates instead that a limited number of Jews continued to live there. It is reasonable to assume that during the reign of Severus, a reputedly liberal administration, Jews succeeded in settling in the city while the rulers turned a blind eye. The Talmud describes a group of the disciples of Rabbi Meir (who was the student of Rabbi Akiva) who lived in Jerusalem during the third century C.E. and were called in Aramaic 'The Holy Congregation of Jerusalem.' In Eretz Israel sources they are referred to as 'Edah Kedoshah' the Holy Community. The character of the scholarly deliberations attributed to members of this community indicate that they were strict with themselves, especially regarding the rules of ritual purity and *separateness* (prishut). They also had a singular life-style, dividing their waking hours into three parts: one third for study, one third for prayer, and one third for work. "Some maintain that they studied all winter and worked in the summer," (Kohelet Rabbah 9:9). Either division implies that the members of the group worked their own fields, or worked in a managerial capacity, for had they been salaried workers, they would not have been able to set their own schedules. Aside from the scholars of the Holy Community, there appear to have been other Jews living in Roman Jerusalem. A burial cave thought to be of the third century, discovered near kibbutz Ramat Rahel, has yielded remains which indicate there were Jewish residents in the vicinity of Jerusalem during this period. In addition, mention is made in the Jerusalem Talmud of one Nehemiah of the Sihin village "who was attacked by a Jerusalemite..." This might indicate that there were ordinary working folk, 'ordinary Jerusalemites,' living in the city.

There is evidence of a first century C.E. structure on Mount Zion. Its remains are incorporated into the structure known as the Tomb of David, which dates to the Middle Ages. It may be the remains of a synagogue mentioned by the pilgrim of Bordeaux, a fourth century Christian pilgrim who notes in his diary that there used to be several synagogues on Mount Zion, one of which is still standing.

A Roman City

Roman Jerusalem does not easily lend itself to theoretical reconstruction, as very few archeological finds remain from this period. It is particularly difficult to differentiate between structures of the Roman and Byzantine periods, for many Byzantine structures were built atop Roman buildings and incorporate the earlier structural elements into their design.

Aelia Capitolina, like other Roman towns, was built in the shape of a square Roman camp, with some changes to accomodate local topography. It was planned on a rectilinear grid, with emphasis on the major axes, a north-south road called the Cardo Maximus, and an east-west road

Part of the Roman arch discovered under the Ottoman-built Damascus Gate. This gate led to the highway to Neapolis (Nablus/Shekhem) and could be used to reach Caesarea as well

The Ecce Homo arch, part of a Roman triumphal arch in Aelia Capitolina

called the Decomanus Maximus. The main roads were replete with monumental buildings which included ornate statuary and facades, memorial columns and triumphal arches. It is likely that at the major crossroads of the north-south and east-west roads stood a tetrapylon, or four-arched gate. Roman urban aesthetics favored grand buildings, paved squares, forums and colonnaded streets. There was no priority given to green areas as modern urban planners might do.

There is no concensus regarding the date of construction of the city walls of Aelia Capitolina, however the course of the eastern and western walls, based on physical evidence, seems to have followed the course of the Second Temple period walls. Triumphal arches were

inset into the walls of Aelia Capitolina; the main one was at the Neapolis Gate. Its remnant has been unearthed below today's Damascus Gate. The highway which began at this gate led to Neapolis (Nablus/Shekhem), and could be used to reach the capital of Roman Palestine, Caesarea.

The Cardo Maximus, the main thoroughfare of Aelia Capitolina, had two colonnaded lanes. It began near the present-day site of the Damascus Gate. New excavations indicate that the southern part of the Cardo was added in the Byzantine period during the reign of Justinian. The Cardo was probably extended in order to reach the Nea Church, whose construction Justinian initiated. Part of the southern section of the Cardo Maximus has been unearthed and restored, and can be seen in the Jewish Quarter of Jerusalem's Old City.

At the intersection where the tetrapylon marked the crossing point of the Cardo and the Decomanus, stood the forum, where most civic and commercial activity took place and which was the scene of large public gatherings. Scholars assume that the forum covered all of today's Muristan area. Another smaller forum stood in the eastern part of the city, north of the Temple Mount. Remnants can been seen in the impressive pavement and part of the triumphal arch called 'Ecce Homo', near today's Convent of the Sisters of Zion.

In the vicinity of present-day Hagai Street, remains of another important Roman street have been revealed, apparently an auxiliary Cardo built parallel to the Cardo Maximus. In the center of the forum from which these two streets emerge stood a column whose existence is still preserved in the Arabic name of the Damascus Gate: *Bab-el-Amud* or Gate of the Column.

Jerusalem as Aelia Capitolina was not a capital city; it was a distant provincial town occasionally visited by Roman dignitaries. Little is written of it immediatley prior to the fourth century, when a Christian community developed in it and its character changed consirably. A small number of Jews lived in Roman Aelia Capitolina, and many more visited as pilgrims.

THE BYZANTINE PERIOD

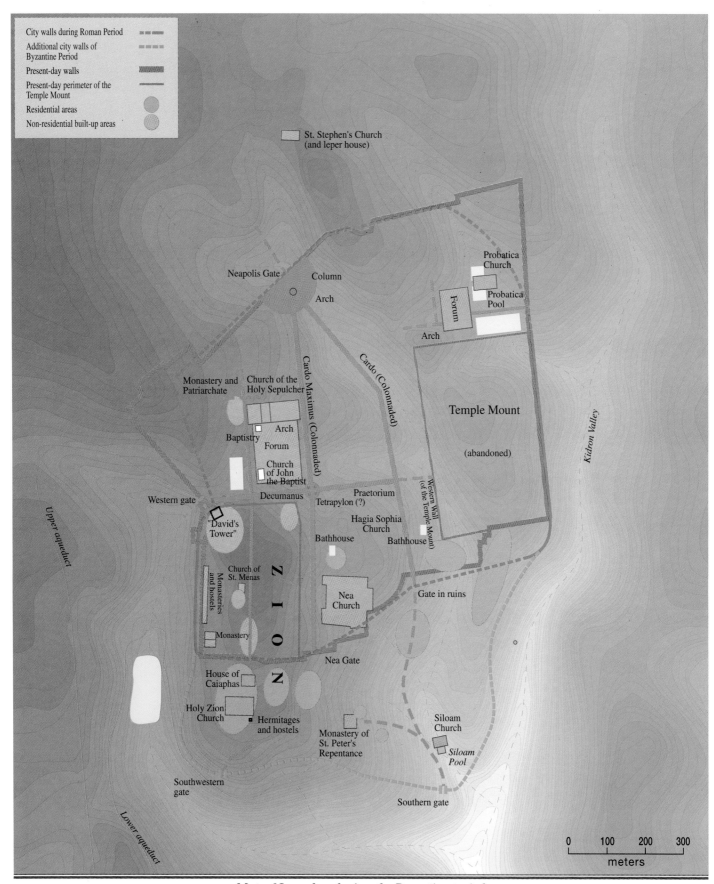

City walls during Roman Period

Additional city walls of
Byzantine Period

Present-day walls

Present-day perimeter of the
Temple Mount

Residential areas

Non-residential built-up areas

St. Stephen's Church
(and leper house)

Probatica
Church

Probatica
Pool

Forum

Arch

Neapolis Gate

Column

Arch

Temple Mount

(abandoned)

Kidron Valley

Monastery and
Patriarchate

Church of the
Holy Sepulcher

Cardo Maximus (Colonnaded)

Cardo (Colonnaded)

Arch

Baptistry

Forum

Church
of John
the Baptist

Western gate

Decumanus

Praetorium

Tetrapylon (?)

Western Wall
(of the Temple Mount)

"David's
Tower"

Hagia Sophia
Church

Bathhouse

Bathhouse

ZION

Church of
St. Menas

Monasteries
and hostels

Gate in ruins

Nea
Church

Monastery

Nea Gate

House of
Caiaphas

Holy Zion
Church

Hermitages
and hostels

Monastery of
St. Peter's
Repentance

Siloam
Church

Siloam
Pool

Southwestern
gate

Upper aqueduct

Lower aqueduct

Southern gate

0   100   200   300

meters

Map of Jerusalem during the Byzantine period

The Byzantine period in Jerusalem's history was inaugurated far from the city itself, when the emperor Constantine, in his new capital on the shores of the Bosporus, focused attention on Jerusalem as the site of the crucifixion and tomb of Jesus. The year 324 is commonly accepted as marking that moment, which initiated a gradual elevation of Jerusalem's status, by contrast with what the city had been for pagan Rome: a minor, distant colony on the edge of the desert.

In 313 Constantine had conferred upon Christianity the status of recognized religion, and subsequently made it the official religion of the Roman empire. This gesture achieved a distinct stabilizing influence on the population of Syria-Palestine, although perhaps half or more of the residents were Jews and Samaritans, who did not take on the new religion. A slow process of Christianization began throughout the Roman empire. The land of Israel, or Syria-Palestine as Hadrian had named it, gradually took on the character of the Christian Holy Land, *terra sancta*. (The term *terra sancta*, 'holy land' in Latin, first appears in the Book of Maccabees II. It was rejected by early Christian thinkers as being too Jewish in connotation, however by the fifth century,

largely due to the writings of Judean monks, the term began to acquire a distinctly Christian content.).

The Christianization of the empire coincided with an emerging trend among Palestinian Christians to determine the exact sites related to the life of Jesus, the members of his family and his apostles, as well various biblical figures. In 326 Constantine decreed that the location of the crucifixion site should be determined and a splendid church built upon the spot. This initiated a process by which Jerusalem rose to special status as a spiritual center for Christians.

Jerusalem – 'The Mother of All Churches'

Constantine's mother, Helena, a devout Christian, visited Aelia Capitolina and during her stay the temple of Venus-Aphrodite, which had been erected at Hadrian's direction, was destroyed. According to Christian tradition, the cross on which Jesus was crucified was found in a crypt beneath the temple. The Church of the Holy Sepulcher was built over the spot, and dedicated with great pomp in September 335. Helena lived in Jerusalem for several years and built a number of churches. According to later Christian legend, she also travelled in the countryside and designated sites that are honored in Church tradition to this day. The trend of venerating Christian holy places continued to

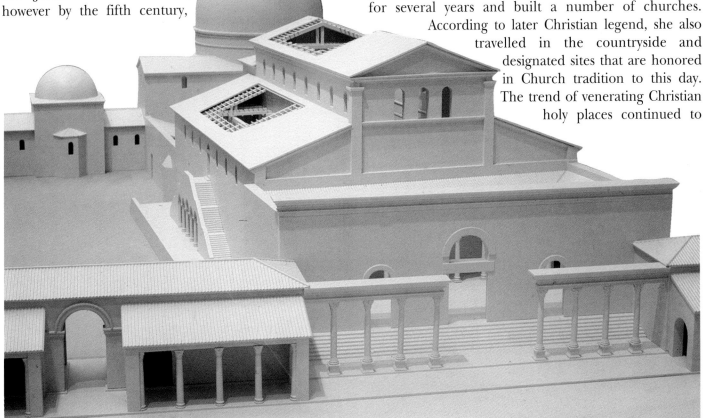

A contemporary model of the Church of the Holy Sepulcher as it appeared in the fourth century

Gold ring of the Byzantine period, unearthed in excavations near the Western Wall. Its design depicts the Church of the Holy Sepulcher

grow, and Christian pilgrimage arose along with it.

The Church of the Holy Sepulcher was one of four in Jerusalem and its environs erected with the encouragement and financial support of the emperor. The other three were the Church of Eleona on the Mount of Olives, the Church of the Nativity in Bethlehem, and the Church of Mamre north of Hebron.

A struggle for ecclesiastical supremacy ensued between Jerusalem and the capital city of Caesarea, which lasted several hundred years. At the first Ecumenical Council which met at Nicaea in 325, it was decided that while the status of Caesarea would be maintained (its bishop would also act as metropolitan, or bishop of a leading city of a province) the Jerusalem church and its bishop would have honorable status within this arrangement. The decision at Nicaea was in essence belated recognition of the apostolic status of Jerusalem. The Nicaean decision was further enhanced in 382 when the Jerusalem church was recognized as "The Mother of All Churches." Due to the energetic political activity of Juvenal, the bishop of Jerusalem in the second quarter of the fifth century, Jerusalem in 451 received the status of patriarchate, and became one of five patriarchates of the Christian world, along with Constantinople, Alexandria, Antioch and Rome. However, this status was achieved in spite of Jerusalem's insignificant size and power by comparison with the other four cities, and Jerusalem never rose to the importance of the other patriarchates.

A description of Byzantine Jerusalem appears in the writings of an anonymous French traveller known as the pilgrim of Bordeaux. He visited the city in ca. 333 C.E. and described the Temple Mount and two statues of Hadrian which were still standing on it, not far from 'the hollowed stone' which the Jews would visit every year and anoint with oil while rending their clothing and lamenting over the destruction of the Temple. The pilgrim marvelled at the magnificence of the vaulted area beneath the surface of the Temple Mount. This was the Herodian substructure for the Temple esplanade and the entryway to the ruined Second Temple. His record provides clear evidence that these sites were viewable in

the early fourth century. He makes no mention of any structure or building activity atop the Temple Mount.

The pilgrim of Bordeaux also visited Mount Zion and described the Siloam Pool which "has four porches and a second pool outside..." from which, he reported, water flowed six days a week but stopped on the seventh, the Sabbath. He pointed out the location of King David's palace on the site of today's Tower of David, and mentioned that before his time, Mount Zion had had seven synagogues but that only one was still functioning. He paid a great deal of attention to Christian sites, particularly those connected with the birth of Christianity, such as Pontius Pilate's house and the hill of Golgotha where Jesus was crucified. The pilgrim of Bordeaux was a reliable witness to the construction of the Church of the Holy Sepulcher, which was dedicated approximately two years after his visit. He wrote: "On the emperor Constantine's orders they are now building a basilica that is most beautiful and which has beside it cisterns of remarkable beauty." On the road to the Mount of Olives, he noted two handsome tombs: one the grave of the prophet Isaiah, and the other the grave of Hezekiah, "king of the Jews," as he designates him.

Fifty years later a wealthy woman named Egeria (or Etheria) came from Spain as a pilgrim to Jerusalem. She lived in the city for a number of years and recorded her impressions, in order to enable her sisters, the nuns in faraway Spain, to enjoy something of Jerusalem's character. In her day there were already a number of Christian communities in the city. She mentions people speaking a mix of languages, among them Syriac, Greek and Latin. At this time the liturgy of the Jerusalem church was being formed. It was to have great influence on the liturgies of the other churches of the east and west. Egeria describes numerous processions of monks and pilgrims who lent a Christian atmosphere to the city as they moved from one Christian site to another, praying and chanting as they went.

Julian 'the Apostate' and the Effort to Rebuild the Temple

The Christianization of Jerusalem – and of the entire empire – did not proceed unopposed. Evidence of this can be seen in the short reign of the emperor Julian

(361-363) dubbed 'the apostate,' who had a negative attitude towards Christianity. Julian viewed the Jews as a component in his endeavor to build a 'pagan church' which would arrest and indeed reverse the process of Christianization of the Roman empire. In order to strengthen his relationship with the Jews, Julian planned to return Jerusalem to them and rebuild the Temple. Apparently the process of reconstruction actually began. Jews were permitted to settle in the city, and Julian appointed Aliphius of Antioch, one of his respected dignitaries, to take charge of the repair of the Temple precinct and reconstruction of the building. It can be assumed that the Jews reacted with enthusiasm to these developments, though the Jewish leadership may have had qualms about this plan, since this episode is not mentioned in Jewish sources. According to Christian sources, Jews began to settle in Jerusalem. They apparently built a synagogue near the Temple Mount, and perhaps other buildings within the city. In the spring of 363, a short time after Julian set out on his campaign against the Persians, the inhabitants of Jerusalem witnessed a great deal of activity on the Temple Mount as ruins were cleared, building materials delivered, and workers began reconstruction. This enterprise did not last long. A great fire broke out on the building site, devouring the building materials and equipment and bringing the work to a halt. Scholars offer different scenarios regarding the outbreak of the fire. It may have been caused by a huge earthquake, or it may have been an act of arson undertaken by Christians. Christian sources of that period and later, interpeted the fire as divine punishment inflicted on Julian 'the Apostate' and other non-believers who supported him, among them Jews and Samaritans.

In Jewish sources there are only faint hints concerning this aborted attempt to rebuild the Temple. Archeological excavation has revealed a Hebrew inscription of five words on one of the stones of the Western Wall at a height of street level of the Byzantine period (several yards above the then buried paved street of the Second Temple period). The inscription quotes part of a verse from the book of Isaiah: "You shall see (this) and your heart shall rejoice, Your limbs shall [flourish like grass]"(Isaiah 66:14). This is a short section

This Hebrew quotation from the the book of Isaiah was found incised on one of the stones of the Western Wall. It is believed to date to the reign of the emperor Julian, and is regarded as evidence of an attempt to rebuild the Temple. Text reads: "You shall see (this) and your heart shall rejoice, Your limbs shall flourish like grass"

of a prophecy of comfort which speaks of the rebuilding of Jerusalem and the rejoicing of all who love her. Scholars date the inscription to the fourth century, and some suggest that a Jew who took part in preparations to rebuild the Temple during the short reign of Julian carved this verse into the wall.

Approximately a month after the beginning of work on the Temple Mount, Julian, according to Christian sources, was assassinated by a Christian soldier in his army. With his death, his plans came to an end and the Christianization of the empire, and of Jerusalem, proceeded.

The Empress Eudocia

The Empress Eudocia in Jerusalem

Among the important personages who spurred the development of Byzantine Jerusalem was the empress Eudocia, wife of the Byzantine emperor Theodosius II. The palace in Constantinople was a long way from Jerusalem; imperial visits to the Holy City were very rare. Given this situation, Eudocia's protracted stay in Jerusalem takes on great significance. In 438 she decided on a pilgrimage to Jerusalem, and upon her return, brought holy relics back with her. A feud with the emperor's older sister, Pulcheria, resulted in an accusation of betrayal against Eudocia, who undertook to return to Jerusalem as place of exile. She lived the last fifteen years of her life in Jerusalem, and saw to the building of churches, hospices, charitable institutions and monumental buildings such as the house of the bishop. Using her private fortune she underwrote the building of the city walls, whose course included the southern portion of Jerusalem, including Mount Zion, the Pool of Siloam and City of David hill, areas which had been included in Second Temple Jerusalem but excluded from the area encompassed by the walls of Aelia Capitolina. Regarding this project, Eudocia was inspired to recall the verse from Psalms (51:20): "May it please you to make Zion prosper; rebuild the walls of Jerusalem." The empress' name, Eudocia, appears in the Greek translation of this verse.

Christianity's Relationship to Jerusalem

Jerusalem has great importance in Christianity. It is the scene of significant events in the life of Jesus, and contains supremely sacred sites for Christians – the places where Jesus was crucified and where his tomb is located. In addition, Jerusalem as abstract concept plays an important role in Christianity; however the well-known ideas of Heavenly Jerusalem and New Jerusalem were not intrinsically rooted in the earthly, or real, city. The question of Christian attachment to earthly Jerusalem challenged framers of the Christian faith, and extensive discourse on this subject is found in their writings. The issue reflects the tension between Christianity as new religion and Christianity as a faith

Old City of Jerusalem: Corner of Eudocia's wall (Byzantine era) where it touches the southeastern corner of the Ottoman wall, not far from the Dung Gate

Fifth century mosaic floor in the Christian chapel north of the Damascus Gate, depicts Orpheus playing his lyre, with a satyr, centaur and animals listening attentively

century, had come east to study the monastic way of life. He wrote of Jerusalem: "Jerusalem according to history is the city of the Jews, according to allegory it is the city of Christ, according to the Anagog it is the heavenly city that is the mother of us all, and according to Tropology it is the soul of man..." (John Cassianus, Conlatio XIV, cap. VIII)

There were even churchmen who were troubled by the phenomemon of the large numbers of Christian pilgrims visiting Jerusalem. The pivotal church father Jerome (Hieronymus), who lived ca. 342-420, for instance, was uncomfortable with this trend, and the veneration of the city's holy places. Although he considered Jerusalem the epitomy of holiness, he observed that "Britain, like Jerusalem, is open to the parlors of heaven." As Jerusalem was a spiritual idea, "cities of Jerusalem" symbolizing the real Jerusalem, sprang up all over the Byzantine empire, from the banks of the Tiber to the shores of the Bosporus.

There is evidence that the early Christian attitude to Heavenly and Earthy Jerusalem was frought with ambivalence, yet the presence of Jews in the land, their persistent efforts to come to Jerusalem, and their teachings, considered along with the Christian hostility toward the Jews and their faith, in all likelihood forced early Christian thinkers to emphasize the doctrine of a purely spiritual Jerusalem. From the fourth century onwards, it seems that the spiritual concept of Jerusalem was 'brought down to earth', so to speak, while the Earthly Jerusalem took on increasing importance. However, the ambivalence lingered on among Christian thinkers.

Jerusalem figures in the attitude of Christianity to Jews and Judaism. Jesus prophesied the destruction of the city and Temple, and the coming about of these events confirmed to early Christians his prophetic powers and messianic nature. The destruction took on doctrinal significance, particularly in light of the emperor Julian's failed effort to rebuild the Temple – which, according to Christian sources had been aimed at the nullification of Jesus' prophecy. After Julian's failure, the destruction of Jerusalem was cited as evidence that the Jews had sinned by refusing to recognize Jesus' messianic nature. Christianity taught that the Jerusalem of the Jews would never be rebuilt, and that the Jews had no further entitlement to the city. In fact, once Jerusalem

emerging from Jewish belief. Much of Judaism's view of redemption is centered on Jerusalem. Although the concept of Heavenly Jerusalem first developed in Judaism, in that religion it is to be achieved through the fulfillment of biblical prophecy: the renaissance of the earthly city, re-establishment of the Sanhedrin, rebuilding of the Temple etc. Christianity's view of salvation and redemption is centered on belief in Jesus and the transforming nature of his death and resurrection. How literally, then, could the framers of Christianity take biblical claims and promises? How could claim be made to Jerusalem's long history if Christianity was a completely new, spiritualized beginning? These questions were largely resolved by viewing Jerusalem as spiritual construct or allegory. For example, the church was the New Jerusalem in which all prophecy would be fulfilled. In the Revelation of John the city is described as the capital of the Kingdom of Heaven, needing no sun and no moon. The monk John Cassianus who lived in Bethlehem during the fourth

Mosaic in archway of the Church of Santa Maria Maggiore, Rome, fifth century. The walls of 'Heavenly Jerusalem' are studded with precious stones, and six lambs symbolize six of Jesus' disciples

was in Christian control, Jews were legally barred from living there, although they were allowed entry one day a year in exchange for a punitive fee.

The Christian Appropriation of Jerusalem

Christianity adopted many biblical and rabbinic traditions while distancing itself from the Jews. In Jerusalem this involved transferring sites associated in Jewish tradition with biblical characters or events, to Christian locations. Thus, Christianity transferred to the Church of the Holy Sepulcher events which in Jewish tradition occurred on the Temple Mount – the sacrifice of Isaac and the murder of Abel at the hands of Cain. The tradition concerning the site of Adam's resting place was moved from the Temple Mount to the hill of Golgotha. A Christian tradition tells how the pilgrim Egeria saw in the Church of the Holy Sepulcher not only the cross upon which Jesus was crucified, but also King Solomon's ring, and the horn from which oil was taken to annoint the kings of Israel.

The biblical account locates the burial place of King David somewehere in the City of David (I Kings 2:10), that is, the southeastern hill on which stood the original fortress Zion which David conquered and made his capital. Christian tradition transferred King David's burial site to Mount Zion (the Western Hill) and the Holy Zion Church was erected there. It became known as the Mother of all Churches. Another Christian tradition set David's tomb in Bethlehem (the town of David's birth, according to I Samuel, and in the Gospels, the town of Jesus' birth). This second Christian tradition in all likelihood originated with the work of Jerome, translator of the Bible into Latin, who understood the term 'City of David' to mean Bethlehem. The Christian community in Jerusalem remained loyal to the Mount Zion setting. A ceremony in memory of King David, conqueror of Jerusalem and founder of the 'Old Zion' (biblical Jerusalem) is integrated into the ritual honoring James, the first bishop of Jerusalem and brother of Jesus, who was considered founder of the 'New Zion', i.e. Christian Jerusalem.

The connection between King David and James illustrates the early Christian effort to establish historical and ideological continuity between the Jewish past and Christian future. The ritual honoring David and James was central, and it was celebrated in the Church of the Apostles on Mount Zion. The Armenian rite, dating to the early fifth century, has a holiday called "The Consecration of All the Altars," which is also held on Mount Zion. It and the annual ceremony of the dedication of the Church of the Holy Sepulcher hearkened back to consecrations of the Temple in Jewish history, for example Solomon's weeklong dedication ceremony for the First Temple, and the Maccabees re dedication of the Temple altar. On the site considered

David's tomb, there are remains of a Crusader church built over the ruins of Zion, Mother of all Churches, thus illustrating the prominence of the site.

Christian Ritual in Jerusalem

Capital of a Byzantine column

Over time the Jerusalem church introduced prayers, rites and rituals related to the city's Christian holy sites. Egeria tells of the singularity of the local liturgy: Jerusalem ecclesiasts adapted readings and special prayers to dates and sites commemorating events in the history of the city and the church. There were holidays celebrated only in Jerusalem and nowhere else in the Christian world, such as the Revelation of the Cross, and memorial days during the month of May for the Emperor Constantine and his mother, Helena. As mentioned above, it was also customary to celebrate the Consecration of All the Altars.

Much pious excitement surrounded the celebration of Easter in Jerusalem. The week prior to Easter Sunday was known as "the Great Week." Thousands of the faithful arrived in the city, and would view and participate in re-enactments of the last week of Jesus' life. On Sunday, his entry into the city would be replayed, with someone of Jesus' age mounted on a donkey while small children announced, "Blessed is he that cometh in the name of the Lord," and spread palm fronds before him, as before a king. Re-enactments continued, culminating with a re-enactment of the crucifixion on Friday, accompanied by fasting and lamenting on the hill of Golgotha. On Easter Sunday there was a celebration of Jesus' resurrection.

Pilgrimages to Jerusalem

Jerusalem's major attraction for Christian pilgrims lay in the opportunity to experience religious ceremonies in the very places where events recorded in the Gospels occurred. As the Byzantine period progressed, pilgrims were probably no longer content with the limited number of sanctuaries venerating key events in the life of Jesus. Every detail mentioned in the Gospels was localized, and Jerusalem came to feature a plethora of

churches, monasteries and holy sites, the most important of which was the Church of the Holy Sepulcher. It was composed of four sections, from east to west: an atrium, a covered basilica, another atrium in whose corner was the stone venerated as Golgotha (the site of the crucifixion), and the tomb of Jesus in a circular structure called a rotunda.

From there, pilgrims generally followed a route to the Zion Church on Mt. Zion, where he could view relics. Pilgrims also visited the Church of Saint Sophia which was said to stand on the ruins of the palace of Pontius Pilate, the procurator who condemned Jesus to death. In the vicinity of the church, there was a pit into which the prophet Jeremiah was said to have been flung by King Zedekiah. Pilgrims also viewed the Temple Mount – not only because its desolation was prophesied by Jesus, but because the southwest corner (also known

Fourth century drawing of a boat used by pilgrims, found in the Church of the Holy Sepulcher

as the Ophel corner, or 'the pinnacle of the Temple wall' in Eusebius' writings) was, according to Christian belief, the place where the devil tried to tempt Jesus, and where his brother James was thrown to his death.

Pilgrims would also visit several sites outside the city walls of Jerusalem, including a number on the Mount of Olives. A small industry developed in Christian keepsakes. In this regard, pottery flasks of the Byzantine period, bearing the image of the Church of the Holy Sepulcher, have been found in Italy, and it is assumed they came from Jerusalem.

*Section of a Byzantine period street, Via Dolorosa,
Old City of Jerusalem*

Cosmopolitan Jerusalem

Christian pilgrims came to Jerusalem because of its sanctity, but the crowding together of masses of people from all over the world contributed to a decidedly non-spiritual atmosphere in the streets. Byzantine Jerusalem gradually assumed the character of a lively international tourist center. In the streets a number of languages could be heard, among them Greek, Armenian, Syriac, and Georgian. Guides and translators accompanied pilgrims. Dealers and craftsmen sat at street corners hawking souvenirs and holy memorabilia. Pilgrimage in fact supported a variety of industrious

service purveyors, among them providers of food and shelter. There were also many hostels in the city; the huge Nea Church, initiated by the emperor Justinian and dedicated in 543, boasted a shelter with three thousand beds.

Not all the pilgrims' activities in Jerusalem were holy. There were frequent licentious scenes in the city's streets and houses, and spiritual leaders found that Jerusalem was becoming like a den of iniquity. Gregory, the bishop of Nyssa who made a pilgrimage to Jerusalem, was shocked, and wrote bitterly of the vices of "prostitution, adultery, burglary, idol-worship, poisoning, jealousy, and murder" which he had witnessed or heard of.

A reflection of this social situation could be seen in Byzantine church architecture. Several churches had entry areas in the form of large halls where worshippers could undergo a change of mood from secular to holy. They changed clothing and absorbed the mood inspired

*Byzantine era 'Birds Mosaic,' discovered in the remains of
an Armenian church of the Byzantine period,
north of Damascus Gate*

by the entry atrium, which helped them recall their reason for coming to Jerusalem and prepared them for the spiritual experience awaiting them.

During the fifth and sixth centuries Jerusalem became an important ecclesiastical center, not only for the church hierarchy but also to many monks, who by education and inclination were very different in character from the members of the episcopacy. A monastery was founded in Jerusalem, however, the monastic way of life favors asceticism and modesty in all things, and apparently could not exist tranquilly in Jerusalem's overly worldly atmosphere. Monasteries were established at a distance from the city, on the fringe of the Judean desert. The monasteries of Euthymius (Khan el Ahmar) and Gerasimus (Deir Hajla) were established southeast of Jerusalem and not far from Bethlehem, and Great Laura (Mar Saba) and Choziba (Ein Kelt) were established in the desert. The dramatic, starkly isolated desert surroundings contributed the proper atmosphere for the austere lifestyle the monks required in order to strive for spiritual perfection. There came a point when the desert east of Jerusalem became home to thousands of monks. A complex relationship developed between the church hierarchy in Jerusalem and the monasteries. Technically the monasteries were subservient to Jerusalem owing to the structure of church organization, and to economic considerations. However their purity of lifestyle lent them considerable prestige. On a number of occasions, the monks were called upon by the patriarch of Jerusalem to express opinions on matters of faith – with the expectation they would be in keeping with the patriarch's judgment. This was not always the result.

The Jews in Jerusalem

Various sources confirm that Jews were not permitted to live in Jerusalem during the Byzantine period, and could visit only one day a year, on the ninth of the month of Av,

Jews mourning over the ruins of the Temple on the one day a year they were permitted to enter Jerusalem - the Ninth of Av. Tableau, Tower of David Museum, Jerusalem

for which privilege they paid a fee. Otherwise they could only view the city from afar and weep for its fate and theirs. The pilgrim of Bordeaux describes a pigrimage of Jews to the Temple Mount, remarking that they mourned on the site of the destroyed Temple, rent their clothing, and afterwards descended in sorrow and returned to their homes.

The renowned church father Jerome points out in his commentary on Zephaniah 1:15, "Until this very day, those hypocritical tenants (Jews) are forbidden to come to Jerusalem... unless (they come to) weep, for then they are given permission to lament over the ruins of the city in exchange for a payment. Just as they purchased the blood of the Messiah, now they are purchasing their own tears; therefore, even the lamentation is not given to them for naught. On the day that Jerusalem was taken and destroyed by the Romans, one could see this people, the women dressed in rags and the old bearing their tatters and their years, gather for a time of mourning..."

There was an interval in which the Jews may have experienced a somewhat more liberalized policy, or at least managed to conduct negotiations over the issue of increased access to Jerusalem. This occurred when the empress Eudocia was developing Jerusalem, (see page 82) investing a fortune in the construction of churches. It is possible that she needed funds to continue her endeavors and hoped to secure them from the Jews of the Galilee. She was inclined to respond positively to the Galilean Jews' request for permission to visit Jerusalem and live there. Both the request and Eudocia's positive response are addressed in a partly legendary biography of the monk Barsauma. He was severely contemptuous of Jews and opposed Eudocia's decision to allow them to visit Jerusalem on the Jewish pilgrimage festivals. The text of a letter from Galilean Jews, as it appears in his biography, invites suspicion as to its authenticity, and there is no confirmation from any other source that it was ever written or received by Eudocia. At one point Barsauma mentions more than a hundred thousand Jews who came to Jerusalem on the Sukkot holiday, when a miracle occurred and a shower of hailstones sent them running from the Temple Mount. The figure of a

Mosaic floor in the synagogue of Hamat Tiberias, with motifs suggesting the Temple ritual

hundred thousand is perhaps intentionally exaggerated, however it is possible that large numbers of Jews approached and entered Jerusalem as a result of Eudocia's leniency. Barsauma reports organizing his followers and rioting against the Jewish pilgrims, stoning and bludgeoning several to death. Undoubtedly these were the same stones he attributed to miraculous intervention. Barsauma had a reputation as a zealot and brigand who previously vandalized synagogues on his way to Jerusalem from Syria. The outcome was that the Jerusalem church did not approve of the relationship between Eudocia and the Jews, and the empress finally acquiesced and cancelled the arrangement with the Jews.

Jerusalem in Prayer and Liturgical Poetry

Jerusalem continued to be central to Jewish spiritual aspirations during the Byzantine period, notwithstanding the prohibition on Jewish entry into the city. Jews signed their letters with the words: "May you see the coming of Redemption, the building of Ariel (Jerusalem) and the gathering of Israel." In the developing liturgical poetry of the synagogue, Zion, Jerusalem, Salem, and the Temple were repeatedly mentioned. The best known such works were composed for the lengthy prayer service on the Day of Atonement; they are filled with yearning for Temple rituals, and mournfully confront the condition of destruction.

In daily life, Jerusalem and the Temple rituals were referred to frequently. Groups of priests residing in Galilean villages preserved memory of Temple routines by adhering to the schedule of priestly watches used in the Temple. There were also Jews who numbered years from the starting point of the destruction of the Temple, rather than the creation of the world. Instances of this appear on gravestones of the Byzantine period discovered in Zoar, south of the Dead Sea.

In liturgical poetry and the legends of the Jews, many names were applied to Jerusalem which expressed longing, as well as various spiritual and intellectual outlooks: Gilead, Zion, City of Israel, Joy of All the World, City Knit Together, Ariel, Abundant Beauty, Sacred City, Temple City, City of David, House of Prayer, City of Gold, Tranquil Dwelling, City and Mother, Bride, City of Peace, Navel of the Universe, and more.

Inscription on a sixth century gravestone in Zoar, south of the Dead Sea. The year of death is recorded according to the date of the Temple's destruction

The Appearance of Byzantine Jerusalem

While illustrations of Jerusalem adorned the books of pilgrims and clerics, and appeared in murals and mosaics in various European churches, these lacked detail and could have been fanciful representations. The appearance of Byzantine Jerusalem remained a mystery until the extraordinary discovery in 1884 of the Madaba map, a mosaic floor map of Syria-Palestine and its surroundings, with Jerusalem at its center. It was found in Madaba, a village in today's kingdom of Jordan. Ever since its discovery, the Madaba map has been an important source of information on Palestine, Egypt and parts of Jordan, in the Byzantine period. Archeological excavations in Jerusalem and other sites have substantiated the correctness of the map's details. It is the first map of Jerusalem, a bird's-eye view of the city at the height of its development in the sixth century. The Church of the Holy Sepulcher is in the center; running from north to south is the colonnaded main street, the Cardo Maximus; a secondary colonnaded street runs along today's Ha-gai Street; and the entire city is enclosed in a wall. Additional streets, buildings and gates are easily identified by comparing them with structures which have survived to the present-day, or with

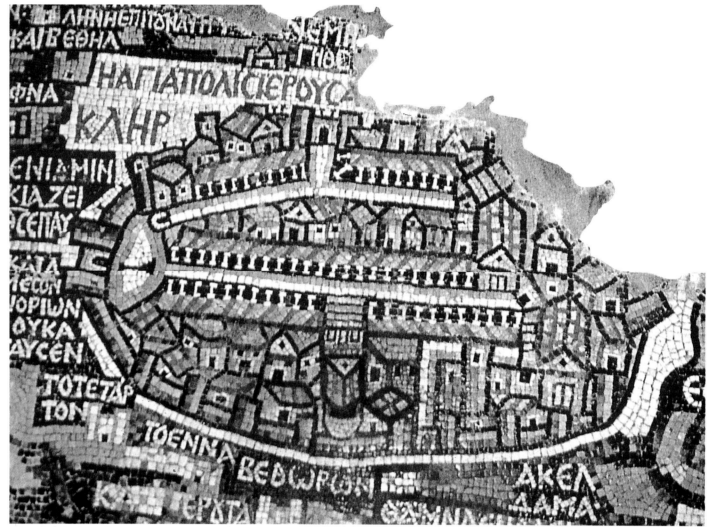

The Madaba map, late sixth century. This section shows Jerusalem, with the central colonnaded street, the Cardo, readily apparent. Also visible, lower center, the Church of the Holy Sepulcher. At the right end of the Cardo, the Nea Church and south of the Cardo on Mount Zion, the Holy Zion Church

archeological remains. The absence of the Temple Mount is conspicuous and not unintentional. It reflects Christian teaching regarding the destruction of the Temple of the Jews, as well as the physical reality that the desolate Temple Mount was actually not a living part of Christian Jerusalem.

Byzantine rule in Jerusalem lasted more than three hundred years, from the fourth to seventh centuries. From its small size and somewhat spartan character as Aelia Capitolina, the city was transformed into a large and beautiful place, with wide streets, monumental buildings, churches and markets. The Byzantine rulers held Jerusalem in high esteem and invested in its development, thus the city grew during the Byzantine era. Its name during this period was first shortened to Aelia; the pagan 'Capitolina' was dropped. Then it acquired the Greek name, Hierosolyma (Hieros means holy in Greek, and solyma is a derivation of the Hebrew Salem [Shalem] peace). This name echoed the sound of the Hebrew *Yerushalem*, however, throughout the Byzantine period the name that predominates in primary literary sources is still Aelia. Jerusalem's population increased over the Byzantine period. Its estimated population at the end of the Roman period is some ten thousand inhabitants. At the height of the Byzantine period, during the sixth century, it had fifty to eighty

Subterranean vaults in a huge reservoir discovered beneath the Nea church

thousand residents. At the beginning of the Byzantine era parts of the city were uninhabited, but in the fifth century, residential areas had been extended and encompassed sections north of the Damascus Gate and outside the Jaffa Gate, which until then were not even considered part of the city.

The Byzantine planners of Jerusalem based their construction on the square Roman colonia plan of Aelia, and extended it; this was a conscious combination of tradition and continuity. In the northern part of the city, the Roman plan of the city was retained, and additional churches were integrated into it. The southern part of the city was planned anew, and additional sectors were

Greek inscription found beneath the Nea Church, mid-sixth century

added, among them Mount Zion, the Siloam neighborhood and Tyropoeon Valley, near today's Western Wall. The newly-planned areas had wide and attractive streets linking them to the areas which dated to Roman times.

Uncovering the Byzantine Past

After the Six-Day War of 1967 extensive excavations were carried out in the Jewish Quarter of Jerusalem. Among the Byzantine structures discovered was the enormous Nea Church, built by the emperor Justinian. On the southern slope of the hill on which the church stood, an enormous set of cisterns were unearthed which were used for storing water and were also intended to support the southern end of the church. At the entrance to these cisterns was an inscription in Greek: "This is the work which our most pious emperor Flavius Justinian carried out with munificence, under the care and devotion of the most holy Constantine, priest and superior, in the thirteenth year of the indiction."

Another captivating find from the Byzantine period is the Cardo, of which a strip more than two hundred yards long was unearthed after 1967. This section dates to the reign of the Emperor Justinian (sixth century) and completed the Roman Cardo Maximus built centuries earlier. It is astonishly spacious, measuring over 22 yards in width, with two lines of columns dividing it into a main uncovered passage (the road) and two covered passages (the sidewalks) on either side. The sidewalks were approxiamtely nine feet wide and were actually covered shopping arcades. There were drainage canals along the row of columns and under the paving. The original side passages had tiled roofs resting on wooden planks. Though the wooden planks did not survive antiquity, the niches in the walls into which the planks were placed, can still be observed. In the unearthed section of the Cardo the remains of shops were revealed along the western perimeter. Near the site of the excavated Cardo, remains from much earlier periods were discovered (the First and Second Temple periods) as well as remains from later periods, when the Cardo was no longer in use. An effort has been made to leave some finds of these various periods open to public viewing.

The Byzantine period provided Jerusalem with a wealth of church structures, architectural and artistic monuments all of which constitute a treasure for archeologists and historians. Archeologists have uncovered the Zion Church on Mount Zion, the Siloam Church, and the New St. Mary's or Nea Church. Excavations have also been conducted in the area of the Church of the Holy Sepulcher and the Church of St. John the Baptist. The wall of Byzantine Jerusalem, and remains of Byzantine period structures were uncovered near the Tower of David. Outside the city walls, the Church of Eleona was found on the Mount of Olives.

Along with the public buildings which have been unearthed, archeologists have revealed remains attesting to the appearance of and everyday life in Byzantine

Restoration of a Byzantine era room found in the excavations south of the Temple Mount. The mosaic floor is original, the walls reconstructed

A restored section of the magnificent Cardo of Byzantine Jerusalem. This broad thoroughfare boasted wide, collonaded sidewalks, a central, uncovered roadway, and well-designed water drainage

Silver coin minted in Jerusalem 614 by the emperor Heraclius

The Persian Conquest

In the early seventh century the Byzantine empire was shaken by political uprisings and internal religious strife. During the reign of the emperor Phocas, riots broke out in various cities, including Jerusalem, where the populace was outraged by the emperor's dismissal of Jerusalem's patriarch. The Persian empire, long the rival of the Byzantine empire, exploited the unrest by mounting repeated attacks on Byzantine-held lands. In 610 the talented military commander Heraclius became Byzantine emperor, but could not resist the Persians. In 614 Jerusalem fell to the Persians.

During the years of conflict, the Persians were assisted by the Jews of the region, those living in Persia as well as those in Syria-Palestine. They took part in the conflict not as mercenaries, but as people who hoped for relief from oppressive Byzantine Christian policies, and permission to return to Jerusalem and rebuild their Temple. The Persian campaign post-dated by many decades the rule of Justinian, under which persecutions of the Jews were widespread, and anti-Jewish legislation was reaffirmed. In the new law code promulgated by Justinian, old imperial provisions safeguarding the rights of Jews and status of Judaism were omitted, while new rules discriminated

Jerusalem. Remains of populous residential sections have been uncovered including wide streets and commercial areas. In excavations just south of the Temple Mount, a number of Byzantine residences have been discovered which were originally several stories high, and had mosaic flooring of sophisticated design, in which geometric patterns predominate, while specimens featuring floral patterns or rare birds have also been found. Water-supply was accomplished by the collection of rain-water drained into cisterns via ceramic pipes.

Structures from the early Byzantine period (fourth-fifth centuries) lack evidence of any facilities for crafts or cottage industries, however, structures of the sixth and seventh centuries display these facilities. In the area south of the Temple Mount evidence of small workshops was revealed, including devices for dyeing cloth, machinery for leather tanning and furnaces for heating metal, possibly used in the production of souvenirs for pilgrims.

West of Jaffa Gate, in the Valley of Hinnom, another Byzantine commercial and industrial quarter was unearthed. North of the Damascus Gate, a large building complex was discovered which included monasteries, hostels and a cemetery.

Silver coins, period of Persian ruler Chosroes II, early seventh century

Drawing of an excavated residential threshhold, late Byzantine period. The cross over the lintel was scratched off by Jews during the short period of Persian rule. Clearer carvings show images of candelabra, shofars, and incense bowls

against them and stressed the inferior status of their religion. Thus the Jews had no interest in supporting Byzantine Christian rule, and it is likely that a good number of them took up the struggle on the side of the Persians. The Persian king at the time was called Chosroes II, a name reminiscent to the Jews of the Persian king in antiquity, Cyrus, who allowed their ancestors to return to their land and rebuild their Temple. When the Persian army invaded Palestine from the north, it was joined by Jews from the Galilee. The Persians advanced toward Jerusalem in two columns, one through Samaria and the other via the coastal plain. Heraclius attempted to forestall the Persians but did not succeed.

The Persians initially tried to take Jerusalem without a battle, besieging the city and negotiating with the patriarch. When negotiations failed, a pitched battle ensued in which tunnels were dug under the city walls, that were breached in the summer of 614. Persian soldiers rampaged through the city's streets for three days, murdering inhabitants, setting fire to churches and plundering. The Christian clergy were particular targets. Christianity was the official state religion of the Byzantine empire, and had been used to advance political aims. The Persians did not distinguish between the enemy regime and the churchmen who had served its ends. Hence the targetting of clergy ensued. The Church of the Holy Sepulcher was burned. The Persians plundered church treasures throughout the city. The patriarch Zacharias was taken into exile, along with the relic of the true cross.

The Persians had made promises to the Jews in exchange for their support and participation in the war. Upon defeating the Byzantines in Jerusalem, the city was turned over to Jewish administration, which lasted for three years. The head of this administration was a man known only by his symbolic name, Nehemiah.

Messianic Hopes and their Collapse

From the standpoint of the Jews, being given authority over Jerusalem was a step on the road to Redemption. Many of the city's churches had been sacked and destroyed in battle; this process is likely to have continued under the Jewish administration of Jerusalem.

There is a distant possibility that the Jews introduced sacrificial rites on the Temple Mount. Hints of this are found in the pietistic poetry (*piyyut*) of Eleazar haKalir, the greatest Hebrew poet of the period, who lived in Syria-Palestine. One of his works alludes to sacrificial rites on the Temple Mount, but indicates that work on the Temple had not commenced.

The period of Byzantine rule, and particularly the period of the Persian conquest, prompted the appearance of Jewish apocalyptic works, a development not surprising for a time of persecution and conquest. Two prominent works were the Book of Elijah and the Book of Zerubabel. Each is named after a biblical figure linked in Jewish tradition with the ultimate Redemption and deliverance of the Jewish people: Zerubabel would reveal the time of the coming of the messiah, and the prophet Elijah would proclaim his coming. The themes of these works reflect the Jewish conception of the historical sequence of events prior to the Redemption: humiliation of the Jews, followed by renewed hope, a great conflict, victory, the restoration of Jerusalem and of the Jews to that city. Clearly the Persian campaign caused the ageless hopes of the Jews to rise to the surface in a particularly powerful manner.

The Book of Zerubabel preserves the messianic name of the Jewish leader Nehemiah son of Hushiel son of Ephraim son of Joseph, as the man who headed the Jewish administration of Jerusalem. (Nehemiah was the name of the Jewish governor under Persian rule a thousand years earlier). This commentary conveys the message that although Redemption was delayed, the Temple would finally be rebuilt. Jerusalem is at the very heart of the work. The process by which the city would be rebuilt is described in more detail and at greater length than the entire process of Redemption. In the later record of Jewish apocalyptic literature, many oft-repeated motifs hearken back to the Book of Zerubabel. In it, Jerusalem is allotted a central role in the Redemption process. Its destruction presages a general destruction, and it is destined to have a central role in the conflagration that precedes the End of Days. Its rebuilding is regarded as more than a symbol of Redeption; it is its aim. The rebuilding of Jerusalem is coupled with the notion of the return of the exiled Jewish people, the resurrection of the dead and the renewal of the sacrificial rite in the Temple. Jewish apocalyptic

authors all envision a miraculous defense of the city of Jerusalem and its inhabitants, even in the time of the apocalyptic destruction. The Book of Zerubabel pictures a fully rebuilt Jerusalem descending from the heavens to rest again on earth, its borders able to expand without measure.

The support of the Persian rulers for Jewish administration lasted three years. The turnabout in Persian policy is not sufficiently understood, but is perhaps attributable to Persian desire to guarantee the permanence of its conquests through negotiation with the major political force that might threaten its flank (the Byzantines) before setting out on a campaign against Egypt. In reaching an accord, concessions would have had to be made, and Jerusalem would have topped the Byzantine's list. On Chosroes II's orders, the Jews were ousted from Jerusalem – with Persian forces violently evicting them. Under a Persian governor, the Christians were permitted to restore ruined churches and re-assert the Christian character of the city. The paramount Christian concern was restoration of the Church of the Holy Sepulcher and the return to it of the relic of the true cross.

Return of the Byzantines

Persian dominion over Jerusalem lasted fifteen years. In 627 the emperor Heraclius launched an attack against the Persians and succeeded in reaching Ecbatana. The

Imaginative depiction of the Cardo in its prime, during the Late Roman and Byzantine periods.
Tableau, Tower of David Museum, Jerusalem

Persians were forced to sue for peace, agreeing to withdraw from all previous Byzantine possessions. In July 629 Heraclius, preparing to enter Jerusalem and reinstate the relic of the true cross, met with Jewish leaders in the Galilee, accepted their gifts, and promised to pardon them, even signing a treaty. This and other evidence indicates that he was apparently not inclined to persecute them. On March 21, 629 Heraclius entered Jerusalem and in a grand procession returned the relic of the true cross to the Church of the Holy Sepulcher. Thereafter the clergy of Jerusalem pressured him to break his promises to the Jews, assuring him they would assume responsibility for his perjury. (A special fast was instituted for this purpose.) The Jews were expelled from Jerusalem and a persecution initiated in which many were put to death; others fled to the desert, Persia, or Egypt. A campaign of forced conversion was begun, in accordance

Pottery oil lamp with seven-branched candelabrum, early Byzantine era

with the apocalyptic Christian vision of a holy land without foreigners and infidels. Thus the victorious campaign of Heraclius was also a campaign of retaliation against Jewish communities throughout Palestine.

The Muslim conquest of Jerusalem occurred less than a decade after Heraclius' victorious entry into the city. It prompted apocalyptic yearning in the Jews and was seen as part of the same context of pre-Redemption conflict as had the Persian invasion.

In 638 Jerusalem fell to the Muslims. The Jews of Syria-Palestine undoubtedly looked forward to the fall of the Byzantine kingdom, however they expected little benefit from the Arab victory, and there are no reliable reports of Jewish assistance to the Arabs. Similarly, there are no indications of any special favorable treatement for Jews. The main advantage derived by the Jews from the Muslim conquest was the right to live in Jerusalem.

THE EARLY MUSLIM PERIOD

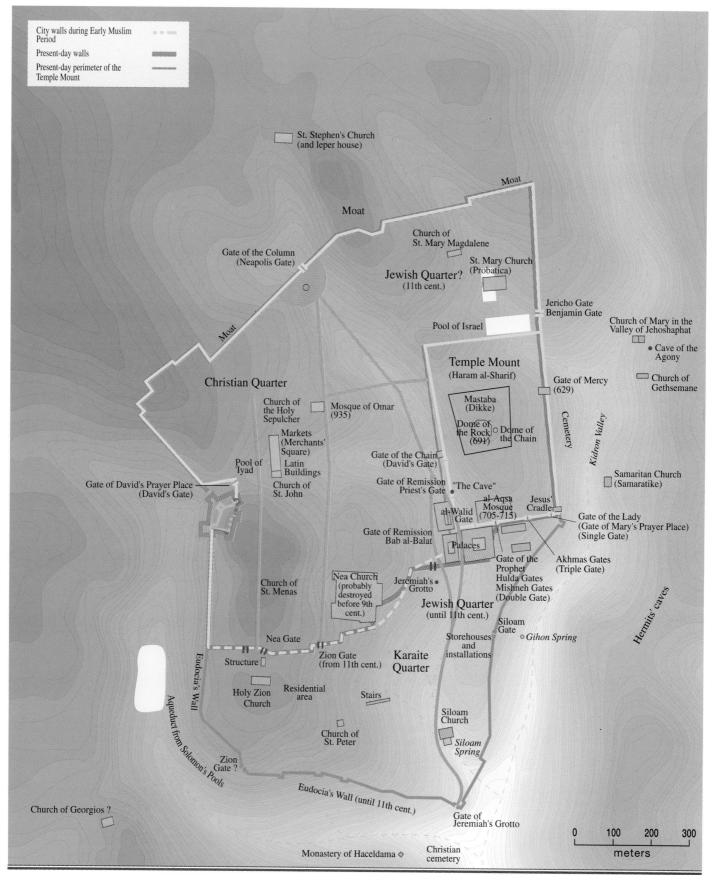

City walls during Early Muslim Period

Present-day walls

Present-day perimeter of the Temple Mount

St. Stephen's Church
(and leper house)

Moat

Moat

Church of
St. Mary Magdalene

Gate of the Column
(Neapolis Gate)

St. Mary Church
(Probatica)

Jewish Quarter?
(11th cent.)

Jericho Gate
Benjamin Gate

Pool of Israel

Church of Mary in the
Valley of Jehoshaphat

Moat

Cave of the
Agony

Christian Quarter

Temple Mount
(Haram al-Sharif)

Gate of Mercy
(629)

Church of
Gethsemane

Mastaba
(Dikke)

Church of
the Holy
Sepulcher

Mosque of Omar
(935)

Dome of
the Rock
(691)

Dome of
the Chain

Cemetery

Kidron Valley

Markets
(Merchants'
Square)

Latin
Buildings

Gate of the Chain
(David's Gate)

Pool of
'Iyad

Church of
St. John

Gate of Remission
Priest's Gate

"The Cave"

Samaritan Church
(Samaritike)

Gate of David's Prayer Place
(David's Gate)

al-Walid
Gate

al-Aqsa
Mosque
(705-715)

Jesus'
Cradle

Gate of the Lady
(Gate of Mary's Prayer Place)
(Single Gate)

Gate of Remission
Bab al-Balat

Palaces

Akhmas Gates
(Triple Gate)

Church of
St. Menas

Nea Church
(probably
destroyed
before 9th
cent.)

Jeremiah's
Grotto

Gate of the
Prophet
Hulda Gates
Mishneh Gates
(Double Gate)

Jewish Quarter
(until 11th cent.)

Siloam
Gate

Hermits' caves

Nea Gate

Storehouses
and
installations

Gihon Spring

Zion Gate
(from 11th cent.)

Karaite
Quarter

Structure

Eudocia's Wall

Holy Zion
Church

Residential
area

Stairs

Siloam
Church

Church of
St. Peter

Siloam
Spring

Aqueduct from Solomon's Pools

Zion
Gate ?

Church of Georgios ?

Eudocia's Wall (until 11th cent.)

Gate of
Jeremiah's Grotto

0   100   200   300
meters

Monastery of Haceldama

Christian
cemetery

Map of Jerusalem in the Early Muslim period

The Temple Mount area, Haram al-Sharif in Arabic. The golden domed Dome of the Rock was erected by the caliph Abd al-Malik in 691. The al-Aqsa mosque (upper right), first erected by al-Walid in 705, was destroyed in an earthquake in 1033. It was restored by A-Tahr but suffered serious damage numerous times over the centuries. Its current appearance differs from the original (see p.108)

Early in 638 Jerusalem fell to Muslim forces led by the caliph Umar ibn al-Khattab. The conquest of the city was part of the dramatic sweep of Arab conquests during the seventh century, which carried the authority of Islam from Mecca and Medina on the Arabian peninsula to the gates of Constantinople, the approaches to India, and the shores of the western ocean. The caliph Umar received the surrender of Jerusalem from the local patriarch, Sophronius, and promised not to destroy churches or force conversion upon the Christian inhabitants of Jerusalem. Muslim Arab rule over Jerusalem would last more than four

The massive vaulted arch known as Wilson's arch after its discoverer, the British archeologist Charles Wilson. During the Second Temple period it supported a bridge connecting the Temple compound with the Upper City along the route of today's Street of the Chain. The arch was restored during the early Muslim era

hundred and sixty years, during which the city would be gradually transformed in culture, language and dominant religion. The change was anything but rapid; Jerusalem's Byzantine character lingered for many years. Byzantine architectural style continued to dominate its appearance, and the population figure long remained steady and of Christian character.

The Muslim conquest was a positive development for the Jews of Syria-Palestine. After centuries during which they were forbidden to enter Jerusalem and lived under the burden of hostile Byzantine law, the Jews, once under Muslim rule, were soon permitted to return to the city as pilgrims, and to reside in it. They could pursue their unique way of life based upon the Written and Oral Law and the heritage that had continued to accrue to it through the generations.

Almost sixty years after the Muslim conquest, a magnificent new structural silhouette appeared on the skyline of Jerusalem. The Muslim shrine called the Dome of the Rock was built upon the ruined Temple Mount and vied with the Church of the Holy Sepulcher for symbolic dominance over the character of the city, just as the fighting forces of Islam and Christianity were battling for dominance over much of the known world. Each of the contending faiths had roots in Jewish belief and teachings.

In Jerusalem a passionate three-way clash of consciousness was created that has no parallel in the religious history of the world: one city sanctified by three faiths, whose adherents met there, lived and prayed there, and all understood that on the religious and spiritual level they were vying for it. The Jewish heritage placed Jerusalem at its very core, from biblical times onward. Christianity adopted elements of the Jewish heritage regarding Jerusalem, and added to it central events connected with the life and death of Jesus. Islam arose and attached its own tradition and sense of holiness, which focused on a miraculous night journey of Muhammed to Jerusalem and his ascent to heaven to meet Moses, Elijah the Prophet and Jesus. The three monotheistic faiths considered Jerusalem a precious and holy city, each from its own point of view, and with certain elements in common. This triangle of commitment began in the seventh century with the conquest of Jerusalem by the Muslims, and has continued to the present day.

From the historian's standpoint, it is doubtful whether the Muslim conquest of Jerusalem was originally motivated by religious considerations. In early Islam there were attempts to decide on the place of Jerusalem in the new religion, but only after debate and after overcoming opposition in orthodox Islamic circles, was Jerusalem granted the status of the third ranking holy city, after Mecca and Medina. Muhammed, after praying for a time in the direction of Jerusalem, established the *kibla* or direction of prayer as being toward Mecca (Koran: Sura 2:136).

Sometime after the conquest of Jerusalem a modest wood and stone mosque was erected on the southern end of the Temple Mount, over the area where Herod's Royal Portico had stood during the Second Temple period. This mosque was called al-Aqsa, meaning 'the outer.' A Moslem tradition had it that this was the 'outer mosque' mentioned in the Koran (Sura 17) in relation to Muhammed's night journey on his wondrous steed al-Burak, when, accompanied by the angel Gabriel, he experienced a heavenly visit with Moses, Elijah and Jesus and was recognized as the foremost prophet among them. A geographical location is not mentioned in the Koran in connection with Muhammed's heavenly journey, while every other tale in the Koran relating to Muhammed's life mentions a specific place name. Many scholars of Islam maintain that the Koranic reference to the 'outer mosque' refers to a mosque at the outskirts of the city of Medina. Some hold that it is in heaven. However, Jerusalem's identity as the location of the 'outer mosque' ultimately took hold in Islam.

The Muslim conquest proceeded at an astounding rate for many years after Jerusalem was taken. At the same time there was great rivalry for leadership of the ever-growing Muslim world. In 659, the same year in which an earthquake shook Jerusalem, an alliance was contracted which shook the foundations of the Muslim empire.

Muawiyah, commander of the army in Palestine and Syria, was a scion of the Omayya clan, the last of the families of Muhammed's tribe to embrace Islam. He was the first caliph to establish the principle of dynastic succession, rather than election to the caliphate. This change came after a period in which the Muslim empire was involved in savage struggle against Omayyad rule. Once in control, Muawiyah signed an agreement with Amr ibn al-As, who had been governor of Egypt, in which the two retracted their recognition of the fourth caliph, Ali ibn Abu-Taleb, who was in Mesopotamia at the time. Ali was assassinated and Muawiyah was pronounced caliph in Jerusalem, from where he departed, to establish his seat of power in Damascus. Damascus became the capital of the Ummayad caliphate. These events mark the beginning of the great schism in Islam between Muawiyah and his heirs, the Sunnis, and the followers of Ali, the Shiites. It was also at this time that efforts were made to aggrandize the status of Jerusalem, which a modern historical interpretation would suggest was an effort to establish a sacred Muslim site close to the Ummayad seat of power, Damascus. With a mind to strengthening their hold over the area, the Umayyads encouraged the elevation of the Temple Mount to sacred status within Islam. They built impressive structures on it. Construction began on the Dome of the Rock in 688, and was completed in 691, during the reign of the caliph Abd al-Malik. The large octagonal structure was meant to serve as a shelter over the holy rock known in Judaism as the *even hashetiyah* or Foundation Stone, which is the likely site of the Holy of Holies of the Temple of the Jews. The rock was called *al-Sakhra* (the rock, or foundation stone) in Arabic. In Islam the rock (and by

Coin from the beginning of the Muslim conquest. To the left of the letter M is the inscription 'Aelia', the Roman name for Jerusalem still in use at the onset of the Muslim era

extension, Jerusalem) was sacred not for any prior association with the Jews, their Scripture and history, but because it marked the jumping off point for Muhammed's heavenly journey. Nevertheless Muslim traditions accrued to it which echo Jewish tradition. For instance, in Jewish tradition it was the site of the binding of Isaac. In Muslim tradition it is associated with the binding of Ishmael. Similarities with Judaism notwith – standing, it should be noted that Islam does not regard itself as a daughter religion of Judaism, but rather as a unique revelation.

Prior to the building of the Dome of the Rock over the stone, the stone seems not to have had significance in Islam. In worhipping at the al-Aqsa mosque, which stood at the southern extreme of the Temple Mount, worshippers would pray with their backs toward the rock. A Muslim tradition indicates that this turning away from the rock was the deliberate intent of the Caliph Umar, who wished to dissociate Muslim prayer from any Jewish

context. However, decades later, once the Dome of the Rock was built (691) and the al-Aqsa mosque rebuilt in a grander style (705-715), the Temple Mount took on an enduring aura of holiness in Muslim eyes, and is known in Arabic as Haram al-Sharif. A literature 'in praise of Jerusalem' emerged in Muslim tradition.

The struggle between Christianity and Islam during the early seventh century engendered messianic hopes in the Jews. Apocalyptic literature of the period predicted the conflict between *Edom* (the Christians) and *Ishmael* (the Muslims) which would ultimately effect the triumph of the people of Israel. Then the Redemption would come, and Jerusalem would return to its rightful people, those who had made it the Holy City.

The fall of Byzantine Jerusalem brought about its increased importance in the Christian world, and even the Jews wherever they lived were influenced by this mood. It was as if all the world now sanctified Jerusalem.

Conquest and its Aftermath

The entrance of Umar Ibn al-Khattab to Jerusalem in 638 is described in a series of Muslim sources in which reality and imagination merge. According to one tradition, he entered riding a camel, dressed in simple clothing, and this annoyed his fighters who thought that their leader should appear more impressive – at the very least mounted on a pure Arab steed. As was customary at the time, Umar sent the people of Jerusalem a letter of protection (*aman*) which was worded as follows, according to the famous Arab historian Tabari:

"In the name of God the merciful and compassionate. This is the covenant given by God's servant 'Umar, commander of the Believers,' to the people of Aelia: He grants protection to each person and his property; to their churches, their crosses, the sick and the healthy, to all the people of their creed. We shall not station Muslim soldiers in their churches. We shall not destroy the

A depiction of the Heavenly Jerusalem in a Spanish manuscript of the eleventh century. According to the Christian conception, the city is square in format.
At twelve gates stand twelve apostles, above the head of each is one of the gemstones of the high priest

churches nor impair any of their contents or their crosses... We shall not compel them to renounce their beliefs and we shall do them no harm. No Jews shall live among them in Aelia. The people of Aelia are obliged to pay the *jizia* (head tax) we impose on the inhabitants of other cities. They must rid themselves of the Romans (Byzantine army) and any local militia. We ensure the safety of these people on their departure, both of their persons and their property, until they reach their asylum. To those who wish to remain, we ensure their safekeeping but they are obliged to pay the *jizia* that the other inhabitants of Aelia pay. To those inhabitants of Aelia who wish to join the departing Byzantines in person and with their property, to vacate their churches and abandon their crosses, we pledge to ensure the safety of their persons and that of their churches and crosses, until they reach their destinations."

The attitude toward non-Muslims was shaped in accordance with the concept of *dhimma*, meaning protection granted by treaty. Members of religious groups that were allowed to live according to the terms of this protection were called *ahl al-dhimma*; individual infidels came to be known as *dhimmi*. Many provisions, such as the prohibition against bearing arms and riding horses, had the purpose of honoring Islam and Muslims and humiliating non-believers. *Dhimmis* were subject to the head tax (*jizia*) and a special land tax (*kharaj*). They were afforded protection and permitted to worship and organize themselves as they wished. These conditions changed for better or worse over the course of history. In principle these parameters, established in the early days of Islam, continue to serve as the basis for relations between Muslims and *dhimmis* to the present day.

The transfer of authority in Jerusalem was not characterized by the violence that on many previous occasions befell the city when it passed from one ruler to another.

From Aelia to al-Kuds

The sociological composition of Byzantine Jerusalem – Hierosolima or Aelia – changed slowly. In accordance with the above-mentioned pact, the remnants of Byzantine authority and their garrison left the city, but

Map of Jerusalem from the ninth century drawn according to the description of the monk Arculf, who visited the country in the seventh century

the majority of the Christian population remained. For generations it was a central factor in the city's fabric. At the same time, Jews became a component of the population, in spite of what is written in the letter of protection. The Muslim community grew, partly through immigration and partly due to the conversion of local inhabitants. The Arabic language also began to gain precedence among Jerusalemites, regardless of religion or origin. The city's name changed. For many years the new rulers continued to call it Aelia, or Iliya, as did many of its citizens. With the passing of time, they adopted Arabic names of Jewish origin, such as *bait al-makdis* (*Bet Hamikdash*, the Holy Temple). From the eleventh century onward, the name *al-Kuds* (The Holy) supplanted all others and is still in use today. The

Hebrew word Zion – one of many names of Jerusalem in Jewish tradition – was also adopted in a slightly distorted version: *Sahyun*, or *Sihyun*.

Jews Return to Jerusalem

In keeping with the above-mentioned covenant, Jews at first were not permitted to live in Jerusalem. Apparently this was due to pressure from the Christian populace for whom theologically motivated contempt for Jews was a deeply ingrained attitude. While the above text indicates that the Muslims accepted this condition, there is evidence that Jews began living in Jerusalem almost immediately after the conquest. This is not necessarily contradictory. It is possible that the Muslim conquerors

agreed to keep the Jews out of Jerusalem, and after a short interval changed their minds. One explanation for the change is that the new rulers concluded that no logical reason existed for giving Christian attitudes more weight than those of the Jews. It was the Jews and not the Christians who were the earliest occupants of Jerusalem, and the Muslims recognized the Jews' spiritual ties with Jerusalem in general, and the Temple Mount in particular. In addition, the Jews were members of a faith community unconnected with a political entity that threatened the Muslim empire; it would probably be correct to assume that the Muslims wanted to reduce Christian influence in Jerusalem as part of a general move to prevent a Byzantine effort to retake the city.

An eleventh century Jewish chronicle found in the Cairo Geniza (a *geniza* is a repository for damaged manuscripts) recounts that the Jews requested permission from the Caliph Umar to settle in southern Jerusalem, and that this request was granted. The petition mentioned two hundred families; the Christians objected to this number. The caliph finally decided, in a spirit of compromise, to allow seventy families to settle. This was apparently in the year 640. At first the Jewish settlement in Jerusalem was a small and impoverished, but with the passage of time it grew in size and numbers, as Jews arrived from Babylonia and North Africa during the period of Umayyad rule.

Jerusalem under the Umayyads

Muslim Jerusalem remained a provincial town during Ummayad rule. It was not granted the status of a capital, but instead was made subordinate to Lydda (Lod) at first, and later to the new administrative center of Ramle, which Sulayman, one of Abd al-Malik's sons and successors, founded. Jerusalem began to decline in importance; trade routes bypassed it.

The Gallic bishop Arculf, who came to Palestine some decades after the Muslim conquest, relates that "near the

According to Muslim tradition, Abraham bound Ishmael (and not Isaac) for sacrifice on the Foundation Stone. After the Dome of the Rock was built over Foundation Stone, to mark the site where Muhammed leaped up to the heavens, further Muslim traditions accrued to the spot, one of which was this tale. Oil on wood, Iran, late 19th century

eastern wall, in this famous place where the magnificent Temple once stood, the Saracens (as the Arabs were called by the Europeans) built a house of prayer in the form of a square made of wooden planks and large beams which they constructed over the remnants [of ruined buildings], a work of inferior quality... some say that the building can hold three thousand men." He is referring to the mosque of al-Aksa, which was re-constructed in a far more substantive manner in the early eighth century.

The Dome of the Rock, noted for its size and splendor, was built on the Temple Mount during the reign of the Caliph Abd al-Malik. It has stood for more than thirteen hundred years, making it the oldest surviving shrine of the early Muslim period. It has been suggested that by erecting a beautiful building Abd Al-Malik's purpose was to instill a sense of pride in Muslims who were overawed by the majestic churches of Jerusalem, tours of which were conducted by the Byzantines for simple nomadic Arabs whose culture equated grandeur with power. A further symbolic purpose is attributed to Abd al-Malik, that of conveying to Jews and Christians that their traditions had been superceded by Islam. His building stood at a higher elevation than the Church of the Holy Sepulcher. It was intended to speak symbolically to Christians by virtue of its elevation and splendid decoration, and to speak to Jews because of its location.

The mosque of al-Aqsa situated on the southern part of the Temple Mount, was from the very outset intended as a place of prayer, as opposed to the Dome of the Rock, which was conceived of as a shrine. Al-Aqsa was built during the caliphate of al-Walid I in the early eighth century, and underwent many changes over time, unlike the Dome of the Rock. Some scholars attribute the numerous repairs and alterations to its structure to its location on the southern end of the Temple platform, an area not resting on bedrock, but suspended over vaulted arches and earthen fill built during the Second Temple period. As the substructure is less stable than on other areas of the mount, al-Aqsa suffered collapses and severe structural problems as a result of earthquakes.

The Umayyad dynasty ruled in Damascus for ninety years, with Jerusalem functioning as a religious site in the region near the capital. Muslim pilgrims who had visited the holy cities of Mecca and Medina, would

Illustration of Muhammad's legendary nocturnal journey from Mecca to Jerusalem and his ascent from there to heaven. On the right is the Ka'ba, the holy stone of Mecca, and in the center, Muhammed on his mythical winged horse; to the lower left, the Foundation Stone

proceed to Jerusalem as well; gifts would stream to the Islamic holy places on the Temple Mount, and to the area south of the Temple platform, where the Umayyad rulers built an impressive administrative quarter, which was uncovered during archaeological excavations after 1967.

Abd al-Malik, the caliph who constructed the Dome of the Rock, displayed tolerance toward the Jews and tacit acknowledgement of the role they played in Jerusalem.

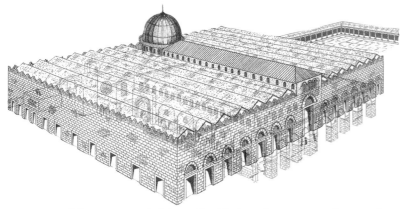

The mosque of al-Aqsa (in blue) as it appears today, against the background (in red) of the hypothetical appearance of the seventh century structure

He appointed some Jewish families as guardians of the Temple Mount, or Haram al-Sharif, and determined that these families whould be exempted from the poll tax.

Abbasid Rule

In 750 the Umayyads were dethroned in Damascus and replaced by the Abbasid dynasty. The last stage of the struggle between the two powers took place not far from Jerusalem, near the sources of the Yarkon River in Rosh Ha-ayin. Jerusalem's standing dwindled further after the transfer of the center of Muslim power from Damascus to the more distant Abbasid capital of Baghdad.

From the very beginning of their reign, the Abbasids displayed little tolerance towards Christians and Jews. They demanded each group strictly observe a discriminatory dress code for non-Muslims, in which they were made to wear special badges to denote their lesser status as members of inferior but tolerated faiths. The Christians were required to wear distinctive blue symbols, while the Jews had to wear yellow symbols. It seems clear that some Abbasid caliphs tried to reduce Christian influence in Jerusalem, however the Abassids' own power diminished following a series of rebellions throughout their kingdoms, including Palestine and Jerusalem. These rebellions recurred from time to time.

From 878 the Abbasids began to lose their hold over Syria-Palestine, as Ahmed ibn Tulun, Egypt's ruler, annexed it to his dominion. Later on, when Egypt became independent of Abbasid rule in Baghdad, the latter started a campaign to return Syria-Palestine to its fold. The country became a battlefield in the struggle between the caliphs of Baghdad and the rulers of Egypt. This unrest continued into the tenth century. In 969, a new dynasty assumed the throne in Egypt; the Fatimids. Their army also conquered Syria-Palestine. They soon came into conflict with the Karmatis, members of a Shiite sect which originated in Persia. The Fatimids gained the upper hand. In this quarrel, the Muslims exploited the Byzantines who had been trying to return to the country ever since they were expelled from Syria-Palestine in the seventh century. In the years 969-975, the Byzantine army

Top: Colonnade or porch from one of the grand Umayyad structures uncovered south of the Temple Mount
Left: A capital in the al-Aqsa mosque which is from the original Umayyad structure

The Foundation Stone beneath the ornate inner surface of the Dome of the Rock. In Jewish tradition the world was founded on this spot, hence the name Foundation Stone

A letter from the Eretz Israel Yeshiva in Jerusalem, to the Jewish communities of Eretz Israel and Egypt

conquered Cyprus, Syria and parts of Palestine. In 974, the Byzantine emperor, John Tzimisces, reached Damascus. In a letter sent in that same year to Ashot, King of the Armenians, John Tzimisces boasts of his conquests and victories in Palestine, and claims that Ramle and Jerusalem succombed to his forces. But this was simply vain bragging.

The Eretz Israel Yeshiva in Jerusalem

Strange as it may seem, during these very troubled times, the Jewish community in Jerusalem enjoyed a relatively comfortable existence. The spiritual center of the Jews which had until then been Tiberias, was transferred to Jerusalem, where the Eretz Israel Yeshiva (academy of Talmudic study), considered the successor of the Sanhedrin, was active for a long time. This was the authoritative institution representing the Jewish community in Syria-Palestine. Its members, judges and other prominent figures, exerted authority over the Jews of Eretz Israel and the Jewish communities in Syria and Egypt. Their influence reached as far as Greece, Byzantium, and North Africa. Their advice and judgment on Jewish law was sought even by far-off communities in Germany, during the tenth and eleventh centuries.

Owing to the discovery in nineteenth century Cairo of an incredibly abundant trove of manuscripts in a synagogue *geniza*, (see p.106) information on the activities of the Eretz Israel Yeshiva is now becoming available. It is apparent, for instance, that the Italian-Ashkenazi school of liturgical poets was influenced by their Eretz Israel counterparts. Synagogue services in Italy and medieval Ashkenaz also followed the Eretz Israel tradition. Many other German-Jewish customs at this time originated in Eretz Israel.

During the tenth and eleventh centuries, with the unsettled circumstances in Syria-Palestine and in Jerusalem in particular, the influence of the Eretz Israel Yeshiva diminished, while the influence of the Babylonian Yeshiva, (essentially the great academies of Sura and Pumbeditha) with which it was in perpetual competition for influence over world Jewry, increased.

At the head of the Eretz Israel Yeshiva stood the *rosh ha-yeshiva*, also called the *gaon* (evidently a term only used during the Muslim period) and he was supported by a council of six members of the Yeshiva. The Yeshiva would appoint the heads of the Jewish communities under its authority. Other positions within these communities were appointed in the same manner. In the Cairo Geniza were found more than six hundred and fifty letters relating to Eretz Israel, among them many sent from the Yeshiva in Jerusalem; most are written in Judeo – Arabic and a few in Hebrew, and almost all were written during the Fatimid period. From these letters, a great deal is revealed about Jewish life in Jerusalem during the tenth century. It can be inferred from the letters that the Jewish neighborhood in Jerusalem was in the south of the city, and that in the community were a good number of immigrants from North Africa and Spain. These immigrants continued to maintain close ties with their original congregations and with one another. During the seventh and eighth centuries, many immigrants from Babylonia also arrived in the country. One of the Babylonian sages provided the information that in certain Eretz Israel cities, immigrants from Babylon had the greatest influence on the community, at times even greater than the indigenous members of the community.

Some of the letters also describe the conditions of life in Jerusalem. The economic situation is generally depicted as being on the decline. Quite a number of immigrants who had brought with them substantial sums ended up impoverished. Much of this was due to Jerusalem's isolation, its distance from the large commercial centers and its uncertain state. Some improvement was felt when thousands of pilgrims arrived in the city – mainly Christians and Muslims – on their holidays or in connection with the Muslim pilgrimages to Mecca or Medina, when Jerusalem incidentally benefited

The Gate of Mercy (Golden Gate). In popular Jewish tradition, the Messiah is to enter Jerusalem through this gate. Jews customarily clustered alongside it in prayer

from their patronage as well. Jewish visitors and pilgrims also came to the city, mostly in the Hebrew month of Tishri (September) for the Sukkot pilgrimage festival. Jews living in Jerusalem who were obliged to pay an annual tax to the Muslim rulers. In exchange, they were permitted to reside in Jerusalem and enjoy the

The Mount of Olives was the major site where Jewish pilgrims to Jerusalem congregated. Here it is represented in an illumination from the Saragossa Bible depicting the prophet Zechariah's vision of the coming of the Messiah at the End of Days: "And his feet shall stand on that day upon the Mount of Olives, which is before Jerusalem…"

protection of the authorities. The payment of this tax also afforded the Jews of the Diaspora the right to make pilgrimages to Jerusalem.

The destination of Jewish pilgrimage during this period was the Mount of Olives. This holy site is mentioned in the Bible and various commentaries as the refuge of the *Shekhina* (Divine Presence) after the destruction of the Temple. According to a document found in the Cairo Geniza, after the Muslims took Jerusalem, the Jews bought the Mount of Olives from

them. The Jews of Jerusalem, together with masses of pilgrims, would assemble on the mount annually in the month of Tishri and pray in the direction of the Temple Mount, on which, it will be remembered, stood Muslim prayer sites. Jews were forbidden entry to it. The major assembly of Jews on the Mount of Olives was conducted on Hoshana Rabba, (the 21st of Tishri, seventh day of the Sukkot festival). The head of the Eretz Israel Yeshiva, (the Jerusalem Gaon) would speak to the assembly. This was also the occasion for important appointments to be announced, contributions collected to support the Jerusalem community and Yeshiva, and to announce the festival calendar for the coming year.

Aside from the Mount of Olives, other sites of Jewish prayer were the entry gates to the Temple Mount, in particular the area alongside the Gate of Mercy in the eastern city wall. Prayers recited there included appeals for the healing of the sick and for the abolition of decrees issued against the Jews.

The Karaites Come to Jerusalem

The Karaites were a Jewish sect which emerged in the late eighth century in Persia and Iraq. They differed significantly from mainstream Judaism in their rejection of the traditions of the Oral Law, reliance on rabbinic authority, and the ancient systems of houses of prayer. The Karaites emphasized the individual's understanding of the Bible text, however they eventually developed their own oral tradition, which differed from mainstream rabbanite tradition. The Karaites were viewed as a threat by the rabbinic authorities, as they attacked the premises upon which Judaism was based, as well as the communal foundations on which the unity of the Jewish people rested. While the Karaites eventually became a small but vibrant presence in Jewish history, in the period under study they might well have become a major force, due to the fierceness of their faith and their proselytizing activities. In the tenth century, Jerusalem became a focal point for the Karaites, and over time their community in the city developed considerably. They

Page from an illuminated Karaite Pentateuch, ninth century

were known as *Avelei Zion* ('Mourners of Zion') or *Shoshanim* ('Roses') by their admirers. They lived in austerity in Jerusalem, mourning the destruction of the Temple and praying for its restoration – activities they regarded as the essence of their religious experience. Many adhered strictly to the wearing of mourning attire, fasted frequently, and abstained from such indulgences as eating meat and drinking wine. They also engaged in proselytizing activity.

The relationship between the Rabbanites and the Karaites were generally tense, sometimes becoming sharp and even violent. Their different customs and holidays and their religious fanaticism were among the reasons for endless confrontations with the Rabbanites, who frequently declared bans of excommunication upon the Karaites during the assembly on Hoshana Rabba on the Mount of Olives. Sometimes the conflict extended beyond the borders of Eretz Israel. This happened in the eleventh century, when the Gaon Solomon ben Judah, head of the Eretz Israel Yeshiva, wanted to cancel the ban on the Karaites. Other Rabbanite leaders, among them the Gaon's own son, were of a different mind, and the ban continued. They also demanded that the Karaites keep the dates of the holidays according to the Jewish calendar. The Jerusalem Karaites brought complaints against the Rabbanites before the Fatimid authorities in Cairo, who issued an order granting the Karaites complete religious freedom. Moreover, the order stated that whoever disturbed the peace between the factions would be severely punished. The Rabbanites did not observe the conditions of the order and as a result, three Rabbanite leaders were arrested and sent to Damascus. Through efforts made in Cairo, the three were eventually released, but the governor of Jerusalem did not allow them their freedom. Once again Cairo was called on to intervene. Finally, the three Rabbanites were set free, while new orders were issued which absolutely forbade further contention between the two communities. In Jerusalem, the Karaites emerged from this struggle in a more advantageous position, as the Fatimid rulers had recognized them as a separate Jewish community. They continued to live in Jerusalem until the Crusader conquest.

Jerusalem in Muslim Tradition

In Islam there are three sites to which special holiness is attached. In descending order of importance they are the Ka'ba in Mecca, the mosque of Muhammed in Medina, and the Haram al-Sharif in Jerusalem. While Jerusalem is not mentioned in the Koran, tradition associates the Temple Mount with "the outer mosque" from which Muhammed ascended to the heavens, accompanied by the angel Gabriel. The tomb of Mary is also regarded as holy, as indicated by the fact that Muawiya, the first Umayyad caliph, prayed there. Jerusalem was rejected as the focus of Muslim prayer and Mecca received this

Illustration in a Turkish manuscript depicting King Solomon praying to God after the completion of the Temple. Solomon is shown on the roof, with a halo of fire around his head, and his features concealed because of their holiness

honor. Jerusalem's special holiness was elaborated upon in later Muslim tradition. The Muslim oral tradition attributes to Muhammed sayings indicating that prayer in Jerusalem has great value. Regarding the Foundation Stone (*al-Sakhra*) on the Temple Mount, Muslim tradition indicates that it is located beneath Allah's throne and above "the well of the spirits," where the souls of the dead gather twice a week. It is part of paradise and all the world's sweet waters emanate from it. Many of these beliefs have parallels in earlier Jewish legend. Muslim legend connects Jerusalem with the day of judgment. Muslim mystics, believing that living in Jerusalem purifies the soul, came to the city.

An extensive body of Muslim literature developed in praise of Jerusalem in both this world and the next. According to this literature, whoever lived in Jerusalem was assured of his livelihood; the source of the purest water in the world was in Jerusalem; whoever visited Jerusalem or even stayed there for a short time, had his sins forgiven; and all of Jerusalem's qualities in this world were nought when compared with what awaited those who believed in the End of Days: on the Day of Judgment a narrow bridge would stretch from the Mount of Olives to the Temple Mount, and only Muslims would cross the bridge, while infidels would fall into hellfires. On the Temple Mount, 'the great trumpet shall be blown' for the resurrection of the dead, and all mankind would gather in Jerusalem to be judged. (The latter bears striking resemblance to Isaiah 27:13.)

Some scholars explain the appearance of an extensive literature 'in praise of Jerusalem' as an Umayyad attempt to elevate the city's status and attract Muslim residents. The problem, which from the Muslim point of view became exacerbated with the passage of time, was that Christians and Jews made up the majority of the city's population, as much evidence shows. The tenth-century historian al-Mukadassi complains bitterly that Islam in Jerusalem was something of a stepchild: "the Christians and the Jews have taken it over and its mosques have no congregation of worshippers and students of the law." This situation was probably attributable to Jerusalem's relative unimportance to the Abbasid dynasty, whose attention was focused on distant Iraq.

This does not mean that the various Muslim rulers (Abbasids, Fatimids and others) paid no attention to Jerusalem: the mosques on the Temple Mount were always important, but it is doubtful whether the city itself demanded any special interest. Apart from the period of the Umayyads, Jerusalem was not at the height of its glory in the early Muslim period.

In the eleventh century, new works of 'praises of Jerusalem' appeared. Some scholars ascribe this development to the wars in Syria-Palestine during the rule of the Shiite caliph al-Hakim. Another explanation links it to the extensive damage to the Dome of the Rock in 1016-1017 and the need to organize a fundraising campaign to rebuild it. It was not unusual for praises of a Muslim city to appear when the city's reputation or status was on the decline.

Jerusalem attracted masses of pilgrims of all religions. According to Nasir-i-Khusraw's remarks in the eleventh century, some ten thousand Muslim pilgrims visited the city annually, mostly from Syria and Syria-Palestine. Many of them had to be satisfied with a pilgrimage to Jerusalem as they were unable to cover the greater distance to Mecca.

Christians in Muslim Jerusalem

The Muslim conquest brought an end to hundreds of years of Christian domination of Jerusalem. The city's Christians experienced a diminution in status and felt themselves on the defensive in this new era. They were still the majority but their power was on the wane. The fact that the Muslims allowed the Jews to return and settle in the city was irksome and offensive for the Christians. Despite Muslim domination, Jerusalem was still a focal point of Christian identification, of pilgrimage, and hopes for a better Christian future. During the eleventh century, Christian apocalyptic literature concerning the End of the Days which would take place in Jerusalem, increased. The Greek Orthodox was the largest Christian community in Jerusalem. They were headed by the Patriarch of Jerusalem, who was appointed to this role in Constantinople. In the early Muslim period the Jerusalem patriarchate went for long periods without a patriarch in residence. Later, the status of the Jerusalem patriarch rose. With the disappearance of competitors like the bishop of Caesarea, he became responsible for the Holy Land. His position also became stronger because the Muslim rulers recognized him as head of the large Greek Orthodox congregation in financial as well as religious matters.

The Eastern Orthodox church in Jerusalem had to tread warily in its dealings with the Muslim authorities on the one hand and with the rulers of the Byzantine empire on the other. Its leaders and members lived in a Muslim world without cutting off contact with Byzantine Constantinople, which was the enemy of the Muslims. Communication was maintained via priests travelling between the two cities. A number of the patriarchs took part in important councils in Constantinople. The Jerusalem patriarchs were also involved in various church controversies, and not infrequently, expressed unacceptable positions because of their special status in the Muslim world. Some of them also had special connections with certain royal courts in Christian Europe.

In the early period of their reign, Muslim rulers did not destroy churches or monasteries but forbade any further building activity, renovation or repair. This resulted in the serious deterioration of Christian structures. In the eighth and ninth centuries, the Christians' relationship with the Muslims began to decline and Christian buildings were attacked and robbed, at times on the instructions of the authorities and at times by Bedouin tribes or thieving peasants. Jerusalem also experienced a number of severe natural disasters. From the seventh to the eleventh century, more than twenty earthquakes shook the city. Many buildings were affected, among them churches. In 1033 the Church of the Holy Sepulcher suffered serious damage in an earthquake.

Over time Christian Jerusalem underwent a process of Arabization and Islamization. The latter involved the conversion of Christians to the dominant religion of Islam. Arabization meant the adoption of the Arabic language in everyday life as well as for religious ritual. Arabic eventually supplanted both Syriac and Greek. Arabization also meant the adoption by Christians of the Muslim calendar which numbers years according to the

The Monastery of the Cross was first built in the sixth century, destroyed during the Persian invasion and restored by a Georgian monk in the eleventh century

hejirah or flight of Muhammad from Mecca to Medina in 622.

Among the Greek Orthodox in Jerusalem, there were Asian Georgians who maintained churches and monasteries. An early source mentions ten Georgian monasteries in the city. Perhaps the best known is the monastery in the Valley of the Cross some two kilometers

Depiction of Jerusalem from the Abbasid period, on a mosaic floor in Um-Rasas in Jordan. Above the city, the words 'the holy city' are written in Greek

west of the Church of the Holy Sepulcher. According to a Christian legend, the Muslims attacked this monastery at the end of the eighth century and murdered all the monks, so that no one survived who knew the site of the Jewish holy vessels (of the Temple) which had been hidden in the monastery on instruction of the Emperor Justinian centuries earlier. This mystery continued to

occupy the imaginations of future generations. The Georgians memorialized Jerusalem and its holy sites in their own country. Many Georgian churches were named after the churches of Jerusalem; their capital was surrounded by places named the Valley of Kidron, Gethsemane, and so forth, and the capital itself was dubbed the 'New Jerusalem.'

Along with the Greek Orthodox congregation in Muslim Jerusalem, there were also a number of dissenting Christian congregations, such as the Monophysites and Nestorians. Until the Muslim conquest, the imperial church made great efforts to suppress dissidents. However the Muslim rulers would not permit this and in addition, the difficulties Christians endured under Muslim domination brought the different congregations closer together. The Copts and Armenians were also among the Christian congregations in Jerusalem during that period.

Sixty Years War

The tenth and eleventh centuries witnessed a lengthy war – or to be more precise, a series of wars – with Jerusalem occasionally at the center of events. The fighting began in 969 and ended in 1029, hence the appelation 'Sixty Years War.' Forces opposed to the Fatimid regime dominated the city from time to time and both sides caused considerable damage to buildings, among them the Church of the Holy Sepulcher. The Fatimids, whose political base was in Egypt, reached accords with the Byzantines on a number of occasions, but each was quickly violated. In 1003, the Christians in Jerusalem were the target of harassment. Five or six years later the Church of the Holy Sepulcher was destroyed in an attack ordered by the Fatimid caliph al-Hakim. (It was rebuilt but destroyed by earthquake in 1034, and not rebuilt again until the Byzantines provided funding, in 1048). The reaction to the Fatimid destruction was the entry of the Christians into a series of pacts with Bedouin tribes who opposed the Fatimid regime. Only in 1013 did the Fatimids succeed in suppressing this rebellion. Uprisings led by Bedouin tribes and supported by Christians again took place in 1024. The Bedouin managed to overcome Jerusalem and Ramle and inflict mayhem among the Jews. In 1029, the Fatimids suppressed the Bedouin.

Everyday Life of the Jews in Jerusalem

At the beginning of the Muslim period the Jewish Quarter was situated in the southern part of the city, not far from the Temple Mount and the Siloam Spring. Apparently it continued to exist on this site for hundreds of years before relocating to the northern part of the city. On the eve of the crusader conquest, the section bordering on the northern wall was called the Jewish Quarter. Evidence from the tenth and eleventh centuries indicates trade and commercial dealings among the Jews of Jerusalem. We know, for instance, that Jewish-Maghribi merchants (from the Maghrib, North Africa) were a central factor in the import and export of various types of goods.

The first page of the 'Scroll of Evyatar,' which describes the history of the Eretz Israel Yeshiva during the eleventh century. The scroll emphasizes the involvement of North African Jews in the yeshiva's affairs

A dyeing installation found in excavations south of the Temple Mount. Dyeing was one of the typical Jewish crafts in Jerusalem during the Muslim era

Jews had shops in the Jewish market of the city, particularly during those periods when many pilgrims visited Jerusalem. The Jews also engaged in banking, textile dyeing, tanning, and money changing. They were also weavers and spinners. Another aspect of Jewish craftsmanship was the copying of holy books, which were then sold to Jewish congregations in the Diaspora.

The economic distress and heavy taxes imposed on the Jewish community resulted in the fact that the Jews of Jerusalem, and primarily the Eretz Israel Yeshiva in Jerusalem, made every effort to gain permanent support from the Jews of the Diaspora. The contributions that streamed into Jerusalem resembled, to a certain extent, the tithes to the priests in the period of the Temple. In this manner, contact with the city was maintained by Diaspora Jewry. The eleventh century 'Scroll of Ahimaaz' tells that Samuel, the son of Paltiel, who brought the remains of his parents and relatives to Palestine, also brought with him a sum of money from his congregation to Jerusalem. R. Shmuel ha-Nagid ('Samuel the Prince'), the renowned Jewish aristocrat of Muslim Spain, who was responsible for the foreign and interior policies of the kingdom of Granada, would annually forward olive oil to the synagogues of Jerusalem. It was said at the time that anyone who gives charity to Jerusalem, is assured of a place in the next world.

The steadfastness of Jerusalem's Jews to the city during the difficult times of the Fatimid regime testifies to their devotion to it. The Fatimid authorities regularly imposed heavy taxes on them. The Jews groaned under the burden, made strenuous efforts to collect the necessary funds, sent pleas to their brethren in Egypt for help, and did not abandon the city. In a letter in the

Page from the 'Guide to Jerusalem', a manuscript found in the Cairo Geniza. It is written in the Arabic language in Hebrew characters, and was intended as a pilgrim's guide to the holy sites of Jerusalem. It includes information on the structure and topographical lay-out of the city and is an important source of information on the city in the tenth century

Cairo Geniza which dates to 1025, Solomon ha-Kohen Gaon, son of Joseph, of Jerusalem, writes to Ephraim, son of Shmarya, in Fustat, (ancient Cairo), that the Bedouin uprising caused much suffering among the Jews in the city, that Ramle was destroyed, and that the income regularly received by the Eretz Israel Yeshiva of Jerusalem from the Jewish inhabitants of Ramle was no longer forthcoming. In addition to their heavy debts, a special tax of 15,000 dinars was levied on the Jews of Jerusalem and a special additional payment of 6,000 dinars on the Jews apart from that – half to be paid by the Rabbanites and the other half, by the Karaites. The writer adds, "and we gave two thousand five hundred and nothing remained [at home] even the chairs or household goods, and many had to mortgage their homes at interest [in order to pa]y, and there were those who sold everything, and many died from their suffering..." The Jews of Jerusalem considered it their duty to remain despite all the difficulties. Among their reasons was concern for the Jewish pilgrims who might otherwise arrive to mourn Jerusalem's ruins and worship in its dust, and find none of their brethren there.

The Links between the Diaspora and Jerusalem

During the Muslim period, Jews living in distant lands continued to preserve and reinforce their connection to Jerusalem. The classic Hebrew literature and liturgical poetry of the period contains innumerable expressions of desire for the city's and the Jewish people's intertwined redemption. Many documents contain references to Diaspora Jews who immigrated to Jerusalem for the purpose of settlement, and to many others who journeyed to there on pilgrimage. It was a well-known Jewish practice to bring the remains of deceased family members to be buried within sight of Jerusalem; and finally but significantly with regard to ties to the city, Diaspora Jewry contributed financial support for the scholars of Jerusalem and the city's Jewish community.

Jewish immigrants to Jerusalem during this period came from all parts of the Diaspora. The greatest numbers came between the seventh and ninth centuries. An instance of the impact of Diaspora Jewry upon

Jerusalem's Jews is the adoption by the Jerusalem community of the prayer rite then prevalent in Babylonia. This important development for Jewish culture is likely to have occurred due to the influence of learned and determined Jews from Babylonia.

During the period of the Sixty Years War (969-1029) involving the Fatimids, Byzantines, Bedouin tribes and peasants, the number of immigrants and pilgrims to Jerusalem lessened considerably owing to often treacherous conditions in the country. Yet one pilgrim, the French sage Rabbi Eliahu ben Menahem, recounted that he made pilgrimage to Jerusalem on four different occasions, and that during the Sukkot festival there were twelve thousand Jewish pilgrims in Jerusalem who had come from all over the world. While the figure would appear to be exaggerated, it is an indication of a very large number of Jewish pilgrims even during difficult times. For Jerusalem's Jews this stream of pilgrims had a threefold significance: it was a means by which contributions from abroad were transferred to them; it was a source of moral support for Jerusalem's Jews, who understood themselves to be the keepers of the spiritual light of Judaism even in the most difficult of times; and it helped maintain contact in the fields of literature and rabbinic correspondence with the scholars of the Eretz Israel Yeshiva in Jerusalem.

A letter from the Gaon Rabbi Solomon b. Judah, in which the controversies among the Rabbanites are mentioned, as well as the ban on the Karaites pronounced publicly each year on the Mount of Olives on Hoshana Rabba

Contemporary artist's rendering of the main Jewish gathering which took place annually during the Muslim period, on Hoshana Rabba on the Mount of Olives. Tableau, Tower of David Museum, Jerusalem

The Jewish pilgrim to Jerusalem is likely to have had one or both of the following motivations for making the journey: the desire to pay homage to Jerusalem's glorious past, when pilgrimage to the Temple was a major factor in the life of the Jewish people; and to achieve expiation from sin. Jerusalem was the quintessential place where, since ancient times, Jews could hope to unburden themselves and achieve atonement. A piece of advice ascribed to the great Babylonian sage Saadia Gaon says that, "One who seeks divine pardon for sins, should go up to Jerusalem and pray there." This understanding of the efficacy of pilgrimage to Jerusalem is often repeated in Jewish writings of the Middle Ages. Special prayers were composed for recital in Jerusalem during the pilgrim's stay. In addition there are popular works advising the Jewish pilgrim how to behave in and near Jerusalem. "If you merit the privilege of going up to Jerusalem, when you gaze upon it from Mount Scopus, if you are on donkeyback, get down. And if you are shod, remove your shoes, and tear your garment... Enter (into Jerusalem) in mourning, somber. And when you get to the city, tear your garment again because of the (destroyed) Temple, and (think of) the House of Israel and the Jewish people, and pray..."

Pilgrimage to Jerusalem was fraught with danger owing to the unstable political and military situation in the land, and also because of the abundance of thieves and highwaymen on the roads. A tale has come down to us of a Babylonian Jew who made pilgrimage to Jerusalem. On his return journey he was attacked by Arabs who stole everything he owned. His life was spared.

The Jewish custom of bringing the dead to Jerusalem for burial was ancient. Throughout the Middle Ages, Jerusalem was one of the most preferred and sacred of sites for this purpose. Al-Jahat, a prominent Muslim writer of the early ninth century, tells that it was customary for the prominent leadership of the Babylonian Jewish community, and the priests, to bury

The first page of a Hebrew primer written in Egypt, 10th-11th century. It features an illustration of the Temple Candelabrum

their dead temporarily in Babylonia and later on, bring the remains for permanent burial in Jerusalem. There is also evidence of this custom having been carried out by other Diaspora Jews, during the entire early Muslim period. Death played an important role in people's consciousness during the Middle Ages, hence the widespread understanding of the significance of transferring the dead to Jerusalem for burial.

Financial support of Diaspora Jews for the Jerusalem community was both widespread and organized. Contributions for the Eretz Israel Yeshiva in Jerusalem, collected in the synagogues of the Diaspora, were critical to the survival of the Jews of Jerusalem. Many documents from the Cairo Geniza refer to this support. At times, special emissaries were sent from Jerusalem to the Diaspora to collect these funds. There were congregations that levied special taxes intended for Jerusalem, and particularly for the Yeshiva. Many Jews set aside a sum for the Jews of Jerusalem in their wills. As we learn from the 'Scroll of Ahima'az', donations came from far and wide. It was the custom to mention the names of generous contributors and to bless them in the course of impressive ceremonies on the Mount of Olives on the day of Hoshana Rabba during the autumn Sukkot festival.

Hebrew liturgical poetry reached its high point, in terms of both quantity and quality, during the Middle Ages. This body of work is replete with evidence of Diaspora Jewry's attachment to Jerusalem. It is referred to in hundreds of liturgical poems as the symbol of Redemption – regardless of the the city's sorry physical and political state at the time. Rabbi Saadia Gaon of Babylonia mentioned Jerusalem in his liturgical poetry, and at the opposite end of the known world, rabbis of Sepharad (Spain) and Ashkenaz referred to the city with great longing. Jerusalem was the symbol of the hope for physical and spiritual

Illustration depicting the Temple's holy implements dates to tenth century Egypt. Leningrad Bible

redemption. The great Ashkenazi sage Rabbeinu Gershom, 'the Light of the Exile,' described Jerusalem in his liturgical poems as a place where one could reach the most profound understanding of the Torah's secrets.

Among the Jews of Spain the tradition developed that they were the direct descendants of the ancient exiles from Jerusalem. They contended that this gave them preferred status over all other Diaspora Jewish communities, and served to explain why Sephardi Hebrew poetry, Torah commentaries,and letters had a superior ring and quality to those produced in any other Jewish community.

Jerusalem in Jewish Apocalyptic Literature

A citation from the early collection of Jewish legends on the book of Genesis (*Bereisheet Rabah*) states: "If you witness powerful kingdoms battling one another, you are beholding the footsteps of the messiah as well." This sentiment lies at the heart of the great body of Jewish apocalyptic literature which arose during the Byzantine period, and continued with the Persian conquest, the Byzantine reconquest, and the Muslim conquest. The turbulence, persecution and occasional catastrophe through which the Jews lived inspired a longing for and expectation of Redemption. The Muslim conquest inspired hope of a great easing of living conditions and even of Redemption. When these hopes were disappointed, a paradoxical result occured. Rather than wallowing in depression and hopelessness, messianic expectation grew, and a number of apocalyptic works were written in the waning days of the Ummayad dynasty, and again towards the end of Abbasid. Pseudo-prophetic works were authored, supposedly from the late Second Temple period, which foretold the downfall of Edom (Rome) by a new power that believed in the word of a prophet. This power would conquer the land of Israel and transfer possession of it to the Jews. Various caliphs are referred to in thinly veiled descriptions, and their decisions viewed in apocalyptic terms. Jerusalem is at the core of this literature.

Among the best known of these works are the 'Secrets of Rabbi Shimon bar Yohai,' and the 'Visions of Rabbi Shimon bar Yohai'. These were written in the

"Jeremiah bar Gedaliah bar Rabbi Joseph", a Jew who came to Jerusalem and etched his name on a stone of the southern wall of the Temple Mount

mid-eighth century during the decline of Umayyad power. Works of a similar genre are the 'Deeds of Daniel' and 'The Vision of Daniel' which date from the mid-tenth century, when Abbasid rule was in decline.

The work, 'Secrets of Rabbi Shimon Bar Yohai' was attributed to a scholar of mystical bent who lived in the second century and whose teachings are cited in the Mishnah. Rabbi Shimon is described in the Mishnah as having lived for thirteen years in total isolation in a secluded cave, in order to escape Roman persecution. According to the aforementioned ninth century work, the 'secret' (referred to in the title) which was revealed to Rabbi Shimon was that the end of the Edomite kingdom (i.e. Rome) would not come directly through the endeavors of the people of Israel, but through a new

kingdom headed by a 'prophet', (clearly a reference to Islam) and that this kingdom would conquer Eretz Israel and give the land to the Jewish people. The book echoes such earlier apocalyptic works as the Book of Zerubabel. It goes on to tell of the conquest of Jerusalem by the Muslims, mentioning names of rulers and hinting at their actions. For instance, the activities of the caliph Abd al-Malik and other rulers are described. The book also depicts the internal struggles, wars with other countries, and the disappointment of the Jews in the Umayyad dynasty. But "the kings of Ishmael would fall," and the visionary author describes a series of events which would ensue beginning with a great catastrophe and ending with consolation and redemption. The pre-messianic character, Messiah son of Ephraim appears in this work, as does ultimately the Messiah, son of David. Jerusalem figures prominently in the plot. After two thousand years, the Lord sits in the seat of judgment in the Valley of Jehoshaphat in Jerusalem; He opens the gates of Paradise and Hell, while before Him pass nations who worship the gods of silver and gold. The Lord sentences them to be burned in hell, while the people of Israel advance to their redemption through hell, led by the Almighty, and some come to no harm, the criminals among them are sent to hell for one year, and are then permitted to enter Paradise. Jerusalem is at the heart of this apocalyptic work, as it is in most of the other works of this kind.

The anticipation of salvation and the rebuilding of Jerusalem as the center of the Jewish nation was also expressed in messianic movements which arose in Diaspora centers of Jewish life. The Cairo Geniza contains a number of correspondences, including those dealing with commerce, which contain blessings for the redemption and salvation of Jerusalem. The apocalyptic writings undoubtedly fostered this tendency, which became stronger just when the likelihood of accomplishing real achievements in the 'earthly Jerusalem' was at its lowest.

The Last Seventy Years

The interval from 1029, the year in which the Sixty Year War ended, until autumn 1099 when the Crusaders conquered the city, was relatively calm in political and military terms. Neveretheless, earthquakes occurred twice, in 1033 and 1068, and caused considerable damage to such monumental structures as the mosque of al-Aqsa, the Dome of the Rock and the Church of the Holy Sepulcher. Their repair sometimes took decades.

"It is better to eat onions in Jerusalem than chicken in Egypt," implores the Jerusalem teacher Amram of his son-in-law Joseph in Fustat, Egypt. The exclamation appears along the upper margins of a document of the eleventh century

Jerusalem during this period was ruled mostly by the Fatimid dynasty of Egypt. Their attitude to Jerusalem and its inhabitants was inconsistent, and depended upon conditions in Egypt proper, as well as on a variety of external circumstances. When, for instance, it was decided in Byzantine Constantinople that in the local mosque, prayers would be recited for the welfare of the Abbasid rather than the Fatimid dynasty, the Fatimids reacted by taking action in Jerusalem – confiscating precious items and documents from the Church of the Holy Sepulcher. This provoked a military response on the part of the Byzantines which ended in the siege of Cairo.

From documents in the Cairo Geniza, we learn that during the second half of the century, a Karaite Jew governed Jerusalem for a short time, and was replaced by a Christian. In the period under the Christian's authority, the Christians attained a greater hold on Jerusalem. This could also be seen in the activities of the Latins (Roman Catholics) who began to encroach on the hegemony of the Greek Orthodox over ecclesiastical matters in Jerusalem. In 1054 the Great Schism took place between Byzantine and Roman Catholic Christianity, and the disputes between the two continued to multiply.

The sixth decade of the eleventh century was difficult for Jerusalem because of the decline of the Fatimid regime in Egypt. Seven years of drought around the sources of the Nile resulted in crop failures and widespread starvation in Egypt. Fatimid power was weakened and public and individual safety was threatened by various lawless elements. An external threat emerged from the east, in the form of the Seljuk Turks, a fierce Turcoman tribe that conquered Baghdad in 1055 and advanced towards Syria-Palestine, reaching Jerusalem in 1073. This brought a marked decline for Jerusalem. In a liturgical poem discovered in the Cairo Geniza, written by the rabbinic judge Solomon b. Jehoseph, the first four years of Seljuk domination in Jerusalem were characterized by murder, plunder and the destruction of buildings. The inhabitants were goaded into rebellion and rose up against the new regime when the Turkoman despot, Atsiz b. Uwak, was away from the city carrying out a campaign against the Fatimids. In the early stages of the rebellion the

Jerusalemites were successful. In keeping with the custom of the day, the Turcoman women and property were seized and divided among the rebels, and the children were taken as slaves. Atsiz hastened back to Jerusalem and slyly offered the rebels an *aman* (letter of security). Then he wreaked havoc on the city, slaughtering three thousand people, among them the Muslim khadi and a group of notables who had supported the rebellion.

The Jewish community of Jerusalem underwent a marked decline as a result of Seljuk domination of the city. The major testimony to a severe reversal was the withdrawal of the Eretz Israel Yeshiva from Jerusalem to Tyre. This institution had until then preserved for Jerusalem a role as beacon for the Jewish Diaspora. The gatherings of Jews on the Mount of Olives ceased as well. These two reversals mark the end of an era in the annals of Jewish national existence, in which Jerusalem had an important influence on Jewish life in the Diaspora. This foreshadowed the decline of Jerusalem as a major Jewish center which began with the era of the Crusades and continued thereafter.

The Fatimids did not give up Jerusalem. They waited patiently for Seljuk power to diminish, and in 1098 sent an army to Jerusalem and laid siege to the city. This situation lasted more than forty days and in the course of the fighting, part of the city wall was destroyed. On August 26, 1098, Jerusalem was again under Fatimid control, however not for long. The First Crusade had been launched two years earlier and crusading armies were even then making their way toward the Holy Land. A year later the Fatimids were defeated by the Crusaders, a turning point which ushered in a period of distinct Christian control over the city after more than four centuries under the crescent.

On the eve of the Crusader conquest, Fatimid soldiers buried their valuables and money not far from the Temple Mount. These gold dinars were discovered during excavations at the foot of the southern wall of the Temple Mount

CRUSADER AND AYYUBID JERUSALEM

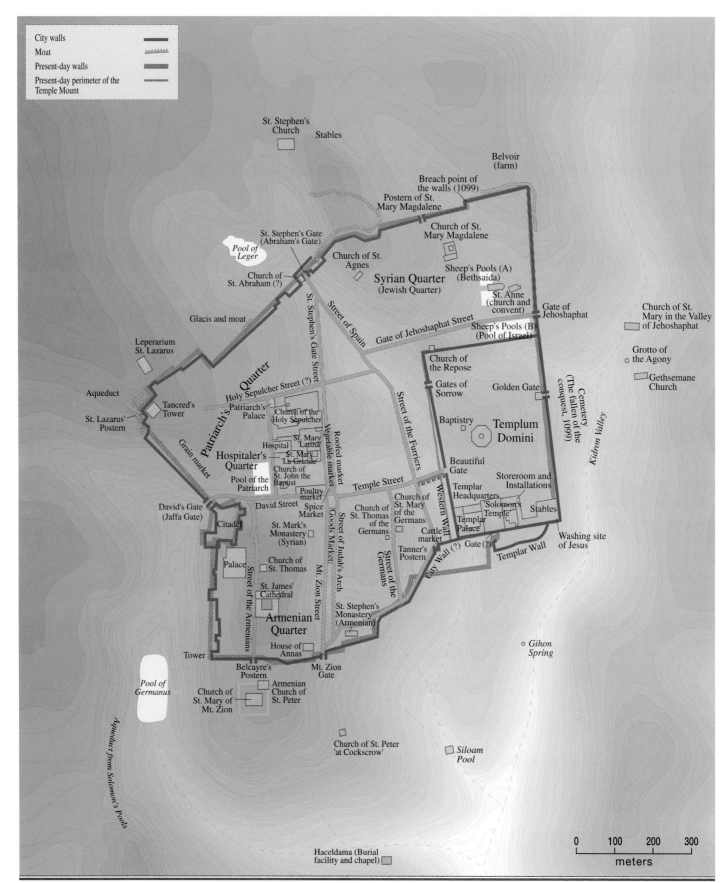

City walls

Moat

Present-day walls

Present-day perimeter of the Temple Mount

St. Stephen's Church

Stables

Belvoir (farm)

Breach point of the walls (1099)

Postern of St. Mary Magdalene

Church of St. Mary Magdalene

St. Stephen's Gate (Abraham's Gate)

Pool of Leger

Church of St. Agnes

Syrian Quarter (Jewish Quarter)

Sheep's Pools (A) (Bethsaida)

Church of St. Abraham (?)

St. Anne (church and convent)

Gate of Jehoshaphat

Church of St. Mary in the Valley of Jehoshaphat

Glacis and moat

Gate of Jehoshaphat Street

Sheep's Pools (B) (Pool of Israel)

Leperarium St. Lazarus

St. Stephen's Gate Street

Street of Spain

Church of the Repose

Grotto of the Agony

Gethsemane Church

Patriarch's Quarter

Holy Sepulcher Street (?)

Gates of Sorrow

Golden Gate

Cemetery (The fallen of the conquest, 1099)

Kidron Valley

Aqueduct

Tancred's Tower

Patriarch's Palace

Church of the Holy Sepulcher

Street of the Furriers

Baptistry

Templum Domini

St. Lazarus' Postern

Grain market

St. Mary 'Latina'

Vegetable market

St. Mary 'Lu Grande'

Hospitaler's Quarter

Hospital

Roofed market

Beautiful Gate

Storeroom and Installations

Church of St. John the Baptist

Pool of the Patriarch

Poultry market

Temple Street

Templar Headquarters

'Solomon's Temple'

Stables

David's Gate (Jaffa Gate)

Spice Market

David Street

Street of Judah's Arch (Goods Market)

Church of St. Thomas of the Germans

Church of St. Mary of the Germans

Western Wall

Templar Palace

Washing site of Jesus

Citadel

St. Mark's Monastery (Syrian)

Mt. Zion Street

Cattle market

Palace

Church of St. Thomas

Street of the Germans

Tanner's Postern

City Wall (?)

Gate (?)

Templar Wall

St. James' Cathedral

Street of the Armenians

Armenian Quarter

St. Stephen's Monastery (Armenian)

Gihon Spring

Tower

House of Annas

Belcayre's Postern

Mt. Zion Gate

Pool of Germanus

Armenian Church of St. Peter

Church of St. Mary of Mt. Zion

Church of St. Peter 'at Cockscrow'

Siloam Pool

Aqueduct from Solomon's Pools

Haceldama (Burial facility and chapel)

0	100	200	300

meters

Map of Jerusalem in the Crusader and Ayyubid periods

In the summer of 1099 Jerusalem was besieged and conquered by the European, Roman Catholic forces of the first crusade. Having breached the city walls, the crusaders massacred the residents and wreaked havoc in the streets, plundering everything in sight. A new period in the city's history was ushered in; Jerusalem became the capital of the Crusader, or Latin Kingdom of Jerusalem. Its former population – Muslims, Jews, and Eastern Orthodox Christians, had either been wiped out or had fled, and the city remained in a severely depopulated state, which soon became a problem for the crusader administration. It was eventually partly corrected by the transfer to the city of Christian Arab tribes and the settlement of some European crusaders. The Crusader Kingdom of Jerusalem adopted a ban on Jews similar to that first imposed by the Byzantines centuries earlier. Nevertheless, a Jewish physical presence in and around the city was preserved by a few Jews who managed to remain, and by others who continued to come on pilgrimage.

While Jews were not welcome in the 'earthly Jerusalem' of the crusaders, their sentiments toward 'heavenly Jerusalem' were, if anything, strengthened during the Crusader and Ayyubid period. The struggle between Christians and Muslims over Eretz Israel, and Jerusalem in particular, was viewed as the dawn of Redemption. Literature of solace and salvation was created which foretold the end of foreign domination and the coming of the messiah. Jerusalem's position as the focus of ongoing conflict between Christians and Muslims increased the yearning of Diaspora Jewry. From Spain in the West to Iraq in the East, Jews produced liturgical poetry, legends and works of philosophy which expressed longing for Jerusalem.

The crusaders left a distinct imprint on Jerusalem, but did not radically alter the city physically. It retained a distinct eastern character in its architecture and the commercial life of its bazaars. The Muslims did not reconcile themselves to the Christian conquests in the east, nor did they forget about Jerusalem. After fewer than a hundred years, Saladin, the Ayyubid ruler of Egypt, managed to reverse crusader successes, and the crescent supplanted the cross in Jerusalem. This state of affairs lasted for an initial stage of forty-two years, after which which there was another interval of limited crusader rule of Jerusalem, during which the Temple

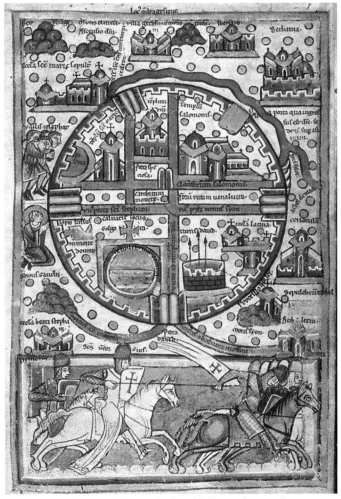

Depicting the world as a circle with Jerusalem at its center was common during the Middle Ages. Beneath the city, crusaders are attacking Jerusalem and one of them drives a spear into the back of the Muslim enemy
Map from the Hague (1170)

Mount was held by Muslims. Before the mid-thirteenth century, the Crusader Kingdom of Jerusalem relinquished its capital, Jerusalem, to the Muslims. For the following seven centuries the city was to be ruled by a number of Muslim regimes, the longest being a four hundred year period under Ottoman Turkey.

Between the two periods of crusader rule, the Muslim Ayyubids of Egypt controlled Jerusalem for several decades, and made efforts to restore the city's Muslim character. The rulers encouraged a Muslim population, and especially wise men, to settle in the city. At the same time they annulled the prohibition on Jews living in Jerusalem, whereupon Jewish settlement was renewed.

Some Jews who settled were natives of Eretz Israel, while others were from North Africa, France and Yemen.

In modern-day Jerusalem there are many physical remnants from the crusader period, and to a lesser extent from the Ayyubid period. Through these remains, and the extensive written documentation of the period, in the form of letters and chronicles, material in the Cairo Geniza, and art and architecture throughout Europe and the Middle East, historians have assembled a record of the phenomena of the crusades, which occupied center-stage for two centuries of European life in the Middle Ages, and had an immense influence on Europe, the eastern Mediterranean basin and Jerusalem in particular.

From Clermont to Jerusalem

The first crusade was an important movement which there is every reason to believe astonished its initiators. It gripped the hearts and imaginations of many Europeans, of a variety of social classes, on a scale the continent had not experienced before. There are an abundance of historical viewpoints concerning the causes of the first crusade. A number will be mentioned here. One key element was the mindset of medieval Europeans. Not without reason, the period has been called "The Age of Faith." Particularly during the first third of the eleventh century, Christians in central and western Europe were excited by the belief that with the end of the millenium (the end of the first thousand years since the crucifixion: 1033), the Day of Judgment was at hand, and with it the Second Coming. A new period in the history of mankind would begin. The date passed without the unfolding of the anticipated dramatic events. In consequence, all manner of natural disasters, human catastrophes, and mundane struggles between the eastern Byzantine church and the Roman papal authorities, prompted interpretation in apocalyptic terms, as presaging the Second Coming of the Messiah. Pilgrimages to holy places and primarily to the holy city of Jerusalem, considered a religious act of the first order, increased. Christian pilgrims visited Jerusalem in the course of that century despite the hardships involved in the journey, particularly in light of chaotic conditions caused by the Seljuk invasions. Pilgrims actually merged with the arriving crusaders, who may perhaps, in this context be regarded as militant pilgrims.

While the central factors explaining the first crusade were religious in nature – Christian millenial beliefs and scandalized Christian sensibility at the violation of Christian holy places and mistreatment of pilgrims by the 'infidel,' – several other, less spiritual factors were also at work. Europe was experiencing a population explosion which was forcing widespread migration to relatively unoccupied areas, a growth in the size of villages, and a migration from villages to cities. These migrations affected not only the actions but the thinking of Europeans; the impulse to leave home for unknown territories became common, and this set the stage for participation in a crusade to a distant land. At the same time, fighting noblemen appeared who were looking for employment, excitement and an opportunity to make their fortunes and acquire inheritances which were denied them under the strict guidelines of the medieval institution of primogeniture. There was also ample economic motive on the part of European traders, first and foremost the great trading cities of Italy, who were concerned by the disruption to international commerce occasioned by the Seljuk invasions.

Regarding Pope Urban II's motive for calling for a crusade, the competition between his western, Roman Catholic church and the eastern, Byzantine church provided ample context for a call to liberate the Church of the Holy Sepulcher from infidel hands – a feat the Byzantines were unable to accomplish, even though Jerusalem was, figuratively speaking, at their back door. Success in liberating Jerusalem promised the potential of healing the schism between the two churches, with Rome in the dominant position. The Byzantine emperor had once before called upon a pope for help against the Muslims. In 1074 Pope Gregory VII had sent military help to preserve the Byzantine capital of Constantinople, which was severely threatened by Seljuk Turks. A force of knights from Flanders had thwarted the Seljuk assault. Twenty-one years later another Byzantine call for help reached the pope at the Church Council of Piacenza. Pope Urban II brought up the issue at the later Council in Clermont, France in 1095, altering somewhat the aim of his call, beseeching the Catholic faithful to rescue not Constantinople, but Jerusalem. He granted crusaders remission for their sins and promised to protect their families and property while they were away. He appealed to the vanity, and chivalric values of feudal nobles, telling them that upon them "above all others, God has conferred remarkable glory in arms, great bravery, and strength to humble the heads of those that resist."

Four Crusader Armies

In Christian Europe there was a gradual but ultimately massive response to Pope Urban II's call. The first to go were a disorganized rabble of peasants, townspeople, simple priests and passionate if unlettered leaders with names like Walter the Penniless and Peter the Hermit. In 1096, these groups set out for the Rhine and Danube regions, and thence further east. On the way, they perpetrated unspeakable violence on the Jews of France and the Rhineland.

A twelfth century Jewish chronicler relates that as they passed through the towns where there were Jews,they said to one another: 'We are going on a distant journey

to seek the (Church of the Holy Sepulcher) and to exact vengeance on the Ishmaelites; yet here are the Jews dwelling in our midst whose forefathers slew Him and crucified Him without reason. First let us take vengeance on them and destroy them as a people...' That the pope had not targetted the Jews of Europe was immaterial.

Calamity struck the Jews of France at Rouen; then the route of the peasant crusaders turned to the Rhine Valley, the core of Ashkenaz, where there were a number of revered Jewish communities which thrived under the official protection of local bishops and nobles. The Rhine Valley communities were warned but could not imagine violence on a scale so massive that the bishops could not control it. Nevertheless, thousands of Jews were murdered and their belongings looted. A slaughter was perpetrated, amidst which there were acts of martyrdom on the part Jews who chose death over forced conversion. All along the route these crusaders continued to ravage and loot. This crusade never reached its destination; only a few even reached Constantinople.

By contrast, four large armies were recruited in France and Flanders, and they formed the backbone of the first crusade. Together with them came simple believers, and perhaps stragglers from the earlier group. The four armies made their way southeast, and in the spring of 1097, arrived in Constantinople. Then their pace slowed, but they eventually reached the Holy Land in the summer of 1099. On the 3rd of June, they took Ramle, and three days later began to make their way to Jerusalem. In less than two days, they stood facing its walls.

The Conquest of Jerusalem

For thirty-nine days in the sweltering summer heat, the crusaders besieged Jerusalem. The fortified city was defended by a Fatimid force of hundreds of soldiers, but the main defense was left to the city's inhabitants – Muslims and Jews (the Christians had been ousted from Jerusalem beforehand, as they were considered an unreliable element. They sought refuge in Bethlehem). The Jews were responsible for the northeastern section of the wall adjoining the Jewish Quarter.

The combined crusader force was not very large, consisting of of twelve thousand infantry and only twelve

The northern sector of Jerusalem's city wall, opposite the Rockefeller Museum, where the Crusaders broke through in 1099

Illustration of the attack on the wall of Jerusalem from the Bari Bible (early eleventh century). Over the heads of the attackers, Jeremiah is seen prophecying the destruction of the city

The crusaders built wooden battering rams and long ladders which they placed at the southern end of the city, at the disposal of the Provencale army of Count Raymond of St. Gilles. This section of wall enclosed the Temple Mount and was especially difficult to conquer due to the steep ravine of the Kidron (or Jehoshaphat) Valley which is found just outside it.

The second crusader force, under Duke Godfrey of Bouillon (in modern-day Belgium) chose the northeastern sector of the wall opposite the Jewish Quarter. The forces in this area included some of Tancred's units, as well as those of Robert, Duke of Normandy. An enormous battering ram was brought up to the wall, along with three catapults which were used to hurl stones in order to drive the defenders back from the parapets. In addition, the crusaders had a seige tower through which the first of the attackers were to enter the city and on which the commanders of the operation could stand. The Muslims lowered sacks filled with straw from the wall to absorb the impact of the battering ram, while the crusaders showered the defenders with burning arrows which set fire to the straw. Then the battering ram went into action, with its pendulum activated by many fighters. The wall was soon breached. The attackers began to bring the tower nearer but something prevented it from moving. On the morning of the 15th of July, the Crusaders succeeded, after five hours of fighting, in breaking through the wall, near the Jewish Quarter. Thousands of crusaders poured into the city. They hurried to open the Gate of Jehoshaphat in the eastern wall to enable additional crusader forces to surge into the city. Many hours later, the southern forces managed to break in, and by using ladders, reached the citadel near the Jaffa gate. The commander of the Citadel surrendered according to the terms of a pact (*aman*) which gave them permission to withdraw to Ashkelon. Some of the Jews of Jerusalem who had taken refuge in the Citadel after the first of the crusaders had broken into the city, succeeded in saving their lives because they were in the right place. The rest did not fare well. The two crusader armies met at the entrance to the Church of the Holy Sepulcher at midday on that same day.

In the early afternoon hours of the 15th of July 1099, Jerusalem was entirely in the hands of the crusaders. From the moment they broke into the city, they sowed

hundred cavalry. When they spread out along the 2.4 miles of the walls of Jerusalem, they were too thinly distributed to determine the outcome of battle quickly. They failed in their first attempt on the 13th of June, 1099, which focused on the northern wall. At the same time, forces under Tancred, the Norman prince of Sicily, managed to destroy the 'small wall' and after that, attempted to break through the 'great wall', and even placed a ladder which the crusaders climbed to engage the defenders in hand-to-hand combat.

The crusaders gave expression to the religious nature of their cause by assembling long processions of barefoot Christians bearing crosses, led by solemn-faced priests, to walk round the walls while praying. Perhaps this was meant to recall the biblical achievement of the Israelites in toppling the town walls of Jericho.

Church of St. Anne, built by the Crusader queen Melisende, ca. 1140. The architectural style is a combination of the eastern Byzantine tradition and the western Romanesque. With the Ayyubid conquest, the church was made into a Muslim religious college, the Salahiyya madrasa, as indicated by the inscription over the entrance

mayhem. It is said that Tancred, who was the first to reach the Dome of the Rock, robbed it of all its valuables. The battalions of Godfrey of Bouillon at first occupied the Jewish Quarter near the site of the breach in the wall, and massacred its inhabitants.

Jews and Muslims who had fled for their lives, were in many cases caught and killed. The chronicler Albert of Aachen provides a hair-raising description of the slaughter in Jerusalem on that day, and among other things, he writes: "All gripped their weapons and wrought a terrible slaughter on all the people (Muslims and Jews) who yet remained in the city... Others, whom (the crusaders) had earlier spared were now killed where they stood, outside the walls of the city: girls, women, noblewomen, pregnant women who were killed along

with their unborn children... Some were killed by the sword and others stoned, no one was shown mercy, regardles of age or sex. The first to burst into a house or palace became its master, with no possibility of appeal, and took possession of all its contents... Thus the crusaders became masters of the city."

Redemption of Prisoners and Holy Books

The killing in Jerusalem went on for four days, until July 18, 1099. Some Muslims met their deaths inside the mosque of al-Aqsa, and Jews were burnt alive in a synagogue. Yet it seems that there were Jews who

*Ruins of the Church of St. Mary of the German Knights,
which the Order of Knights Teuton built on a slope of what
is today the Jewish Quarter of the Old City.
A mid-13th century pilgrim mentions, "a hospice and
church built recently in honor of St. Mary but popularly
called the German building, for only German-speaking
people are accepted there"*

survived, and these were taken prisoner and sold as slaves; they brought a poor price – thirty Jews for one gold coin, on Tancred's orders. Others were sent to Europe.

There is a clear-cut Jewish law concerning the redemption of Jews from slavery, to which medieval Jews felt legally and morally bound. The medieval rabbinic scholar Maimonides details this halakhah in his major opus, the Mishneh Torah. "The captive is in the category of 'the hungry, the thirsty and the naked' and lives in peril for his life... There is no greater obligation than the redemption of captives" (Mishneh Torah, Laws of Donations to the Poor, 8:1).

The Jews of Ashkelon (which was not occupied by the crusaders), and the Jews of Egypt, ransomed their brethren who had fallen into crusader hands. A letter in the Cairo Geniza which was to be sent from Ashkelon, tells of an emergency meeting of Egyptian Jews in the home of the community's leader, the Nagid, Mevorakh b. Saadia. The issue was the ransom of sacred Jewish texts and of prisoners taken by the crusaders. A special envoy was sent to Ashkelon with a large sum of money which had been collected at the meeting in Egypt. Letters from Karaites indicate that they too redeemed holy books and people held in bondage by the crusaders.

Crusader demands for ransom – for people and for holy books, were among the baser examples of the economic motive which animated many to embark on a journey to the Holy Land. A letter found in the Cairo Geniza makes it clear the crusaders were not above selling children into slavery. They also made an effort to convert prisoners among the Muslims and Jews whom they held. Another letter from the Geniza reads as follows: "We redeemed (from slavery) anyone whom we were able to purchase, and only a few stragglers remained (in crusader possession). Among them was a boy of about eight... whom the Franks tried to pursuade to convert of his own will. They promised to be good to him... (and he remained with them) since he had been in that situation for many days, and it was impossible to redeem him, because he had no hope that they would allow him to leave..."

The Beginning of Crusader Rule

In the weeks after the conquest, the crusaders organized governing institutions in Jerusalem, but rivalries erupted among the conquerors. Members of the church who had accompanied the crusade from its onset, demanded that a Latin patriarch be appointed master of Jerusalem. Heads of the different military entities did not agree, and chose a secular governor – Godfrey of Bouillon, who gave himself the title *Sancti Sepulcri Advocatus* Defender of the Holy Sepulcher, rather than king. He explained that he refused to wear a royal crown where Christ had worn a crown of thorns. Godfrey demanded command over the citadel, which had been taken by Raymond of St. Gilles, and the latter agreed only under duress. Later on, governance of the city was divided between the patriarch and the secular governor. The Latin patriarch became the most important religious personality in Jerusalem, since the Greek Orthodox patriarch left the city on the eve of the conquest and did not return.

Eventually most of the leaders of the first crusade departed. Only two remained in the city: Godfrey of Bouillon (who was the secular governor) and Tancred, the Norman ruler of Sicily. A year after the conquest only a small force of crusaders was left in Jerusalem – not more than three hundred, even though there was still a threat from the Muslims, who had not given up their hopes for the city. Nevertheless, the crusaders were able to complete their domination of the rest of the country.

An internal threat existed among the crusaders, primarily due to the endless friction between clerical and secular authorities in Jeruslem. These became even more complex when Godfrey died, in late 1100, after ruling Jerusalem for only one year. The Latin patriarch tried to sieze control of the city, but Godfrey's supporters occupied the Citadel and summoned his brother Baldwin, prince of Edessa (a newly created state Baldwin had acquired as a result of his participation in the first crusade). He came to Jerusalem and the patriarch was obliged not only to accept his authority, but to crown him King of Jerusalem, in a ceremony which took place in the Church of the Nativity in Bethlehem on Christmas, 1100. The coronation in Bethlehem was intended to symbolically associate the crusader king with David King of Israel, suggesting that Baldwin was his heir and descendant. Of course, the location of the ceremony in the Church of the Nativity linked the crusader king with Jesus, who in Christian tradition is a descendant of David, and with a holy place which the crusaders had come to the Holy Land to liberate.

King Baldwin and the Patriarch Diambert continued to confront one another in subsequent years. Early in his reign Baldwin founded a number of monasteries and churches in Jerusalem and its environs. Their clerical administration was loyal to him. Among them were the Monastery of Templum Domini (Temple of the Lord) located in the Dome of the Rock shrine, which had been consecrated as a church, and the Monastery of St. Anne,

David granting Solomon the right to build the Temple. Initial letter illumination ("E") of a manuscript of twelfth century England

north of the Temple Mount. The patriarch found himself increasingly isolated in the Church of the Nativity, and was deposed in 1105.

Crusader Jerusalem

Crusader Jerusalem maintained its original configuration for less than ninety years. The main problems facing its leaders during its early years were demographic – that is, where to find inhabitants for the city? The Jews and Muslims had been killed, sold as slaves, or had fled, and crusader law distinctly forbade their return. The crusaders were few in number and the local, eastern rite

Christians, known as Syrians, who returned after the conquest did not add much of a presence and were in any case distrusted by the Roman Catholic crusaders. The crusader rulers tried to attract to Jerusalem merchants from the Italian trading cities of Pisa, Venice, and Genoa, but these merchants set up their own districts in the port cities or prominent trading cities of the various crusader kingdoms, such as Acre or Antioch. They showed no inclination to settle in Jerusalem.

The crusader rulers of Jerusalem invited groups of 'Syrians' from Trans-Jordan to settle in Jerusalem. In 1120, King Baldwin II introduced the economic policy of free trade, cancelling customs fees and allowing non-Christians to carry on commercial dealings in Jerusalem. A number of Muslims and Jews returned to engage in trade but not to live there. Yet, as a result of these moves, the population of Jerusalem increased towards the mid-twelfth century. In 1160, the number of inhabitants had risen by thirty thousand – mostly Roman Catholics from Europe and Eastern Christians.

Jerusalem was the capital of a centralized feudal state. The inhabitants of the city, as well as the state, consisted of two main social classes: the aristocrats and the bourgeoisie, hailing from various parts of Europe. People from the same area of origin generally lived clustered on the same streets. Most of the Europeans in Jerusalem came from areas of present-day France; the vernacular in Jerusalem was French.

A unique form of knightly organization developed in Jerusalem: associations of warrior-priests whose members combined the fighting ideal with religiously motivated service to mankind. Nine French knights who had taken vows as canons of the church organized the "Knights Templar" in 1129 and the prominent churchman Bernard of Clairvaux drew up monastic rules for them to follow. Their mission was to aid and protect pilgrims to Jerusalem. Later, two orders with similar purpose were created, the Knights of St. John in Jerusalem, usually called the Knights Hospitaler because they were attached to the Hospital of St. John, and the Order of Teutonic Knights, a German breakaway group from the Hospitalers. In addition to aiding the sick and caring for the needy and for pilgrims, these knights were also involved in fighting, and were part of the regular army of the Crusader Kingdom of Jerusalem. Members of these orders saw themselves as the perfect crusaders:

During the first crusader period the mosque of al-Aqsa was renamed Templum Solomonis and became headquarters of the Knights Templar. They stabled their horses in the vaulted area beneath the Temple Mount plaza, which was given the name 'Solomon's Stables'

simultaneously monks and fighters. The Order of Knights Templar was stationed in the mosque of al-Aqsa on the Temple Mount, known in Latin as the *Templum Solomonis* (Solomon's Temple), hence the name Templars. The Templars won the admiration and sympathy of the Christian world and for many years made an important contribution to the kingdom's army, defending fortresses and initiating campaigns against the Muslims. On occasion, they also adopted independent policies which did not meet with the approval of the heads of the realm.

The Kings of Jerusalem

The monarchs of the Crusader Kingdom of Jerusalem ruled from Jerusalem, although the capital was not always their main seat of power. They were absent from the city for lengthy periods, on long journeys or military campaigns. They often stayed in the port city of Acre, which was the prime city and main economic center of the country. They made a point of returning to Jerusalem for the Christian holidays in order to participate in religious processions and in ceremonies at the Church of the Holy Sepulcher.

Baldwin I reigned from 1100 until his death eighteen years later. He extended the borders of the Crusader Kingdom of Jerusalem through military conquest. His heir was his cousin, Baldwin II, who was also Count of the crusader County of Edessa. Baldwin II ruled in Jerusalem for thirteen years, until 1131. During his time the Kingdom of Jerusalem reached the height of its influence over the northern crusader states of Tripoli, Antioch, and Edessa.

Detail from the marble lintel over the western entrance to the Church of the Holy Sepulcher. The influence of Romanesque art on crusader illustration is evident here

During the first fifty years of crusader rule, Jerusalem experienced a number of tense years owing to the repeated attempts of the Muslims to conquer it or to reduce crusader sway over Syria-Palestine. Muslims mounted attacks on Jerusalem in 1113, 1124, and 1152. Although these were repelled, often victory occurred only when it seemed that all was lost. In addition, internecine quarrels continued to threaten the kingdom. The most serious of these occurred in 1152. Its plot involves intrigue, forbidden love, and betrayal.

The beginning of the affair is connected with Fulk, Count of Anjou, who married Melisende, the daughter of Baldwin II. After the death of his father-in-law, Fulk was crowned king of Jerusalem, and reigned for twelve years over a peaceful kingdom. When he died at the age of forty-eight, the crown prince was very young and Melisende acted as Queen Regent in his stead. After her

son Baldwin III was crowned, the kingdom was divided between Baldwin and his mother. Melisende received Jerusalem, Nablus and its environs, while Baldwin ruled in Acre and Tyre. But this arrangement did not last long; Melisende demanded control over the entire kingdom and Baldwin reacted by starting a campaign against his mother, supported by a number of nobles of the realm who hated her, together with the commander of the army who had evidently been her lover. Baldwin III took Nablus and pursued the army loyal to his mother as far as Jerusalem. Most of the city's inhabitants joined his camp and opened the city gates to him. The queen fled to the Citadel and Baldwin's army besieged her. The nobles of the city mediated between the two and Melisende finally decided to forgo Jerusalem, retiring to Nablus.

Baldwin III frequently waged war, and he finally succeeded in taking Ashkelon, more than fifty years after

The Spice Market, one of three covered markets built by the crusaders east of the Church of the Holy Sepulcher, and which still serve as public markets today

PLATE A

PORTRAIT OF SALADIN (?)

FATIMID SCHOOL
About A.D. 1180

Saladin, the talented Ayyubid warrior. Illustration from a 15th century book whose author claims that this drawing was done at Saladin's court

twelve years of Baldwin IV's reign, each side experienced victory and defeat in turns. Baldwin IV contracted leprosy and died in 1185. In the last two years of his reign, his brother-in-law Guy de Lusignan acted as regent for Baldwin V, and was later replaced by Raymond, Count of Tripoli.

The next king of Jerusalem was Baldwin V, a minor who ascended the throne at age five and died when he was seven. A struggle over the succession ensued between the two regents, Guy de Lusignan and Raymond, Count of Tripoli. Guy succeeded, and was the last ruler of Jerusalem in the first crusader period. The armies of Saladin stripped him of parts of his kingdom. The summer of 1187 proved catastrophic for the crusaders, who suffered repeated defeats. In the battle of the Horns of Hattin they almost lost their entire army, the king of Jerusalem was taken prisoner, and the realm's fortresses fell one after another to Saladin's advancing forces. On September 17, 1187, the Muslims laid siege to Jerusalem. In the surrounding Christian settlements, the churches and monasteries were sacked and laid waste. Saladin himself commanded the attacking forces.

The patriarch of Jerusalem sent a letter to Pope Urban III pleading for crusading armies to rescue the Crusader Kingdom, however, the Europeans were not able to rush to Jerusalem's aid on such short notice even had they been inclined to do so. Saladin at the height of his power, was determined to conquer the city. The siege lasted for two weeks and during the fighting, the attackers destroyed some of the city's fortifications as well as the spirit of its defenders. Negotiations began over the terms of surrender. At first Saladin stated his unwillingness to reach any agreement. His aim was to conquer Jerusalem and avenge the slaughter of its Muslims eighty-eight years earlier. However, elements among the crusaders threatened to commit suicide and destroy the city, and this apparently persuaded Saladin to come to terms with them. The crusaders, at their own suggestion, would hand over the city to the Muslims; they would be considered prisoners-of-war, but would be ransomed immediately for a sum agreed upon in advance.

On October 2, 1187 Jerusalem again came under Muslim control. Thousands of destitute Christians who

the crusaders had dominated most of Syria-Palestine. He reigned until 1163 and seems to have died of poisoning. His successor was his brother Amalric, during whose reign the Crusader Kingdom reached its height.

The kingdom of Baldwin IV, son of Amalric, was constantly engaged in fighting the forces of Saladin, a military commander of Kurdish-Armenian origins, who was the leading minister (*wazir*) and afterwards Sultan of Egypt. During these campaigns which continued for the

had no one to pay their ransom, were sold as slaves. Refugees made their way to cities still under Christian control. Some reached the coasts of Palestine, Egypt, and Syria and boarded ships for Europe.

Jerusalem's fall aroused an angry response in Europe. Some of the Christians in Syria-Palestine criticized the humiliating terms of surrender of their brethren in Jerusalem. An anonymous beleaguered Christian expressed his rage and frustration: "How great the pain! Is there any pain to compare with it? Have we ever read that the Jews abandoned the Holy of Holies without bloodshed and bitter battles, yielding if of their own volition? May these fiends who willingly betray the Holy City and the Messiah perish!"

Jews in Jerusalem and the Jewish Conception of Jerusalem

Only in isolated instances were Jews permitted to live in crusader Jerusalem, but they preserved the memory of their prior presence under Muslim rule. In the crusader period, the inhabitants of the city still called the area where the Jews had lived, the 'Jewish Quarter'. Although there were almost no Jews residing in Jerusalem, many came on pilgrimage from Diaspora communities, in particular those of Spain, France and Ashkenaz (Central Europe). Their visits were short and concentrated, lasting for but a few days. They were of a very personal nature, for the open conduct of religious ceremonies which had been possible under Muslim rule was forbidden under crusader rule.

Several outstanding Jewish personalities of the Middle Ages came on pilgrimage to Jerusalem during the crusader period. One was Rabbi Judah Halevi, the greatest medieval Hebrew poet, who was also a physician and developer of a unique philosophy concerning the character of the Jewish people and the sanctity and centrality of the land of Israel for them. He reached Jerusalem some forty years after the crusader conquest. While still in Spain, he ended one of his letters with the phrase, "Spain is my country and Jerusalem, my destiny." Judah Halevi seems to have toured Jerusalem and other parts of the land, and died shortly afterwards.

*The opening page of 'Sefer Haavodah' ('The Book of Worship') the eighth of fourteen sections of the **Mishneh Torah** of Maimonides. This book deals with the rituals in the Temple and laws governing those who work in it*

Some twenty-five years later the giant of medieval Jewish thought, Moses Maimonides (1135-1204), visited Eretz Israel and Jerusalem, and in a description attributed to him, wrote: "On (October 1, 1165) we left Acre on our perilous journey to Jerusalem, and I entered the great structure (the Temple Mount area) and prayed there..." Maimonides remained in Jerusalem for five days, then left for Hebron and other parts of the land. He settled in Egypt, where he had a life of great accomplishment. When he died, his body was brought to Tiberias for burial.

A noteworthy medieval Jewish traveller and pilgrim to Jerusalem was the Spanish Jew,

Portait of Maimonides, Rabbi Moses ben Maimon

Left: part of a manuscript of the travelogue of Benjamin of Tudela. Below: A letter of Rabbi Judah Halevi in which he expresses his hope to go to the holy land

From Benjamin's account historians learn that there were four Jews living in crusader Jerusalem toward the end of the twelfth century, probably with their families. From a further description we learn that there were a number of other Jews in the city or surroundings, who observed practices of mourning and abstinence. Thus, despite the crusader ban, there seem to have been a small number of Jews living in Jerusalem at the time.

Ten years after Benjamin of Tudela's visit, another European Jewish traveller visited Jerusalem. He was Petahiah of Regensburg in Germany. In his journal he mentioned a Jew called Abraham the Dyer "who gives large sums to the king to permit him to stay there."

The sorry condition of the miniscule Jewish presence in Jerusalem under crusader rule did not diminish its vaunted spiritual status in the eyes of Diaspora Jewry. Jerusalem and Eretz Israel occupied an important role in medieval Jewish consciousness, for the Holy Land, so remote in actual terms, was at the center of world events, and often brought to mind predictions in Jewish apocalyptic literature. In Jewish eyes, Eretz Israel and Jerusalem had become the focus of a world struggle involving European and Byzantine Christians and the Muslim world. The conflict was the war between 'Edom' and 'Ishmael.' Perhaps higher forces were leading both camps to destruction, so that the promised land and chosen city would finally be returned to their rightful residents, the Jews. The Jews viewed this tremendous struggle as the prologue to their return to Zion. The crusader failure to hold the country was validation of this belief.

Benjamin of Tudela, who made a five-year journey to Italy and the East, and after returning home wrote a travel journal which has endured as a precious historical resource. Benjamin of Tudela visited Jerusalem 1170 and wrote of it: "(Jerusalem) is a small city fortified by three walls... it contains a dyeing house for which the Jews pay a small rent annually to the kng, on condition that besides the Jews, no other dyers be allowed in Jerusalem. There are about four Jews who dwell under the Tower of David in one corner of the city."

These beliefs were expressed in Jewish spiritual life in the form of prayers, liturgical poems and songs. The twelfth-century Hebrew poets in Spain, chief among them Judah Halevi, viewed the crusader conquest of Jerusalem and the Temple Mount as the seizure of the most precious assets of the Jewish people. Even when the city was in Muslim hands and Jews were permitted relatively unrestricted residence and worship, they considered the fact of Muslim control of the city and Temple Mount a form of slavery for them. How much

ספר

הלכותינו תטעה. וזהו סדרן: הלכות בית הבחירה: הלכות כלי המקדש: והעובדים בו: הלכות ביאת המקדש:
הלכות מעשה הקרבנות: הלכות תמידין ומוספין: הלכות פסולי המוקדשין: הלכות עבודת יום הכפורים: הלכות מעילה" וכו' :

הלכות בית הבחירה

פרק ראשון

Title page of **Sefer Haavodah** ('The Book of Worship') of Maimonides' **Mishneh Torah**. This manuscript from northern Italy dates to the late fifteenth century. During this era Italian Jewry was more exposed to general culture than were other European Jewish communities, and were therefore the first to use a likenesses of the Dome of the Rock in their depictions of the Temple

During the crusader era, the Latin patriarch's residence in Jerusalem was situated opposite the Church of the Holy Sepulcher. With the Ayyubid conquest, the building became a 'khanka' or home for Muslim mystics

moreso was this the case when harsh 'Edom' (Christianity) replaced 'Ishmael' (Islam).

Judah Halevi's poems express bitterness regarding Jerusalem's change of masters and the fact that it was not returned to its genuine owners, for, "Edom is resident in my Palace, Arab and Edomite hands control it..." Halevi expresses a desire to dwell in the desolate Eretz Israel over the aristocratic circles in which he dwelled in Spain: "Better a day in the land of God, than a thousand on foreign soil, the ruins on the Holy Mount than a coronation hall. For by these I shall be redeemed, and by those held in thrall." And, in one of his most famous lines, "My heart is in the East, and I am in the distant West, How shall I taste food and be sated, how shall I fulfill my oaths, while Zion is tethered by Edom and I am by Arabs (alt. the West) chained..."

Halevi was not alone among the Hebrew poets of his century, in expressing distress over the possession of Jerusalem by foreign masters, or in expressing longing for an apocalyptic righting of the situation, and the restoration of Jerusalem to the Jews.

The stormy events of the first crusader period led to a widespread trend among many peoples, of reckoning the End of Days. This was true of the Jews, among whom there were a number of announcements of the anticipated arrival of the messiah. This happened in 1107, which was the five-hundredth anniversary of Muhammed's appearance. Even Judah Halevi made such calculations, expecting the messiah in 1130. In 1186 Jews, Christians and Muslims all made detailed calculations of the End of Days, and a year later Saladin's stormy conquest of Jerusalem and defeat of the crusaders took place. This added to the hope that "Edom's end was near and that it would subsequently be the turn of 'Ishmael'."

Another factor which raised hopes of redemption in Zion and increased the emotional attachment to Jerusalem, was the worsening condition and status of the Jews of Europe, particularly after the Fourth Lateran Council in 1215, led by Pope Innocent III.

Jerusalem under the Ayyubids

The crusader conquest of Jerusalem in 1099 seems to have taken a somewhat lethargic Muslim world by surprise, however this interval of inactivity did not last. With the passage of time the influence of the extensive Muslim literature 'in praise of Jerusalem' drove Muslims to rise and rescue the city from the Christian infidels. Sayings such as "He who lives in Jerusalem is as one who fights for Allah," and "He who cleanses his body and prays in Jerusalem merits forgiveness for his sins and becomes as pure as a newborn babe," left a deep impression on the Islamic world, from Persia to Spain. Time and again, believers were called on to embark on a *jihad* or holy war, to liberate the Islamic holy places on the Temple Mount from the Christians. In 1187 Saladin the Ayyubid succeeded in doing just this, and without a fight.

For more than forty years, Jerusalem and large areas of Syria-Palestine were ruled by the Ayyubid dynasty. Saladin set about restoring Jerusalem's Muslim character. The golden cross which the Templar order had set above the al-Aqsa, which they had renamed Templum Solomonis, was torn down and dragged through the streets, and al-Aqsa resumed functioning as a mosque. Churches throughout the city were converted into mosques, and mosques which had been turned into churches became Muslim institutions once again. The Church of Saint Anne, for instance, became a Muslim *madrasa* (religious seminary) called *Salahiyya* after Saladin (*Salah-a-din*). For all this restoration of the city's Muslim glory, Jerusalem was no longer the capital of the land, a situation which parallels its status in the early Muslim period.

Under Ayyubid administration, neither Jews nor Christians were permitted on the Temple Mount, and whoever violated this ban was punishable by death. The new rulers encouraged the settlement of Muslims in the city. Veteran fighters were granted stretches of land outside the city and Muslim neighborhoods sprung up around the graves of two old fighters – these neighborhoods retain their names to this day: Sheikh Jarrah and Abu Tor. The Christians lived in a concentrated area around the Church of the Holy Sepulcher, while the Jews too had their own quarter. The status of non-Muslims was again that of protected people (*dhimmis*) (see p. 105) and they were obliged to pay the discriminatory head and property taxes, in exchange for which they received official protection.

Jews in Jerusalem under Ayyubid Rule

Saladin's conquest of Jerusalem revived Jewish settlement in the city, and the passage of time inspired a mythical interpretation of the Ayyubid conquest. The Ayyubids in banishing the 'uncircumsized' had acted as a tool of the Almighty, for the Christians had not allowed Jews to live in the city, and this was an intolerable situation – as it appeared that God despised his first-born, the Jews. Thus the Ayyubids conquered and cleared the way for "the Israelites" to return to the city from many lands and pray in its dust. This mythical interpretation is at the heart of an account written by the Spanish-Jewish poet, Judah Alharizi who visited Jerusalem some thirty years after it was again under Muslim rule and spoke with a Jerusalem Jew about the return of Jews to the city: "He said: the Lord was zealous of his name and pitied his people. (The Lord) said, 'It is not good that the sons of Esau [Christians] inherit my Holy Temple while the sons of Jacob are expelled from there, lest the Gentiles say, 'God abandoned his first-born in hatred'...'"

Judah Alharizi describes the Jews of Jerusalem and their various communities in his work *Tahkemoni*. The largest group were Jews from Ashkelon, who originated in North Africa (the Maghrib) and France. Those from Ashkelon were the first allowed to settle in Jerusalem. Their move there was connected with the 'scorched earth' policy adopted by Saladin in his war against the leaders of the Third Crusade. When Saladin's armies approached Ashkelon, he ordered the town's fortifications destroyed, on the assumption that the crusaders had insufficient human and financial resources to rebuild and maintain the city. Ashkelon's

Inscription from 1212, during the reign of the Ayyubid ruler al-Malik-al Mu'azzam, which was discovered in the remains of a tower of the Ayyubid period near Zion Gate

Muslim and Jewish inhabitants, left unprotected, abandoned the city and some of the Jews moved to Jerusalem. The leader of the North African Jewish community was Elihu the Maghribi, who was appointed *ra'is al-yahud*, or leader of the Jews.

The Jews who earned Alharizi's greatest praise were those from France who established a community in Jerusalem a few years prior to his visit. Many sages from England and France, undoubtedly accompanied by a variety of companions and dependents, immigrated to Eretz Israel and some settled in Jerusalem. In some sources they are described as 'three hundred rabbis'. While during crusader rule, Jews would generally come to Eretz Israel as pilgrims, now they came to settle, especially in Jerusalem and Acre.

There is evidence of another Jewish community in Jerusalem, hailing from the Yemen. Documents in the Cairo Geniza indicate that the Yemenites in Jerusalem maintained their own synagogue.

During the first two generations after Jerusalem's conquest by Saladin, there was evidently a Jewish presence in the city, and there is a warranted assumption that the different communities set up common institutions which would represent them when dealing with the Muslim authorities.

Life among the Jews of Jerusalem was difficult during the Ayyubid period. Their livelihood was barely sufficient and in addition, their notables frequently clashed with pilgrims and immigrants who had settled in the town. The latter claimed they were greater scholars of Torah, and criticized the level of spiritual leadership in Jerusalem. There is evidence, for instance, of complaints relating to this subject which were sent to the *nagid* or head of the Jews in Egypt, Abraham ben ha-Rambam, the son of Moses Maimonides. Most of the important rabbis who emigrated to Eretz Israel from France and England in 1210-1211, preferred to settle in Acre, not Jerusalem, and it may be assumed that the reason for this otherwise perplexing choice is that the immigrant scholars did not care to be subordinate to people of inferior knowledge.

Remains of an Ayyubid tower in the western course of Jerusalem's Old City wall. It was part of al-Mu'azzam's fortifications. Some three hundred years after al-Mu'azzam destroyed his own fortifications, the Ottoman emperor Suleiman the Magnificent built the current Old City walls along the lines of the ruined Ayyubid walls

The military and political upheavals during the first decades of the thirteenth century gave rise to confusion in both the communal and private lives of Jerusalemites. The Jews of Jerusalem, like the Muslims, were exposed to danger when Crusader forces approached or when Ayyubid rulers decided to destroy the city's fortifications (see below). The problems increased when Jerusalem again fell to the crusaders in 1229. The Muslims along with the Jews, abandoned Jerusalem, though there is no known renewal of the ban on non-Christians living in the city. Past experience had apparently taught Jews and Muslims alike to regard the crusaders with suspicion. This interval of crusader rule lasted fifteen years, during which Jews came to Jerusalem as pilgrims but evidently only one lived in the city.

The Destruction of Jerusalem's Fortifications

After Saladin's conquest of Jerusalem, heads of the Christian regimes in western Europe organized a Third

Crusade with the aim of freeing Jerusalem from the Muslims. (The Second Crusade occurred in 1147-1149; it was primarily a rescue campaign for the County of Edessa. For various reasons its strength was dissipated before it got near Jerusalem.) A sizable army came to Palestine in 1191, and among its commanders were Richard the Lionheart, king of England, King Philip II Augustus of France, and Emperor Frederick I of Germany. Acre fell once again to crusaders on July 12, 1191, and Saladin could not block renewed Christian control over the narrow coastal strip from Lebanon to Jaffa, with its ports. Jerusalem, however, remained unobtainable as far as the crusaders were concerned, although in their agreement with Saladin, Christians were permitted to visit Jerusalem and Bethlehem.

For Jerusalem, the reign of the Ayyubid ruler al-Malik al-Mu'azzam proved disastrous. In 1212 he fortified the walls of Jerusalem, but seven years later, in an unusual step, destroyed the fortifications and wreaked destruction in the city as well, apparently to convince an advancing crusader army not to come any closer to Jerusalem, and to further convince them to depart from Egypt as well, for they had set out from Europe on the assumption that Egypt's conquest would facilitate an easy seizure of Jerusalem and all of Syria-Palestine. The crusader army he feared was that of the Fifth Crusade, a force consisting of the armies of King Andrew II of Hungary, Prince Leopold of Austria, and the navies of various European states. In order to relieve the pressure on Egypt, al-Malik al-Mu'azzam set out from Damascus, attacked crusader fortresses, and, as mentioned, ordered the demolition of Jerusalem's fortifications.

According to traditions found in Muslim accounts, al-Mu'azzam's order regarding Jerusalem's destruction was so cruel that even his commanders were reluctant to execute them. He set out from Damascus to Jerusalem to supervise the destruction personally. The inhabitants of the city were appalled by the extent of the ruination; many remained without a roof over their heads, while others fled. A year later, al-Mu'azzam returned to Jerusalem and finished off whatever was still standing, this time for fear that Mongol forces advancing from the north would conquer the city. Another seven years passed, and al-Mu'azzam, apprehensive about a new crusade, gave orders to eliminate fortresses, cities and settlements throughout Syria-Palestine, apparently in

*Crusader architectural details are integrated into the Gate of the Chain leading to the Temple Mount. It was called The Beautiful Gate by the crusaders, who invested both planning and money in its appearance. An inscription tells of restorations during the Ayyubid period (1203). It is possible this gate stands where the former **Ksistos Gate** stood, which led to the Temple Mount during the Second Temple era*

order to give the crusaders pause for thought. He did not believe they could summon the manpower and financial resources to rebuild and hold on to fortresses so far from Europe. In destroying the fortresses he hoped to retain the territories they were meant to defend. For the third time in eight years, Jerusalem fell victim to al-Muazzam's battle tactics.

For the next three hundred years, Jerusalem was an unwalled, defenseless city, much shrunken in size, and greatly marginalized in status. This, however, did not detract from the aspirations of Christians to rule it. What their armies had not accomplished by military means, a Catholic ruler achieved by political means.

Chandelier from the cathedral of Hildesheim, Germany, ca. 1060. The fixture is fashioned in the form of the walls of Jerusalem, showing twelve gates. Similar chandeliers adorned Romanesque cathedrals throughout Europe during the Middle Ages

Another Fifteen Years of Christian Rule

Christians returned to Jerusalem in the wake of the Sixth Crusade led by Frederick II Barbarossa, Emperor of Germany and King of Sicily, who was involved in numerous confrontations with the popes, one of which was because he had not fulfilled his pledge to crusade in 1221. Frederick married Yolande (Isabella), the daughter of John of Brienne, ruler of the crusader kingdom of Jerusalem, and by virtue of this marriage was heir to the title, King of Jerusalem. When he reached the Holy Land in the summer of 1228, most of the Christian forces, including the military orders, refused to come to his aid because of his conflict with the pope. Only the Order of Knights Teuton joined him. He began negotiating with the Sultan of Egypt, Al-Malik-al-Kamil, who agreed to return to the crusader kingdom parts of the country, including Jerusalem (without the Temple Mount), Bethlehem, Nazareth and sections of the Galilee. The agreement was signed in February 1229 and Jerusalem once again passed to Christian hands.

The Temple Mount became a Muslim enclave in Christian Jerusalem. The keys of the Temple Mount gates were entrusted to Muslim guards, but Christian pilgrims were allowed to enter the area, visit the 'Templum Domini' (Dome of the Rock) and pray on the site. In exchange, Muslims were permitted to visit Bethlehem. The agreement caused hard feelings on both sides. As far as the Muslims were concerned, giving up Jerusalem was a sacrifice, and there was widespread sentiment that too much had been given up without a battle. A chronicler of the time writes: "In Jerusalem, the expelling of the Muslims was announced and the city transferred to the Franks (French-speaking European Catholics). The Muslims went on their way feeling their pain and full of bitterness at the loss of the holy city, and cursing the name of Al-Kamil."

Many Christians including the pope and the Latin patriarch of Jerusalem (who had been living in Acre for years), considered the agreement a betrayal, for Frederick had received only parts of the crusader kingdom, and not even the whole of Jerusalem. The patriarch refused to return to the city for a number of years. Frederick's consent not to rebuild the walls of Jerusalem was also severely criticized.

On March 18, 1229 Frederick II was crowned king of Jerusalem. He arrived at the Church of the Holy Sepulcher with great pomp, wearing royal robes. He took the crown which had been placed on the altar and placed it on his head. This was the last Christian coronation in Jerusalem. This second period of crusader rule lasted less than twenty years. The crusaders did their best to develop the city, but could not approach the level achieved during the first Crusader Kingdom. Frederick II returned to Europe. Jerusalem remained a Christian city until 1244, when it fell to the Khorezmians, mercenaries hired by the ruler of Egypt al-Malik al-Saliah Ayyub, to help repel an anticipated Syrian-Frankish (Christian) attack. The Khorezmians (Tartars), known for their ferocity, poured into Syria-Palestine, destroying whatever stood in their way. The Christian inhabitants of Jerusalem fled in the direction of Ramle, but the Khorezmian battalions slaughtered thousands of them. According to the chroniclers, only three hundred of the seven thousand Christians who left Jerusalem reached the port of Jaffa safely.

In Jerusalem the Khorezmians killed everyone they found and destroyed every building they could. Their effort was directed at Christian holy places in particular, such as the Church of the Holy Sepulcher in Jerusalem and the Church of the Nativity in Bethlehem. Afterward they joined forces with the Egyptian army and confronted the Syrian Franks in a decisive battle south of

Ashkelon. The Mamluk sultan, Baybars, commanding his Egyptian armies, first overcame the Syrian forces, and then the Franks. The Mamluks captured most of the Crusader Kingdom, including Jerusalem.

Jerusalem in Jewish Thought

During the Crusader and Ayyubid era, Eretz Israel and Jerusalem in particular, were exceedingly important elements in the development of Jewish thought. Several literary works emerged from this period which became highly influential. Their appearance can be understood in good part as efforts to understand the significance of the Exile, in which events of great cruelty and humiliation had occurred: the violence of the crusades and the taking of Jerusalem, the 'normal' humiliation at the hands of Muslims, the slaughter by Christians of Jews, in Europe and the Holy Land, and the diminution of the status of Jews all over Europe in the wake of the crusades. All these caused Jewish thinkers to seek some meaning for the suffering of the Jewish people, and a reason for the weakness of the nation chosen by God. In addition, the flourishing of rational thought and philosophical creativity among the Jews of Spain, and the increasing interest in Jewish mysticism, all brought about the emergence of influential gems of medieval Hebrew literature, in which Jerusalem is contemplated and glorified, and its significance in Jewish consciousness raised to a new height.

Rabbi Judah Halevi (see pp.137-138) in his elegant prose and poetry, stressed the merits of Jerusalem and Eretz Israel even in their destroyed state: only a life lived in Eretz Israel, he posited, allowed for fulfillment of the special bond between the Jewish people and their God. The sanctity of Jerusalem for Jews, and the blessed influence of Eretz Israel over Jews, were everlasting and not dependent on physical conditions. Sanctity and blessedness are inherent in certain geographic locations. "Heart and soul can be clear and pure only in the place which they know is dedicated to God" (The Kuzari, V, para. 23). The patriarch Jacob, as Halevi saw it, was granted divine revelation only when in a holy place. Jerusalem is the most holy place on earth. The doctrine of Judah Halevi is found in his prose masterpiece, The Kuzari as well as in his poetry. The boundless attachment

Page from an illuminated manuscript of Maimonides' commentary on the Mishnah, with a depiction of the candelabrum of the Temple

Halevi felt toward Eretz Israel and Jerusalem is even expressed via allusions to Christian and Islamic teachings: "Jerusalem is the gateway to heaven; all the nations of the world agree on this. The Christians say that souls gather unto Jerusalem and from there rise to the heavens. The Ishmaelites say it is the place of the ascendance of prophets to the heavens, and the place where the Day of Judgement will occur."

Judah Halevi seems to have been arguing against those who rejected *aliyah* (going up) to Eretz Israel on the grounds that it was in ruins, that Christians were ruling it, that the Jews should not abandon the graves of their fathers. He addressed himself above all to a wealthy and prominent social circle, to which he himself belonged. He acted on his principles, and in 1141, with great public demonstration, left for the Holy Land.

Another Spanish Jew produced writings during this period which have had lasting impact in Jewish thought. He was Nahmanides (Rabbi Moses ben Nahman or Ramban, 1195 – ca. 1270) whose widely studied Torah commentaries reflect a sense of the eternal bond Nahmanides felt existed between the Jew and the holy city. He believed that aliens could not succeed in settling the land because it did not wish to have them, and did not flourish under them. Rather, it was waiting for its sons – hence, the desolation of the land was seen as a sign of promise to the Jewish people. Nahmanides also complained bitterly to God regarding the situation of the Jews in exile. He left Spain to settle in Jerusalem, where he arrived in 1267, re-established the Jewish community and then settled on the coast, in Acre (see pp. 156-158).

A new ideology relating to the place occupied by Eretz Israel and Jerusalem in Jewish thought emerged in the area of medieval Jewish mysticism, *Kabbalah*, which grew in influence during the twelfth and thirteenth centuries. Kabbalists began to view the Exile as a divine cosmic catastrophe, the downtrodden position of Israel reflecting the defective state of the universe. The Redemption of the

people Israel would mean the redemption of the universe. In the kabbalist conception, Jerusalem, and to a lesser extent the whole of Eretz Israel, is described as directly receiving 'the divine flow'. The great work of Jewish mysticism, the Zohar, praises one who lives in Eretz Israel, who merits the bringing down to earth of 'divine abundance' from heaven, while one who lives in Jerusalem is rewarded with a direct flow of holiness.

The End of the Crusader Kingdom of Jerusalem

In 1250 with the fall of the Ayyubids, Egypt came under Mameluke rule, and so did Jerusalem, which would remain under Mamluk domination for two hundred and fifty years. Christian hegemony over areas of Syria-Palestine continued for slightly more than forty years, until 1291. After the fall of the port of Acre to the Mamluk al-Ashraf Khalil, the last crusaders left the ports of Atlit and Tyre for the isle of Cyprus. From the middle of the thirteen century onward, various Muslim rulers dominated Jerusalem. Jews returned to the city and remained uninterruptedly until today.

Battle between crusaders and Saracens (Muslims) from a stained-glass window of the Abbey of St. Denis in Paris. This window no longer exists

THE MAMLUK PERIOD

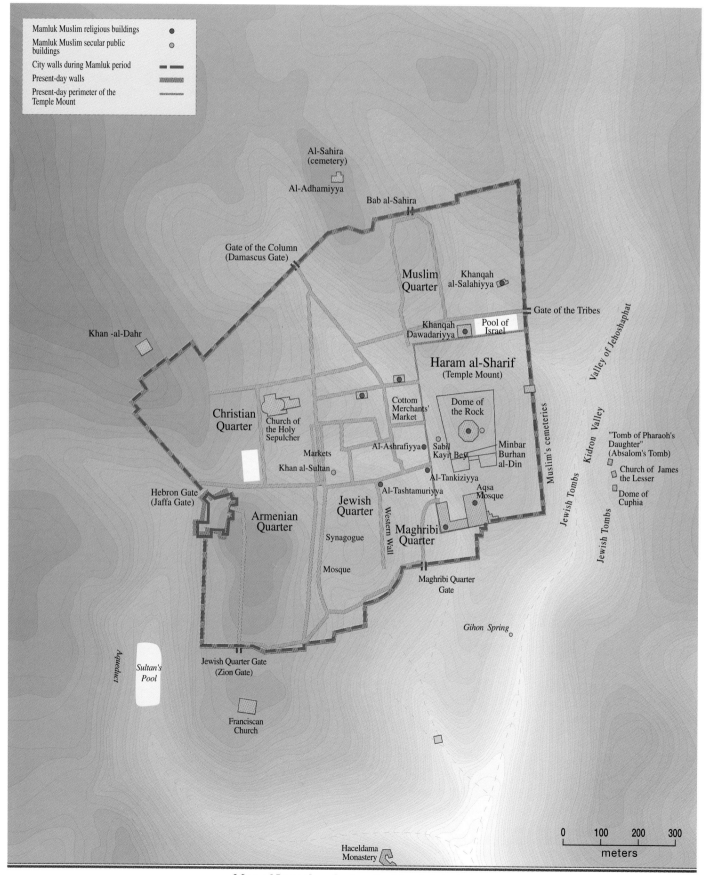

Al-Sahira
(cemetery)

Al-Adhamiyya

Bab al-Sahira

Gate of the Column
(Damascus Gate)

Muslim
Quarter

Khanqah
al-Salahiyya

Gate of the Tribes

Khan -al-Dahr

Khanqah
Dawadariyya

Pool of
Israel

Haram al-Sharif
(Temple Mount)

Christian
Quarter

Church of
the Holy
Sepulcher

Cottom
Merchants'
Market

Dome of
the Rock

Al-Ashrafiyya

Sabil
Kayit Bey

Minbar
Burhan
al-Din

Markets

Khan al-Sultan

Al-Tankiziyya

Hebron Gate
(Jaffa Gate)

Al-Tashtamuriyya

Aqsa
Mosque

Armenian
Quarter

Jewish
Quarter

Maghribi
Quarter

Synagogue

Western Wall

Mosque

Maghribi Quarter
Gate

Gihon Spring

Aqueduct

Sultan's
Pool

Jewish Quarter Gate
(Zion Gate)

Franciscan
Church

Valley of Jehoshaphat

Muslim's cemeteries

Kidron Valley

Jewish Tombs

"Tomb of Pharaoh's
Daughter"
(Absalom's Tomb)

Church of James
the Lesser

Dome of
Cuphia

Jewish Tombs

Jewish Tombs

Haceldama
Monastery

Mamluk Muslim religious buildings
Mamluk Muslim secular public
buildings
City walls during Mamluk period
Present-day walls
Present-day perimeter of the
Temple Mount

0   100   200   300
meters

Map of Jerusalem during the Mamluk period

Gateway to the Cotton Merchants' Market, a monumental structure built by the Mamluks in the mid-fourteenth century

Jerusalem endured a harsh period of invasions before coming under Mamluk rule in 1260. In 1244 it was overrun by Khorezmians, who spent their energies on it in a matter of weeks. The Mongols sacked it in 1260, and that same year were defeated by the Mamluks near Ayn Jalut (present-day Ein Harod in Israel).

The character of Mamluk rule over Jerusalem can be understood against the background of the Mamluk rise to power. They were not native Egyptians, but were imported as young slaves from the steppes of southern Russia, forcibly converted to Islam, and trained as archers in the army of their patrons the Ayyubid rulers of Egypt. The Mamluks (the term means 'owned') accrued a history of fierceness on the battlefield and unquestioned loyalty to their patrons. They became so powerful in Egypt that in 1250 they were able to overthrow the Ayyubid regime, which was rife with dissension and intrigue. Once in power the Mamluks continued the policy that they had been raised with, of promotion to positions of importance, rather than the bequeathing of authority from father to son. The success of the Mamluks on the battlefield can be attributed to a number of factors: intense military training, strict discipline, and their newfound religion, Islam, which gave them a sense of identity and purpose. They tried to repay their debt to Islam whenever and wherever possible, including in Jerusalem. During their 260 year rule over the city, they largely rebuilt it, guided by religious

considerations and the desire to perpetuate their names in a system that did not allow for dynastic succession. They erected mosques, *madrasas* (religious colleges) *khans* (hostels) for Muslim pilgrims, and *khankas* or hostels for Sufis (Muslim mystics).

In 1260, ten years after they had taken power in Egypt, the Mamluks defeated the Mongols, driving them out of Syria, which they then integrated into their kingdom. In the following years, the Mamluk commander Baybars, who had become sultan, engaged the crusaders, and by the year of his death (1277) managed to shrink the area under crusader control to a narrow strip along the coast between Atlit and Acre. (The crusaders retained northern enclaves such as Tripoli). In 1291 the crusader presence in the Holy Land was eliminated, and the Mamluks came into total possession of Syria-Palestine. They ruled Egypt and adjoining lands from their capital of Cairo, until their defeat by the Ottomans in 1517.

Jerusalem on the Periphery

In political terms, Jerusalem was a peripheral city of third or fourth rank during the Mamluk period. It did not function as a capital or provincial center, as did Safed or Gaza, nor was it directly subordinate to the central authority in Cairo. Rather, it was usually under the control of Damascus, a secondary capital, the primary city of Syria. From the Mamluk viewpoint, Jerusalem had little strategic significance. Its destroyed walls were not restored until the beginning of the Ottoman period, and no major highway led to it. Evidence that its political and economic stature was very low was its exclusion from the mail routes established by Baybars to maintain steady and swift communication with major cities of his empire. The infrastructure for the mail routes included postal relay stations, new roads and new bridges (one of the latter still stands near Lod); these routes reached centers such as Damascus and Kerak but not Jerusalem. A road from Ramle to

Mamluk horseman. For hundreds of years the Mamluks controlled Egypt and an extensive area to its northeast

Jerusalem served pilgrims, and was not well maintained by the authorities.

Jerusalem's lack of importance is also testified to by the lowly stature of its Mamluk governors. The city was a place to which disgraced officers were sent in exile, as well as a place where older officers retired. The governor of Jerusalem had little responsibility, and every matter, large or small, had to be referred to his superior, the commissioner in Damascus.

Of the forty Mamluk sultans who ruled during this period, fewer than ten visited Jerusalem. Those who did,

came in the context of a *hajj* (pilgrimage) to Mecca, generally on the return journey. The visit was undertaken from religious considerations; these sultans did not visit governmental institutions, as rulers might have been expected to do when touring an important city. In 1376 Jerusalem experienced a slight improvement in its status when its governor began being appointed directly by Cairo, rather than by officials in Damascus. The city's role was also somewhat broadened, however it remained peripheral, small and undefended.

The Lions' Gate got its name from the pair of beasts (actually leopards) adorning the facade on either side of the gate. The leopard was the insignia of the Mamluk Sultan Baybars. The design was integrated into the wall built by the Ottoman, Suleiman the Magnificent

Mamluk Construction

In Jerusalem some seventy buildings have been preserved from the Mamluk period, among them impressive and architecturally interesting structures. This period was characterized by a surge of building in the city despite Jerusalem's minor political or military stature. It was a holy city to Muslims, and the fact that it was reconquered from the crusaders added to its importance. As the Mamluks were comparatively 'new' Muslims, historians have suggested that they tried to demonstrate fidelity to Islam by, among other things, undertaking construction of a religious character. Baybars renewed the outer mosaic panels on the octagonal-shaped Dome of the Rock; Kalawun, who followed him, repaired the ceiling of the al-Aqsa mosque; his son al-Nasr Muhammad regilded the domes of the Dome of the Rock and al-Aqsa; Sultan al-Ashraf Shaban erected the turret over the Gate of the Tribes in the mid-fourteenth century; and in the late fifteenth century Kayit Bey repaired the fountain that supplied drinking water to believers, and also built the largest Muslim religious college in Jerusalem – the Ashrafiyya Madrasa.

Even those Mamluks who were exiled to Jerusalem contributed to the construction effort. Some had held central offices in the sultanate, and wanted to immortalize their activities by putting up such buildings as madrasas or impressive mausoleums. An example of such construction is the madrasa begun by Argun al-Kamili, who was governor of Aleppo. It was completed after his death in the mid-fourteenth century.

Many Mamluk officers, aware that neither their official position nor the property gained thereby could be passed on to their offspring, erected religious structures for the public benefit, which also insured positions for their heirs. (These structures also frequently house their tombs). The heirs were made responsible for pious foundations or trusts (wakfs), which remained within the family while enhancing the appearance of Jerusalem. Officials from outside Jerusalem also engaged in the same practice. The emir Tankiz, having accumulated a fortune as governor of Damascus and viceroy of Syria (1312-1340) spent a good deal of it in Jerusalem. Three inscriptions on buildings mention his name. He erected a hostel or caravanserai (the Khan Tankiz) a market, two bathhouses (hammams),

The facade of the al-Ashrafiyya Madrasa combines typical Mamluk architectural elements: elaborate pendants over the entryway, interlocking rows of alternate colored stones (Ablak technique), and benches on either side of the entrance

and the best known structure, the Tankiziyya Madrasa (Tankiz religious college) erected 1328-1329, which has a magnificent entrance featuring a large decorative inscription, interrupted by three decorative elements featuring the form of a cup. The cup was Tankiz' blazon, and indicates that he started his career as a cupbearer. Other governors of Damascus and those of other cities also initiated construction in Jerusalem.

During the entire Mamluk period, with the exception of the short period of Mongol raids in 1260, Jerusalem was not involved in warfare. This fostered its reconstruction and architectural development.

Mamluk architecture in Jerusalem is readily distinguishable. It features the decorative use of Arabic calligraphy and Koranic inscriptions in stonework, the use of intricate architectural elements primarily in decorative parts of buildings, such as facades and entryways, and the use of varied types and colors of building stone in visually stimulating patterns, in facades and entryways. Mamluk facades commonly feature combinations of two or three colors of stone, chiseled stonework, and metal grills in which metal balls are inserted at certain design crosspoints. Mamluk entryways are often placed below high vaults enhanced by many bold design elements. Their buildings are generally large, manifesting a conscious display of monumentalism. Today they predominate in the area around the Street of the Chain and northwest of the Temple Mount, as well as on the Mount itself.

Inhabitants of Jerusalem in the Early Mamluk Period

From the outset of their control of Jerusalem Mamluk rulers strove to bolser the Islamic character of the city. The great amount of Mamluk construction was one means to achieve this end. Another was to encourage the settlement of Muslims in the city. Muslim immigrants came from Persia, Afghanistan, Kurdistan, India, Egypt and Spain. The *Maghribis* – immigrants from North Africa, had arrived as early as Saladin's reign and set up their quarter west of the Temple Mount. Their institutions are still present in the area. Another section of the city was called Harat al-Akrad, the Kurdish quarter. Muslims of the towns and villages of Syria-Palestine and its surroundings were also invited to settle in the holy city, while others sought refuge in Jerusalem from repeated Bedouin incursions.

During the Mamluk period, many Sufis (Muslim mystics) settled in Jerusalem. Most lived in hostels, *khankahs* meant specially for them, the most famous of which was the Khankah al-Salahiyya, established by *Salah-al-Din* (Saladin). It was the former residence of the Latin patriarch during the crusader period. Some Sufis served as teachers in various *madrasas*, making their influence felt on spiritual and religious life in the city for many years to come.

Jerusalem's Christians were relegated to secondary status as tolerated or 'protected peoples,' or *dhimmis* (see p.105). Most Christians had left the city when Jerusalem's

crusader era came to an end in the mid-thirteenth century. Those who had remained, their descendants, and later Christian arrivals, lived in the vicinity of the Church of the Holy Sepulcher. Almost all the Christians living in Jerusalem during this period were of the Eastern (or Greek) Orthodox church as they were better tolerated by the Mamluks than were the Latins.

Kayit Bey fountain, erected in the mid-fifteenth century. Water flowed into it from the upper conduit which came from Solomon's Pools to Jerusalem

Among the Europeans (Latins, or Catholics) remaining in the city, there was a small group of Franciscan monks who resided mainly on Mount Zion, having arrived in 1335 to serve the needs of pilgrims. The Vatican granted them the rank of protectors of holy Christian sites, and to the Mamluk administration they were considered the representatives of European interests in Jerusalem.

Above: The al-Khalidiyyah Library, founded at the end of the nineteenth century in a Mamluk structure. Right: Illuminated manuscript of a fifteenth century volume on medications, collection, al-Khalidiyyah Library

Christians in Mamluk Jerusalem suffered both legal and social discrimination. The crusader threat to Jerusalem and the region was still in the air despite the defeat of the Crusader Kingdom. The Mamluks considered it within the realm of possibility that Christian Europe would again attempt to conquer Jerusalem, and regarded Christians in Jerusalem as a fifth column. In addition, the Mamluk regime was severely troubled by Christian pirates in the Mediterranean, who seriously affected their trade with Europe. As they could not surmount this difficulty, they often took out their frustration on Christians living in their realm. Churches, including the Church of the Holy Sepulcher, were often closed or vandalized in retaliation for Christian attacks on Mamluk bases in Egypt and other areas. On a number of occasions Christian monks in Jerusalem were arrested, exiled and even done physical harm. These instances typically provoked a European response, a Mamluk counter-response and a repetition of the same cycle.

The Mamluks displayed greater tolerance towards eastern rite Christians than towards Latins. The Armenians, for instance, were granted a letter of protection from the Sultan Jakmak relating to their property, even though Jakmak was known for his religious fanaticism. (The text of this letter of protection can be found carved in the stonework over the entranceway to the Armenian Church of St James, and again in the entrance corridor.) Aside from the Armenians there were also small Christian denominations resident in Jerusalem: Copts, Ethiopians, Syrians and Greek Orthodox.

The Church of the Holy Sepulcher was reconsecrated in ca. 1370 by the Russian archimandrite Agrefenii, who made a pilgrimage to Jerusalem. He called it the Church of the Blessed Resurrection. According to the archimandrite, there were six pastors living in Jerusalem at the time: Greek, Georgian, Armenian, Frankish, Jacobite, and Ethiopian. The Church was opened only on Easter, when thousands of Christians would stream towards it, to remain through the night until the following day. It was during this period that the phenomenon known as the Miracle of the Holy Fire took place. It was, according to the archimandrite, "an indescribably miraculous event." The Christian notables in Jerusalem and the East, headed by the Patriarch Sophronios IV, the Metropolitan of Egypt and the Bishop of Damascus, encircled the tomb of Jesus three times, until a thin plume of smoke began to rise from under the cupola. The smoke became thicker and in its wake "the hall became filled with a heavenly fire." The patriarch lit candles from the holy fire, "and all those present lit their candles from the patriarch's candle, and a great cry arose from the whole church."

The Mongol 'Conquest' and the Crusading Spirit in Europe

In the late fourteenth century, Jerusalem again suffered a Mongol raid. Although the Mongol ruler of Persia, Ghazan, had converted to Islam in 1295, he maintained the traditional antagonistic stance of his forefathers

A pulpit in Re'han a-din, also called the Summer Fountain, erected in the fourteenth century using stone and marble. Crusader materials are incorporated in secondary usage

toward the Mamluks. In 1299 his forces defeated the Mamluk army near Homs in Syria, and he was able to occupy Damascus. His scouts and raiders advanced southward into Syria-Palestine, reaching as far as Gaza and Hebron. A number of writers report how Mongols raided Jerusalem. A contemporary Egyptian historian writes that they killed both Muslims and Christians, and drank wine on the Temple Mount. "They did despicable deeds, destroyed, killed, looted and captured children and women."

The Mongol occupation of Syria, however, was short lived, and after several months they withdrew back across the Euphrates. The Mamluks were able to reoccupy Syria, including Eretz Israel and Jerusalem. Interestingly enough, reports of this Mongol victory and their 'conquest' of the Holy Land and Jerusalem reached Europe and brought about a flurry of apocalyptic expectations and hopes for the liberation of Jerusalem. In spite of Ghazan's conversion to Islam, in the West it was reported that he had become a Christian, and had conquered Jerusalem in order to return it to the Christians. There were even some preparations for a new crusade. The pope in 1300 contacted the English king and called upon the faithful to go to Jerusalem immediately, offering remission for sins, as had been done during earlier crusades. In Italy and Spain as well, preparations were made, but in the long run, nothing of substance came of these efforts. They did, however influence Jewish thinkers as well as Christians. Joseph Ibn Caspi, who lived in the mid-fourteenth century, expressed the hope that the Mongol khan would help establish the Jewish kingdom in Eretz Israel, and that the Jews of his realm and those of the rest of the world, would gather there.

Nahmanides in Jerusalem

Primary testimony to the size of the Jewish community of Jerusalem in the early Mamluk period is found in the letter of a towering figure of medieval Jewish scholarship, Rabbi Moses ben Nahman, or Nahmanides

In his letter from Jerusalem dated 1267, Nahmanides mentions a building which was turned into a synagogue. That synagogue was destroyed and another built in its place. The four pillars in the center of this structure led to its identification by a sixteenth century author as the Ramban (Nahmanides) Synagogue. The structure still bears this name

*Depiction of
Jerusalem and the
roads leading to it in
a French manuscript
(1455)*

ספר כפתור ופרח

אשר נמצא בבית גנזי החכם סיני ועוקר הרים הלא הוא
הגאון נגיד ממצרי עשיר עניו בו נמצא תורה וגדולה
במקום אחד כמהרר יצחק כהן שולל ובו
נמצא רוב התועלת שמדבר בדיני
ארץ ישראל הנהונות היום
בארץ ובשאר דינים יפים
כאשר תראה בסימני
פרקים שלו:

אותו העיר: הבחור מאיר: במשפחתו הצעיד:

פה ויניציא

Title page of the Provencale Rabbi Ashtori ha-Farkhi's book
Kaftor va-Ferakh, *'Calyx and Petals.' The book was printed
in 1549, according to a manuscript found in the home of
Rabbi Yitzhak ha-Cohen Shulal, the* **nagid** *in Egypt*

(see also, page 146). He described Jerusalem as having very few Jewish residents; however over time the community grew to several hundred families. He arrived in Jerusalem after having been forced to flee Spain. (At age seventy he was called upon to represent Judaism in a debate before King James I of Aragon. His opponent was a convert from Judaism who had become a Dominican monk. Nahmanides was an aggressive debator who, given the tenor of the times, could not have been allowed to win the debate, but who managed to be very persuasive, so much so that he was obliged to leave Spain for his own protection. Shunning refuge in a comfortable community, he fulfilled a longstanding dream and settled in Eretz Israel). He arrived in Jerusalem on

September 1, 1267 and described the city in a letter to his son: "There is much desolation in the country. The general rule is, the more holy the place, the greater its state of destruction. Jerusalem is more destroyed than the rest..." Despite Jerusalem's destroyed state, "(it is) very good." There were about two thousand inhabitants in it of whom three hundred were Christian and a few were Jews, because most of the congregation fled from the city seven years earlier during the Mongol threat, and had not returned. In accordance with past practice, two Jews had purchased dyers licenses from the governor in the city and it appears that they were not the only Jews in Jerusalem. According to Nahmanides, "They are joined by a *minyan* (ten worshippers) in their home on the Sabbath."

Nahmanides urged the Jews of Jerusalem to develop their spiritual and religious life. "We encouraged them," he tells. "We found an unclaimed decaying house built with pillars of marble and a lovely dome and turned it into a synagogue." This was not a difficult task for "the city is abandoned and whoever wants to take over ruins, does so." On Nahmanides' initiative the building was repaired and messengers sent to Nablus to bring back the Torah scrolls which had been spirited away from Jerusalem lest the Mongols destroy them. "Shortly," he tells his son, "the synagogue will be standing firm and we shall pray there. It is needed," he explains, "(because) many come to Jerusalem regularly, men and women from Damascus, Aleppo and Egypt, and from all over, to see the Temple and mourn over it." And, "whoever beholds Jerusalem in its desolation, will be worthy of beholding it in its renewal, when the Shekhinah (Divine Presence) returns to it..." The return of the Torahs from Nablus indicates that Jerusalem was judged safe enough at the time.

The early period of Mamluk rule also witnessed the arrival in Jerusalem of Jewish settlers from Ashkenaz (Central Europe) and the sources even make mention of convoys of Jews attempting to reach Eretz Israel. Leading such a group was Rabbi Meir of Rothenburg, who set out on this journey with his family in 1286. He and his caravan reached northern Italy and were to have met up with another group of emigrants. As the result of an attempt to malign him, Rabbi Meir was taken hostage by officers of the Habsburg monarch Rudolf and held for seven years, until his death. His fellow travellers dispersed.

During the fourteenth century, the Jerusalem community grew and became the most important Jewish

Nabi Samwil, believed in the Mamluk period to be the tomb of the prophet Samuel, was a site of Jewish pilgrimage. The site is also significant for Christians, as from this spot Jerusalem was first visible to the armies of the first crusade

community in Eretz Israel. It was founded by local Jews and was home to many new immigrants, mainly from neighboring countries and a minority of European Ashkenazis. The leadership generally derived from the Oriental or eastern community, and Ashkenazi Jews did not play a prominent role in communal life. For a considerable span, the Jews of Jerusalem were subordinate to the *nagid*, the highest Jewish office under Mamluk rule. The *nagid* was a resident of Egypt. At first the deputy *nagid* officiated from Damascus, and extended his authority over Jerusalem as well. From 1376, however, Jewish Jerusalem had a deputy *nagid* of its own. On occasion, when Mamluk rule was weakening, the status of the *nagid* and his deputy, in Egypt, weakened as well, and the influence of the local leadership became stronger.

In Muslim law the Jews of Jerusalem had the same status (*dhimmi*) as Christians, however their actual condition was better than that of the Christians; in Jerusalem they were rarely subject to attacks. In the fourteenth century there were a number of riots by Muslim fanatics against Christians, and in these, Jews

were also affected, but less so than the prime targets. In times of natural disaster adherents of the three religions were united, as was the case in 1317 when there was a serious drought. From an Egyptian document relating to this matter it appears that there was a reward for this inter-religious effort. As there was no water in Jerusalem, according to a contemporary writer of the time, "all the inhabitants left the city, Muslims, Christians and Jews, and went out into the open and prayed to Allah for rain, and their prayers were answered on the third day."

The Jewish quarter in those days, was situated in the neighborhood of Mount Zion, not far from the Armenian quarter.

Immigration to Jerusalem in the Fourteenth Century

As Nahmanides remarked in his letter to his son, pilgrimage to Jerusalem was a common practice among the Jews of neighboring countries. Ashtori ha-Farkhi, who settled in Jerusalem from a more distant locale,

Provence in southern France, toured Eretz Israel in the early fourteenth century. He recorded his observations including the social customs and traditions of the people. His work, *Kaftor va-Ferakh* ('Calyx and Petals') was the first descriptive geography of the Holy Land in Hebrew. He noted, "Our brethren, of the Exile, who live in Tripoli (Syria) Hamat, Damascus, Aleppo, Egypt, Alexandria, go up to Jerusalem on holidays and festivals..." Pilgrimage was undertaken during the spring in the month of Iyar, and included the ceremony of 'Ziarah' or visit to the traditional gravesite of a charismatic religious figure, such as Rabbi Shimon bar Yohai in Meron or the prophet Samuel in Nabi Samwil, north of Jerusalem.

During the Mamluk period there was immigration to Jerusalem as well as pilgrimage. Jews came from the East and from Ashkenazi centers in Europe. Persecution of the Jews of Spain for instance, accounted for a marked increase in Jewish emigration, while messianic hopes inspired many toward the Holy Land. Among the new immigrants were scholars and sages, such as Rabbi Ashtori ha-Farkhi and Rabbi Jacob Sikili, and a group of scholars from Ashkenaz who established a yeshiva in Jerusalem in the mid-fourteenth century. In this period the first written evidence appears indicating that money was collected in Ashkenaz to support "the poor of Jerusalem."

From about the same time we are aware of a phenomenon known as 'the agreements' or the 'bonds,' joint ventures of sages to migrate to Jerusalem. Thus, for instance in 1317, Rabbi Jakob Sikili and his friend Hezekiah signed the 'bond,' in which they pledge: "to go up to Eretz Israel... and live in or near Jerusalem... for there fulfillment of the commandments and acceptance of the obligations of Heaven, and worship, are preferred, because there (was) the House of God, and there is the gateway to heaven..." In the continuation, it states: "We have taken upon ourselves to dwell in Jerusalem for one year, with no one forcing us, and with worldly possessions. (We will perhaps stay longer), and will not stay shorter." The group of immigrants agreed among themselves on joint financial arrangements which would enable them to live in Jerusalem. There were also groups of sages who undertook to go up to dwell in Jerusalem. On occasion they were led by important rabbinic personalities. There was Jewish immigration to Jerusalem for the purpose of achieving atonement for sins. Finally,

'David's Tomb' on Mount Zion

Rabbi Dosa 'the Greek,' a fourteenth century commentator on the work of Rashi, mentions the custom of Ashkenazis and Sephardis settling in Jerusalem when nearing old age, so that they might upon their deaths be buried there.

The Black Death and the Increase in Jewish Immigration to Eretz Israel

The terrible plague that decimated the population of Europe beginning in the mid-fourteenth century had the indirect effect of increasing Jewish immigration to Eretz Israel. In the atmosphere of hatred for Jews prevailing in Europe in the fourteenth century, it did not take long for the outbreak of the Black Death (bubonic plague, today known with absolute certainly to have been spread by flea-infested rats that had carried it from Asia to Europe) to be blamed on the Jews. In scores of communities they were viciously attacked. The death toll was unprecedented by comparison with the harm done in previous medieval persecutions. Some survivors of the persecution made their way east to Eretz Israel.

This was the case as well with Spanish Jews after the attacks and forced conversions which began in Spain in 1391: Jews left for other countries and some turned eastward toward the lands of the Mediterranean basin, including Eretz Israel. However, as was previously noted, Jewish migration from Spain to Eretz Israel and Jerusalem pre-dated the persecutions of 1391, and could be ascribed to the emotional appeal of Eretz Israel and the awareness of the religious significance of ascending to Jerusalem (see also pp. 171-172).

The Struggle for Mount Zion

Mount Zion had been a holy site for hundreds of years, and was the subject of ideological clashes between Jews, Christians, and Muslims. According to ancient tradition, King David and King Solomon were buried on the mount, and folk legends added that silver and gold treasures were buried with famous kings. The site known as David's Tomb had been sacred to Jews for generations, and during the Mamluk period, they tried to claim it. Of course Mount Zion was also sacred to the Christians, for on it, according to Christian tradition, stood the Coenaculum, where Jesus and his disciples partook of the Last Supper. During the Mamluk period the Coenaculum hall was in the custody of Franciscan monks. It seems that Jews offered to purchase the buildings on Mount Zion from the monks, who refused to sell. According to some sources, the Jews appealed to the Mamluk sultan in Cairo on a number of occasions, asking for possession of Mount Zion. Felix Fabri, who visited Jerusalem towards the end of the fifteenth century, mentions that the sultan wished to investigate the origins of the site's sanctity. When he was told that King David and his heirs were buried there, he said: "We also consider David holy, just as the Christians and the Jews do, and we believe in the Holy Book just as they do. Therefore neither Jews nor Christians will possess this place; we will keep it for ourselves."

By the sultan's command, the church on Mount Zion was destroyed and the Franciscans ousted. They did not give up easily and for decades pressured Cairo to allow them to re-occupy Mount Zion. They managed to return to the site for a short period, however were forced away again. Finally they were permitted to build a monastery

there. Early in the sixteenth century, all the Franciscans' property in Jerusalem was confiscated, the monks were arrested, and some were imprisoned in Egypt.

The Spanish traveller, Guillem Oliver, who visited Jerusalem in 1464, noted that the Muslims were the keepers of the chapel on Mount Zion where the tombs of King David and King Solomon were located, "and they prevent Christians from entering, under pain of death." Jews too were not permitted to enter.

There were distant ramifications of the Mount Zion dispute. In various European countries, all of Jewry was blamed for the aspiration of the group of Jews of Jerusalem to control Mount Zion. It was this, to the European mind, which had brought about the mount's domination by the Christian-hating Muslim infidels. European Jews were punished in a number of ways. The pope decreed that Italian Jews must pay a heavy tax whose proceeds would be turned over to the Franciscan

The Coenaculum above David's Tomb. Crusader inscriptions can be seen on the Gothic arches left of the **mihrab** *- the niche indicating the Muslim direction of prayer*

order which had been discriminated against on Mount Zion. He also forbade Christian sea captains to carry Jewish passengers to the Holy Land. This decree endured, with some interruption, throughout the fifteenth century. Jews who wanted to go to Eretz Israel had to travel overland via roundabout routes for months and sometimes years. It was only towards the end of the fifteenth century that this decree was withdrawn.

Christian and Muslim Pilgrims Describe Jerusalem

Pilgrims and travellers from various countries frequently arrived in Mamluk Jerusalem, and a number left records from which impressions emerge of the city, its sites, and the life of its inhabitants.

Wilhelm von Boldensele was a German Dominican monk who in 1333 set out for the Mediterranean and the East, with Jerusalem as his eventual goal. In the work he wrote upon his return, he described holy places of the different religions in Jerusalem. He noted that the Temple Mount plaza was paved with fine white marble, and that the Muslims were exacting about its cleanliness. They tread on it cautiously after removing their shoes, they prostrated themselves and often kissed the ground. Non-Muslims were not allowed into the Haram compound since "so holy a place, which alone is the House of God, must not be desecrated by Christians and Jews..."

Von Boldensele happened upon a Jew from Germany (Ashkenaz), whom he described as "a knowledgeable fellow" and hired as a guide. It seems that Jewish guides in Jerusalem were in demand. This is reflected in the account of Jacob of Verona, an Augustinian monk who visited Jerusalem in 1335. "A pilgrim who wishes to visit cities and ancient fortresses in the Holy Land could not find any of them without the help of a good guide, who knows the country well, or one of the Jews who live in these places. For the Jews know all the ancient places, as they are well-versed in their law and the sites from the writings of their forefathers and sages. Hence... I asked for and frequently acquired a good guide from among the Jews living there."

Jacob of Verona noted that the Jewish Quarter in Jerusalem was situated not far from Mount Zion. In addition, he noted that Jews from Jerusalem and from other places were in the habit of making pilgrimage outside the city, to the tomb of Samuel the Holy (Nabi Samwil) and Jacob, who had joined a party of them, had to ride a donkey, for a Christian, no matter of what rank, was forbidden to ride a horse.

The archimandrite Agrefenii who lived in Jerusalem in the late fourteenth century, describes among other things, the Tower of David in the west of the city: "...a small but strong fortress where the guilty are imprisoned, and in its halls a treasure is kept, and the weapons of the Emir of Jerusalem. If someone resides there for a year, he will die."

Another pilgrim who visited Jerusalem some twenty years later, near the end of the fourteenth century, was the French aristocrat, Seigneur d'Anglure. Jerusalem seemed to him a large and lovely city, despite the fact that the Saracens maintained it in a filthy state and lived in crowded conditions. There were a few pleasant streets

The German aristocrat Bernhard von Breydenbach accompanied Felix Fabri on his tour of Syria-Palestine in the fifteenth century. Von Breydenbach made drawings of the country's landscape and its peoples. Depicted here are Turkish Janissaries in the Mamluk army

Arabs in Jerusalem of the late Mamluk period, as depicted by von Breydenbach

and vaulted arches embellished with ornamental stonework, and the light caught their beauty when it penetrated windows set in the upper part of their arches. Passageways between buildings ran above the arches and formed a network of overhead streets. As to the Jews and Christians, they lived in special streets, in different parts of the city.

D'Anglure explained that the observer could differentiate the various nationalities in the city by noting headgear. The Muslims wore a white headcovering, the Christians blue and the Jews, yellow. Samaritans wore a spotted headdress of white and apricot tones.

Ibn Batuta, a Muslim traveller from North Africa who visited Syria-Palestine and Jerusalem on a number of occasions during the first half of the fourteenth century,

The Valley of Jehoshaphat (alt. Kidron Valley) and Mount of Olives, with ancient Jewish cemetery. This slope was a gathering point for Jewish pilgrims during the Mamluk period

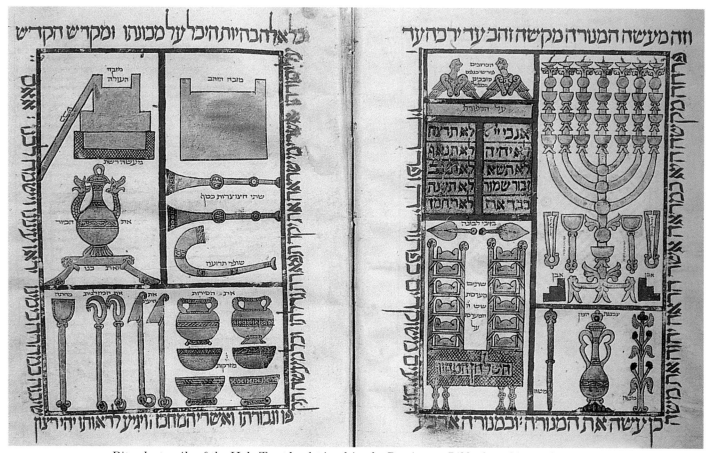

Ritual utensils of the Holy Temple, depicted in the Perpignan Bible, late thirteenth century

provides important information, confirming that Jerusalem was unwalled because Saladin and his successors destroyed the city walls to prevent crusaders from fortifying themselves within the city. He describes the mosques on the Temple Mount in detail and in an awed tone, using such adjectives as "rare," "the largest in the world" and "wondrous." The Christians, he says, dwell around the Church of the Holy Sepulcher. Whoever wanted to visit the church had to pay a tax to the Muslims. The Christians, he reported, were also continually humiliated by being a minority under Muslim rule.

Travellers and pilgrims from Europe continued to visit the country in large numbers during the fifteenth century and their descriptions suggest that Jerusalem underwent little change in this era. Brother Felix Fabri, a German-Swiss, visited Jerusalem twice during the 1480s and wrote a three-volume work, *The Wanderings* (*Evagatorium*), which became a well-known travel account of the late Middle Ages. It contains much detail about

Jerusalem towards the end of Mamluk rule. Fabri relates that Jerusalem suffered from a shortage of water, and placed the blame on the Muslims, who washed everyday, a practice apparently not customary in Europe at the time. The majority of Jerusalem's inhabitants were Saracens, he noted, though the city included about one thousand Christians, five hundred Jews, and "many others from every nation and speaking every tongue under the heavens."

From Fabri's book, a lesson is learned about the tourist guides of the period, who made zealous attempts to capture the business of pilgrims: "It (often) happened that two or three drivers were dragging one pilgrim in one direction, another in another; for when the country people... heard that pilgrims were come, they brought many asses, more than there were pilgrims. So each man tried to bring a pilgrim to his asses; for one Saracen brought seven or eight asses, of a sort, and hence it happens that when there are not above two hundred pilgrims, there will be four hundred asses, (which is why) the drivers fight for pilgrims and drag them hither and thither... He to whom no pilgrim comes has made his journey for nothing."

The Jews of Jerusalem in the Fifteenth Century

There were good and bad times for the Jews of Jerusalem during the fifteenth century. The unevenness of their situation was attributable to problems that arose from their relationship with the regime, with the Christian and Muslim communities, and from internal communal strife. In this period the Jewish Quarter was located in the southeast, not far from Mount Zion. It remained there for several hundred years. In about 1400, the Jews acquired a building and set up a synagogue for use by all the different Jewish congregations. This synagogue was named for Nahmanides, although it was opened more than a hundred and thirty years after his visit to Jerusalem.

Jewish immigrants continued to come to Jerusalem. Among them were rabbis and scholars from the East and from Europe. The Ashkenazi community grew and the immigration from Spain also increased. There are hints that after Constantinople fell to the Ottomans (1453), there was a revival of messianic ideas in Spain and a

Minaret of mosque located in the center of the Jewish quarter in the Old City of Jerusalem. The mosque was erected near a synagogue and caused it considerable damage. In a later period, that synagogue was replaced by another, the Hurvah ('Hurvat Rabbi Judah Hasid') which was destroyed by the Jordanians in 1948. One of the supporting arches of its walls was restored after 1967 and is visible, lower right

consequent increase in the number of immigrants to Eretz Israel. There was continuous immigration from North Africa, and these Jews who were closer in language and customs to the Muslim inhabitants of Jerusalem were more easily absorbed into the social fabric than the Ashkenazis.

Jewish pilgrims to Jerusalem usually followed a regular route which included the Western Wall, where they mourned the destruction, and then two sites which were related to the Jewish idea of the messianic future of Jerusalem and the Jewish people, the Mount of Olives and the Valley of Jehoshaphat. The route began at the Gate of Mercy, through which, according to Jewish tradition, the Divine Presence passed from the Temple and ascended to heaven, and through which it was expected to return.

From the late thirteenth century onward, the slope of the Valley of Jehoshaphat-Mt. of Olives, developed into the cemetery of the Jews of Jerusalem. Another site that attracted the Jewish pilgrims was Mount Zion where, according to tradition, the kings of Judah, with David at their head, were buried.

The Impoverishment of the Jews

The economic situation of the Jews was more often than not precarious, in good part due to periodic extremely heavy taxes imposed on them by the authorities, and collected by local governors. The tax burden in the second half of the fifteenth century brought about the utter impoverishment of the Ashkenazi community and a severe decrease in the status of the Oriental Jews, who lost all their property and assets, their religious foundations, and their holy books and utensils.

In mid-century, the Jews of Jerusalem were ordered to evacuate the city, and only the payment of 'compensation' could cancel the decree. The organization of the congregation and the collection of taxes to be paid to the rulers was the responsibility of the 'elders', heads of the community, and for this reason, they were blamed for what was considered their collaboration with the Muslim rulers.

According to various sources, tens and perhaps hundreds of Jewish families were living in Jerusalem in the fifteenth century, but evidently the size of the Jewish

Facade of the house of Rabbi Obadiah, in Bertinoro, Italy

community fluctuated. Thus, Rabbi Yitzhak Latif, who arrived in Jerusalem during the 1450s, tells of 150 Jewish families living in the city, while Rabbi Obadiah of Bertinoro, who settled in the town only a few years later, speaks of only seventy families.

At times, the Jews were involved in long quarrels with their Muslim neighbors, and surprisingly, the Mamluk regime as often as not stood by the Jews. This was the case in the days of the Sultan Kayit Bey during the 1470s. An Ashkenazi Jew, who was at loggerheads with his community, converted to Islam. His mother had a house near the synagogue, and as she was also angry with the community, she gave the house to the Muslims to establish a mosque there. The Muslim judges of Jerusalem considered the matter and decided that the nearby synagogue should be taken from the Jews. In their distress, the Jews of Jerusalem appealed to Sultan Kayit Bey in Cairo, who examined the matter and ordered the local government in Jerusalem to cancel the decision. The Muslim religious leaders met in the al-Aqsa mosque and decided that the building would be returned to the Jews, who were however forbidden use it as a synagogue. (They could use it as a shop.) The local authorities, in keeping with the Sultan's orders, rejected this decision and permitted the Jews to set up a synagogue in the building. The Muslim religious leaders continued their struggle and spread the rumor that the Jews had bribed the Sultan, who was very cross with his detractors and demanded that they be put on trial. A further deliberation was held in which it was proven that the synagogue belonged to the Jews. Muslim fanatics angered by the final decision destroyed the synagogue in November 1474. The matter was again brought before the Sultan, and he ordered the synagogue's reconstruction, and even sent two Egyptian judges to Jerusalem to supervise it.

The Letters of Rabbi Obadiah of Bertinoro

Rabbi Obadiah of Bertinoro was an Italian Jew who in 1485 embarked upon a journey to Jerusalem. He was three years on the road before reaching the Holy Land. Three letters which he sent from there (two from Jerusalem and one from Hebron) include a wealth of material about the period generally, and the Jews in particular. He arrived in Jerusalem on the eve of Passover, on March 25, 1488, and was received by an Ashkenazi rabbi, originally from Italy, Rabbi Jacob Columbano, with whom Rabbi Obadiah spent Passover.

Jerusalem made a poor first impression on Rabbi Obadiah: "It is mostly destroyed and in ruin, and it goes without saying that (the city) has no wall around it." He went on to describe the city's four thousand households, among which were only seventy Jewish households. In an

earlier period there had been three hundred Jewish families, however most left because of exploitation by 'the elders' or established 'lay' leadership of the Jewish community. He deemed the attitude of the Muslims toward the Jews to be good: "The Jews do not experience (the harshness of) the Exile here... and if many Jews are seen congregated together... this does not arouse anger."

Rabbi Obadiah recorded that the greatest trouble for the Jews of Jerusalem was actually a communal one, perpetrated by the class of leaders known as 'the elders,' of whom he wrote: "All of them are uncouth misanthropic, and think only of their personal profit." It seems it was common knowledge among Jerusalem's Jews that these 'elders' collaborated with the authorities to the detriment of elderly childless widows, whose worldly possessions, according to Islamic law, would become the property of the state upon their deaths. Payment for

"The Temple will be built quickly in our day," illustration in the Sarajevo Haggada, Catalonia, mid-fourteenth century. Through the entrance to the Temple are depicted the Ark with cherubs' wings over it and the Tablets of the Law resting within

pointing out such women to the authorities, came in the form of a portion of the confiscated estate. The 'elders' claimed that monies from these sources were used to reduce the debt incurred in establishing the synagogue, however the debt endured "forever," in an unreduced state. Those same elders were the government's representatives for tax collection among the Jews, and no means of collection, however despicable, was beneath them.

In Rabbi Obadiah's estimation, the diminished state of the Jewish community of Jerusalem was directly attributable to the immoral character and evildoings of the 'elders.' Both Ashkenazim and Sephardim left the city in great numbers, and only the poorest remained, many of whom were women. The 'elders' stooped even to selling Torah scrolls and synagogue ritual objects to non-Jews, who would resell them in other lands.

Rabbi Obadiah offers descriptions of Jerusalem which parallel the accounts of other travellers and pilgrims of his time. He remarks favorably on the cool and beautiful bazaars of the city, mentioning four: a main market, the spice market, the vegetable market, and a fourth "for all manner of cooked foods and bread." Three kinds of honey were available in Jerusalem: bee, carob and grape. However date honey was not to be found, nor were fresh dates, and this surprised him. Even in Jericho (known in the Bible as "the city of datepalms") they were not available.

Rabbi Obadiah described the period of his visit as a peaceful time under Mamluk rule. The land's residents related well to strangers and those who did not speak the vernacular. Jerusalem was filled with gentile visitors who spoke "all the languages of the nations." They came from the East, and even from Ethiopia. Muslims and Christians came to visit their holy sites. Jewish pilgrims came from Egypt, Damascus, Aleppo and other places. There were even Jews who had come from Aden, a place which Rabbi Obadiah thought to be the location of the Garden of Eden, and which is in all likelihood modern-day Aden and Yemen.

The Christians of Jerusalem he described as belonging to one of five groups: Latins, Greeks, Jacobites, Armenians and Ethiopians. As he described it, each group rejected the faith of the other, and they guarded against one another in the Church of the Holy Sepulcher.

Rabbi Obadiah noted that Jews were not permitted on the Temple Mount or in its mosques. He recorded a description he had heard – that the interiors of the mosques were splendid, for all the Muslim rulers had endowed in them rooms lined with gold. About the Western Wall Rabbi Obadiah observed, "Its stones are very large and thick. I have never seen such large stones in any other building, not in Rome or anywhere else."

The account of Rabbi Obadiah of Bertinoro at times depicts reality in overly rosy terms. He no doubt wished to convey a positive message in his letters to Italy, and turned a blind eye to certain hardships. It is likely that his attitutde to Jews, Christians and Muslims was influenced by the treatment he received by one or another official. This might account for the great variation between his description of Jerusalem and that of a Bohemian Christian pilgrim, Martin Kabatnik who visited the city only three years later than Rabbi Obadiah. He described, "Christians and Jews totally impoverished, and the infidels (Muslims) exploit them in different ways." Kabatnik supplied the detail that a Jew whose house fell into ruin was not permitted to build a new one, but only to rent again and again from his Muslim landlord. The Jew was not permitted to make repairs to the house. Jews and Christians could wear only ragged garments, and could not carry metal tools or utensils, but only those made of wood or clay.

A Russian pilgrim, the monk Zosima, who visited Jerusalem in the early fifteenth century, wrote an account paralleling the difficult conditions for foreigners and Christians mentioned by Kabatnik. In his words, "because of wicked Arabs, we barely managed to reach holy Jerusalem." He remained in Jerusalem all summer, for he was unable to leave the confines of the city. "For if a man reach Jerusalem and see the Sepulcher of Our Lord, because of wicked Arabs who beat him without mercy, he cannot pass beyond Jerusalem."

Rabbi Obadiah of Bertinoro was well received in Jerusalem; even the notorious 'elders' of whom he wrote, did not bother him. He became a teacher of Torah and continued to write his great commentary on the Mishnah, which he finished in Jerusalem, where he lived out his long life. The exact year of his death is not known, but apparently he lived to the end of the Mamluk period (1516).

Golden candelabrum with two olive trees from which oil is poured via golden pipes. A depiction of the vision of Zechariah.
Illustration from the Cervera Bible, Spain 1300

Rabbi Obadiah did not depict a time in which the Jews of Jerusalem lived in their glory. Rabbis and scholars did not flock to the city, nor were any masterworks of Jewish culture produced. Still, Jewish settlement in Jerusalem during the Mamluk period can be viewed as connecting a great past and a hopeful future. There is a clear continuity of Jewish settlement in Jerusalem from the mid-thirteenth century until the present day.

The Longing for Jerusalem in Late Medieval Jewish Thought

In the aftermath of the Black Death the political and social position of European Jews plunged dramatically. In less than one hundred years, from 1349 onward, both Ashkenazi and Sephardi Jewry, each of which by that time had developed a distinctive subculture within Judaism, suffered traumas which wrought great changes in their thinking and actions. Across the lands of Ashkenaz (primarily the German Rhineland and adjacent areas of Germany and France) the downturn in the status of Jewish communities which had begun after the first crusade, reached new depths. Ashkenazi Jews suffered from Christian persecution on a hitherto unknown scale. From 1391 onward the situation of the Jews of Spain worsened rapidly as well, as a period of bloody Christian persecutions and forced conversions occurred.

In both these significant Diaspora Jewish populations, harsh realities stimulated a turn in intellectual trends from the rational to the mystical; interest in kabbalah grew. Longing for Eretz Israel, and for Jerusalem in particular, found expression in literary works in which the hope of Redemption in Zion was the major theme. In the last half of the thirteenth century, a number of outstanding Ashkenazi and Sephardi rabbinic scholars, emigrated and settled in Eretz Israel, or tried to do so. Knowledge of this activity lent greater weight to the general rise in expectation of the Redemption.

The Sephardi scholar Nahmanides' ideas differed from a commonly accepted idea that the obligation of a Jew to move to Eretz Israel was linked to the coming of the messiah, and thus practical action toward realizing that ideal could wait until the messianic era. Nahmanides proposed a more activist position, namely that it was the

"Next year in Jerusalem." The last page of the Birds' Head Haggada, the oldest illuminated Haggada of Ashkenaz, late thirteenth century. Instead of human heads, the figures have birds' heads, with exaggerated beaks. Jerusalem is depicted as a Gothic castle

obligation of a Jew to live in Eretz Israel no matter what historical period he lived in, and irrespective of whether or not the messiah had come. To Nahmanides the obligation to reside in Eretz Israel, preferably in Jerusalem, was not time-dependent. The commandments and obligations of the Torah could be completely fulfilled only in Eretz Israel; only there, and particularly in Jerusalem, could mystical or prophetic experience (the apex of the spritual experience) be realized. It is not surprising that one of Nahmanides students could later write that the massive *aliyah* ('going up') of the Jewish people to Eretz Israel and Jerusalem was a necessary condition for the coming of Redemption. Without its happening first, the messianic era would not come.

Rabbi Hasdai Crescas, one of the great intellects of late fourteenth century Spain, contended that Jerusalem was chosen as God's holiest spot because of its geophysical properties. The offering of sacrifices in Jerusalem had a strong impact upon the Upper World, and brought down spiritual power which made Jerusalem a place suited for human spirituality and excellence. Crescas devoted a good deal of thought to the subject of prayer, and maintained that prayer offered up in Jerusalem was especially efficacious, if somewhat paradoxical in nature. So dense with the Divine was the atmosphere of Jerusalem, that people there were too awestruck to utter meaningful words of prayer. Yet God is particularly attentive to prayers offered up in Jerusalem, as an act of lovingkindness on His part. To Crescas, Jerusalem is the most fitting locale for true joy, and joy is a necessary precondition to worship.

Among Ashkenazi scholars of the period, a great longing for Jerusalem can also be detected. Rabbi Meir of Rothenberg would bow during prayer whenever Jerusalem was mentioned. After he had recited his nightly devotion prior to sleep, he would recite the 122

Psalm: "I rejoiced when they said to me, we are going to the House of the Lord. Our feet stood inside your gates, O Jerusalem, Jerusalem built up, a city knit together, to which tribes would make pilgrimage, the tribes of the Lord..." These words which expressed his hope of reaching Jerusalem, were the last thing he said each night. In 1286, five years before the fall of Acre, the last crusader outpost in Eretz Israel, Rabbi Meir of Rothenburg attempted to reach Eretz Israel, together with members of his family, and at the head of a group of settlers who were followers (see p. 149). The journey was undertaken even though there was a common awareness that the end of the Crusader Kingdom was near, and the future of Eretz Israel was uncertain.

After the Black Death, certain Ashkenazi scholars went up to Jerusalem and established a yeshiva there. German Jewish scholars who came to Jerusalem to study at this yeshiva met scholars from other places, and in this manner Ashkenazi thinkers first encountered Sephardi mysticism. A leading scholar of the yeshiva was Rabbi Isaac *Asir Tikva* (Prisoner of Hope), whose very name belied his attitude toward Jerusalem. The tale of an Ashkenazi Jew of Austria also indicates the grip Jerusalem had upon the mind of Ashkenazi Jewry. An Austrian Jew wrote of his dream that a great catastrophe was about to befall the Jews of Austria. There was only one way to avert it, and this was to choose twelve of the greatest Austrian

A depiction of the destruction of Jerusalem and the Temple going up in flames, Hartman map, 1439. Alongside the Temple are depicted Christian and Muslim structures

rabbis, send them for a year's sojourn in Eretz Israel and especially Jerusalem, where they would pray and beseech God as they stood beside the graves of scholars, and where they would study Torah. Engaging in these activities in Jerusalem had the power to avert an evil decree.

The End of Mamluk Rule

Mamluk rule weakened with the passage of time, both from economic decline and growing political instability. Confronted by threats on any number of occasions, the Mamluks managed to overcome them until their nemesis emerged from the north: the Ottomans Turks. The Ottomans did not at first turn their attention toward the Mamluk realm; they attacked Byzantium and southeastern Europe, and in 1453 conquered Constantinople. Then in 1512 the Ottoman sultan Selim I defeated the Shah of Persia, and thereafter turned his attentions upon the Mamluks. Selim had established a modern army replete with the newest technological advances in warfare: rifles and cannon. In addition, he built up a large navy which sailed the Mediterranean Sea.

The Mamluks were armed with their tried and true weaponry – swords, spears, bows and arrows. They did not realize that a new age in warfare had dawned.

Mamluk forces headed by eighty year old sultan Kantsu al-Ghawri were fooled by Selim in a battle which took place in northern Syria, a frontier zone between the Mamluk and Ottoman kingdoms. The Ottomans were waiting for the Mamluks, their heavy weaponry trained down upon them. On the 24th of August 1517 the Mamluk sultan and many of his officers lost their lives or were captured. Selim I marched southward across Syria-Palestine, all the way to Cairo. The entire area of this route was conquered by the end of 1516, and the Mamluk empire was absorbed into the newer entity, the Ottoman Empire.

In Syria-Palestine two battles associated with this war occurred, one near Beth Shean and the other south of Gaza. Both resulted in Mamluk losses. Jerusalem stood totally unprotected and had no choice but to surrender. Selim I was well received by Jerusalem's populace. He stayed for two days in the city and its vicinity, including Hebron, and then went on his way. With this Jerusalem was launched upon yet another new era, the Ottoman period, which was to last for four hundred years.

UNDER OTTOMAN RULE

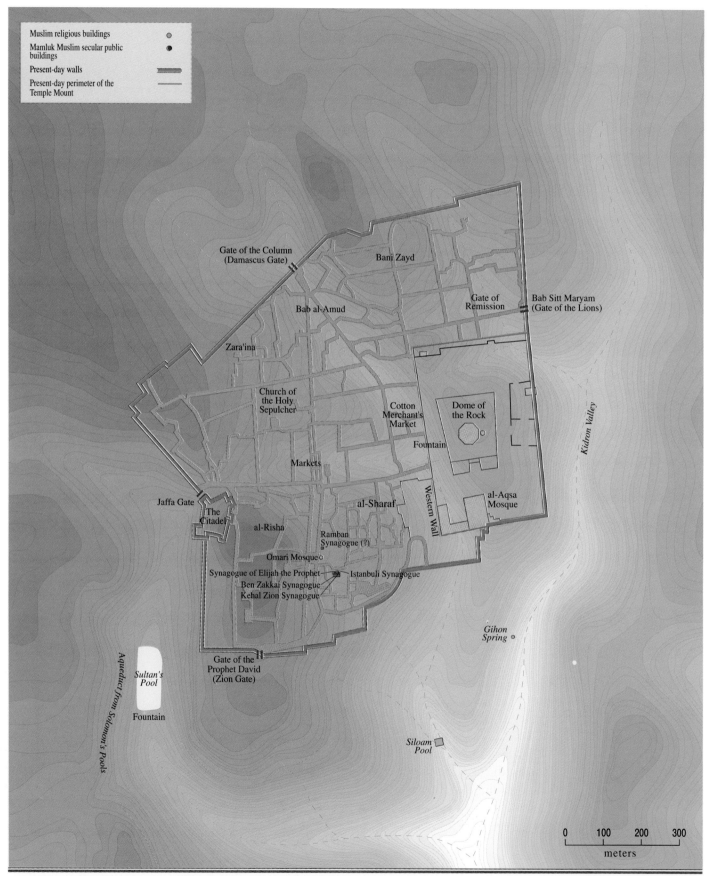

Muslim religious buildings
Mamluk Muslim secular public buildings
Present-day walls
Present-day perimeter of the Temple Mount

Gate of the Column
(Damascus Gate)

Bani Zayd

Gate of Remission

Bab Sitt Maryam
(Gate of the Lions)

Bab al-Amud

Zara'ina

Church of
the Holy
Sepulcher

Cotton
Merchant's
Market

Dome of
the Rock

Fountain

Markets

al-Aqsa
Mosque

Western Wall

Jaffa Gate

al-Sharaf

The
Citadel

al-Risha

Ramban
Synagogue (?)

Omari Mosque

Synagogue of Elijah the Prophet
Ben Zakkai Synagogue
Kehal Zion Synagogue

Istanbuli Synagogue

Gihon
Spring

Gate of the
Prophet David
(Zion Gate)

Aqueduct from Solomon's Pools

Sultan's
Pool

Fountain

Siloam
Pool

Kidron Valley

0   100   200   300

meters

Jerusalem during the Early Ottoman Period (16th - 18th centuries)

The restored Rabban Johanan ben Zakkai synagogue in the Jewish Quarter of Jerusalem's Old City was founded in the early Ottoman period and named for the revered Second Temple period scholar

Ottoman rule over Jerusalem commenced in 1517 and can be divided into three periods, the last of which coincided roughly with the nineteenth century, and will be treated in a separate chapter. The earlier two are of unequal length, the first a period of some fifty years initiated by the Ottoman conquest, and the second spanning some two hundred years. The initial period was one of reconstruction and fortification for Jerusalem, and was a prosperous time for the city. In the second and far longer period, Jerusalem receded to the position it had had in former centuries: that of a political and economic backwater on the fringe of the desert.

The Ottoman empire in general experienced its finest era during the sixteenth century. Its great military achievements occurred during that period as its armies conquered lands from North Africa to the frontiers of Iran, and from the Black Sea to southern Arabia. Its leadership had a grip on economic and political conditions of the empire. After the sixteenth century Ottoman power gradually dissipated. The central authority's former involvement in the affairs of the empire shrank, administration became provincial and more subject to political and economic corruption.

For many years the situation of Jews within the Muslim Ottoman empire compared favorably with the condition of Jews in Christian Europe. Many Jews of Spain, after the expulsion in 1492, sought refuge in North Africa, first in Portuguese-controlled areas and after the Inquisition reached them, in the Muslim environment of Ottoman-held territories. They were invited by the Ottoman Sultan Bayezid (father of Sultan Selim I, conqueror of Jerusalem) to settle within his realm, and many did so. Rabbi Eliahu Capsali, a member of the veteran Jewish population in the Ottoman Empire and a contemporary of the expulsion, wrote of the Ottomans: "They received all the Jews pleasantly. They had protection day and night... there came to the Ottoman Empire thousands and myriads of the expelled Jews so that the country... was filled with them."

Some Spanish exiles travelled through Ottoman territory to reach Eretz Israel and Jerusalem. Beginning in the sixteenth century there is considerable information regarding the presence in Jerusalem of scholars who were the driving force behind the spiritual life and creativity of the Jews of the city. When the Ottoman empire began to decline, the situation of the Jews deteriorated as well.

Suleiman the Magnificent

A major attraction of visitors to modern Jerusalem are the impressive 2.4 miles of Old City walls. They are generally assumed to date back thousands of years,

Aerial view of the Old City walls of Jerusalem, looking north. The walls were rebuilt during the sixteenth century upon the initiative of the Ottoman sultan, Suleiman the Magnificent

however they are approximately five hundred years old, and were built during the early period of Ottoman rule. Sultan Suleiman, the son of Sultan Selim I ordered the rebuilding of Jerusalem's walls. From the perspective of Jerusalem's history, Suleiman can be added to the roster of its master builders, for during his reign imposing and monumental structures were constructed, and the city took on a new look which has been preserved for centuries. Suleiman, known in the west as 'the Magnificent,' reigned for almost fifty years (1520-1566) and is known for his military achievements, the legal system he instituted, and his building activities throughout the empire.

Suleiman's engineers and constuction workers were active at many sites in Jerusalem. Among others, they refurbished the religious structures on the Temple Mount, built new markets and rebuilt older ones, overhauled the aqueduct south of the city and the reservoir near Mount Zion, which took on the name 'Suleiman's Pools,' today *Breikhat Hasultan* ('the sultan's pool'). Near the reservoir, a *sabil* (or elaborately designed water fountain) was built which provided drinking water for man and beast. Additional *sabils* were built on the Temple Mount and its surrounding area. A new *hammam* (bathhouse) was erected, and the poor were provided with a free soup kitchen, part of the large

*This **sabil** (fountain) near the Sultan's Pool was erected in 1536-37. It is one of six built by Suleiman the Magnificent.*
Its water supply came via an ancient aqueduct from Solomon's Pools near Bethlehem

institution for the poor built on the initiative of the Sultan's wife, Roxelana.

Suleiman's most conspicuous contribution to Jerusalem, however, was the great wall surrounding the city – the first to be erected since the thirteenth century. Because of it, Jerusalem was once again a fortified city. The northern sector of the wall is 1,398 yards long; the western sector, 962 yards, the southern sector, 1,221 yards; and the eastern sector 838 yards. Its construction was remarkable in several respects, not least of which was the speed with which the work was accomplished. The major part was done in only five years, from 1537 to 1541, using local materials. Hundreds of workers carried out the construction; the walls by and large followed the course of earlier city walls, whose vestiges were still visible in the form of sometimes massive foundation courses and the lower courses of defense towers.

Simultaneously with the construction of the walls, repairs went forward on the Citadel or Tower of David, as it was popularly designated – an important feature of the

city's fortification system. It abuts from the western facade of the city walls, just south of the Jaffa Gate. The Ottoman garrison was stationed in the Citadel and from it dominated the city and the surrounding area.

Suleiman's walls followed the topographical contours of the city; their relative height above sea-level changes from place to place. Thus, for instance, to the northwest of the city, the site of the today's New Gate, the height of the wall is 2,580 ft. above sea level, while near the Dung Gate, it is only 2,400 ft. above sea-level. At a number of places above the gates the builders left inscriptions in praise of Sultan Suleiman, by whose grace and financial support the work was executed.

Suleiman expressed the wish that large gates be inserted in the wall which could be locked at night. The gates were designed in a highly stylized manner reflecting the conventional Ottoman architectural characteristics of the sixteenth century. The most prominent of them is the Jaffa Gate, in Arabic, *Bab al-Khalil*, the Hebron Gate. It was erected in 1538 and faces west, at the meeting point of southern-facing and western-facing sections of the city wall. The area around Jaffa Gate was a hub of commercial and public activities of Ottoman Jerusalem. The gate's proximity to the Citadel lent it great importance.

Another prominent gate was located in the northern sector of the city wall, and is today called the Damascus Gate, then called the Neapolis or Nablus Gate, or in Arabic, *Bab al-Amud* (Gate of the Column). Above it is an inscription dedicated to the one who "commanded the building of this blessed wall... Suleiman, son of Selim Khan, may Allah preserve his reign."

Another gate in the northern wall is Herod's Gate, in Arabic *Bab al-Zahra* or Flower Gate, which possibly derives from 'Sahira' – the site of the Resurrection in Muslim tradition and the name of a nearby Muslim cemetery.

Another gate is the Lions' Gate, the only opening in the eastern facade of the city walls. Its date of construction (1538/39) appears in an inscription on the lintel. Its name is derived from the two lions (actually leopards) which appear in the facade on either side of the gate, and which were the insignia of Baybars, the thirteenth century Mamluk conqueror.

Like the Lion's Gate, the Gate of Mercy was also located in the eastern wall. Its double-arched entryway was sealed. This gate is regarded as sacred in all three religions which revere Jerusalem: Judaism, Christianity, and Islam. It seems that the Ottoman builders of the walls did not want to tamper with these traditions and preferred not to open it, despite the fact that it provides easy access to the Temple Mount.

Two gates were erected in the southern sector of the wall: the Dung Gate not far from the Western Wall, and the Zion Gate, close to the southwestern corner of the city wall. The Zion Gate is called in Arabic *Bab al-Nabi Daud* (the Gate of the Prophet David – King David) as it opens onto Mount Zion, regarded since Byzantine times as the burial site of King David. It was also known as the

Gate of the Jewish Quarter, as it provided access to the sector of the city where Jews lived.

Evidently an essential reason for Suleiman's re-fortification of the city was the threat posed by Bedouin incursions. The nomads would emerge from the

The Tower of David, in the western facade of the city walls. It stands on foundations that go back to the Second Temple period. The minaret, added by the Ottomans, has become the most distinctive visual element of the fortress tower. Pilgrims and visitors to Jerusalem associated the minaret with the biblical verse "Your neck is like the Tower of David..." (Song of Songs 4:4)

An imaginative depiction of Jerusalem: detail from 'Jesus in the garden of Olives' by the Renaissance artist
Andrea della Mantegna 1431-1506

nearby Judean desert to raid the city, threaten the lives of its inhabitants – and subject the city's rulers to ridicule. The desert was also an entry route for marauders from across the Jordan River. Another perhaps even greater concern of Suleiman's was the massive development of the Venetian fleet which might well have initated a course of events in which Christian longings combined with the varying aspirations of popes and merchants to result in a new crusade for Jerusalem. Wishing to make Jerusalem an unattractive target, Suleiman put up the massive walls.

Ottoman Jerusalem: Society and Economy

Two major Ottoman undertakings, the reconstruction of Jerusalem's walls and the refurbishment of its water supply system, were important factors in the economic development of the city. Indeed, the first few decades of Ottoman rule were years of prosperity. The Ottomans

saw themselves as the rising power that bridged three continents, Europe, Asia, and Africa, and all the trade routes associated with them. The commercial potential which their geographical position represented was not lost upon the Ottomans; economic matters were at the forefront of their interests.

The general Ottoman interest in reaping the economic rewards of conquest was felt in Jerusalem, as its governors made efforts to encourage local industry and trade. The Ottomans built new markets and restored old ones which were in a decrepit state owing to prolonged neglect on the part of the Mamluks. There were olive presses, flour mills and workshops for producing weapons, and various industries developed alongside them, one of the most prominent being the manufacture of soap.

Travellers and pilgrims continued to reach the country, and some of them left descriptions of Jerusalem and its inhabitants during this period. Ulrich Prefat was a Czech traveller who visited Jerusalem in the mid-sixteenth century. From his memoirs, we learn that many

Syrian Arabs and Christians, the latter including Catholics, Greeks, Armenians, Jacobites, and Ethiopians, lived side by side with the Ottomans. There were also a large number of Jews who occupied a street of their own. "There are no rich people in Jerusalem," remarks Prefat. The Ottomans did not allow Christians or Jews to accumulate wealth, though the Christians enjoyed greater freedom of action.

There were four population censuses in Jerusalem in Suleiman's time, which provide many instructive details relating to the inhabitants of the city in the sixteenth century. According to the first census, held in 1525-1526, there were 5,607 people living in Jerusalem, of whom two-thirds were Muslims (3,369), a fifth Jews (1,194) and an eighth Christians (714).

Thirteen years later, during 1538-1539, the number of Jews in Jerusalem were 1,363 (14.5%), 884 Christians (9.5%), and 7,117 Muslims (76%) – in all, 9,364 souls. From this data, it appears that although the number of Jews and Christians increased, their proportion within

The Damascus Gate (alt. Nablus Gate, Shechem Gate) with its ornate crenellations is perhaps the most elegant in appearance of all the gates built by Suleiman the Magnificent

The Jewish longing for Jerusalem as expressed in a woven synagogue ark curtain, Venice, seventeenth century

the entire population diminished. This was attributable to the greater number of Muslims returning to the city, apparently those inhabitants who had fled during the conquest and had not been present during the first census. Another fifteen years passed, and in the year 1553-1554, the city had a population of nearly 16,000 people. The Jewish inhabitants reached their peak at the time, with 1,958 souls (12%) the number of Christians was almost identical, 1,956 souls, and the Muslims numbered more than 12,000, keeping their proportion of three quarters of the city's population. The last census during the reign of Sultan Suleiman was taken in 1562-63. There was a certain decline in the number of the inhabitants of all religious denominations. Out of 15,066 inhabitants, there were 1,434 Jews (9.5%) 1,830 Christians (12%) and 11,802 Muslims (78%). This downward trend continued during the next generations,

as the glorious reign of Suleiman became a distant memory.

In addition to the permanent Muslim community, there were also many mystics and pilgrims crowding into the city, encouraged by Ottoman efforts to cultivate Jerusalem's reputation as a religious center. Christians and Jews were considered *dhimmi* (see p. 105) and were subject to the poll tax (*jizya*). There were no restrictions on their business dealings. Nevertheless, beginning in the second half of the sixteenth century, when the authority of the central government in Istanbul (the Ottoman name for Constantinople) began to wane, an increasing number of irregular taxes were imposed on Jerusalem's non-Muslim inhabitants, which at times amounted to exploitation and blackmail.

The largest Christian community was the Greek Orthodox. Most of its adherents were natives of

Syria-Palestine whose lifestyle was similar to that of the Muslims. The second largest Christian community was the Armenian. They lived in a separate quarter and preserved a distinct character. The third group was the Catholic community, most of whom were Latins of European origin, among them many monks, mainly Franciscans, who were appointed by the pope as guardians of the holy sites of the Holy Land. For hundreds of years, the various Christian sects carried on an internecine struggle over the rights of each over Christian holy places, particularly the Church of the Holy Sepulcher.

A rich source of information concerning life in Jerusalem in general and of the various sects and communities in particular, has recently been made available to scholars: the records of the local Muslim court in the city, the *Sijill*. In the sixteenth century, these courts dealt with every aspect of life – economic and social, the functioning of the civil service, religious institutions, quarrels between members of the public and between a husband and wife (or wives), and naturally litigation concerning debts, commercial conflicts and questions of inheritance. Details emerge from the court protocols which shed light on social and economic phenomena in Jerusalem during the Ottoman period. Thus, for instance, forty shops were rented in the 'new market' completed in 1563. They were divided almost equally among the Muslims (14) Christians (13) and Jews (13). At the time, the Jews of Jerusalem were less than ten percent of the population and the Christians slightly more. The explanation for this distribution, which gave preference to Jews and Christians, evidently lies in their noted familiarity with the commercial world, which can also be seen in other parts of the *Sijill*.

The Jewish Community in Jerusalem

During the sixteenth to eigtheenth centuries the Jews of Jerusalem were engaged in a range of typical occupations, from working-class to professional. There are records of Jewish physicians as well as cobblers, jewelers, cheesemakers and ironsmiths.

In 1521, Rabbi Moses Bassola made a pilgrimage to the Holy Land and in his painstaking travel account described the composition of the Jewish community:

The Elijah the Prophet Synagogue in the Jewish Quarter of the Old City dates to the early Ottoman period

"The community is of all kinds. There are fifteen Ashkenazi and Sephardi householders, and Mustaribs who were the indigenous Jewish inhabitants, and 'westerners' who came from the Berber area (i.e. Jews of North Africa)."

The Portuguese traveller Pontaleo de Aveiro who was in Jerusalem in 1565, tells of a visit he made to the synagogue during prayers for a holiday in the month of September (evidently the New Year or the Day of Atonement – Yom Kippur). "The synagogue is old, gloomier and more dreary than those I visited in all the countries of the East, but because of their holiday, (the Jews) adorn it with priceless fabrics embroidered with gold and silk, the likes of which they have in abundance in the Holy Land. For this purpose they receive donations not only from the Jews of Portugal and Spain, but from Jews in every corner of the earth."

Some sixty years later, the Italian Pietro Verniero describes Jewish society in Jerusalem: "They come from various places and countries. One may hear among them almost every language, though the most common is Castillian Spanish. They include Romaniotes, Italians, Germans, Poles, Russians, Greeks (former residents of) Dubrovnik (on the eastern shore of the Adriatic) and from all parts of Turkey and Persia." From these reports it is clear that Jerusalem's Jewish community comprised elements from many countries, in addition to those who were indigenous to the country. The latter, who had in the past been the dominant element in the community and provided its leadership, lost this status, to the Ashkenazi community. This shift in favor of the Ashkenazis had occurred even prior to the Ottoman conquest. The indigenous 'Eretz Israel' Jews found it difficult to tolerate immigrants whose mentality was so different from their own. As a result there was constant tension between them, particularly with the increasing flow of immigrants toward the end of the sixteenth and beginning of the seventeenth centuries. This state of affairs was probably also due to the lower intellectual level of the indigenous Jews. Economically the indigenous Jews were the poorer element in the Jewish community, petty traders or peddlers. Eventually they assimilated into the Sephardi group.

Refugees of the expulsion of Spanish Jewry settled in Jerusalem, forming a large and distinctive minority. Among them were scholars who ranked among the top Jewish intellectuals of that generation. Rabbi Moses Bassola noted that the order of the synagogue service in Jerusalem's one permitted synagogue was akin to that of the Sephardim (Jews of Spain and Portugal). Evidently the Sephardi heritage of synagogue ritual and prayerbook liturgy was imposed by social coercion (threats of excommunication) on the rest of the community. With the passage of time the superior status of the Sephardis within the Jewish community of Jerusalem solidified. They were the social elite and left their imprint on the lifestyle and culture of the whole community, except for the Ashkenazis.

In the early sixteenth century the Ashkenazis formed one sixth of the Jewish community of Jerusalem. They preserved their uniqueness and conducted their lives as a separate entity. They were insistent on their right to send their own emissaries to collect donations in the Diaspora, and maintained their own institutions.

All dealings of Jews with the Ottoman authorities were handled by the Sephardi leadership; in this area the Ashkenazis were not independent. The Sephardis were responsible for the payment of taxes to the authorities, and this put them in the dominant position. As might have been expected, there were frequent quarrels between the Sephardi and Ashkenazi communities over the sums each group was required to pay.

The Relationship between Jews and the Central and Local Authorities

The Jews' relationship with the Ottoman authorities was complex. As far as the central authorities were concerned, the Jews were a single religious community belonging to the category of 'protected peoples.' They enjoyed protection in exchange for the payment of a poll tax. It can be inferred from decrees issued by the central authorities to the governors of Jerusalem that the local authorities frequently imposed extra restrictions and humiliating decrees on the Jews. Often the leaders of the Jewish community would ask the Jews of Istanbul to plead for them before the central authorities, and at times they even appealed directly to the sultan's court. The more the influence of the central authorities waned, the greater the pressure of the local authorities on the Jewish community of Jerusalem, to the point where synagogues and communal property were confiscated.

The local Muslim community was also oppressive toward the Jews, on occasion. The Jewish cemetery on the Mount of Olives was part of a Muslim religious foundation (*wakf*) which demanded high rent for its use, while the Jews considered that they had the right to bury their dead at the site. Another area of contention had its origins in the Mamluk period. The Ramban synagogue was very close to the al-Amri mosque, and Muslims attempted to oust the Jews from the synagogue, claiming part ownership and complaining that the Jews "raise their voices in words of heresy in the synagogue every morning and evening." The central authorities accepted the Jewish claim that the synagogue had been there before the mosque, and allowed them to use it. But in 1587 the ruling was reversed when the *kadi* of Jerusalem issued an order barring Jews from praying in their synagogue. At the same time a decree of the sultan was published declaring that Jews could not build new synagogues. From that time onward, the Jews of Jerusalem were obliged to pray in private homes and later on in schools, which in the course of time became prayer sites. This was the history of the four attached Sephardi synagogues which are a popular site for visitors in the modern-day Jewish Quarter of the Old City.

The Muslims of Jerusalem frequently treated the Jews with contempt. Rabbi Israel of Perugia, Italy, wrote in 1520: "Their (the Muslims') hatred is great, for they have slandered and plotted against us this year and we thought they would expel us from the country, had it not been for the mercy of Heaven." The Jews collected a large sum "in order to placate the anger of the masters of the country." The money was borrowed on interest from rich Muslims "and the interest grew from day to day." The Jews of Europe had to come to the aid of their brethren in Jerusalem.

Leadership of the Jewish Community

The Ottoman conquest led to the abolition in Egypt of the institution of *nagid*, which had been the government appointed medium answerable for the Jewish communities in Egypt, Syria-Palestine and Syria. The

The messiah before the gates of Jerusalem - a page from the Washington Haggada, Florence, Italy, 1478

conquest also brought about an end of the domination of the 'elders,' however in the sixteenth century, 'the eldest of the Jews' (*sheikh al-yahud*), still stood at the head of the Jerusalem community. In the second half of the century, that position was voided of all meaningful content. A new institution was set up – the *parnassim*, (leaders) who were chosen by the socially prominent Jewish circle – generally members of the wealthier families. The role of the *parnassim* was to collect taxes and decide on matters of finance, bans of excommunication, etc. When they had difficulty fulfilling their function, the *parnassim* were aided by the 'seven good men of the city', seven notables who, were guarantors for the community's debts. Another

An Ottoman fortress west of the Old City walls

important office was that of *dayan* (judge) who was responsible for the Jewish communal judicial system of Jerusalem.

The changes in the appointment of decision-making roles led to a division between the 'secular' and 'religious' leadership. Among the Ashkenazis, the institution of the rabbi became defined while in the Sephardi community, the analogue was the *hacham* or sage. Each group had its rabbi or sage who acted as the authority for religious and judicial decisions for the group. This was a salaried position chosen by the *parnassim* of the community.

The Jewish community saw to the orderly functioning of its various institutions: the synagogue and bakery, kosher slaughter, and provision for funerals and burial.

It also maintained an educational system which included schools for young children (*Talmud Torah*) and a yeshiva for adults. Voluntary community welfare institutions cared for the poor and sick.

Muhammed Ibn Faroukh's Reign of Terror

In the late sixteenth century and throughout the seventeenth, the condition of Jerusalem and its inhabitants worsened. The prosperous days of the early Ottoman period passed, owing in part to the rising power of the Bedouin. The Ottoman rulers had restrained them for many years, however the Bedouin eventually gained strength, attacked and plundered villages and towns, and plagued pilgrims on the roads. Even caravans of Muslim pilgrims on their way to Mecca and Medina were not safe. The situation worsened further when the Bedouin gained access to firearms, which had formerly been the province only of Ottoman soldiers.

The governors of Jerusalem strove with only partial success to defend the city. The Turkish troops shut themselves up in the Citadel and other fortresses in the area, and travel on intercity roads became very dangerous. The economy deteriorated and Jerusalem's population began to shrink. A time of particular trouble occurred early in the seventeenth century under the governor Muhammed Ibn Faroukh. He imposed heavy taxes on the city's inhabitants, particularly the Jews, some of whom he arrested and had tortured. It is known that he arrested prosperous Jews and seized their assets. There is also a record of his having forced Jews to dig defensive trenches before the walls of Jerusalem, apparently because he suspected that the sultan would send another governor to Jerusalem to replace him. During this period the number of Jewish inhabitants in Jerusalem dropped from 3,000 to 1,000.

Ibn Faroukh was finally dismissed, an eventuality which resulted from the intervention of the Jews of Istanbul on behalf of their brethren in Jerusalem. It took the Jews of Jerusalem a long time to repay debts they had incurred in an effort to pay Faroukh's exhorbitant demands. Emissaries were sent to every corner of the Jewish world to ask for assistance for their brethren in the holy city.

Safed and Jerusalem

The sixteenth century saw the rise to prominence of the Galilee town of Safed. Its Jewish community began vying with that of Jerusalem for the status of leading Jewish community of Eretz Israel. The contention between the two had an impact upon Jewish scholarship, culture, and the dynamics of charitable donations, far beyond the confines of Eretz Israel.

Safed is far north of Jerusalem and not far from Syria proper. It became prosperous as an outcome of the Ottoman takeover of the land, benefitting from new links with commercial centers in Syria and Egypt. The Jewish community of Safed which had been insignificant earlier, became a major cultural and economic entity when it swelled with Sephardis – Jewish refugees of the Spanish and Portuguese expulsions, who chose the pristine mountain location for several reasons. It was the town of Jewish population closest to Syria and the land route by which Jews arrived in Eretz Israel from other parts of the Ottoman Empire, and by which goods were transported. Also, Safed was not sacred to any other faith, and the

*The courtyard of a **khan**, or roadside inn built early in the Ottoman period for use by travellers coming to Jerusalem from the south*

exiles would not have to endure a tense and contentious atmosphere, with all that that could imply. Finally, Safed was close to the burial sites of rabbinic sages. In particular, the tomb of Rabbi Shimon bar Yohai, regarded as the author of the central mystical work, the Zohar, was in nearby Meron (see p.160). The Jewish community of Safed established a broad economic and social base, and prospered. Although the many scholars in the community depended upon charity, many Jews engaged in trade and commerce.

By contrast, Jerusalem's Jewish community was much more dependent upon charity, and the city was enduring hard times owing to the disruptive activity of the Bedouin and the policies of Ibn Faroukh (see above). During the sixteenth century Safed's Jews embarked upon a brilliant cultural period, while in Jerusalem this was not the case. In Safed there resided a number of great rabbis and kabbalists who ultimately achieved wide impact in the Jewish world well beyond Eretz Israel. Among them were the giant of Jewish mysticism Rabbi Isaac Luria (known as "*Ari Hakadosh*" The Saintly Lion,) Rabbi Solomon Alkabetz, composer of the liturgical poem *Lecha Dodi* still sung in synagogues worldwide on Sabbath eve, Rabbi Joseph Caro, author of the great codification of Jewish Law the *Shulchan Aruch*, and Rabbi Jacob Berab, who took the major step of attempting to re-establish the ancient institution of *semikhah* (ordination) by which high level Torah scholars had been ordained in ancient times.

Among Jewish scholars, Rabbi Jacob Berab's renewal of the *semikha* would have been immediately understood as having implications for the reconstituting of a Sanhedrin, and the intiation of a process leading to the Redemption. It was highly controversial. The common view was that the Redemption was to be patiently and humbly awaited, not initiated. Also, it was viewed as an attempt to give the Safed community and its rabbis superior standing over Jerusalem's. Jerusalem's rabbis entered the fray against Berab's move, and the two communities, Safed and Jerusalem, began a period of fierce dispute.

The argument had implications for the distribution of charitable funds sent to Eretz Israel but not earmarked for a specific purpose. There were various formulae proposed for the division of these funds, and as might be expected, claims and counter-claims were brought before various rabbinic authorities in and beyond Eretz Israel (in Istanbul for instance).

For a time Safed's Jews basked in prosperity. Scholars and schools relocated there, and Jewish culture flourished. During the latter half of the seventeenth century, however, people began to leave Safed for economic reasons. The centers of wool production in the East, of which Safed was one of the most prominent, lost importance with the rise of wool manufacture in Western Europe. This led to the migration of many Jews to Jerusalem, among them scholars and their schools. The generation of kabbalists and well-known rabbis of Safed passed away, and their heirs did not attain their level of achievement.

As Safed's prestige decreased Jerusalem regained its role as the leading Jewish community of Eretz Israel. There was an influx of immigration which included rabbis and scholars. The outstanding personality in this group was Rabbi Jacob Hagiz, a native of Fez, Morocco, who travelled throughout the Ottoman empire and stimulated rabbis and public figures to settle in Jerusalem. He settled there in 1658, opening a talmudic academy which trained rabbis for the communities of Eretz Israel and the Diaspora.

Shabbetai Zevi in Jerusalem

Shabbetai Zevi was a messianic pretender who arose in Smyrna, Turkey in the seventeenth century and created a movement of great impact on Jews across Europe, Asia, and the Mediterranean basin. He was not the only claimant to messianic status in a long period of messianic ferment, however he was by far the one who attracted the most attention. He had a 'prophet,' one Nathan of Gaza, who went before him to visit communities and send instructions to many more, calling for harsh penitence. These calls awakened the ascetic zeal within many Jews and became a unifying element across broad geographical areas. In most places they were willingly accepted, and the

Portrait of Shabbetai Zevi

opponents to the idea that Zevi was the messiah had to suppress their serious reservations.

Jerusalem is of necessity central to any Jewish dreams of the Redemption and End of Days. The rise of Shabbetai Zevi coincided with the arrival in the city of many Jewish mystics. It coincided, for example, with the decline of Safed and the resettlement of many of its kabbalists in Jerusalem. The prior centuries had been ones of great persecution and disruption for Ashkenazi and Sephardi Jewry, and the cultural atmosphere within Jewry at such times was ripe for messianic longing. This would have been at least as true in Jerusalem as it was elsewhere in the Jewish world.

Shabbetai Zevi was thirty-three when he arrived in Jerusalem in 1662. He had become known in his native Smyrna for his ethereal manner and tender character, which tended to changeability. Contemporary descriptions allude to his periods of 'illumination,' when he was ready to perform great and revolutionary deeds, and periods when his 'visage was averted,' apparently times of depression, when he expressed humility and regret for the revolutionary deeds he had already performed. In Jerusalem Shabbetai Zevi behaved with persistent abstinence, prayed at the graves of the saints, and attracted followers among the common people as well as the scholars. The notables of the town were impressed by him and decided to send him to Egypt as a good-will emissary, to collect funds for the Jerusalem community. En route, he passed through Gaza and there made the acquaintance of Nathan ben Elisha, who from that time onward was given to prophecying and was called Nathan of Gaza. During a stay in Egypt, Zevi was given money for the Jerusalem community and married a woman called Sarah, a refugee from the Ukraine who miraculously survived the pogroms of 1648-49, (and had foretold of herself that she would marry the king messiah). Shabbetai Zevi returned to Jerusalem, where he was openly presented as the messiah of the Jewish people. Jews of Jerusalem followed him (no precise information exists as to how many did so) while others were extremely perplexed by the phenomenon. In Jerusalem Shabbetai Zevi publicly taught that the Jewish fast days of mourning for the destruction of the Temple and of Jerusalem, were to be abrogated. In so doing, he moved to eliminate commands and prohibitions of the halakha – and crossed a 'red line' well known to any

The only extant sample of the handwriting of Shabbetai Zevi, with his signature "Shabbetai Muhammed Zevi." (Collection, Ben-Zvi Institute)

educated Jew. The rabbis of Jerusalem warned him to recant his heresy, even while emissaries appointed by Nathan of Gaza and some self-appointed emissaries, went off to the Diaspora to spread the news of the messiah's arrival. In Jerusalem, Shabbetai Zevi refused to hand over the charity funds he had received in Egypt. The *parnassim* of the city and the rabbis cautioned him as to the consequences but to no avail. He was excommunicated in Jerusalem, and the heads of the community reported him to the Turkish governor. He fled to Gaza and from there sailed to Smyrna. Nathan of Gaza raged against the Jerusalemites and declared that Jerusalem was no longer a holy city and that Gaza had taken its place. Thus ended Shabbetai Zevi's physical involvement with Jerusalem. But Sabbateanism had many followers in Jerusalem and throughout the Jewish world for many years. (Shabbetai Zevi was eventually arrested by the Ottoman authorities and chose to convert to Islam, whereupon his movement for the most part collapsed, although it had reverberations through Jewish history for some time to come).

Pilgrims and Settlers in Jerusalem

Despite the hazards and arduousness of the journey, pilgrims and travellers of all the religions represented in Jerusalem continued to come to the city. The Franciscan monk, Eugene Roger, who visited the city in the 1630s, noted that pilgrims stemmed from all peoples, from every race and religious sect. He mentions Jews, Muslims, Christians (Catholics), Protestants (whom he called "radical secessionists") Greek Orthodox, Armenians, Copts, Ethiopians, natives of India, Yemen, Egypt, and the Barbary coast (North Africa) and other countries. Muslims vistors were permitted everywhere in Jerusalem and its environs and paid no special taxes. Jews and the Christians were obliged to pay a heavy tax and were allowed to enter Jerusalem for the first time only through the Damascus Gate – where they would have to identify themselves to the guards, state their ethnic group or religious sect, and wait until the head of their sect received an entry permit from the Pasha.

Jews continued to flow into the country, mainly from Spain and the East but also from parts of Central and Eastern Europe. The latter groups were Ashkenazis. Among the factors that led numbers of them to journey to Jerusalem to re-settle there, were the horrible Cossack pogroms of 1648-49 which swept the Ukraine and Poland, and the mood of messianic yearning touched off by Sabbateanism. Some were unable to adapt to life in Jerusalem and settled in other parts of the country or the Ottoman empire. Others returned to Eastern Europe. Hunger and disease took a toll among them. However, until their last moments, they were reluctant to leave Jerusalem.

A particularly large caravan of Ashkenazi immigrants arrived towards the end of the seventeenth century, headed by Rabbi Judah Hasid, a charismatic preacher and teacher of somewhat Sabbatean style who travelled from city to town in Poland calling for Jews to ascend to Jerusalem and await the messiah there. Early in 1699 he set out at the head of a large group of followers, stopping in Moravia, from where, together with the leaders of his entourage, he made a circuit of Austrian and German communities. The number of his followers grew steadily and reached some 1,300 souls. The size of the group contributed to a particularly lengthy journey to Jerusalem, which, according to some sources, accounted

for the deaths of hundreds of the travellers en route. Rabbi Judah Hasid and some three hundred of his followers arrived in Jerusalem in October 1700, and lodged in the 'Ashkenazi Courtyard.' Three days after their arrival, the rabbi took ill, and two after that, died. Internal squabbles ensued in his group, mainly between overt and the covert Sabbateans. Some of the new immigrants returned to Europe.

The debts of the Ashkenazi sub-community of Jerusalem were large even before they were obliged to absorb these new immigrants. They grew huge. Muslims who had lent money to Ashkenazi Jews demanded repayment and when it was not forthcoming, confiscated Jewish property. These complications continued for years and reached a climax in November 1720, when, on a Sabbath, Arabs broke into the synagogue in the 'Ashkenazi Courtyard,' burned sacred books, and had the leaders of the congregation arrested. The Muslims took control of the synagogue

Above: A widespread custom among Jewish pilgrims to Jerusalem during the Ottoman period was to set down an account of their visit, with illustrations, on a scroll
Below:
A scroll illustration depicting the Western Wall, the Temple Mount and David's Tomb

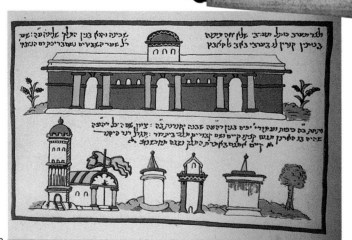

*The upper decorative panel of a 1732 **ketubah**, (Jewish marriage contract) from Padua, Italy features a depiction of Jerusalem and the Temple Mount*

building. Ashkenazi Jews were banned from Jerusalem pending the repayment of the communal debt, and for more than one hundred years Ashkenazis could not live in Jerusalem. When a new synagogue was finally erected on the same site in the mid-ninteenth century it was called 'Hurvat Judah Hasid' (The Ruins of Judah Hasid). It became a domed landmark, the central synagogue of the *Prushim* or disciples of the Gaon of Vilna.

In 1702, another group of Jews arrived in the city, led by Rabbi Abraham Rovigo of Modena, Italy. For the next two decades, there was a steady flow of immigrants, among them well-known biblical scholars: Rabbi Haim Ben Attar (author of the commentary *Or ha-Haim*) from Morocco; the Yemenite kabbalist Rabbi Shalom Sharabi (*ha-Rashash*); in the mid-eighteenth century, Rabbi Gershon of Kutov, the brother-in-law of the Ba'al Shem Tov, who moved to Jerusalem after first settling in

Hebron. For Rabbi Gershon settling in Jerusalem was no small matter, as he was an Ashkenazi. Like other Ashkenazi Jerusalemites, he was not officially known as an Ashkenazi, but appeared in the records as a Sephardi *haham*. In his wake, immigration of Hasidim from eastern Europe to Eretz Israel increased. Of particular note is a group of three hundred who arrived in 1777 headed by the revered hasidic leader, Rabbi Menahem Mendel of Vitebsk. They settled in Safed but after some time, some moved to Jerusalem.

Ties with the Diaspora

Rabbinic attitudes in sixteenth and seventeenth century Europe leaned toward viewing settlement in Eretz Israel and Jerusalem as a step toward Redemption – a positive perception – while in earlier times, the same movement of settlement might have been perceived as 'hastening the coming of the messiah' – a negative judgment. An atmosphere was fostered which was sympathetic to the migration of individuals and groups to Jerusalem for profoundly pious purposes, and the same atmosphere encouraged contributions for the upkeep of the Jews of Jerusalem, so that they could constantly pray and study, and in this manner foster conditions leading to messianic Redemption. In Jerusalem, the impoverished condition of the Jews coincided with growing demands of the Ottoman authorities. Appeals were sent out to the Diaspora, and arrangements organized for the regular collection of money. For instance, the community of Venice imposed an annual tax on its members for the Jews of Eretz Israel. Those who refused to contribute were punished. In other countries as well, organizations were set up and various systems introduced to collect money for the holy communities of Eretz Israel.

The permanent and continuous assistance on the part of Diaspora Jews gave rise to an adjustment of rabbinic attitudes and general outlook which justified contributions for the Jews of Eretz Israel. According to it, the holy Jewish communities in Jerusalem and Eretz Israel endured great privations and suffering in order to hasten the Redemption of the entire Jewish people (the common good). Hence sustenance was owed them. This same period saw a renewed emphasis on burial of the dead in Eretz Israel, in Jerusalem in particular. A folk belief widespread among Ashkenazis taught that Jews who were buried at a distance from Jerusalem would have to endure a kind of penitential 'rolling of the dead' all the way to Jerusalem, to achieve their resurrection in the messianic era. Hence it was better to be buried near the city, or at least in Eretz Israel, and spared this form of penitence for having lived a life outside the Holy Land.

These Diaspora attitudes influenced the Jews of Jerusalem to understand themselves in a noble way. They viewed their lives as a form of sacrifice for their people. The funds that arrived were not viewed as demeaning, but rather as compensation for forgoing the pleasures of this world.

A noteworthy Diaspora association which helped support the Jews of Jerusalem during the eighteenth century was the Istanbul Committee of Officials for Palestine, formed in 1727 to extricate the Jerusalem community from the entanglement they had landed in owing to the above-mentioned debts of the Ashkenazis. The Committee appointed officials whose function was to intervene with the Ottoman authorities and otherwise help with every aspect of the lives of the Jews of Jerusalem, including the appointment of rabbis and kosher slaughterers. In fact, these officials became the leaders of the Jewish community in Eretz Israel and Jerusalem. The fruit of their effort was the increase in the Jewish population of Jerusalem to 3,000 souls by the 1840s. Later on the impact of this organization was dissipated by quarreling between representatives in Constantinope and in Jerusalem and mismanagement of finances. This was all exacerbated by a general decline in conditions in Syria-Palestine at the end of the eighteenth century. Once again, the Jerusalem community had to resort to sending emissaries to collect donations from the Jews of the Diaspora. The best known of these was was Rabbi Hayyim Joseph David Azulai (*Ha-Hida*), a native of Jerusalem and one of its important sages.

Yeshivas in Jerusalem

According to the account of Rabbi Moses Bassola mentioned earlier in this chapter, in the transition between Mamluk and Ottoman rule, the character of the yeshivas in Jerusalem underwent change. Until then, it was not customary to categorize them on a sub-communal basis (Ashkenazi, Sephardi, etc.) but this changed. The manner of study and of reasoning also changed, under the influence of the Ashkenazi settlers. There is no written evidence of formal Torah study institutions in Jerusalem during the 1530s, however, in view of what is known of the later period, it

Rabbi Hayyim Joseph David Azulai (acronym: 'Hida') was a communal rabbi, bibliographer, and emissary on behalf of Jerusalem to Diaspora Jewish communities. He authored more than 150 works. His signature appears to the left of the portrait

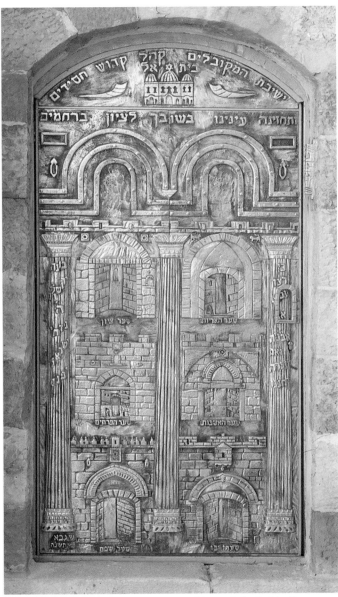

The entrance to the Bethel Yeshiva of the kabbalists.
The yeshiva is still functioning

is reasonable to assume that the number of such institutions grew with the influx of Jewish settlers. At the end of the sixteenth century a *takanah* (rabbinic dictum) was published originating in the court of Rabbi Isaac Shul'al, exempting Torah scholars from the tax burden placed on the Jewish community by the Ottoman authorities.

Various sources reveal that students at the yeshivas were adults, among them some of high reputation. Torah study was also engaged in outside the formal yeshivas, for all the householders met in synagogues during off-work hours. Financial support of the educational institutions was too heavy a burden on the Jerusalem community, and the Jerusalemites required the assistance of Jews of the Diaspora, as described above.

During the eighteenth century there were more than twenty yeshivas in Jerusalem, attended by hundreds of scholars. An outstanding example was the Bethel yeshiva established in 1737-1738. Its pupils studied kabbalah under Rabbi Shalom Sharabi (*ha-Rashash*). Most of the scholars came from the Sephardi community but, notably, they were joined by Rabbi Gershon of Kutov who headed the small Ashkenazi community. From this it can be inferred that there was collaboration between the different Jewish sub-communities, as Ashkenazis were forbidden to reside in Jerusalem.

During this time in the Ottoman period, Jerusalem became an important center of Torah study, and its rabbis received inquiries from all over the Diaspora on complex questions of interpretation of halakha. Jewish books were authored in Jerusalem and published in Istanbul, Smyrna and Salonika.

Jerusalem in Books and Maps

The world experienced an Information Revolution as an outcome of the Renaissance and Age of Discovery, which coincided with the invention of the printing press. In the wake of these developments Jerusalem was described in books and depicted in maps to a much greater degree than ever before. The first printed map of Jerusalem appeared in 1486, to be followed by many others, however most were highly imaginative, based upon the mapmakers' awareness of various literary sources, including works of pure fiction and the accounts of pilgrims. An interesting example of this phenomenon is the 1581 map of Heinrich Bunting, which depicts the world as cloverleaf, with each leaf representing a continent (Europe, Asia, and Africa) and Jerusalem a circle at the center, characterized by lofty towers (see p.195). In a number of maps Jerusalem resembles a European city, while in others it appears more as an ancient Oriental city.

In illustrated Hebrew books published during the centuries of the Ottoman period, Jerusalem is generally depicted in an imaginative fashion. The Temple Mount and Dome of the Rock occupy a prominent position. Often the headline 'site of the Temple' appears above them. From the eighteenth century on, Hebrew books as well as Jewish home and synagogue ritual objects frequently display decorative motifs symbolizing Jerusalem: the Temple, sacred sites in the city and its surroundings, the Temple Mount and Western Wall. In Jewish folk art these motifs appeared on synagogue ark curtains, marriage contracts, jewelry boxes and embroidered Sabbath tablecloths.

Jerusalem's Status in the Seventeenth and Eighteenth Centuries

Beginning in the last quarter of the seventeenth century and for the following three hundred years, Jerusalem was a peripheral city on the fringe of the Ottoman empire. The central authorities paid it little heed. The infrastructure of the entire country became dilapidated. The roads, unguarded and unmaintained, were plagued by wild animals and highwaymen. All of this adversely affected Jerusalem – and almost every other town in Ottoman ruled Syria-Palestine. Jerusalem came to resemble nothing so much as a large and grimy village. Within its walls large areas became rubble strewn lots, in which grain, vegetables and fruit were grown. Its streets were a maze of narrow, refuse-littered lanes.

Yet Jerusalem was the largest city in Syria-Palestine. In the mid-sixteenth century, its population reached a peak – more than sixteen thousand souls; then it began to dwindle. Most of the population was Muslim and among them the clans of Husseini, Nashashibi, and Khalidi rose to local prominence. Their influence has endured into the twentieth century. The rise of these families derived primarily from the weakening of the Ottoman central government and the custom of local officials to bequeath civil functions from father to son.

The number of Jews living in Jerusalem in the seventeenth and eighteen centuries ranged from 1,000-3,000. The Christian population, was larger than that of the Jews, and made up of different denominations, with the Greek Orthodox having the highest status as a result of its influence within the Sultan's court in Istanbul. The other Christian denominations experienced continual fluctuations in their status owing to changing policies of the Ottoman regime. Early in the seventeenth century, France became the patron of the Catholic sects in the Holy Land, and together with Venice, whose influence was at its height, looked after their interests in Jerusalem and the rest of the country.

The contention between various Christian denominations over control of the Church of the Holy Sepulcher, or parts thereof, repeatedly erupted into disputes during the Ottoman period. In 1629, the governor of Jerusalem, Muhammed Pasha, decided in favor of the Franciscans, having been paid ample *bakshish* (bribe) to do so. The Greek Orthodox patriarch, with the support of a number of Jews close to the Sultan's court, managed to obtain a *firman* (decree) favoring the Greek Orthodox. The Franciscans in turn recruited the support of European diplomats in Istanbul who from time to time managed to obtain what they wanted through influence peddling and bribery. In September 1756, the rivalry between the Greek Orthodox and Roman Catholic establishments erupted anew. Armed Catholics burst into the Church of the Holy Sepulcher, injured members of the Greek Orthodox community, and damaged ritual vessels. The Greek Orthodox seized control of the church, and a *firman* came from Istanbul authorizing the move.

The Muslims – Arabs and Ottoman Turks – were generally tolerant towards the Christians, principally from economic motives. Christian pilgrimage brought a welcome stimulus to the forlorn economy of the country and of Jerusalem. Pilgrims were charged any number of fees, including one for entry into the Church of the Holy Sepulcher and another for travelling from Jaffa to Jerusalem. The trip to Jordan River baptism sites near Jericho also cost pilgrims a pretty sum. During the seventeenth and eighteenth centuries, when the state of security in the country was uncertain, the number of pilgrims decreased but never ceased.

During the eighteenth century there was a change in the type of Christian visitor who arrived in Jerusalem. Along with pious pilgrims whose motivation was to visit and worship at Christian holy places, there arrived Christian Europeans whose motive was more worldly. They came as part of the 'grand tour,' considered an essential to the education of well-born young men. Their

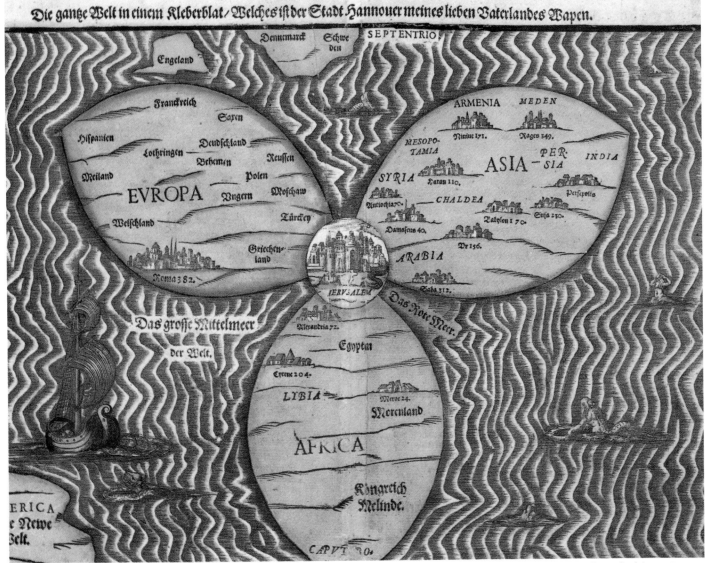

The Bunting Map (1581) – The world is represented in cloverleaf form with Jerusalem at the center, even though this map was printed long after cartography had advanced beyond such stereotypes

visit was part of an itinerary by which they toured major sites and ruins of the classical world in order to understand the sources of European culture. This phenomenon would grow during the nineteenth century; many scholars, writers – and tourists who were simply curious and could afford the trip – visited the country and Jerusalem.

In 1703-1705 civil unrest erupted in Jerusalem, as part of an uprising of fellaheen (peasants) and Bedouin in the southern part of the country. The revolt in Jerusalem has been named after the leader of this revolt, Nakib al-Ashraf, a descendent of Muhammed. The causes of the uprising were all attributable to the ebbing power of the Ottoman regime. As was mentioned earlier in the chapter, the heavy hand of the Bedouin nomads was upon the roads and villages of the country, while the heavy tax burden and tyranny of the governor, Muhammed Pasha, brought matters to the boiling point. The uprising and revolt in Jerusalem were eventually suppressed.

In the second half of the eighteenth century, power struggles for control of the country occurred in the north, in Acre and areas of the Galilee. They had little effect upon Jerusalem. Although there were occasional incidents over tax matters or Bedouin raids, the violence that took place only some dozens of miles from Jerusalem did not affect it. At the end of the eighteenth century, Jerusalem stood behind its Ottoman walls, removed politically, economically and culturally, from the rest of the world.

THE LATE OTTOMAN PERIOD

Jerusalem the Old City and environs towards the end of the Ottoman rule

Worshippers at the traditional Tomb of King David on Mount Zion. Drawing by Ulrich Halbreiter, early 19th century

The neglected city of Jerusalem underwent a dramatic rise in status during the nineteenth century, as it increasingly attracted the interest of European leaders intent upon empire building. In 1799 a young and ambitious Napoleon Bonaparte could allow himself to retreat to Egypt after an unsuccessful campaign against the port of Acre without ever turning east toward Jerusalem. By the century's end, a spectacular visit to Jerusalem was the chief objective of a tour by Germany's Kaiser Wilhelm II. For Napoleon, Jerusalem was, apparently, neither an achievable nor a

sufficiently worthwhile objective. For the ambitious Wilhelm, a gaudy and very public visit to the city was the perfect gesture to demonstrate his imperial interests.

Jerusalem's rise in status during the nineteenth century was accompanied by a significant rise in population. At the turn of the century the city had 9,000 inhabitants – seven thousand Moslem and Christian Arabs, and two thousand Jews. By the end of the century, the population numbered 55,000, of whom 35,000 were Jews and 20,000 Arabs. In the course of a hundred years, the population of Jerusalem increased more than sixfold, while the Jewish population grew to more than seventeen times its former size. Jerusalem became a city with a Jewish majority, a condition it had not known since the Second Temple period eighteen hundred years earlier.

1840: Messianic Expectations

Change in Jerusalem was negligible during the first three decades of the nineteenth century. It was a small, dilapidated provincial town occupying an area of no more than a half mile square. Enclosed within city walls erected by the Ottomans in the early sixteenth century, it could be entered via four massive gates which were barred every evening to prevent the entry of thieves, bands of highwaymen and wild animals all of whom made travel treacherous anywhere in Palestine.

Within the walled city, buildings were in various stages of disintegration. There were empty areas between them, long and wide strips of twenty to a hundred yards which served as garbage dumps, fallow ground, or small patches for planting grain. The Turks, for reasons of their own, forbade the restoration of buildings, including great Muslim and Christian monumental structures such as the Dome of the Rock and the Church of the Holy Sepulcher. The latter was seriously damaged by fire in 1808.

Jerusalem's economic base was severely limited, and poverty was rampant. Living quarters were crowded, means of water delivery primitive, and means of sanitation virtually non-existent. Rainwater which fell during the short winter season was stored in cisterns in nearly every courtyard, and these often became depleted during the long dry season. Water from natural springs was hauled into the city on the backs of human water carriers or donkeys, and was sold at high prices.

The imperious and unaccountable Turkish sultan placed a heavy tax burden on every sector of the population. At the turn of the nineteenth century, the taxes imposed on Jerusalem's residents were out of all proportion with their ability to pay. The plight of non-Muslims (Jews and Christians) was particularly unbearable. They were considered inferior subjects and had to pay a poll tax (*jizya*). They could not bear arms or give evidence in a Muslim court of law, and their entire existence hung by a thread. One of the first scholars to visit Palestine, the Swiss, Burckhardt, wrote: "There is almost no instance in which a Jew or Christian could enjoy power or property for any length of time. Such people are always ruined at the height of their success."

The three large religious communities of Jerusalem were crowded into their own quarters: the Muslims to the north and west of the Temple Mount, the Christians mainly around the Church of the Holy Sepulcher, and the Jews in the southeastern sector of the city, near the Western Wall. The official Turkish institutions were located mainly in the west. At the Citadel, there was a Turkish garrison and adjoining prison. The Turkish governor's residence stood on the Via Dolorosa.

Early in the nineteenth century, the Jews of Jerusalem, mostly members of the Sephardi community, were the smallest and most vulnerable group in the population. At the time, Ashkenazi Jews were not permitted to live in Jerusalem, and did not do so openly – an outcome of events which occurred more that a century earlier (see previous chapter). Ashkenazi Jews in their traditional long-coated and fur-hatted costume did not dare appear in the lanes of Jerusalem, for fear of being accosted by Arab and Turkish agents demanding payment of the Ashkenazi community debt. The few Ashkenazis who lived in Jerusalem in the early nineteenth century, did so in the costume of Sephardi Jews.

Political developments resulted in a relaxing of Turkish policy toward Ashkenazis and later on a *firman* was issued annulling the old debt. By the late 1830s more Ashkenazis were settling in Jerusalem. These included a large group of *Prushim*, abstemious ultra-orthodox disciples of the Gaon of Vilna, and other pious Ashkenazis from Russia, Poland, Galicia, and other European countries. A contemporary Jerusalemite, Eliezer Bergman, wrote of "a stream of godfearing Jews arriving to take up residence in the four holy cities (of the

'Mizrah' ('East') Decorative wall hanging indicating the direction a Jew should face in prayer – toward Jerusalem. Drawing on glass by Moshe Mizrahi, latter half of 19th century

The Cotton Merchant's Gate and view of the Temple Mount and Dome of the Rock.
Painting by Gustav Bauernfeind,, 1886

land of Israel) Jerusalem, Hebron, Tiberias and Safed." During the 1840s, hassidic Jews from Safed migrated to Jerusalem in the wake of several calamities: a Druse rebellion, a health epidemic, and an earthquake which struck Safed in 1837, demolishing a good portion of the town. A factor motivating ever larger numbers of pious Jews to settle in Jerusalem was a widespread folk belief in imminent salvation which gripped Jewish communities of the West and East during 1839-40 (5600 according to the Jewish calendar). Since Jewish religious tradition strongly links Redemption and messianic salvation with Jerusalem, the city became the focus of group pilgrimage with the aim of permanent residence.

For centuries, the Jews of Jerusalem clung to the city out of powerful religious motive. Most males spent their days engaged in prayer and study, in keeping with the awesome privilege and responsibility of living in the Holy City. Dire poverty was a necessary consequence of this non-income producing lifestyle, and a method was developed to ensure the sustenance of families. Emissaries of each of the various Jewish communal groups were sent out to Jewish communities of the Mediterranean basin and Europe, to collect charity. The beginning of the nineteenth century saw improvement in the method of collection, with the setting up of an institution in Amsterdam entitled "The Clerks and Administrators." It assumed responsibility for collecting money in Europe and distributing it to support the Jews of Palestine in general and of Jerusalem in particular.

The French writer and publicist, François René de Chateaubriand visited Jerusalem in 1806 and penned a description of 'the Jewish people' of the city. It was "the subject of contempt, bows its head without bitterness... submits to blows without responding and suffers all

"The weeping place of the Jews," description of the Western Wall by the artist William Henry Bartlett. Drawing, 1842

Scale model of the interior of the stately Hurvah synagogue which dominated the skyline of the Jewish quarter of the Old City. Model by Meir Rosen. Collection, Israel Museum

them, rather than being suppressed. Inhabitants of Jerusalem and other cities joined the uprising. A year later, Sultan Mahmud II ordered the governor of Acre, Abdullah Pasha, to put down the insurgency. His forces positioned themselves on the Mount of Olives and bombarded Jerusalem. The rebels returned fire with cannon they had seized when they took the Citadel near the Jaffa Gate. Two weeks of siege and cannon fire wiped out the insurgents, and the city fell to the Turkish attackers on October 4, 1825. In a departure from the cruel common practice in those days, the Turks spared the inhabitants of Jerusalem any further suffering. The Jews, as 'a protected people' had not actively participated in the rebellion, but suffered equally with the other inhabitants of Jerusalem. Jewish property and possessions were destroyed and stolen, and Jews had to pay heavy taxes in order to compensate the authorities for the cost of the uprising. Still, the Jewish community recovered almost completely.

The Western Wall, with cypresses to suggest cedars of Lebanon, from which the Holy Temple was built. Seal of the Kollel Prushim, pious Ashkenazi community

Muslims and Christians

From 1800 to 1830 there was little change in the size of the Muslim community of Jerusalem. At the turn of the century it numbered some 4000 souls, and three decades later, not much more than 4500. The same applied to the Christians, whose various congregations at the turn of the century totalled fewer than 3000 individuals, and in 1830, only slightly more.

The Muslims were Jerusalem's largest and most underdeveloped community. They engaged in menial labor and had a relatively small number of skilled craftsmen. Unlike the Christian and Jewish communities, the Muslims did not have ties with other countries. Later in the century, when distant imperial powers began to represent the interests of various segments of the Jerusalem populace, the Muslims were by and large not supported by the great powers, while Christians and Jews were. The fact that the Muslims were of one faith with the

manner of insult without crying for mercy." And, "although it has witnessed the destruction of Jerusalem seventeen times and can do nothing about it, nothing will prevent it from looking towards Zion."

During the 1820s, various segments of the Muslim and Christian population in the environs of Jerusalem initiated a tax revolt against the Turks, and fled from their homes and villages. Some found refuge in churches and monasteries outside Jerusalem and in Bethlehem. The governor of Damascus, Mustafa Pasha, sent forces to Jerusalem to put down the rebellion. His troops overcame the outlying villages, plundering churches and monasteries. Soldiers burst into Jerusalem, sought out the rebellious sectors, attacked and arrested many, and plundered everything they came across. All segments of the populace suffered – Jews, Christians and Muslims alike. An attitude of rebelliousness increased among

of the Rock and al-Aqsa mosque. The contemporary German scholar Ulrich Jasper Seetzen called this area "the most beautiful site in the entire Ottoman empire." Entry onto the Temple Mount was forbidden to non-Muslims.

The Muslim community was virtually homogeneous, consisting of local Arabs and a minority of Muslims from North Africa (Maghribis), living in the Muslim quarter. There was also a small group of Indian Muslims. Turkish soldiers were another Muslim presence, however they were not permanent residents.

There were three large groups within the Christian community at the onset of the nineteenth century. The Greek Orthodox numbered some fifty percent of the Christian community, the Latins or Roman Catholics numbered thirty percent, and the Armenians numbered eighteen percent. The remaining two percent was made up of very small groups of Copts, Ethiopians and Syrians. The great majority of Christians were ethnically Arab,

Arab peasant women before the Old City's Dung Gate.
Photo Bonfils Studio

Ottoman rulers did not enhance their status. The Turks ruled everyone with an iron hand.

European penetration of Palestine and Jerusalem in particular, was typically viewed with disdain by Muslims. Even in mid-century, an important Muslim personage could comment: "When there is more than enough money, I build a house, buy a slave, a gemstone, a good horse or a wife, but I do not pave a road so that strangers will come to the city. Jerusalem is now the pearl which all Europeans covet, and why should we make it easy for them to achieve this aim?"

The Muslim community was master of the most significant area in the city – the Haram al-Sharif or Temple Mount, with its two grand structures, the Dome

French sailors on pilgrimage to the Church of the Holy Sepulcher

while a small number of clerics came from abroad. The ranks of Christian residents were temporarily swelled several times a year by thousands of Christian pilgrims.

The most important Christian site in Jerusalem was the Church of the Holy Sepulcher. It was administered in a complex manner by various Christian sects, with the Greek Orthodox in a dominant position. In 1808, the Church of the Holy Sepulcher caught fire, and its dome crashed inward after its supporting columns were damaged. The building's restoration served as the pretext for unending quarrels between various Christian

Muslim worshipers in the Dome of the Rock, first half of 19th century

denominations. The Greek Orthodox, who were supported by the Russian Czar, bore the major financial burden of the restoration, and this larger share of the fiscal responsibility further buttressed the dominant status of the Greek Orthodox within the sacred shrine, to the detriment of the French-supported Roman Catholics.

Each of the nineteenth century's great European powers (England, France, Austria, Prussia and Russia) had a long and complex association with one or another branch of the Christian church. In their ruling circles, attention was paid to decisions about refurbishing the Church of the Holy Sepulcher, and to other Christian matters relating to Jerusalem. Interests were expressed and political pressures brought to bear. Jerusalem was a stage on which inter-Christian rivalries were acted out, as well as negative attitudes to Ottoman Turkey.

The Christians of Jerusalem and particularly the masses of tourists who came to the city, celebrated the Christian holidays in the Church of the Holy Sepulcher and other holy sites. Each community observed its festivities separately – watchful lest another congregation infringe on an established site. There was no Protestant community in Jerusalem at the beginning of the nineteenth century, however this changed with the arrival of English and American missionaries. Protestant influence in Jerusalem was increasingly felt as the century progressed.

A Brief Interlude of Egyptian Rule

For nine years, from 1831-1840, Jerusalem was not governed by Ottomans, but by the Egyptian, Muhammed Ali. Together with his adult son Ibrahim Pasha, Muhammed Ali took control of Palestine and Syria, and reached as far as Anatolia. This revolutionary Egyptian annulled previous Ottoman governing arrangements in Palestine and altered the country's division into counties. The entire country was considered one district, administered from Jerusalem. The social and economic situation in Jerusalem underwent change, as Muhammed Ali reversed Ottoman policy of placing lighter legal and tax burdens on Muslims than on non-Muslims. The Egyptian increased the burdens on the Muslim inhabitants while easing the burden on the Christians, and to a certain extent, on the Jews. Jerusalem was opened to the influence of the European powers, whom Muhammed Ali admired. The latter were quick to exploit the opportunities made available to them. The British established the first foreign consulate in Jerusalem in 1839. Other European powers increased their influence in Jerusalem indirectly, by investing their various religious and commercial representatives with greater powers to represent their countries' interests, and extend favors.

The area's Muslim inhabitants were put off by such policy measures as Ibrahim Pasha's ban on private ownership of weapons, and the recruitment of Muslim peasants into the army. The power of the local Muslim leadership was weakened, and the concessions made to non-Muslims were a constant provocation. It is not surprising that less than three years after the Egyptians took control of Jerusalem (1834), its Muslim inhabitants joined the Fellaheen (peasant) Rebellion throughout the country. The Egyptian garrison retreated to the Citadel, which was then besieged. Only when Ibrahim Pasha's reinforcements reached Jerusalem was calm restored to the city. The instigators of the rebellion paid heavily for their initiative, and the Egyptian rulers became even more stringent regarding Jerusalem's Muslim community.

By contrast with the discontented Muslims, the Christian communities enjoyed the Egyptian approach. Christians were permitted to build new churches and restore old ones. They were more likely to be chosen for jobs in public and governmental institutions, and were not burdened with a compulsory military draft of every fifth young man, as the Muslims were.

The Jews, who breathed freely during the early part of Egyptian rule, were disappointed when they realized that no marked difference had occurred in their

Muhammed Ali, the bold Egyptian who briefly siezed control of Palestine and Jerusalem from the Ottoman Turks, 1831-1840

lives. During the Fellaheen Rebellion in 1834, they suffered hostile encounters with the fellaheen peasants, who dominated the city, stole Jewish possessions and murdered some Jews. Even when the Egyptians resumed control, danger to the Jews of Jerusalem did not cease, and there were instances of Jews being attacked by Egyptian soldiers. However, for the Jews, in their perpetually precarious existence, Egyptian rule was a better time than most. One improvement occurred in 1835 when permission was granted to repair and renovate the complex of four ancient Sephardi synagogues in the Old City. A year later, the Ashkenazi Jews received permission to repair the Rabbi Judah Hasid synagogue known as the *Hurvah.*

The more rooted Egyptian rule became, the stronger became the position of the Jews of Jerusalem, not through any deliberate government policy, but because the regime permitted the arrival of pious communities from central Europe. The number of Jerusalem's Jews was augmented by hundreds who arrived mostly from Safed. This relatively large group had an impact on the ethnic character of Jerusalem's Ashkenazi Jewish community, which organized itself in sub-communities (kollel; kollelim) according to region of origin. For the previous twenty years the main Ashkenazi kollel had been the 'Prushim' (literally, 'the opposed,' ultra-orthdox opponents of hassidism), whose origin was Lithuania. Then came the large influx from Safed, and other Ashkenazi arrivals included Jews from Holland and Germany. The effect was the doubling of Jerusalem's Jewish population during the late 1840s, to five thousand. Viewed from a statistical perspective, this made the Jews the largest of Jerusalem's religious groups, however not yet an absolute majority.

Egyptian rule came to an end in 1840. The Turks, assisted by Great Britain and Austria, sent their army and and navy to Syria and Palestine and repulsed Ibrahim Pasha's troops. Acre fell after a siege of six months. Jerusalem was taken without difficulty. The Egyptian army which withdrew from Damascus southward, beyond the Jordan, briefly considered re-taking Jerusalem, however, upon reaching Jericho, Ibrahim Pasha was

Pious Jews of the Old Yishuv. Second half of the 19th century

informed that the city was defended by a strong Turkish force. He decided to continue on to Egypt, and Jerusalem returned to Turkish dominion.

Jerusalem in the Mid-Nineteenth Century

Jerusalem from the 1840s onward was quite different from the city of a decade earlier. A series of changes in the lives of the inhabitants and the laws of the country fostered a new spirit and direction. The more equitable policies of the Egyptian rulers toward non-Muslims had a lasting impact on Turkish policies. The European powers who had helped the Turks rid themselves of the

Egyptians, demanded reforms, and indeed from 1839 onward, the period of *Tanzimat*, a series of far-reaching reforms, began. One of the most important was related to the Capitulations Agreements, according to which citizens of foreign powers did not have to abide by Turkish law, but were the sole responsibility of the consuls of those powers. As a result, Jerusalem became dotted with the consulates of European states, and later also that of the United States. Each consul was a man of power and influence in Jerusalem. His status was only

The European imperial powers made their presence felt in 19th century Jerusalem. Holy Trinity Cathedral, the Russian Compound

slightly beneath that of the pasha, the Turkish governor. When a foreign consul came down a street, he was preceded by two ceremonial attendants. Each consul conducted a court of law in accordance with his country's legal code, judging his Jerusalemite citizens without the Turkish authorities playing any part in the matter.

The consuls sought to broaden their influence through demonstrating to the Turks that they represented large numbers of Jerusalemites. Each was ready to extend citizenship or protection even to Jerusalemites who did not hail from his mother country. The Jews were the main beneficiaries of this effort. Many of them were from Russia, or were descended from Russian-born forebears. Owing to the strictures of Ottoman law, they could not (nor could their descendants) become Ottoman citizens. There was no love lost among the Jews for the harsh czarist regime, and they were pleased to renounce their Russian citizenship in favor of German or British. A number of Sephardi Jews also took advantage of this option, however, as the Sephardis had Ottoman citizenship, they were not as subject to Ottoman xenophobia as the Ashkenazis, and the majority remained loyal to their Ottoman linkage.

The British Consul was widely considered to be the patron of the Jews. Foreign Secretary Palmerston informed the first consul, Young, that "the general patronage of the Jews would be part of his duties." In 1847, Lord Palmerston proposed that all the Jews of Palestine should come under the aegis of the British, but the other powers objected to the idea.

The other segment of Jerusalem's population to benefit from the patronage of the European powers was the Christian sector. Czarist Russia acted as protector of the Greek Orthodox, France supported the Catholics and Great Britain and Prussia supported the Protestants. A burst of Christian-sponsored construction occurred both within and outside Jerusalem's city walls. The first Anglican church was built inside the Old City, not far from the Tower of David, while Greek monks, Protestant missionaries and the British Consul were actively commissioning construction outside the walls. Built at this time were British Consul James Finn's residence in

The Hacham Bashi, Rabbi Saul Eliachar, prominent Sephardi rabbi, early 20th century

what would become the Talbieh neighborhood, and Bishop Gobat's school on Mount Zion, among other structures.

The condition of the Jews also improved. The Turks issued an edict in 1841 recognizing the Sephardi chief rabbi, known as the 'First in Zion' (*Rishon le-Zion*) as the *Hacham Bashi*, the highest authority from the Turkish point of view, in all matters dealing with the Jewish community – Ashkenazi and Sephardi. From that time on the *Hacham Bashi* was the official representative of the Jews, and his status was equal to that of the consuls and the various Christian community heads. The first *Hacham Bashi* was Rabbi Avraham Haim Gagin. All those who succeeded him until the end of Turkish rule, enjoyed a similar status.

The Sephardi Jewish community with the *Hacham Bashi* as its head, was a well established one. In the course of the nineteenth century the social profile of the oriental Jewish community changed, with the arrival of immigrants from North Africa, Bukhara, Persia, Yemen, and other lands. The Ashkenazis, were divided, as previously mentioned, into the Hassidic and Prushi (or Mitnagged) major subgroups, and then into *kolelim* (communities), that is, groups hailing from a certain country, district or city (for instance, Kolel Warsaw, Kolel Hungary, etc.) Quarrels among them were quite common, over customs and particularly over funds, and it was only at a much later stage that all these groups set up a "General Committee" to facilitate an equitable distribution of charitable funds.

In the mid-nineteenth century, all the Jews, both Sephardi and Ashkenazi, faced a bitter challenge, which scandalized their communities. Beginning in the 1830s, several conversion-minded Missions to the Jews established themselves in Jerusalem. The missionaries, some German, but mostly British, offered impoverished Jews food, clothing and medical assistance, on condition that they convert. There is vehement antipathy in Jewish culture toward missionizing activity directed at Jews. This is heightened by bitter historical memory of the Middle Ages, when forced conversion was met with martyrdom. In nineteenth-century Jerusalem the numbers spoke for themselves; very few Jews converted. Still, the perception of a threat hung over the Jewish community. As the century progressed, more Jewish communal institutions were established (soup kitchens, hospitals and schools) which eliminated the need to turn to non-Jewish service providers. Missionaries generally lowered their expectations. They provided social services without overt attempts to convert Jews, or turned their attentions to the Arab population.

The economic situation of Jerusalem's Jews continued to be bad. A large proportion survived on the *halukah* system (literally, 'division' – of funds) previously described (p.202). Every year, scores of emissaries bearing letters of reference from well-known rabbis in Jerusalem, set off for widely dispersed Jewish centers to collect donations. Competition between them was intense, and much wrangling ensued regarding the collection and distribution of money.

Jerusalem's Jews endured occasional periods of severe destitution whenever it was difficult to collect funds abroad. Another factor contributing to their poverty was the extremely rapid growth of the city's Jewish population during the nineteenth century. At particularly difficult times, a number of European Jewish philanthropists came

to their aid. The most prominent was Sir Moses Montefiore, a wealthy British Jew of Italian descent, who was related to the Rothschild family. Montefiore visited Palestine, and particularly Jerusalem, seven times between 1827 to 1875, and went to great lengths to improve the conditions of the Jews and direct their activities along economically productive lines. Among other enterprises, he helped set up a weaving workshop, provided for a Jewish doctor so the community would not have to resort to the services of a mission doctor, and was connected with a scheme to establish Jewish agricultural settlements. He also played a dominant role in building the first Jewish living quarters outside the walls of Jerusalem.

Sir Moses Montefiore, British Jewish philanthropist and community leader, unparalleled in his charity to the Jews of the Holy Land

Fire Out of Jerusalem

During the mid-nineteenth century the attention of European Christians was drawn to Jerusalem as a result of several tragic events. The first was a conflagration in the Church of the Holy Sepulcher which broke out during Easter week 1834. Death and injury were the lot of many pilgrims when the Greek Orthodox Patriarch, in the presence of the Egyptian ruler Ibrahim Pasha, lit the Holy Fire while almost fifteen thousand Christian pilgrims were pressing into the entrance of the church. The flame leaped out of control, hundreds were crushed in the pandemonium, and others choked on the fumes. The ancient building suffered serious damage.

In the early 1850's, festering tensions between Jerusalem's Greek Orthodox and Roman Catholic clergy ignited the spark that touched off the brutal Crimean War. Clerical accusations and counter-accusations over the theft in 1847 of the Star of Bethlehem, an ornament from Bethlehem's Church of the Nativity, escalated into a dispute over the rights of the Greek Orthodox and Roman Catholic establishments to the Church of the

The hostility of the Jewish community toward missionary activity is reflected in obliterated names of two who converted. Noted beside each name, "May his name be cursed.(He is) ostracized (from the community)"

Holy Sepulcher and other holy places in Jerusalem and Bethlehem. Each branch of Christianity had its empire-minded European sponsor, and each sponsor had as his target the weak Ottoman Empire. A three year conflict ensued on the Crimean peninsula. Half a million British, French, Russians, Turks and Sardinians died, yet very little of substance was resolved.

The Crimean War had a direct influence on life in Jerusalem. From an economic viewpoint, financial aid to the indigent Jewish community ceased entirely, as shipping and land routes were affected by the war. The Jews were a large portion of the city's population, and the resultant plunge from their normal penurious state to utter destitution had its impact. However, the lasting impact of the Crimean War on Jerusalem was positive. The Turks, who had been helped against the Russians by the European powers, displayed a greater sympathy toward European requests that Ottoman governing

policies be eased. From this point onward, Ottoman citizens, whether Jews or Christians, could buy real-estate. For the first time, non-Muslims were allowed to enter the area of the Temple Mount, and tourists and visitors were given permission to enter formerly prohibited areas. The Christians were also granted the privilege of ringing church bells, which until then had been forbidden in the Muslim Ottoman empire.

Settlement outside the Old City Walls

The period after the Crimean War witnessed further progress in construction outside the city walls of Jerusalem. The Russians built a large area called the Russian Compound, which included churches and hostels. The Germans put up the Syrian Orphans Home (Schneller Compound) and the Jewish Mishkenot Sha'ananim complex went up as well.

The spurt in construction outside the Old City walls constituted visual evidence of progress in early 1860's Jerusalem. Yet, these developments did not in themselves alter the city's oriental and backward character. Two developments which contributed to modernization were the establishment of a Jerusalem municipality, and, towards the end of the decade, the paving of the first road in all of Palestine, a narrow thoroughfare which ran from the port of Jaffa to Jerusalem. Until 1869 there had only been a cowpath linking the two cities.

The Mishkenot Sha'ananim ('Tranquil Dwellings') quarter, was built for the poorest of Jerusalem's Jews by Sir Moses Montefiore, using funds entrusted to him in the bequest of the American Jewish philanthropist Judah Touro of New Orleans. A windmill and two rows of simple apartments rose on the western slope of the Hinnom Valley in full view of the Old City. The buildings were enclosed by a wall for protection from the still commonplace attacks of bandits and wild animals. The neighborhood was meant to provide its residents with secure, sanitary conditions, and means of earning a livelihood using the windmill. Though the

The Western Wall, a major focus of pilgrimage in the 19th century. Jews and non-Jews visited this last vestige of the Temple

living conditions were better than anything the residents had known in the Old City, contemporary reports indicate that, gripped by fears of being 'outside the city' after dark, the residents would return every evening to the relative safety of the walled Old City. Several years were to pass, and numerous attempts at persuasion, before Mishkenot Sha'ananim was firmly established. In spite of its slow start, the project made a powerful impression, and was a forerunner of many Jewish neighborhoods which arose mostly to the north and northwest of the Old City.

Among the Jews of Jerusalem there was also progress in the fields of medicine, education and culture. Beginning in the 1850s, Jewish schools and hospitals were set up, and in 1863, the first two Hebrew newspapers appeared on the Jerusalem scene: *Ha-Levanon* and *Havazeleth*. Both represented ultraorthodox communities, the former the Mitnaggedim and the latter the Hassidim. Both were closed by the Turks in the same year, but Hebrew and Yiddish papers were published regularly in Jerusalem from the 1870s onward.

Christian-sponsored construction went on outside the walls, and by the end of the century there were a good number of churches, monasteries, schools, hospitals, hostels and other projects. In addition, groups of Europeans – Russians, French, Italians, Austrians, and British – initiated construction projects, and Muslims began to build outside the walls as well.

In a significant administrative development, the Turks recognized Jerusalem's rising importance and granted it the status of an independent district, no longer subordinate to the governor of Beirut or Damascus, but directly responsible to the sultan in Constantinople.

In 1870 a milestone went largely unnoticed, as the number of Jews in Jerusalem rose to equal the combined total of non-Jewish inhabitants. The Jews thereafter soon became the majority of Jerusalem's population, and in time amounted to a two-thirds majority, a statistic which only changed during World War I, when the hardships of war and Turkish policy brought about a significant decrease in the city's overall population. (The first post-war census indicated that the Jews had remained a majority, but not a two-thirds majority.) In 1870, most Jews lived in the Old City and

Mishkenot Sha'ananim (Tranquil Dwellings), the first Jewish neighborhood outside the Old City walls. Note the protective wall, and roof crenellations echoing the design of the Old City walls

Montefiore's windmill above Mishkenot Sha'anamim, was meant to provide means for economic productivity. Painting, Ludwig Blum

Jewish newspapers of mid-19th century Jerusalem

first the very symbol of progress and innovation. Luncz describes its modern market which featured cleanliness and proper supervision of weights and measures. This quarter also had Jerusalem's first street lighting – kerosene lamps – a feature soon emulated by the Pasha of Jerusalem, who installed a number of street lamps in the major streets of the city. Mea Shearim became an important neighborhood, around which Jewish satellite neighborhoods arose.

Although living conditions for Jerusalem's Jews improved over the course of the nineteenth century, their place within the social structure was still at rock bottom. They suffered from entrenched discrimination and attacks by Muslims, and routinely accepted the lack of legal recourse. In an article Luncz published in the Warsaw, Poland Hebrew weekly *Ha-Zefirah* he described the Muslim attacks upon Jews:

"The Muslims, who cannot vent their fury against Christians, who are protected by the European Powers, vent their rage against the Jews, a scorned and belittled people... and heaven help the man who dares answer them, for then he is not sure of his life, and witnesses would immediately appear who would swear that he had cursed their (Muslim) faith and he would be sent into exile."

only a very few lived outside the walls. However the trend to move outside rose, and by the turn of the twentieth century there were a roughly equal number of Jews living within the Old City walls and in the newly constructed areas outside.

Seal of the 'Ma'aravim' ('westerners') North African Jews who founded Mahane Yisrael, second Jewish neighborhood outside the walls

A Personal Glimpse of the City – 1876

A a vivid account of Jerusalem in the last quarter of the nineteenth century is presented by Abraham Moses Luncz, a contemporary writer, editor and publisher of geographical works on Palestine and Jerusalem. Luncz's pamphlet, *Paths of Zion and Jerusalem* describes the city's inhabitants as mainly poor and residing in abject and filthy conditions. He describes the "white faces and emaciated bodies, the quarter of the poor, which testifies to their sorry state and circumstance, in which poverty rules them with unlimited power and terrible cruelty." A short time before Luncz wrote this, construction began on the new Mea Shearim quarter. This neighborhood, today home to many ultra orthodox Jerusalemites, was at

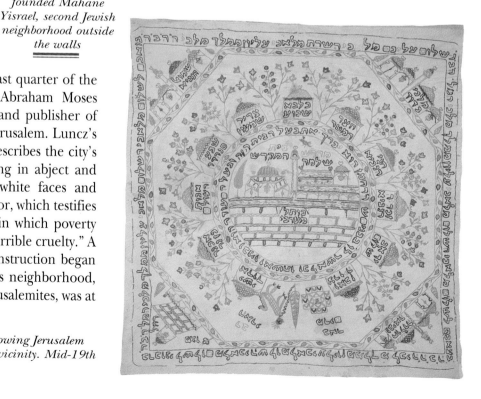

Embroidered cloth for the Sabbath table, showing Jerusalem holy sites and pilgrimage sites in the city's vicinity. Mid-19th century, Sephardi tradition

Tradition and Change

In 1878 a small number of orthodox Jews of Jerusalem, apparently frustrated by the pervasive poverty, abuse by Muslims and lack of economically productive lifestyle, left the city, to set up agricultural settlements in other parts of the country. They did not have a rigorous ideology, and yet their modest break from convention and venture into economic self-sufficiency was the precursor of great change about to take place for the Jews of Palestine. Theirs was the first pioneering venture of what would be called the New Yishuv ('the New Settlement'). Their first farm colony, located northeast of Jaffa, was Petah Tikva (Gateway of Hope).

Jewish Jerusalem continued to grow, particularly outside the walls. Some nine quarters were established in 1877, and after an interval of five years, building began again in the 1880s resulting in another fourteen neighborhoods.

In 1881, an organized stream of European Jewish immigrants began arriving in Palestine who are known as 'the First Aliyah' (the first organized ascension to The Land). Their arrival marked the historical turning point which the farmers from Jerusalem had signalled. Unlike all the pious immigrants of earlier decades, these European Jews were imbued with a national aim, to found Jewish agricultural settlements in the ancient Jewish homeland as the first step towards a massive return of the Jewish people to Palestine. They founded settlements which have lasted to the present day. However, in actuality, only a portion of them were farmers. Many settled in Jerusalem and struck roots within the framework of the Old Yishuv ('Old Settlement').

One member of the First Aliyah who rose to prominence in the annals of Jewish nationalism was Eliezer Ben Yehudah, the father of modern Hebrew. He was a colorful and provocative figure on the streets of

Yemenite Jews study Torah. Several Jerusalem neighborhoods were constructed to absorb the 1881 wave of Yemenite immigration (aliyah)

Exploring the massive remains of Second Temple arches.
Figure ascending the rope ladder is probably archeologist
Charles Warren. Illustration, William Simpson, 1871

Jerusalem, where he put out a Hebrew newpaper and edited his masterwork, a nineteen volume dictionary of the Hebrew language.

In a remarkable coincidence, another migration of Jews to Palestine occurred in 1881, from a completely different point of origin. This was a group of Jews from Yemen, come to settle in the Holy Land, and largely focused on living in Jerusalem. Their numbers augmented a small Yemenite Jewish community which had arrived earlier. Several Yemenite neighborhoods were established in Jerusalem: in the Siloam Village, on the Mount of Olives, and on the slopes west of the Old City, the Mishkenot HaTemanim and Nahlat Zvi neighborhoods.

Group-sponsored construction projects were also undertaken in the Christian and Muslim communities. Two unique groups joined the various Christian communities during the latter years of the nineteenth century: German Templars and American Protestants. The Templars were a breakaway Lutheran group who

regarded the Temple as a source of inspiration and established a series of agricultural and urban settlements in Palestine, one of which, in the Valley of Rephaim south of the Old City was called simply 'the German Colony' and is still known by that name. Some years after their arrival, a group of American Protestants from the United States established themselves in a partially communal set-up. At first they lived in the Old City and later, settled in the Sheikh Jarrah area, in a section known as the American Colony. Over time, dozens of Swedish Christians joined this latter group, and it was owing to their residence in Jerusalem that the writer Selma Lagerlof wrote her book about the city.

Scholars, Writers, Kings and Princes

Nineteenth-century Jerusalem opened itself to the great world like a rare flower, its exotic color and fragrance luring myriads of visitors. Many writers and poets visited the city, as did artists, emperors, savants and historians, Bible scholars, archeologists, botanists and geographers. Developments which contributed to the rise in the number of visitors to Jerusalem were the rise of steamship travel, and the liberalized Turkish attitude towards foreigners. A bi-product of all these visits was the appearance of hundreds of travel books with Jerusalem as a central feature. The city's name and image became familiar to European and American readers. It seems that the nineteenth century witnessed Jerusalem's evolution into one of the most famous cities in the world, despite its remoteness and modest size.

Among the authors and poets who visited Jerusalem were the Frenchmen François Réné de Chateaubriand, Alphonse de Lamartine, and Gustave Flaubert, and the Americans Herman Melville and Mark Twain. Some of the artists were William Holman Hunt, David Roberts and William Henry Bartlett.

During the first half of the century, the first scientific map of Jerusalem was executed. The Germans Gotthilf Heinrich von Schubert and Titus Tobler, the French Félicien de Saulcy and Charles Clairmont-Ganneau, and Edward Robinson the American, brought their research on ancient Jerusalem to the attention of the scientific world. An enormous contribution to the study of Jerusalem's past was made by the British Palestine

Exploration Fund (P.E.F.) which from the 1860s on sent a steady stream of scientific missions to Jerusalem. One of their projects was the digging of shafts (vertical tunnels) alongside the foundations of the Western Wall, to determine the size, strength and depth of the ancient construction surrounding the Temple Mount. Another shaft, cleared by the archeologist Warren in the Siloam Village just south of the Old City, revealed how the waters of the Gihon spring flowed into ancient Jerusalem.

In the wake of the British fund, scholars and scientists from other countries also visited Palestine. In Germany, they established the *Deutscher Verein zur Erforschung Palaestinas* which carried out archaeological excavations in Jerusalem and other sites.

There was a modest Jewish contribution to this field of study. Joseph Schwartz, who came from Germany in 1833, spent twelve years in Jerusalem, and published a book entitled *The Fruit of the Land* (Leviticus: 23:39, in Hebrew: *Tevuot ha-Aretz*) on the geography of Palestine and Jerusalem and also about the growing Jewish community.

Jerusalem attracted the famous personalities of the time. Among them, the English Prince of Wales, Edward VII (later to be king) in the years 1862 and 1869; the Austrian emperor, Franz-Joseph, whose visit in 1869 caused the Turks to hurriedly pave a highway from Jaffa to Jerusalem; the heirs to the Austrian and Swedish thrones, and the former president of the United States, Ulysses. S. Grant. The guest of the century was without a doubt the German Kaiser Wilhelm II. The Turks were eager to receive the Kaiser and spent months cleaning up the town, repairing buildings and even built a new gate in the walls of the Old City, in order to provide the Kaiser and his entourage with easier access to the holy places in the Christian quarter. The extent to which the Turks were prepared to go to ensure this visit's success could be seen in the removal from city streets of all 'undesirables' – individuals the Turks considered 'unrepresentative,' such as thieves, beggars and various troublemakers, who were imprisoned without investigation or trial. Indigent tourists were sent to the port of Jaffa and expelled from the country. When they protested, they were told that these actions were done with the agreement of their consulates.

All of Jerusalem awaited the Kaiser when he entered the city on October 29, 1898. Officially he came in order

Early 20th century montage depicts Theodor Herzl's vision - the walls of Jerusalem and Jewish immigrants. Herzl met Kaiser Wilhelm II in Jerusalem in 1898

to consecrate the (Lutheran) Church of the Redeemer in the Old City. Actually, he was interested strengthening his country's influence on the Ottoman empire in general, and particularly with regard to Palestine and Jerusalem. During the week of his visit, Jerusalemites seemed to do little else save follow the Kaiser's every activity. Everyone spoke of him in superlatives: how he looked, what his consort, the Kaiserin Augusta-Victoria was wearing, and the activities of his entourage. Even the various horses the Kaiser rode were of interest. Whoever managed to be introduced to him considered himself royalty.

A visitor to Jerusalem who succeeded in obtaining an audience with Wilhelm II was the thirty-eight-year-old president of the newly created Zionist Organisation, Theodor Herzl. He met with the Kaiser in the latter's encampment outside the walls of the Old City, explained to him the principles of the Jewish nationalist idea, and asked for his support. The Kaiser listened, made some unflattering comments about Jews, and the visit came to an end. "He did not say yes and did not say no," was Herzl's summary of the meeting.

German Kaiser Wilhelm II passes beneath arch of greeting erected by Jerusalem's Jews, 1898

Late in the nineteenth century and in the early years of the twentieth, the Turks made great efforts to modernize Jerusalem. The roads leading to the city were widened and improved, making the journey from Jaffa shorter. In 1892 the railway line was completed. Built by a French company, it shortened the trip to some four to five hours, compared with the eight to ten hours needed when travelling by carriage. Nevertheless, most travellers still preferred to travel by carriage, as it was by far the less expensive means of transport. The railway was also used by the Turks to haul water to Jerusalem, however this was not a long-term solution for the city's water supply problem.

The Jerusalem railway station, near the German Colony. In September 1892 the first train journeyed slowly up from Jaffa to Jerusalem

The Final Years of Turkish Rule

By the turn of the new century, Jerusalem was the major city of Palestine. Its population was nearly 55,000, of whom some 35,000 were Jews. The new areas of the city had spread far beyond the Old City walls, and this growth began to diminish the importance of the Old City as a commercial and social center. This diminished effect was particularly noticeable with regard to the ever-growing Jewish population. For example, the major Jewish hospital in the Old City, the Rothschild Hospital, moved to large new quarters outside the walls on the Street of the Prophets, while its building in the Old City was taken over by Misgav Ladach, an infirmary for the poor. Even the new Rothschild Hospital could not meet demand, and two additional hospitals joined it, Sha'arei Tzedek, the first Jewish hospital actually founded outside the Old City, and Bikur Holim, another instance of the re-location of an institution from the Old City to the area outside the walls.

The availability of modern urban services contributed to Jerusalem's growth, and credit for this development goes to the consulates of European nations and the United States. Many of the city's inhabitants were citizens of their countries and it was possible, and even preferable, to use their banks and currencies over those of the Turks. The same was true of the great advances in the city's postal services made possible by foreign post offices. In accordance with the Capitulations

Eliezer Ben-Yehudah with wife Hemda. He worked tirelessly for the modernization of Hebrew and its transition from age-old language of prayer and scholarship to a modern spoken language

Agreements, the great powers were permitted to maintain their own postal services within the Ottoman empire. This taken together with the notoriously ineffective Turkish postal services explains the popularity of the Austrian, German, Russian and Italian post offices in Jerusalem. Jerusalemites and visitors only used the Turkish post office when there was no other alternative.

Parallel with this ongoing growth in Jerusalem, the pioneers of the New Yishuv were growing in number and becoming an increasing percentage of the overall Jewish population of Palestine. Their impact was to be seen mainly in agricultural settlements, particularly those near Jaffa and Haifa. Jerusalem's large pious and non-nationalist Jewish population began to lose social influence. In Jerusalem itself there were pockets of the New Yishuv, including the Bezalel School of Art

Entry plaza just inside the Jaffa Gate, with medieval dry moat and Citadel steps on right

established in 1906, and various newpapers. However, the anti-modern, non-nationalist pious Jewish sector was still very large and influential in Jerusalem, and exerted a considerable dampening effect on modernizing and Zionist efforts. This, coupled with the relative unavailability of agricultural lands around Jerusalem, and the city's location far inland, contributed to the growth of other centers, on the coast, as hotbeds of Zionist activities. The port of Jaffa was such a center, and its new suburb, Tel Aviv, founded in 1909, soon dwarfed it in physical growth as well as importance, becoming a center of modernity and Jewish nationalist activity. Tel Aviv would soon develop into a miniature metropolis – and rival Jerusalem as the principle Jewish center.

Muslims, Christians and Jews

Although the Jews were the majority in Jerusalem since 1870, they enjoyed few rights, and the Muslims were considered the leading religious community. As far as political offices were concerned, the mayor of Jerusalem was a Turkish-appointed Muslim, as were most members of the municipal council and its top officials. Second in line were appointed Christian officials. The Jews were last. The minimal political power of the Jews was partly attributable to the fact that so many of them were not Turkish citizens, but were represented by the foreign consulates.

The local Turkish and Muslim authorities tended to differentiate between the Sephardi and the Ashkenazi Jews, and the Sephardis, in the main Turkish citizens, were given preference, although the traditional scornful attitude towards Jews still prevailed. Though it was unpleasant and widespread, it would be inaccurate to attribute this scornful attitude to the kind of hatred toward Jews that was well known in turn-of-the-century Europe. It would be equally inaccurate to attribute it to a nationalist Muslim awakening. Certainly the Jews did nothing to provoke such an awakening. Most Jews of Jerusalem masked any singular qualities that could be interpreted as superior, and had no nationalist leanings whatever. As to the Christians, the Muslims treated them with even greater antagonism and suspicion than they did the Jews, owing to their exaggerated reliance on foreign consuls.

In 1908, there was a revolution against the Sultan Abdul-Hamid organized by a group of rebels known as the "Young Turks." As was the case in other centers of the Ottoman empire, in Jerusalem the change was accepted willingly, and it was hoped that the new rulers would remedy some of the weaknesses of the Sultan's government. This did not occur and in the course of time it became evident that the new government was as ineffective as its predecessor.

The Young Turks emphasized to a greater degree the Ottoman character of the realm, and without intending

1896 ketubah, Jewish marriage contract of the Georgian (Russia) community, depicting Dome of the Rock and al-Aqsa mosque, thus calling to mind the Temple Mount

to do so, strengthened Arab nationalist sentiments. The Palestinian Arabs, who until then had felt almost no national identity, increasingly considered themselves as one minority among many within the Ottoman Empire. This feeling became obvious in Jerusalem, the major Arab-Muslim center in Palestine, although it should be pointed out that the first Arab nationalist newspaper, *al Carmel* appeared in Haifa, and *Falastin* which succeeded it, in Jaffa. The editors and owners of both were Christian Arabs.

During the last years of Turkish rule, heads of the Arab community in Jerusalem demonstrated their strong anti-Jewish and anti-Zionist stand. In the elections to the Turkish parliament, the candidates from Jerusalem were known for their antipathy towards the Jews and their activities in Palestine. In 1911, the following statement appeared in the Jerusalem newspaper *Ha'or*: "An evil wind has stirred among the Arabs. An evil wind has roused them to acts of hatred and malice against the Jews, for no particular reason."

Jemal Pasha, cruel and unpredictable Ottoman overlord of Jerusalem during the First World War

The City In Wartime

The First World War erupted in Europe in August 1914. It had immediate ramifications in the Middle East, as each of the war's major participants had colonial designs on the territories of Ottoman Turkey. Palestine and the entire region surrounding it were prime objectives, a fact not lost upon the Turks. Their effort to retain control of their empire was typified by harsh and arbitrary measures, imposed in the spirit of their well-known xenophobia. Jerusalem suffered hardships for three years and four months, until the Turks were driven out of the city by the British. Although Jerusalem was in the front line for only a very short period, its residents suffered the ills that a war could inflict – arbitrary recruitment into the army, arbitrary arrests and expulsions, epidemic disease, hunger, scarcity, and a large exodus of refugees.

Thousands of the city's residents left. Many waited out the conflict in British-controlled Egypt. Others fled to nearby villages or other areas of Palestine. Jerusalem's population became greatly diminished. Of the seventy thousand inhabitants on the eve of the war, only some forty thousand remained towards the end of 1917. The Jews were the most affected segment of the population

figures – they numbered just half their former strength, twenty-six thousand reduced from fifty thousand.

For Jerusalem's Jews, physical existence was a critical problem. While all the city's inhabitants were hungry, the Jews suffered more acutely because they had no recourse to farm villages, as the Muslim and Christian Arabs did. Furthermore, their sources of *halukah* charity were cut, because many donor communities were behind enemy lines, and an Allied naval blockade effectively sealed off the coast of Palestine.

Had it not been for donations of food and funds from the Jews of the United States, a country neutral for the first three years of the war, it is doubtful whether the Jews of Jerusalem would have survived until the British take-over. Even with the help, the Jewish community was hungry. Furthermore, the epidemic diseases which typically plagued the city did not spare it in wartime. The hospitals tried to cope with the situation, but their efforts were generally inadequate. Hundreds of people died in the worst year of all – 1917.

The Turkish authorities tyrannized the inhabitants in direct proportion to how their empire was faring in the war. The ruler of Palestine, Jemal Pasha, one of the triumvirate heading the 'Young Turks,' was a cruel and capricious despot who could sentence a suspected spy to be hanged without benefit of inquiry or trial. He detested the local Muslims, hated the Christians, and saw in every Jew a Zionist aiming to undermine the Ottoman empire. Together with his aides, Jemal Pasha terrified Jerusalem and the whole of Palestine. Fortunately for the entire population, his cruelty was only exceeded by his unpredictability, and harsh decrees were changed time and again.

Among those expelled from the country by the Turks in 1915 were two young Zionist leaders, David Ben-Gurion and Izhak Ben-Zvi. In an attempt to get their expulsion edicts cancelled, the two managed to reach Jemal Pasha himself, but were still banished. They were taken to Jaffa in chains and put on a boat sailing to Egypt. In their expulsion order, the Turkish ruler wrote: "Expelled from the Turkish empire, never to return." They returned three years later, to a land from which the

*The surrender of Jerusalem to the two British sergeants,
Hurcomb and Sedgewick. Mayor Hassan al-Husseini leans
on his walking stick, center*

Ottoman Turks had disappeared, and eventually
Ben-Gurion became the first prime minister of Israel,
and Izhak Ben-Zvi its second president.

The End of Turkish Rule

As the war progressed, the Turkish sultan's power waned.
The Ottoman Empire, already known as "the sick man of
Europe," mounted losing battles against several
opponents. Hunger, disease and desertion among the
ranks all shook the empire's foundations. Oppressive
policies and rampant official corruption increased in
Palestine and Jerusalem. When an Arab from one of the
villages tried to bring his farm products to town, he was
immediately pounced upon by police or soldiers. The
arrest of defectors from the army, spies, or those accused
of committing an 'act against the state' was a daily

occurrence. In particular, Jewish leaders who had not
been expelled bore the brunt of Jemal Pasha's ill
treatment. In 1917 rumors were rife that the British army
was advancing from the south towards Jerusalem. The
Turkish authorities behaved even more heartlessly
towards the silent, knowing population. There was every
indication that the Turks were preparing for a long siege
of Jerusalem.

During the first two weeks of November, 1917, British
forces conquered the southern part of Palestine and as
far north as the coastal area, including Jaffa and its
garden suburb of Tel Aviv. They then turned eastward,
toward Jerusalem. By the end of November they had
taken most of the strategic points north and west of the
city, and were preparing to storm it. The Turks, realizing
that their forces were inadequate and the battle lost
before it began, decided to admit defeat, thereby saving
the city from destruction. On December 8, 1917, Turkish
forces stationed in Jerusalem evacuated the city, and on
the following morning, the head of the Jerusalem
municipality, Hassan al-Husseini ventured forth to
surrender to the conquering forces. However, as the
vagaries of war would have it, the surrender was achieved
only after great, if not comic, effort. Armed with a white
sheet obtained from the hospital in the American
Colony, and a note of surrender, the mayor mounted a
horse and led a delegation toward the north of the city to
precede the British reconnaisance unit. He encountered
two army cooks who had been sent by their officer to
fetch eggs from a nearby village. According to one
version of the tale, the perplexed cooks refused to accept
the surrender of Jerusalem. Another version has it that
they returned to their unit in an excited state and
reported that they had no eggs but that they had brought
the document surrendering Jerusalem. In the meantime,
the mayor, unconvinced that he had dealt with the
correct parties, encountered two British sergeants,
Hurcomb and Sedgewick, to whom he handed over the
white flag. Apparently the mayor was obliged to perform
the surrender several more times, and in each instance,
as the stories go, the British recipient was of a higher
rank.

The Briton of unquestionably highest rank was
General Edmund Allenby, who sent units to the city on
that very day, but whose official entry took place a few
days later. Half a year earlier, on the eve of assuming

General Edmund Allenby on the steps of the Citadel officially announces the conquest of Jerusalem by the British,
Dec. 11, 1917

command of the Palestinian campaign, Allenby had heard the Prime Minister of Britain, David Lloyd-George tell him: "I want Jerusalem as a Christmas present for the British people." Allenby fulfilled his mission, assuming control of the city on December 11, 1917, a fortnight before Christmas.

General Allenby entered Jerusalem in a colorful victory procession. It seemed that all the city's residents awaited him along the main street of the new city, Jaffa Road. The parade included all the British imperial units – English, Scottish, Irish, Australians, New Zealanders, Indians, Bantus from Africa, as well as smaller units from the French and Italian armies, and even a liaison officer of the United States army. The parade also featured horses and camels of the cavalry, armored cars, and military orchestras. Allenby, mounted on a magnificent steed, led the parade. When he arrived at the Jaffa Gate, he dismounted and entered the Old City on foot, expressing in this manner his recognition of the city's holiness. In the inner courtyard of Jaffa Gate the conqueror of Jerusalem made a declaration to the inhabitants of the city while photographers recorded the event. Four hundred years of Ottoman rule over Jerusalem had come to an end.

Save for the initial decades of their long rule over the city, the Turks did little to develop Jerusalem. Their indifference to its welfare was blatant. Progress and development during the nineteenth and early twentieth centuries were generally initiated by the Jews, Christians and representatives of the various churches and major European powers, largely against the regime's will. Yet in retrospect, four hundred years of Ottoman Turkish rule was in some way advantageous for Jerusalem. There were few wars and rebellions during that time, no small blessing for a city that had known so many conquerors. Life in the city, despite the scarcity of food and the poverty, was considered relatively endurable for the times.

THE BRITISH MANDATE PERIOD

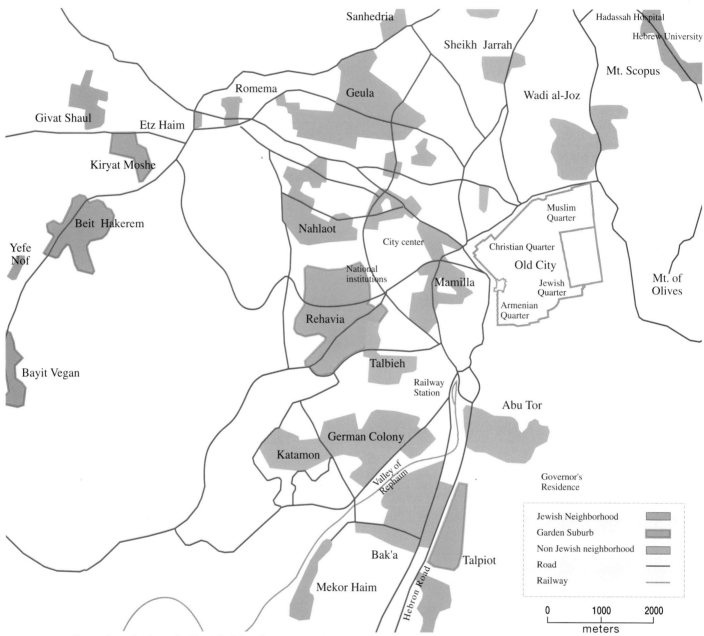

Sanhedria

Sheikh Jarrah

Hadassah Hospital

Hebrew University

Mt. Scopus

Romema

Geula

Wadi al-Joz

Givat Shaul

Etz Haim

Kiryat Moshe

Beit Hakerem

Muslim
Quarter

Yefe
Nof

Nahlaot

City center

Christian Quarter

Old City

National
institutions

Mamilla

Jewish
Quarter

Mt. of
Olives

Rehavia

Armenian
Quarter

Talbieh

Railway
Station

Bayit Vegan

Abu Tor

German Colony

Katamon

Valley of
Rephaim

Governor's
Residence

Bak'a

Talpiot

Mekor Haim

Hebron Road

Jewish Neighborhood	
Garden Suburb	
Non Jewish neighborhood	
Road	
Railway	

0   1000   2000

meters

Jerusalem during the British Mandate years, showing the Old City and the spread of new neighborhoods on the surrounding hills

ירושלם

שאלו שלום ירושלם ישליו אהביך יהי שלום בחילך שלוה בארמנותיך

A romanticized depiction of Jerusalem, one of a series of postcards designed by Zev Rabban
of the Bezalel School of Art, 1931

On December 9, 1917 Jerusalem came under British military control. The First World War was still raging, and General Allenby and his forces soon left the city to resume the campaign against the Turks, both in Palestine and far beyond it. A military governor was left in charge of Jerusalem, whose authority extended over the city and would, in due course, extend over all Palestine. In 1920 military control was replaced by a British-dominated civilian authority. The legal basis for Britain's continuing control of Jerusalem and Palestine was a mandate given to Great Britain by the League of Nations. It was intended as a temporary arrangement, to bring "people not yet able to stand by themselves" to the point where they could be self-governing. In this context, Britain controlled Palestine and Jerusalem, with the understanding that it would encourage and oversee development and modernization, and foster processes leading to self-government. A unique proviso of the British Mandate for Palestine was the obligation to implement the Balfour Declaration, whose brief text was incorporated directly into the Mandate charter. The Balfour Declaration, officially issued by Foreign Minister Lord Arthur Balfour in November 1917, committed Great Britain to fostering in Palestine the establishment of a national home for the Jewish people, while also protecting the rights of the land's non-Jewish communities.

The Jews of Palestine were overjoyed by this succession of fortuitous events (the Balfour Declaration in November 1917 followed by the British conquest of Jerusalem a month later) while Palestine's Arab inhabitants gradually became wary, and then demonstrably discontent over the implications of the very same events. Since Jerusalem was the capital of Mandatory Palestine, it would in the coming decades be at the center of many controversies.

The British would control Jerusalem for thirty years, five months and five days. Having entered as liberators, they would depart in 1948 scorned by all sides, at the height of a crucial struggle between Jews and Arabs over the future of Jerusalem and Palestine.

The British in Jerusalem: Defeating Hunger and Disease

In December 1917 the British were the great hope of a starving and desperate Jerusalem populace. The first military governor, Colonel Ronald Storrs, found the city in a desperate state. Famine threatened to add to the city's death toll, which had reached many hundreds and perhaps thousands. Storrs noted in his memoirs that on the morning of January 1, 1918, he heard a soft sobbing outside his office window. Investigating the source, he found a crowd of veiled women, some of whom had pushed aside their veils to reveal protruding cheek-bones which almost came through their skins. The children were in an even more dreadful state.

The British delivered large aid shipments to the city. First, however, they adopted special measures to ensure equitable food distribution. The military government ordered that bread should first be sold to women, then to children, and only after that to men, for otherwise the weaker inhabitants would not stand a chance against the stronger. Jerusalem was crowded with feeble inhabitants, among them thousands of refugees who were returning to the city from their scattered havens. For quite some time, the military government channeled large quantities of wheat, flour, sugar, and oil into the city in order to keep prices at an affordably low level.

The British repaired roads within and leading to the city as well as the railway connecting Jerusalem with the coastal plain. They made efforts to improve the standards of sanitation by repairing drainage systems and the thousands of leaky cisterns which stored water in almost every courtyard. Jerusalem was perpetually deficient in water reserves. The British Army Engineering Corps put their equipment and know-how to work laying a pipeline to the city from the wells of Arrub in the Hebron mountains. A large reservoir was also built north of Jerusalem, and in a relatively short time, a network of pipelines served a large part of the town.

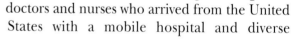

Special attention was paid to the health needs of Jerusalemites. Clinics were established, hospitals enlarged, and immunization drives launched, all of which played an important part in improving public health. The Jewish community also benefitted from the work of a large contingent of doctors and nurses who arrived from the United States with a mobile hospital and diverse

The British were the first rulers in modern times to make Jerusalem a capital city and create Palestinian currency and stamps. Shown: stamps and pound note depicting Jerusalem sites and Rachel's Tomb in nearby Bethlehem

medical equipment. They were sent by Hadassah, the Zionist women's charitable organization founded in 1912.

In sharp contrast to the attitude of Jerusalem's previous Ottoman rulers, the British viewed the city as a worthy capital in which all governing institutions should be centered. In view of its rich and varied past, the city was deemed worthy of special attention. Military Governor Storrs commissioned two urban planners to establish guidelines for preservation of landmark architecture and of the dramatic and evocative vista of the Old City. William McLean drew up Jerusalem's first urban master plan, while Patrick Geddes carefully delineated details. An early decision was to surround the Old City with parkland and a 'no-building' zone.

Ronald Storrs, a classics scholar by education, left his mark on Jerusalem in the eight years that he ran the city, first as military governor and afterwards as civilian district commissioner. Of lasting impact was his order forbidding the use of any material other than local stone for building within the vicinity of the Old City. In order to further the city's prospects, Storrs established the Pro-Jerusalem Society, which took on the task of caring for the city. It was composed of lay representatives of all Jerusalem's religious and ethnic groups, along with scholars and spiritual leaders. One of its suggestions was the removal of an anachronistic and stylistically discordant clock-tower erected by the Turks alongside Jaffa Gate.

Laying the Foundations of the Hebrew University

In July 1918, more than a little optimism was needed to lay the cornerstone for a new Hebrew University on Mount Scopus. The driving force behind this visionary enterprise was Dr. Chaim Weizmann, an Anglo-Jewish chemist and leader of the World Zionist Organization who is generally credited with a pivotal role in achieving the Balfour Declaration. Weizmann succeeded in gathering a distinguished group for a ceremony on Mount Scopus. It was headed by the triumphant General Allenby, whose mission was still not at an end, and attended by heads of the Jewish community and dignitaries of the Muslim and Christian population. Dr.

Purim caricature depicting Sir Herbert Samuel, first High Commissioner of Palestine

Weizmann gave a short speech to the sound of distant cannon shelling Turkish positions north of Ramallah. The ceremony came to an end with the singing of two national anthems: the Jewish 'Hatikvah' and the British 'God Save the King'. Less than seven years later, the Hebrew University opened its gates with a much more impressive ceremony.

In 1920, British military personnel made way for the first civilian governor of Palestine, the Anglo-Jewish High Commissioner Sir Herbert Samuel. At first he and his staff occupied the Augusta Victoria building on the Mount of Olives. Within a short time, Samuel built up an efficient civil service, led mainly by British administrators, with both Arabs and Jews at the lower levels.

Ben-Yehudah Street, the new commercial center of Jerusalem

Who Was Who in Jerusalem

When the British took responsibility for Jerusalem in December 1917, its estimated population was fewer than fifty thousand souls, a decline of forty percent compared with the figure in the summer of 1914. The decline was particularly evident among the Jews, who had lost much of their number through death, deportation, and mass emigration. Even in the first census conducted by the British in late 1922, the city had not regained its former strength. Its population numbered some 62,500 souls, as compared with 75,000 seven years previously. There were some thirty-four thousand Jews (54.8%), 14,700 Christians (23.7%,), and 13,400 Muslims (21.5%).

The results of the second and last census conducted by the British in Palestine at the end of 1931, show the population of Jerusalem numbering 90,500 inhabitants. The Jewish majority rose slightly to 56.6%, the Muslims constituted 22% and the Christians, who lost a tenth of their former number, constituted 21.4%. In the following years, with the increase in Jewish immigration, the number of Jerusalem's Jewish inhabitants grew enormously. In the 1940s, they accounted for 60% of the population. The Arab population was almost equally divided between Muslims and Christians, with a slight edge to the Muslims. At the end of the British Mandate, in 1948, the population of Jerusalem was estimated at 160,000; one hundred thousand Jews and the remainder, Muslim and Christian Arabs, in addition to small groups of Armenians, Copts, Greeks, British and other Europeans.

The Jewish population dispersed geographically and established new neighborhoods while their number within the Jewish Quarter of the walled Old City dwindled. In 1900 there were still 19,000 Jews living inside the Old City. In the 1931 census, it appeared that less than ten percent of the Jews of Jerusalem lived in the Jewish Quarter (5,200), and six years later, on the eve of the British Mandate's expiry, there were only 2,500 Jews living in the Quarter, less than two and a half percent of the entire Jewish population of Jerusalem.

In contrast, the Arab population of the Old City rose. In 1900 17,000 Arabs were living there (as opposed to 19,000 Jews). Two generations later, in 1947, the Arab population of the Old City was ten times larger than that of the Jews, 27,000 as against 2,500.

The Jewish population of Jerusalem during the Mandate period consisted of four main elements: the old, ultraorthodox Ashkenazi community and the old Sephardi community, who together made up 'The Old Yishuv,' the modern Ashkenazi community, and the Oriental communities (Jews from Muslim lands of the East). The 'Old Yishuv' had, until a short time before the Mandate period, constituted the majority in the city. Its percentage declined to the extent that towards the end of the 30s, it consisted of only 20 percent of the total population. The Oriental communities made up a third of the Jewish population and the

The author S.Y. Agnon immortalized Mandate period Jerusalem in his novels.
He later won the Nobel Prize for Literature

Period rooms of Jerusalem in the early Mandate period. On left, a Sephardi salon. On right, an Ashkenazi salon

newer Ashkenazi community a little less than that, while the old Sephardi community were some ten to fifteen percent of the Jewish population.

The Struggle for Control of the Municipality

Despite official statistics which clearly indicated that Jerusalem had a Jewish majority, the British insisted on maintaining the Ottoman status-quo which dictated that a Muslim Arab should be mayor. To offset this decision, a change was made in the composition of the Municipal Council. The British dislodged the Ottoman Municipal Council, which had included seven Muslims, two Christians and one Jew, and appointed a new council consisting of six members – two Muslims, two Christians, and two Jews. The mayor, Hussein Effendi al-Husseini remained in his post, and when he died five months later, his brother, Musa Khazem al-Husseini was appointed. In the spring of 1920, Colonel Storrs dismissed the latter Husseini, after he made sharply critical public remarks about the British government's commitment to the Balfour Declaration. The new mayor, put in place by Storrs, was Ragheb al-Nashashibi, the scion of a prominent family at odds with the Husseini family, and known to be more moderate politically. Storrs also appointed a new Municipal Council of six members with the same set-up of Muslims, Christians and Jews. This council functioned until the first municipal elections in 1927. As a balancing factor, the British appointed two deputies to assist Nashashibi – the Jew David Yellin, and Yakoub Frej, a Christian.

Only a small portion of the inhabitants of Jerusalem participated in the elections of 1927. According to the Ottoman rules suffrage, only males age twenty-five and over who were citizens of Palestine, owned property, and paid some form of government or municipal tax, had the right to vote. Actually, for the first time, those who maintained property but did not necessarily own it, and who paid taxes, were permitted to vote. As a result of these limitations on suffrage, only some 4,000 out of 80,000 inhabitants of Jerusalem were qualified to vote. Of these 1,500 were Muslims, 1,400 Jews, and 1,000 were Christians.

Daniel Auster, the only Jew during the Mandate period to act as mayor of Jerusalem

This limited electorate chose a Municipal Council of twelve, which closely reflected the ratio of enfranchised Muslims to enfranchised Jews. There were five Muslim Council members and four Jews. Muslim representation had risen at the expense of Christian representation, which dropped from four to three seats. Viewed from another, inescapable perspective, the 1927 Council was composed of four Jews and eight Arabs, as both the Muslims and Christians were ethnically Arab. Thus, in a city with an absolute majority of Jews, the Jews' interests were likely to be set aside by a Municipal Council on which their representatives were greatly outnumbered. Once again, the mayor was Ragheb al-Nashashibi and his two deputies were a Jew and a Christian Arab.

In the elections of September 1934, in accordance with the law in force at the time, 8,800 Jerusalemites had the right to vote. Of these some fifty percent were Jews. For the first time the British decided that six Jews and six Arabs (both Muslims and Christians) would participate in the council. As to the mayoralty, British High Commissioner Sir Arthur Wauchope stressed that despite the Jewish majority, he was obliged to appoint an Arab to this role. Ragheb al-Nashashibi was again a candidate, but his opponent, Dr. Hussein Khalidi, was appointed mayor.

There was considerable tension between Mayor Hussein Khalidi and his Jewish deputy, Daniel Auster. After the eruption of riots in April 1936, the Arab representatives on the council boycotted the sessions and it became impossible to hold meetings for lack of a quorum. During the next six months, the British attempted to bridge the widening gap between Jews and Arabs, and almost succeeded. In the summer of 1937, when Khalidi took a long leave, Auster was appointed acting mayor. In October, following a new series of disturbances instigated by the Arabs, Dr. Khalidi was exiled to the Seychelle Islands along with other leading Palestinian Arabs, including a member of Jerusalem's Municipal Council.

During the next few years, matters continued to be troublesome. It was proposed repeatedly that the role of mayor be filled by a Jew and an Arab in rotation. Elections to the Municipal Council which were supposed to take place in December 1939 were postponed indefinitely due to the outbreak of World War II.

To a certain degree, war-time circumstances lessened the tension around the Jerusalem municipality's affairs, although tensions did not disappear entirely. The Muslim Arab mayor, Khalidi, died on August 27, 1944, and his place was taken by the Jew, Daniel Auster. Excitement surrounding this development was rife in the Arab sector, and the demand was made to appoint an Arab mayor. For months there was a great deal of agitation over the

matter, and again the suggestion of rotation was brought up. During this period, Daniel Auster continued to fulfill the function of mayor despite the resentment of the Arabs. In 1945 the Arab Council members resigned, and the British government appointed a committee headed by the former British postmaster, George Webster. This committee ran the city until the end of the British Mandate. The mere fact of its continued existence was an indication that Jews and Arabs were unable to bridge the gap between them, and the British gave up hope of finding a compromise solution.

Mayor Khalidi of Jerusalem

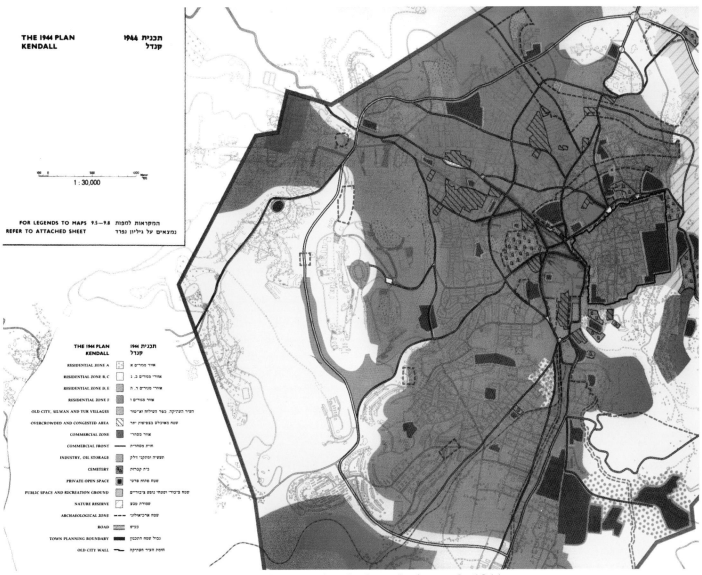

THE 1944 PLAN KENDALL		תכנית 1944 קנדל
THE 1944 PLAN KENDALL		תכנית 1944 קנדל
RESIDENTIAL ZONE A		אזור מגורים א
RESIDENTIAL ZONE B, C		אזורי מגורים ב, ג
RESIDENTIAL ZONE D, E		אזורי מגורים ד, ה
RESIDENTIAL ZONE F		אזור מגורים ו
OLD CITY, SILWAN AND TUR VILLAGES		העיר העתיקה, כפר השילוח ואי־טור
OVERCROWDED AND CONGESTED AREA		שטח מאוכלס בצפיפות יתר
COMMERCIAL ZONE		אזור מסחרי
COMMERCIAL FRONT		חזית מסחרית
INDUSTRY, OIL STORAGE		תעשיה ומתקני דלק
CEMETERY		בית קברות
PRIVATE OPEN SPACE		שטח פתוח פרטי
PUBLIC SPACE AND RECREATION GROUND		שטח ציבורי ושטחי נופש ציבוריים
NATURE RESERVE		שמורת טבע
ARCHAEOLOGICAL ZONE		שטח ארכיאולוגי
ROAD		כביש
TOWN PLANNING BOUNDARY		גבול שטח התכנון
OLD CITY WALL		חומת העיר העתיקה

The Kendall master plan for Jerusalem's growth, 1944

Expansion of the Built-Up Area

The era of British rule in Jerusalem was characterized, among other things, by a notable escalation in all types of construction. After the two master plans prepared by McLean and Geddes during the period of military rule, the British civilian administration continued planning the new city. In 1922, Charles Robert Ashbee, secretary of the Pro-Jerusalem Society, submitted plans for the distribution of residential districts, light industry, and parkland. Three years later, British architect Clifford Holyday submitted more detailed plans, which were

authorized after some years and were still valid in the 1940s. The major emphasis of the plan was its placement of residential districts on the fringe of the city, both to the north and the south. A fifth plan was prepared during the 1940's by Henry Kendall. It served Jerusalem's needs until the end of British rule.

Surprisingly, in view of their interest in the overall planning of Jerusalem, the British did very little actual construction. The number of monumental structures erected by them is comparatively small. Among them, were the High Commissioner's residence on the Hill of Evil Counsel to the south of the city, the Central Post

Office on Jaffa Road, the Police School in the Sheikh Jarrah Quarter, and the Rockefeller Museum which was built with the help of American support. Most British offices were located in pre-existing buildings, such as those in the Russian compound, the Palace Hotel, the King David Hotel, and the David Building.

The bookplate of Prof. Martin Buber, one of a number of Jewish intellectuals and artists attracted to Jerusalem during the 1920s

There was a marked increase in Jewish residential areas in Jerusalem during the 1920s – 1930s. In only a few years, Jewish garden suburbs sprouted – Talpioth and Mekor Haim in the south, Rehavia in the center, Beth ha-Kerem, Bayit Vegan, and Kiriat Moshe in the west. These joined the list of existing Jewish neighborhoods: Romema, Sanhedria, Mahanaim and Givat Shaul. In the center of the city a number of gaps were closed between Jewish areas, as commercial buildings and tall residential projects were erected all along the new street named for King George V, which together with the nearby Ben-Yehudah Street, quickly became the most important commercial area of the new city.

From the late twenties onward, Jewish public buildings went up at a fast pace. These included the Hebrew University campus on Mount Scopus, the Teachers' Seminary in Beth ha-Kerem, the Straus Health Center in the middle of the city and, in Rehavia, the building housing the Jewish national institutions. The latter dignified building with its curved facade, housed the Jewish Agency, the National Council, the Jewish National Fund, and Keren Hayesod. Designed by the architect Jochanan Ratner, it was a landmark in Jewish Jerusalem during the Mandate period.

In addition to the monumental national buildings constructed in Jerusalem during this period, mention should be made of the elegant King David Hotel which opened its doors in 1930, and has ever since functioned as the most prestigious hostelry in Jerusalem; the building of the YMCA with its tall minaret-like tower, inaugurated in 1933, the Hadassah Hospital on Mount Scopus, the Scottish Church of St. Andrew in southern Jerusalem, and the Jerusalem branch of the Anglo-Palestine bank (today's Bank Leumi) in the center of town.

The establishment of the Hebrew University campus on Mount Scopus was an important contribution to the development of Jerusalem. The ceremonial opening of the world's first Jewish university on April 1, 1925 was a national holiday. Heads of the religious communities in Jerusalem, alongside leaders of the Jewish community and senior representatives of the Jewish people, all took part in the festivities. The guest of honor was Lord Arthur Balfour, who drafted the British government declaration bearing his name. Other prominent guests were the High Commissioner Herbert Samuel, and General Edmund Allenby, conqueror of Palestine and Jerusalem during World War I. The chief sponsor of the celebration was Dr. Chaim Weizmann, who had seen this project through, from dream to completion. Weizmann would later become the first president of Israel.

Until 1948, the university was somewhat limited in size (fewer than a thousand students), but it achieved a considerable reputation in the world of scientific research as well as the spirit and nature of Judaism. The Jewish National and University Library had an important role from the outset.

Dedication of the Hebrew University, 1925. Lord Balfour addresses the crowd, Dr. Chaim Weizmann and chief rabbis are among the dignitaries at the dais

Muslim and Christian Construction

The Mandate period witnessed considerable momentum in Arab construction of homes, however Arab public building was quite limited during that period. The Muslim Arabs who left the confines of the Old City were in the main concentrated in the northeastern part of the town, in such quarters as Wadi al-Joz, Bab al-Zahara, and Sheikh Jarrah. The latter began to enjoy a reputation as the most prestigious Muslim neighborhood in Jerusalem. Among the few public buildings built by Arabs was the Palace Hotel in the Mamillah Quarter, which was built on the initiative and with the support of the Muslim Higher Council. Not long after its completion it proved to be an unprofitable venture. It was leased for office space by the Mandate authorities.

Christian construction during the Mandate period was marked by extreme restraint. The initiative for building had in the past come from outside the country, either from foreign states or a major church. The Greek Orthodox Church which had a pivotal role in Ottoman Jerusalem, was in financial crisis during the Mandate period, and had to sell a considerable portion of its land holdings. Christian Arabs built privately during this period, particularly in Talbieh, Katamon and the

German and Greek colonies. Talbieh, bordering on the Jewish quarters of Rehavia and Kiriat-Shmuel, was considered the most prestigious Christian neighborhood. Its elegant houses were occupied by many prominent Christian Arabs of Jerusalem, as well as high officials of the Mandatory government. A number of consulates were situated there, lending the neighborhood an international flavor. A number of wealthy Jewish families also built homes in Talbieh.

The King David Hotel, prime example of monumental architecture during the Mandate period

A Colorful and Variegated City

Jerusalem during the Mandate period was a pluralistic city with a variety of residents. There were the British rulers with their large contingent of civil servants who hailed from various parts of the United Kingdom. Members of the different Christian churches contributed to the city's colorful international atmosphere. Palestine, a country of insufficient rank to merit ambassadors, was nevertheless host to the consuls general of many states, who made their headquarters in Jerusalem and expected to be treated in every way like a diplomatic corps. Jerusalem's Arab inhabitants – Muslims and Christians alike – represented the East, while the Jews added a gallery of personalities from the old Ashkenazi Yishuv, clad in their long coats and fur-trimmed hats, to the veteran Sephardim and scions of the eastern communities and the emigres from Eastern and Central Europe who had settled in new Jerusalem.

High Commissioner Sir Arthur Wauchope in ceremonial dress on the day of his swearing in, 1931

To this great variety were added the tourists who came to the city throughout the year and especially during the holidays of the different religious communities. VIP's and journalists added a final touch to the colorful variety of 'types' walking the streets of Mandate period Jerusalem. Journalists were inclined to stay in Jerusalem for extended periods, in calm times, and moreso during times of stress and struggle, which were not lacking during British rule. During World War II, for instance, the restaurant of the King David Hotel was the lodestone for every journalist in the Middle East. Every reputable reporter or columnist made a point of being there at one time or another.

Jerusalem had always had a social life, even before the arrival of the British, but this increased substantially during their rule. Social gatherings after the fashion of European salons were held at the homes of senior British officials as well as in the homes of Jews and Arabs of certain standing and repute. Katie Antonius' salon was celebrated among the Arabs. A variety of prominent Jerusalemites met there; British officials, Arab notables and intellectuals, Jews such as Dr. Judah Magnes, president of the Hebrew University, and a large

contingent of foreign and local journalists. Among the Jews, the homes of Dr. Arthur Ruppin and the attorney Shalom Horowitz were similarly scenes of large and mixed social gatherings. Finally, the High Commissioner's home was a meeting place for prominent personalities. A strict balance was always maintained there between invitees of Jerusalem's different communities.

The King David Hotel was to Jerusalem what the "Ritz" or the "Grand Hotel" were to other capitals. Built at record speed in 1930 by a group of Jewish investors from Egypt, it was probably unmatched from Cairo to the Far East for beauty and elegance. Kings, statesmen and millionaires were all part of its scene. In its guest book are the names of General Dwight D. Eisenhower and General George Marshall, the family of the Persian Shah, ambassadors, and journalists from every important newspaper in the world.

The building across the street from the King David Hotel – the YMCA – also constituted an important social and diplomatic meeting place. Its construction was the outcome of a 1927 international gathering of the Young Men's Christian Association. They decided to build a center in Jerusalem on a large site. Plans called for an edifice with a tall tower. It is to this day one of the most eye-catching features of Jerusalem' skyline. The building houses meeting and concert halls, a swimming pool, gymnasiums, and a hostel.

The Press in Jerusalem

Until World War I, Jerusalem was the journalistic center of Palestine. The first newspapers (weeklies) were brought out by the Jews in 1863. The first Arab newspaper appeared at the outset of the 20th century, also in the form of a weekly. The first daily *Ha-Zvi* was published in 1908, with Eliezer Ben-Yehudah, the father of modern Hebrew, as its editor. Within the next few years, three Hebrew dailies were on the newsstands as well as a large number of periodicals in Hebrew, Arabic and other languages. After World War I, Jerusalem still maintained superiority as the major journalistic axis but this status was eventually surrendered to Tel Aviv.

The British encouraged tourism. Poster design, Franz Kraus, 1936

Jerusalem lane, 1947. Painting by Ludwig Blum

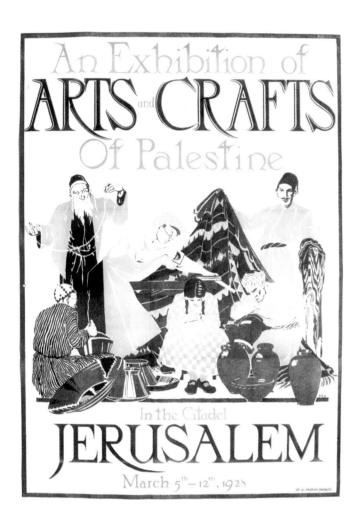

With the onset of British rule, two new Hebrew dailies began to appear in Jerusalem: *Hadashot Ha-aretz* (which became the present-day *Ha-Aretz*) and *Doar ha-Yom*. The latter also published weekly editions in English and Arabic. In 1923, *Ha-Aretz* moved to Tel Aviv, where most of the Hebrew dailies appeared. During the 30s, *Doar ha-Yom* closed down and attempts to publish other Hebrew dailies proved unsuccessful. Newspapers in Arabic also seemed unable to strike roots in Jerusalem. During the 1930s, two dailies – *Marat a-Sharq* and *al-Liwa* – appeared in Arabic in Jerusalem but they did not last long. Arabic dailies in Jaffa were much more successful.

In contrast to the above-mentioned newspapers, the only English language daily, *The Palestine Post*, which first appeared in Jerusalem in 1932, enjoyed a favorable response from the outset. From its pages, its readers – diplomats, officers, British police and soldiers, tourists and visitors, and even Arab intellectual circles – drew their information on local and international affairs. Its editor, Gershon Agron, did not conceal his affinity with the New Yishuv and the Jewish people, but still adhered to high journalistic standards of accuracy and objectivity. After the establishment of the state, this daily changed its name to *The Jerusalem Post*.

Taking Stock

The sustained Jewish majority in Jerusalem was a major success of Jewish national endeavors during the Mandate period. At times, this majority hovered above sixty percent, clear evidence of ardent Jewish attachment to the city, despite Jerusalem's limited economic base and the violence which periodically plagued it during the

Mandate years. Another success was the increase in new Jewish neighborhoods and commercial areas, and their geographical spread. Also of significance was the decision to locate the major Jewish national institutions in Jerusalem. The main offices of the Zionist movement were all there: its elected assembly, National Council, the Zionist Organization's executive, the Jewish Agency for Palestine, and the Chief Rabbinate. They were housed in newly built structures designed especially for Jewish self-government functions. Their location in Jerusalem bonded the Jewish national leadership to the city. In addition, the first Jewish university, the Hebrew University, was located on Mt. Scopus, and became an academic institution of the first order, lending a high tone and prestige to the Jewish national endeavor, and to Jewish cultural life in Jerusalem.

Rabbi Abraham Isaac HaCohen Kook, revered scholar, first Ashkenazi Chief Rabbi

From the 1920s onward, Jerusalem became the home of several spiritual and intellectual giants, among them the rabbinic scholar Rabbi Abraham Isaac Kook, the philosopsher Martin Buber, who arrived in 1938, and the writer S.Y. Agnon, who later in his career would receive the Nobel Prize for Literature.

Jerusalem became the center for nurturing Jewish cultural and spiritual identification in Palestine and around the world. Its Jewish neighborhoods and schools fostered a generation of authors, playwrights and poets who would use the city's features as both backdrop and central imagery in their work. In 1936 the newly established government radio station introduced a daily broadcast in the Hebrew language. It was called *Kol Yerushalayim*, ('the Voice of Jerusalem') and it had a great impact on the spirit of the Jews of Palestine, helping to sustain a sense of fraternity and common cause, and helping to weave a new Jewish culture.

Yet, for all Jerusalem's importance to the dreamers and planners of the New Yishuv, conflicting national priorities and limited financial resources restrained Jewish immigration to and development of Jerusalem. The Zionist dream placed high priority on working the land, and many Jewish immigrants during the Mandate period joined existing Jewish agricultural settlements or founded new ones. Other immigrants went to towns, especially Tel Aviv, which became the first exclusively Jewish city. It was located on the coast, easily accessible from the country's ports of entry, and underwent extremely rapid growth. The Jews of Jerusalem were the majority of that city's population, but were a steadily shrinking percentage of the total Jewish population of Palestine. At the beginning of the Mandate period, the Jews of Jerusalem were 50% of the total Jewish population, while at the end of the Mandate period they were no more than 16% of the total. Furthermore, as far as their impact upon overall Jewish nationalist policy was concerned, Jerusalem's Jews had even less clout than the figures might indicate, for the figure of 16% included many Jerusalemites of the Old Yishuv, the ultraorthodox communities who did not involve themselves in Jewish nationalist issues.

A comparison of 1931 and 1936 population figures for Jerusalem and Tel Aviv offers ample evidence of the contemporary trend. While in 1931 there were ninety thousand Jews living in Jerusalem and half that number in Tel Aviv, five years later the scene was completely changed. Jerusalem's Jewish population had indeed grown and had some 120,000 souls, but Tel Aviv had expanded to three or four times its size, and in 1936 had some 145,000 inhabitants. While Jerusalem absorbed 20,000 new Jewish immigrants during these years, Tel Aviv absorbed a hundred thousand! Jerusalem lost its status as the largest city in Palestine.

The vibrant and energetic secular leadership of the Zionist New Yishuv identified itself with Tel Aviv, a city they had begun from scratch. A new Jewish culture began to grow there, as well as a social scene and an exceptionally lively political life. Running a close second in the hearts of the New Yishuv Jewish leadership were the kibbutz communal settlements and the moshav cooperative settlements, which were fulfilling the Zionist dream of turning the countryside green, and feeding the steadily growing Jewish population. Only after these places came Jerusalem. Passionate claims were made by some of the leaders that priorities should be altered. Menachem Ussishkin, one of the first Zionist leaders and

The conflicting priorities regarding Jerusalem may account for the fact that when the British Royal Commission (Peel Commission) in 1937 proposed a partition plan in which a small Jewish state would exist without Jerusalem (which was to be part of a British enclave), such senior Jewish statesmen as Weizmann,

Jewish workers of the 'Labor Battalions' prepare the ground for the Jewish National Institutions building in Rehavia neighborhood

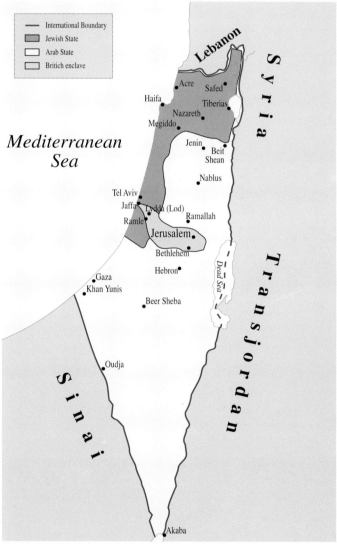

Map of the Peel Commission partition plan, July 1937. Jerusalem was to be a British-controlled enclave within the Arab state

an inhabitant of Jerusalem from the day he arrived in Palestine in 1919, expressed his heavy-hearted feelings on the subject:

"...I must say that the Zionist Organization sinned against Jerusalem since our inception. It neglected the capital... and what did we do about it? We almost delivered our capital to our elders (the Old Yishuv) to sigh, to mourn and bewail it... If we want to be our own masters, we must first of all receive our rights in Jerusalem, as is due to us as the majority of its inhabitants... for if Palestine is holy to us, then Jerusalem is the holy of holies."

Ben-Gurion and Shertok, agreed to the proposal, though others objected. The Arab leadership rejected the commission's proposals on all scores, so the point was rendered moot. Ten years later, the drama was repeated, when the inquiry commission of the United Nations

(UNSCOP) suggested partitioning Palestine between the Jews and the Arabs and establishing two states, with Jerusalem under the aegis of the United Nations. Once again, the Jewish leaders agreed to the proposal while the Arabs rejected the plan in its entirety. It was only when the battles raged which developed into the War of Independence, that Ben-Gurion's approach became solidified: that Jerusalem was part of the emerging Jewish state which could not exist without Jerusalem.

Riots in the Twenties

The Arabs of Palestine became increasingly discontent with the political realities of Mandatory Palestine. Jerusalem became a main setting for violent Arab opposition to the immigration and settlement activities of the Jews, and the policies of the British. The first episode of large scale looting and murder occurred on the Jewish pilgrimage festival of Passover 1920. The trigger that sent an Arab mob coursing through the city was a concocted claim that the Jews were planning to desecrate Muslim holy places on the Temple Mount. In the eyes of the frenzied Arab mob, all Jews and their buildings and property became targets on which to act out their anger. Synagogues and Jewish-owned buildings were destroyed, and Jewish property plundered, mainly in the Old City. Six Jews were killed

Ze'ev Jabotinsky, officer in the Jewish Legion of the wartime British army, tried to defend Jerusalem's Jews in the 1920 riots, but was arrested for his efforts. He later led the Revisionist Zionists

and over two hundred wounded. The British proved inadequate to the task of protecting the Jews and dispersing the rioters. Attempts at organized Jewish self-defense were vigorously discouraged by the British, who refused to allow members of the Jewish Battalion (a unit of the British armed forces which had fought in World War I and was still on duty in Palestine) to defend Jewish life and property. This policy led to the arrest of twenty Battalion veterans led by Ze'ev Jabotinsky. The punishment for their unauthorized self-defense effort was fifteen years of imprisonment. They were all subsequently pardoned, as were the Arab rioters.

British unwillingness to deputize Jews to protect their own community contributed to the establishment by the Zionist leadership of a small underground Jewish fighting force, the Haganah ('self-defense'). In its early stage, the Haganah was caught unprepared by May 1921 Arab rioting outside Jerusalem, in Jaffa and some rural Jewish settlements, but later that same year, on November 2, "Balfour Day," a group of Haganah defenders was able to stop an Arab mob from attacking the Jewish Quarter of the Old City. The Haganah would continue to play a role in the defense of the Jews of Jerusalem, however it was always severely limited by its illegal status.

Although the Arab Nationalist movement was more successful in the coastal cities of Jaffa and Haifa than in Jerusalem, most of the Arabs in Palestine looked towards the Muslim religious establishment in Jerusalem for leadership. The Grand Mufti (supreme religious leader) of Jerusalem, Haj Amin al-Husseini, was appointed to his post in 1921 by the High Commissioner Sir Herbert Samuel. Haj Amin, the scion of a very important Arab clan, was known for his extremism. He was chosen over several more moderate candidates. He gathered strength and influence and came out with sharp anti-Jewish and anti-Zionist pronouncements daily. During the 1920s he incited Arab attacks on the Jews of Jerusalem. The attackers did not distinguish between Zionist Jews and the members of Old Yishuv, who took no part in nationalist activities.

'The Wall,' masthead for the Haganah defense underground's bulletins, with Western Wall motif

Though a level of tension was ever-present in Jerusalem during the 1920s, actual demonstration of discontent mainly took the form of Arab general strikes. Toward the end of the decade a simple mishandled incident triggered an ever worsening spiral of events. On the eve of Yom Kippur (the sacred Jewish fast of Atonement) the 24th of September 1928, Jews preparing the narrow space before the Western Wall for the worship service, set up a temporary cotton screen to divide between men and women worshippers. The Arabs complained to the British that this Jewish alteration of the area was a violation of the status quo. Though the screen was temporary, and was placed in the worship area by ultraorthodox Jews who remained studiously uninvolved in nationalist issues, British police forcibly removed the screen, in the name of preserving the status quo. Nevertheless, the Grand Mufti Haj Amin al-Husseini used the incident to provoke Arab fears by claiming that the Jews intended to gradually take control of al-Aqsa mosque on the Temple Mount. During the next few months, Arabs took several actions which had the dual effect of offending Jewish religious sensibilities and altering the status quo. A noisy Arab construction project broke an opening in a wall near the Western Wall, and turned the narrow Jewish praying site into a passageway for people and cattle. During the daily Jewish prayer services held at the Wall, the Arab neighbors habitually played loud music. And changes were made to the upper courses of the Western Wall itself, Judaism's holiest site. All Jewish protests to the British authorities were of no avail.

In the summer of 1929 there were bloody attacks by Arabs on Jews in various areas of Palestine. The British had police but no military forces in Palestine, and were caught by surprise by the widespread attacks. In Jerusalem, Arab masses left the Temple Mount at noon on Friday, August 23, 1929 and tried to break through to the Jewish areas of the new city. The British were unprepared to control the riot. The number of Jewish victims grew from hour to hour, and on Saturday, the first seventeen dead were buried. During the next few days, Jewish neighborhoods in the north and west of the city were attacked: Beth ha-Kerem, Bayit Vegan, and Givat Shaul, and an even harsher attack was directed at the southern neighborhoods of Talpioth, Mekor Haim and Kibbutz Ramat Rahel. These areas were evacuated on the instructions of the British and their inhabitants returned after several days, to discover that their homes had been robbed and burned. The Jewish sections in the center of the city were also attacked a number of times.

The Haganah, working without British sanction, had a significant role in helping to put down the assaults in Jerusalem and isolated settlements nearby. In addition, until the British managed to mobilize reinforcements, they deputized British citizens and even tourists to assist their overwhelmed security forces. The most publicized of these groups were the 'Oxforders', twenty-eight students from the theological institute of Oxford University who had arrived with their teachers to make a study tour of Jerusalem, and were recruited to help maintain order. The young Britishers who went from quarter to quarter, played an important part in restoring order.

The violence of August 1929 was countrywide. Terrible atrocities against Jews occurred in Hebron and Safed in particular, where there was no British help, and also no Haganah. A detachment of British troops finally arrived in Palestine from Egypt, and order was restored. During the disturbances, the British administration forbade the appearance of newspapers and cut off the country's contact with the rest of the world. Only in September did life slowly return to normal.

The Arab Rebellion

The effect of the 1929 Arab riots in Jerusalem continued to be felt for more than a year. It was only with the onset of the 30s that peaceful conditions again prevailed. This state of affairs continued until the spring of 1936, when a new wave of riots termed the 'Arab Rebellion' erupted. By contrast with earlier episodes, this was not a short-winded outburst; it went on for three years, and Jerusalem was frequently the focal point of the two-sided, and at times three-sided conflict, between Arabs, Jews and British.

Between 1931 and 1935, the Jewish community in Palestine more than doubled in number – from 175,000 to almost 400,000. From 17% of the entire population at the beginning of the decade, the Jews reached approximately 30%, mainly due to the thousands of European Jewish immigrants arriving annually. The

Arabs warned the British administration that they would not stand idly by as this immigration proceeded. On April 19, 1936, riots erupted in Jaffa which quickly spread to the entire country, including Jerusalem. The Arabs also declared a general strike for an unlimited period, until the administration observed the following conditions: the suspension of Jewish immigration, a ban on the sale of land to Jews and the setting up of an administration which reflected Palestine's Arab majority.

From 1936 on, Jerusalem was to experience difficult times. Terror dominated its streets and Jews were shot in various parts of the city. The British strove to suppress Arab terror, but with little success. A disagreement arose within the Jewish leadership concerning tactics for Jewish response to the violence. Members of the Irgun 'B' (later to be named *Etzel* a Hebrew acronym for National Military Organization) responded with counter- terrorist activities and set off explosives in markets and other places where there were concentrations of Arabs, particularly in the Old City. However, the majority of the Jewish community of Palestine stood behind their leaders' adoption of the principle of *Havlaga* ('self-restraint'). This was a refusal to engage in lethal counter-terrorist acts and indiscriminate punishment. The *Havlaga* policy called for vigorous self-defense, and aggression only against actual perpetrators of attacks. A small unit of the Haganah called the "the Mobile Unit" was set up in Jerusalem and was the first to be involved in initiating offensive actions against centers of Arab terrorism.

The Arabs, who at first only attacked the Jews, soon vented their rage against the British as well. This clash reached its peak towards the end of 1937 and in 1938. Owing to the escalation of Arab terrorism, the British reacted harshly against the Arab leadership and in October 1937 arrested some of its leading figures, among them head of the Jerusalem municipality, Dr. Hussein al-Khalidi, and expelled them from the country. The Mufti of Jerusalem, Haj Amin al-Husseini, considered the most important Palestinian leader, fled the country. The months that followed witnessed a veritable war between the Arabs and the British, which for a brief time involved the absolute domination of the Old City, including the Temple Mount, by Arab forces. Only the Jewish Quarter remained outside Arab control. In response the British brought in large military reinforcements, and after a

Buses on the ascent to Jerusalem travel in convoy during the 1936 disturbances

battle lasting several days, regained control of the Old City.

Jewish Jerusalem paid heavily for the terror. In three years of bloody riots, some one hundred Jews were killed in the city and its environs, and hundreds wounded. The Arabs, who were the instigators of the riots, suffered greater losses. They became the targets of both a Jewish and a British response. In addition, they were the victims of bloody internal clashes within the Arab leadership. Haj Amin al-Husseini fled Jerusalem, never to return. and the head of the Jerusalem municipality and other leaders were expelled by the British. These events represented a blow to the Arab community of Jerusalem from which it was difficult to recover.

In 1939, on the eve of the outbreak of World War II, the 'Arab Rebellion' in Palestine subsided and peace returned to Jerusalem.

Jews Against the British

The Arab Rebellion was suppressed by the British against a background of intense political activity whose outcome was to affect the political constellation in Palestine and Jerusalem. Throughout the Mandate years, the British had periodically re-evaluated their commitment to the Balfour Declaration, spurred by the unceasing opposition of the Arabs. In July 1937 the British recommended partitioning Palestine into separate Arab and Jewish states. Jerusalem would become an international enclave within the Arab state. The Jews reluctantly accepted this idea, although the Jewish state would be confined to a narrow strip on the coast, and Jerusalem would be no part of it; the Arabs rejected the plan, and mobilized a rejection front of Arab leaders from lands far beyond Palestine. During the following two years further conferences were held, but no agreement was found. In May 1939 the British published a major foreign policy statement, the MacDonald White Paper, which imposed severe restrictions on Jewish immigration to Palestine over a five year period, and then ordered its complete halt, unless the Arabs approved more. The White Paper also imposed limits upon Jewish land purchase and settlement. For the New Yishuv, the White Paper could not have come at a worse time. In Palestine, it would arrest steady, visible progress toward an economically and politically autonomous Jewish national home, and nullify decades of hard work

and sacrifice. Furthermore, the inability to absorb Jewish immigrants would mean utter disaster for masses of desperate European Jews seeking shelter from Nazi atrocities which had rendered them stateless, penniless and in fear for their lives. Palestine was their last hope, and the British were barring the way.

The Jews of Palestine reacted to the White Paper in a variety of ways: increased efforts to bring Jewish refugees into the country illegally, anti-British demonstrations, and acts of sabotage against British government targets. Thus, in Jerusalem, shortly after High Commissioner Harold MacMichael announced the policy of the White Paper, the line connecting the Palestine Broadcasting Service in Jerusalem with the transmission antennas in Ramallah was damaged. However, all overt acts of sabotage came to an end some months later with the outbreak of World War II (September 1, 1939). The Jewish community was placed in the odd position of opposing the British in Palestine, while mobilizing in support of the British war effort. Opposition took the form of calmly defying British restrictions: new settlements were established, arms were stockpiled, young people received military training, and efforts continued for as long as possible to smuggle illegal Jewish immigrants into the country. At the same time, the leadership of the Yishuv mobilized Jewish resources for wartime agricultural and industrial purposes in support of the British, and as many as 18,000 Palestinian Jews served with British forces.

In late 1942 the direct Nazi threat to Palestine was eliminated when the British general Montgomery drove Rommel's forces entirely out of North Africa. By the winter of 1944 it began to be apparent that the Nazis would lose the war in Europe. Etzel, the military wing of the minority Revisionist Zionists, renewed its military activities against British rule. In Jerusalem, Etzel attacked personnel and buildings used by the British administration, among them the Intelligence and Income Tax Headquarters, army camps, and the railway station in the southern part of the city. This sort of sabotage was at that point opposed by the

"Bevingrad" in the heart of Jerusalem, 1947

The Rockefeller Museum, erected by the British with American support, 1938

Monumental architecture in Jerusalem. The YMCA, built in 1933, housed the UNSCOP delegation in 1947

majority leadership of the Yishuv. However, when the war ended and it became apparent that British policy would remain conciliatory toward the Arabs and detrimental to the interests of the Yishuv, the leadership too adopted an active, militant stance. Towards the end of 1945, a united Hebrew underground movement was set up to carry out coordinated moves against the British in Jerusalem and elsewhere. The British reacted by imposing a curfew on Jerusalem's Jewish areas, and arresting hundreds of suspects. During June and July, 1946, the Jewish-British struggle reached its climax. On Saturday, June 29th, the British took over the National Institutions building in Rehavia, which was the seat of the Jewish administration in Palestine. They confiscated documents and searched for arms. All over Palestine the British arrested some 2700 Jews, among them leaders of the Yishuv such as Moshe Shertok, head of the Political Department of the Jewish Agency, Itzhak Gruenbaum and Rabbi Yehuda Leib Fishman. The only reason that the chairman of the Jewish Agency, David Ben-Gurion, was not arrested was that he was out of the country.

Some weeks later, Etzel blew up the southern wing of the King David Hotel in Jerusalem, which housed British

military headquarters in Palestine and the main offices of the British government. Ninety-one people were killed in the explosion, most of them British, but some were Arabs and Jews. This act aroused considerable dissension in the Yishuv, and resulted in an end to the joint action of the united underground movement.

Jewish sabotage against the British did not cease in 1947, and the authorities reacted by imposing more curfews, carrying out searches for arms caches and interning suspects. The British enclosed themselves in fortified encampments within the city, sardonically known in Jerusalem folklore as 'Bevingrads' (after the British Foreign Secretary at the time, Ernest Bevin).

The British declared a state of martial law, bringing thousands of troops to the country while evacuating the wives and children of British personnel. They prepared themselves for a protracted struggle against the Jewish underground organizations. Concurrently they passed on the problem of Palestine to the United Nations, the young international body in existence only two years. A special assembly of the UN was called in the spring of 1947 and decided to send an inquiry commission to Palestine. This was UNSCOP – the United Nations Special

Jewish State
Arab State
International Boundary

Mediterranean Sea

Lebanon
Acre
Haifa
Nazareth
Nablus
Tel Aviv
Jerusalem
Gaza
Dead Sea
Beer Sheba
Syria
Jordan
Sinai
Akaba

The UNSCOP Partition Plan, November 1947. Jerusalem was to be an international enclave under UN control. The Jews reluctantly accepted the plan, the Arabs rejected it

September 1947 the commission published its conclusions. It recommended ending the British Mandate in Palestine and establishing two states – one Jewish and one Arab.

With regard to Jerusalem, UNSCOP departed from the principle of solution through partition. They recommended that Jerusalem remain united under the auspices of the United Nations, as an enclave within the territory of the Arab state. The Jews accepted the decision in the hope that it would be possible to maintain contact and establish a land bridge between the hundred thousand Jews who were the majority of Jerusalem's population, and the proposed Jewish state. The Arabs rejected the UNSCOP proposal.

The following months witnessed feverish discussions at the UN in New York on the subject of the UNSCOP proposals, and although changes were introduced, they remained essentially similar to the original proposals: the division of Palestine and the designation of Jerusalem as an international area.

Jerusalem in Political Plans, 1937-1947

In summary, during the last decade of British rule, a number of plans were put forward regarding the future of Jerusalem. In the summer of 1937 one of the recommendations of the Peel Commission's partition plan was to leave Jerusalem under British control. Between the Jewish and Arab states, a 'land corridor' would be created, to run from the Mediterranean to Jerusalem. The corridor would include Jaffa, Ramle and Lod, greater Jerusalem and Bethlehem. The Arabs rejected all the Peel Commission recommendations, while the Jews reluctantly accepted them. The assumption of the Jewish leadership was that the Jewish part of Jerusalem would be attached in some way to the future Jewish state.

There were mainstream Jewish leaders who could not countenance renunciation of control over Jerusalem. Berl Katznelson, an influential editor and intellectual guiding light of the Yishuv said: "If we remove Jerusalem from the Jewish state, we make naught of the Jewish state psychologically, politically and culturally... a Jewish state, no matter how small, with Jerusalem, will be accepted by the Jewish people as a beginning. A Jewish state without

Commission on Palestine. Its members remained in Palestine for over a month, and were based at the YMCA in Jerusalem.

The members of UNSCOP encountered a host of typical problems in that Jerusalem summer of 1947: barbed-wire barriers, fortified districts, difficulties getting from one district to another at night, and other restrictions that stemmed from British anxiety over acts of sabotage carried out by the Jews. The Commission met with representatives of the Jewish community, and were coolly received by the British, while the Arabs spurned them whenever they could. At the beginning of

Jerusalem would be like a body without its head... a Jerusalem beyond the borders can lead to the destruction of the Jewish state."

The British government sent another commission to Palestine in 1938, chaired by Sir John Woodhead, which made a number of proposals to put the partition plan into practice. The Jewish State became even smaller in this context, reaching miniature proportions in a strip along the coast. In all three of the commission's proposals, and in all subsequent deliberations, Jerusalem, including its access corridor to the sea, was to remain under British control.

The aforementioned proposals lay dormant during World War II. Then, in 1946, a joint British-American plan was formulated according to the principle of regional autonomy. The Morrison-Grady plan (so called

for Morrison, the Englishman, and Grady, the American) proposed that the Jews receive a sixth of the territory of Palestine; four tenths would be Arab land, and the southern Negev. The corridor from Jaffa to Jerusalem and Bethlehem would remain in British hands. The British High Commissioner would be the highest authority on political issues, finances, taxes, security and the legal system. Both the Jews and the Arabs refused to treat these proposals seriously, and they were removed from the agenda.

In the autumn of 1947, Britain was virtually relieved of its dominion over Palestine and Jerusalem. UNSCOP recommended, as mentioned above, ending the British Mandate conclusively. The two proposed states, one Jewish and one Arab, were to be independent, while maintaining economic unity. Jerusalem and its environs

Overjoyed Jews celebrate the UN partition vote in a parade along Jaffa Street, Jerusalem, November 30, 1947

were to become a "separate body" (*corpus separatum*) administered by the UN Trusteeship Council. A UN-appointed official would govern this international area with the help of a staff composed mainly of native Palestinians. A UN security force would be responsible for order in the city. The area would have an elected legislative body which would be neutral and unarmed. The UN governor would be responsible for the holy places of all the religions and would act in conjunction with representatives of the Jewish and Arab states of Palestine to defend their interests and those of their fellow-countrymen in Jerusalem.

The Arabs of Palestine rejected the UNSCOP partition plan, including its provisions for an internationalized Jerusalem. The Jews accepted the plan half-heartedly: gratified by the recognition of their claims and their aim of statehood, and distressed by the proposed borders of the Jewish area, and the exclusion of Jerusalem. David Ben-Gurion was aware that the city would be separated from the Jewish state, but decided that in spite of this: "Jerusalem does not cease being to the Jewish people what it was during King David's time and still is today: the heart of the Jewish people and its joy. It has not been designated (by UNSCOP) the capital of the Jewish state, but it was and will always remain the capital of the Jewish people, the very core of the entire Jewish people, whether they are in the Land of Israel or in the Diaspora. Jerusalem must become the navel of world Jewry..."

Ben-Gurion proposed that all the institutions of world Jewry join the Zionist national institutions (e.g. the Jewish Agency and the World Zionist Organization) in Jerusalem. He also saw the Jews of Jerusalem as holding citizenship in the Jewish state.

The End of British Rule

Even before the UN partition resolution was adopted, the British announced that they would accept any decision that body reached, and they began preparations to evacuate their military and governing institutions from Palestine. They were unwilling to help the UN during the interim and quickly found themselves in the very midst of the war between the Arabs and Jews. Palestine's Arabs, with the encouragement of the Arab states, proclaimed

that they would "drown the UN decision in blood." And from the morning after the UN decision, the Jews had to respond to this challenge.

The last half year of British rule in Jerusalem saw the gradual dismantling of all Britain's possessions in the city. The High Commissioner continued to occupy his residence and did his best to navigate through the stormy waters surrounding him. The British army attemped to separate the warring parties and both of them accused the British of partiality – toward the opposing party. Within the Jewish community there was bitter feeling towards the British, who were accused of carrying out a deliberately chaotic policy which would lead the UN to call on them to remain in Palestine. From documents published decades later, however, it appears that the chaos was not a British device, and that the British government was determined to end its hold over Palestine in an orderly manner.

The British presence in Palestine was gradually reduced during the winter and spring of 1948. On Friday, May 14, 1948, the last high commissioner, Sir Allen Cunningham, reviewed a guard of honor in the courtyard of his official residence in Jerusalem. The flags were lowered to the moans of the bugle, as the Union-Jack was lowered for the last time. The High Commissioner stepped into an armored car, which took him through the empty streets of Jerusalem to the Kalandia airport (today's Atarot) to the north of the city, and he took off for the port of Haifa. Later that day he boarded a warship, and following precisely the procedural specifics, waited until midnight to leave the territorial waters of Palestine.

During the morning hours of that same Friday, the last British soldiers left their bases in their various 'security zones' in the center and south of Jerusalem. The Jewish forces, while seriously outnumbered, had a superior intelligence system to that of the Arabs, and possessed last-minute details of the British evacuation. They managed, in the course of a few hours, to take over many British 'security zones', a fact which provided them with a definite advantage in the coming struggle.

Bitter battles ensued within and outside Jerusalem, which caused the British to be forgotten at once. The former triangle of conflicting interests was erased. Two sides were left to fight over Jerusalem – Jews and Arabs.

DIVIDED JERUSALEM

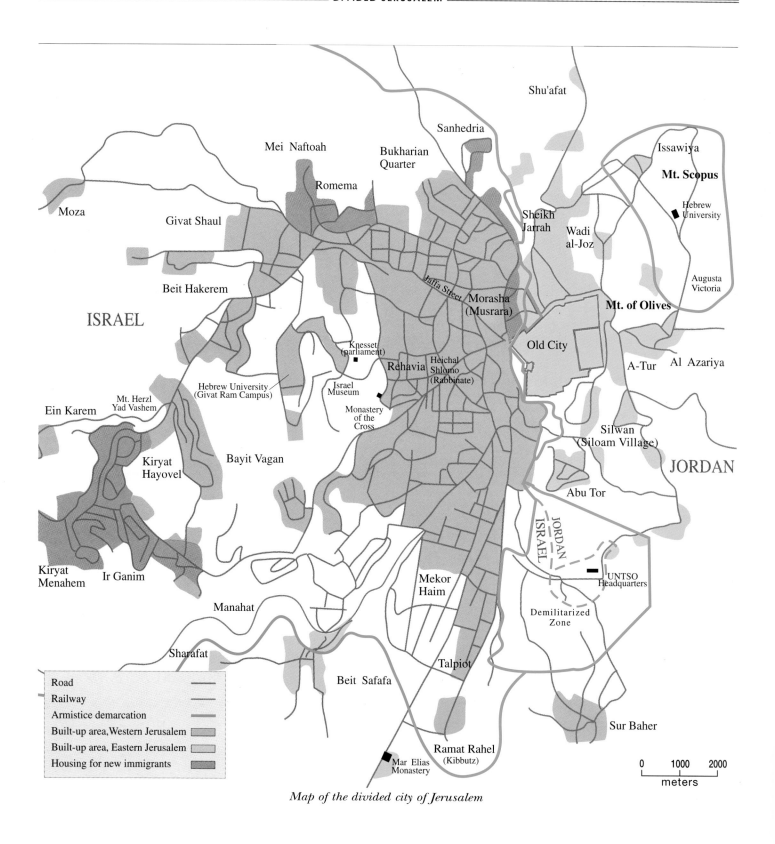

Map of the divided city of Jerusalem

Road

Railway

Armistice demarcation

Built-up area, Western Jerusalem

Built-up area, Eastern Jerusalem

Housing for new immigrants

Shu'afat

Sanhedria

Mei Naftoah

Bukharian
Quarter

Issawiya

Mt. Scopus

Romema

Moza

Givat Shaul

Sheikh
Jarrah

Wadi
al-Joz

Hebrew
University

Beit Hakerem

ISRAEL

Jaffa Street

Morasha
(Musrara)

Augusta
Victoria

Mt. of Olives

Old City

Knesset
(parliament)

Rehavia

Heichal
Shlomo
(Rabbinate)

A-Tur

Al Azariya

Hebrew University
(Givat Ram Campus)

Israel
Museum

Mt. Herzl
Yad Vashem

Ein Karem

Monastery
of the
Cross

Silwan
(Siloam Village)

JORDAN

Kiryat
Hayovel

Bayit Vagan

Abu Tor

JORDAN
ISRAEL

Kiryat
Menahem

Ir Ganim

UNTSO
Headquarters

Mekor
Haim

Demilitarized
Zone

Manahat

Sharafat

Talpiot

Beit Safafa

Sur Baher

Ramat Rahel
(Kibbutz)

Mar Elias
Monastery

0   1000   2000
meters

Convoy sets out from Tel Aviv for besieged Jerusalem. For several months Jerusalem was almost totally cut off from food and supplies

On Sunday morning November 30, 1947, a euphoric mood lingered in the Jewish areas of Palestine after the previous night's celebration of passage of the UN resolution calling for the partition of Palestine into Jewish and Arab states. The Jews of Jerusalem could not hide their joy, even though the city and its outlying area were to be internationalized under UN supervision, and not included in the Jewish state. So great was the mood of celebration that even British soldiers were caught up in it. On various Jerusalem streets their slow-moving patrol vehicles were seen transporting celebrating Jews on hoods and running boards.

The Arabs of Jerusalem like all the Arabs of Palestine, were bitterly disappointed by the UN vote. Extremists immediately resorted to violence. The first attacks meant to prevent the establishment of a Jewish state occurred miles from Jerusalem, but symbolically struck at the city itself. Two buses of the Jewish Egged bus cooperative were fired upon as they travelled to Jerusalem from Hadera and Netanya; 6 Jews were killed and 9 injured.

On the road to Jerusalem, wrecks of Jewish armored vehicles bear silent testimony to the toll from the deadly crossfire of winter 1948

These first casualties of what would later be known as Israel's War of Independence occurred six months before Israeli statehood was declared, in the beginning of the critical period between passage of the UN partition resolution and the departure of the British from Palestine.

On the day of the bus attacks the first shots of the conflict were fired within Jerusalem as well. A Jewish ambulance passing through an Arab neighborhood was attacked as it transported a patient to Hadassah Hospital on Mt. Scopus. The next day, the Arab Higher Committee declared a three day general strike. One day later an Arab mob emerged from the Old City's Jaffa Gate to loot and rampage in the Mamilla Street commercial area. Violence spread throughout Jerusalem. Neighborhoods of mixed Arab and Jewish populations witnessed a flight of residents, as both Arabs and Jews moved to more secure areas. During the early weeks the

military initiative was mainly in the hands of the Arabs, while Jews tended to adopt a strategy of defending their neighborhoods and lines of communication.

Travel by Convoy

Jewish Jerusalem soon came under partial siege. The steep, winding road from Tel Aviv to Jerusalem passed through areas dotted with Arab villages. Ambush and sniper activity against Jewish vehicles became the norm. For self-protection, Jews began travelling the route in convoys. In the early days of travel by convoy, Haganah defenders were prohibited by the British from carrying arms. Wary of British searches, they travelled with their weapons hidden, at times dismantled and concealed under the young women's clothes. At the first sound of gunfire the weapons were speedily assembled. After a time, makeshift armored vehicles were employed. Buses and trucks were protected by panels of wood overlaid on either side by thin metal plating. These ungainly vehicles were sardonically dubbed 'sandwiches'.

Jewish Jerusalem, to a great extent besieged, was responsible for helping to sustain outlying Jewish settlements. Hartuv in the west, Atarot and Neve Yaakov in the north, Kalya and Beit Haaravah in the east, and the four settlements of the Etzion bloc in the south, were dependent upon Jewish Jerusalem for supplies and aid. Travel to these settlements, not far from Jerusalem but isolated in the heart of Arab areas, could also only be undertaken in convoys.

Within Jerusalem as well, some Jewish neighborhoods were partially cut off from one another and suffered shortages. The most threatened area was the Jewish Quarter within the Old City. Unlike the area of Jerusalem outside the walls, where the Jews were a majority, within the Old City there lived only two thousand Jews surrounded by many thousands of Arabs. The British supervised occasional cease-fires in the Old City to allow for a resupply of food, medicine and the like, but not of weapons or extra manpower.

Winter 1948 in Jerusalem

In Jerusalem, the armed struggle between Jews and Arabs went on daily. Neighborhoods and sections of streets turned into fortified enclaves. The British, who administered Palestine and Jerusalem until May 1948, maneuvered between the warring parties, but often took decisions which had the effect of supporting the Arab side. Administrative decisions such as the continued ban

A large explosion destroyed much of Ben Yehudah Street in the heart of Jewish Jerusalem, on February 22, 1948. Painting by Ludwig Blum who lived near the explosion site and hurriedly created this urban landscape. Months later Jordanian shrapnel came through Blum's window and damaged the canvas Inset: Blum in his damaged studio

In besieged Jerusalem three women carry their water allotments

on Haganah possession of weapons, left the Jews with the unavoidable impression that the British were using their powers to favor the Arabs. Events in Jerusalem in winter 1948 deepened the Jews' suspicion and bitterness toward the British. In February 1948 deserters from the British army, dressed in British uniforms, twice managed to pass British roadblocks, penetrate the heart of Jewish Jerusalem and set off vehicle-bombs. In the first instance, saboteurs in a British police truck blew up the offices of *The Palestine Post*, the respected Jewish-owned English language newspaper. In the second instance, three vehicles loaded with explosives managed to reach Ben Yehudah Street, the heart of Jewish Jerusalem, and set off a massive explosion in which 54 people died and 100 were wounded. Less than one month later, an explosion

demolished a large part of the Jewish National Institutions building, killing 12 and wounding 70. The ability of the driver, an Arab employed by the American consulate, his vehicle flying an American flag, to pass British roadblocks and penetrate to the heart of the institutions of Jewish self-government further embittered feelings toward the British.

The Yishuv as a whole felt vulnerable, however morale was remarkably high. The Jewish writer Yeshurun Keshet, who kept a diary during 1948, wrote on March 1: "These are tension-filled days, but perhaps not the most turbulent... People seem to be clad in the armor of a 'come what may!' attitude, but beneath this they are motivated by the powerful, irrational expectation of a miracle." He further observed, "Public life of the Yishuv seems to mirror the climate of the land we live in; one sunny day brings quick forgetfulness of a string of gloomy ones."

Jerusalem's Jewish population had the impression that in these early months of the conflict the Arabs had gained the upper hand, with the help of a biased British policy. Interestingly, the Arabs did not seem to share this assessment. The Christian Arab author and intellectual Khalil al-Sakakini kept a diary during the same time period that Keshet kept his. On March 16 al-Sakakini noted: "By God, I do not know how we will hold out against the Jewish aggression. They are well trained and organized, unified, and possess modern weapons. And us! We are none of those things. Will we ever reach a point of realizing that unity is superior to divisiveness, organization is better than anarchy, and preparedness is better than negligence!"

In fact the Jews were better organized than the Arabs. In Jerusalem the Jewish leadership formed a committee to deal promptly with the daily problems occasioned by the fighting, from rationing of food and water to burial of the dead. As the weeks passed, the Haganah managed to place armed defenders at Jewish enclaves in Jerusalem and its vicinity. And, in spite of the hail of bullets that met food convoys on the Tel Aviv-Jerusalem road, efforts were unceasing to run the gauntlet.

By late March, 1948 the situation of Jewish Jerusalem had seriously deteriorated. Arab dominance of the highway was virtually total. The convoy system had become largely ineffective, and was sustaining a terrible death toll. Under the circumstances, the Jewish leadership in Jerusalem hardly had the means to help outlying Jewish settlements. On March 27, a convoy which had managed to re-supply the Etzion bloc was returning to Jerusalem when it was pinned down by gunfire for two and a half days outside Bethlehem. Its few members held out against hundreds of Arab fighters supported by many villagers from the surrounding hills. Only the arrival of a British unit saved the convoy from certain death. They were extricated from the scene on condition that they relinquish their arms and ammunition. A few days later, a convoy which left Tel

Late in the War of Independence, David Ben-Gurion arrives in Jerusalem as Premier of the State of Israel, and is received by a police honor guard

Aviv to resupply Jerusalem was stopped dead, and the city's large Jewish population was totally cut off from supplies.

The Battles of April 1948

David Ben-Gurion, the leader of the Yishuv who held the defense portfolio in the Jewish Agency Executive, convened an urgent meeting on March 31, 1948 to determine a way to save Jerusalem. Expressing his assessment of the blow Jerusalem's loss would mean to the fighting spirit of the Yishuv, Ben-Gurion challenged the Haganah to find a way to break through to the city. He ordered the re-deployment of 1,500 select Jewish fighters to Jerusalem, even if it meant weakening other frontline areas. 'Operation Nahshon' came into being, its name recalling the Biblical character who, according to tradition, challenged the unknown by boldly striding into the waters of the Red Sea, which parted for the

Night battle, 1948. Jordanian shellfire rains down on the Jewish areas of Jerusalem

Israelites only after Nahshon was in up to his neck. Three battalions of the Haganah launched coordinated attacks on the Arabs lining the hills and on the villages from which they were being summoned. After bitter fighting the road was opened, and two convoys totalling 225 vehicles brought 900 tons of food and supplies to Jerusalem. A week later another two convoys, this time of 500 vehicles, reached Jerusalem in Operation Harel. Among the supplies reaching the city were tons of matzohs for the upcoming Passover festival. On April 21, the Harel Brigade of the special 'Palmah' strike force, still deployed in positions overlooking the highway, was summoned to Jerusalem when intelligence reports indicated that the British (contrary to the skepticism of many in the Jewish leadership) were preparing to pull out of their positions in the city, as the end of the Mandate drew near. It was urgent that British security positions in Jerusalem fall into Jewish and not Arab hands. The Harel Brigade redeployed, and Arabs promptly re-took positions overlooking the highway at Sha'ar Hagay (literally, 'Entrance to the Valley') a narrow pass where the road could easily be cut. Jewish Jerusalem was again under siege.

The Battle for the Kastel and its Aftermath

During the first two weeks in April, 1948, at the very time that Operation Nahshon opened the way to Jerusalem, several events of far-reaching consequence occurred in and around Jerusalem. At the Kastel, the highest vantage point overlooking the Jerusalem-Tel Aviv highway, fierce battles took place between Jewish and Arab forces, to sieze control of the Kastel fortress. From its height the Palestinian irregular forces in the area were commanded by Abd al-Khader al-Husseini. Control of the fortress passed from one side to another, remaining finally in the hands of the Haganah. Abd al-Khader al-Husseini was killed, and his death seems to have been a turning point in the conflict, dealing a blow to the Arab fighters in the area, and to Arab morale in general.

On April 9, 1948, during the offensive in the Jerusalem area in which several Arab villages were conquered, a unit composed of Etzel and Lehi fighters, (non-Haganah paramilitary units of the minority revisionist Zionists) penetrated the Arab village of Deir Yassin on the western approaches to Jerusalem. A battle developed in which the death toll exceeded by far the number of casualties which occurred in any other village. Word quickly spread to the media in Palestine and around the world that a massacre had been committed in Deir Yassin, perpetrated by Jews. The Haganah and the majority leadership of the Yishuv put out a statement condemning the killings. A spokesman for the Etzel underground claimed that advance warning had been given to the townspeople to evacuate.

In the Arab states, spokesmen broadcast hyperbolic accounts of the incident at Deir Yassin to goad the Arab states into action against the Jews. The spokesmen instead seem to have enhanced the motivation for the massive flight of Arab villagers out of Palestine.

Four days after events at Deir Yassin, a Jewish convoy of medical personnel travelled through Jerusalem's Sheikh Jarrah neighborhood toward Hadassah Hospital and Hebrew University on Mt. Scopus. The convoy came under deadly Arab crossfire. Although a British force was standing nearby, witnessing the incident, it did not come to the passengers' aid, and the Haganah could not reach the site. The vehicles were pinned down for hours, and at the end of the day, the casualties numbered 78 dead, with many injured. Among the dead were leading doctors, professors of medicine and nurses of the Hadassah Hospital.

Until mid-May, Jerusalem was essentially an urban battlefield, with Jews and Arabs maneuvering to seize the best strategic positions in anticipation of the British departure on May 14th. The Jewish fighting units were more successful than the Arabs at this effort; their intelligence capabilities were superior although their

Jordanian soldiers of the Arab Legion fire on the besieged Jewish Quarter of the Old City near the Porat Yosef Yeshiva, May 1948

position 'on the ground' was dire (Jewish Jerusalem was again under siege). The Jewish conquest of Jerusalem's southwestern Katamon neighborhood dealt a mortal blow to the Arab effort to hold ground in west Jerusalem. On May 14, 1948, the last day of the British Mandate, the Jews managed to take several strategic locations as the British were evacuating them. However, this success was offset by the loss of the outlying Etzion bloc of Jewish settlements, which was overrun by the Arab Legion. Its loss meant the absence of a Jewish advance presence on the southern approach to Jerusalem.

Jordanians to the East, Egyptians to the South

The day after the British left Palestine, the State of Israel came into being. On that occasion, May 14, 1948, the fifth day of Iyar on the Jewish calendar, ten of the thirty seven delegates of the provisional National Council (parliament) could not be present in Tel Aviv for the declaration of statehood and reading of Israel's Declaration of Independence because they were trapped in besieged Jerusalem. They affixed their names to the declaration at a later date. Their enforced absence was eminently symbolic of the fact that Jerusalem was cut off from the territory of the young Jewish state.

The four weeks following Israel's declaration of statehood were among the most difficult Jewish Jerusalem had known in modern times. Two of the five Arab armies that immediately invaded the new state turned toward Jerusalem: the Jordanian Arab Legion, and elements of the Egyptian force. The Jordanians seized east Jerusalem, which was predominantly Arab, and, after two weeks of fighting, captured the Jewish Quarter of the Old City. The Egyptians approached from the south and seized vantage points between Bethlehem and Jerusalem. Both Arab forces commenced shelling of Jerusalem's Jewish areas. The bombardment went on night and day, causing many casualties and widespread property damage. In the first four weeks 240 Jews were killed, only 40 of whom were soldiers, and 1,400 were wounded. In further fighting in and around Jerusalem, another 250 fighters fell. The Arab Legion cut the road to Jerusalem at Latrun, the half-way point from Tel Aviv. The Legion also made several efforts to seize further

Jewish areas inside Jerusalem, but was repulsed by desperate Jewish defense efforts, undertaken in one instance by teenagers of the Gadna youth para-military organization. David Ben-Gurion who was both Prime Minister and Minister of Defense of the new state, recorded in his memoirs that the focus of his concerns at that time was Jerusalem, whose value to the Jewish state was beyond assessing, "for, if a land can have a soul, Jerusalem is the soul of the land of Israel. The battle for the city would be the decisive one, for more than military reasons."

He directed his command staff to open the road to Jerusalem, and specifically ordered the deployment of the new Seventh Brigade, even though senior commanders did not think it was ready for battle. Two assaults on Latrun were costly failures. By the end of May 1948 Jewish Jerusalem continued to be cut off. A measure of its desperation can be inferred from the telegram the military commander for Jerusalem, Dov Yosef, (Canadian-born Bernard Joseph) sent Ben-Gurion. "I don't wish to burden you with yet another difficulty, and I am trying to keep up people's morale, however, there are only a few days rations left. Any further delay courts disaster. Can you see your way to supplying us by air?" (Jerusalem had two small landing strips at which light planes from the coast could land).

Creating the 'Burma Road'

To Ben-Gurion it was clear the situation in Jerusalem was stretched to the breaking point. The only good news was that the failed battle for Latrun had the indirect effect of reducing direct attack on Jerusalem, as the Jordanian Arab Legion was forced to divert forces from the city to the Latrun area. During the battle for Latrun, Jewish forces gained some ground to the south, where the Palmah strike force discovered a path leading up into the hills, skirting the embattled Jerusalem road and enabling passage on foot to Jewish held areas in the Judean hills and thence to Jerusalem. Manpower was thrown at the task of removing boulders and widening the path enough to take jeep traffic. At the point where vehicles could no longer go on, supplies were transferred to the backs of 'porters' (men too old or infirm to be in uniform) and carried to waiting vehicles higher up the hill. The 'Burma

Members of the 'National Front' (Lehi) demonstrate against UN mediator Count Folke Bernadotte, who was later assassinated

Road' (named for a strategic road-building drama in Asia on the eve of World War II) could not have been opened at a more timely moment. The UN was brokering a cease-fire to go into effect on June 11, 1948. Had a way not been opened to Jerusalem, no further effort would have been permitted. Because the way was opened, the Jews were able to consolidate control of western Jerusalem.

Within a few weeks, thanks to the efforts of hundreds of laborers and heavy equipment, the entire road was passable to vehicles. In addition, a makeshift water pipeline was laid along the 'Burma Road' taking over the function of the Latrun pumping station which the Arab

Legion had blown up. The city's thirsty residents were afforded a water supply just a few days before the last of the city's antiquated cisterns would have run dry.

Jerusalem, the Eternal Capital

The UN brokered cease-fire lasted four weeks, every moment of which was used by the Jews to strengthen their hold on Jerusalem. The intense fighting over Jerusalem seemed to demonstrate that the UNSCOP plan for the city fell short of what would be required to restore peace. The UN called for the services of its mediator Count Folke Bernadotte, who introduced a plan to end the Arab–Israeli conflict in which the issue of sovereignty over Jerusalem figured prominently. Bernadotte suggested the turnover of Jerusalem neither to the Jews nor the Arabs of Palestine, but to the Kingdom of Transjordan, which would receive it together with the Judean and Samarian Hills and the Negev desert. To satisfy the interests of the Jews, autonomous status was to be given to the Jewish population of Jerusalem. In the rest of the plan, Bernadotte recommended that the territory of Israel be composed of the north of the country and the coastline until Ashkelon.

The Israelis and all the Arab states rejected this plan, and Bernadotte revised it. In his revised plan he returned to the previous UN recommendation that Jerusalem be an international enclave within Jordanian territory. The city itself would be divided into two zones, one Arab and one Jewish, each with municipal autonomy. The UN would protect holy places and disallow any immigration that would alter the status quo. The immediate reaction of Jews and Arabs to this plan was negative. (King Abdullah, whose forces controlled the Arab part of the city, warned that it would happen only over his dead body.)

Public deliberations at the UN had not yet begun on Bernadotte's second proposal when he was assassinated in September 1948 by an extreme faction of the Jewish Lehi underground, motivated by the desire to stop Bernadotte from wresting Jerusalem from the State of Israel. The killing was condemned by the Israeli government, which proceeded to arrest many members of Lehi. The assassination occasioned an outpouring of sympathy for Bernadotte's proposals, affording them a greater measure of international attention than they might otherwise have received. This prompted a re-assessment by Israel of its position regarding Jerusalem.

In the summer of 1948, Prime Minister David Ben-Gurion formulated the Israeli position on Jerusalem, asserting that it be included in the State of Israel. He based his position on two points. The first was that Israel was physically in control of large sections of the city and the route connecting it with the coast. The second was that the Arab side, in rejecting the UN partition plan (which was to bring into being an Arab as

well as a Jewish state) had in effect nullified the UN's proposal for internationalization of Jerusalem, thus freeing Israel from the obligation to accept it.

By declaration and practical action, Israel demonstrated its intent to make Jerusalem the capital of the Jewish state. On September 13, 1948 Israel's Supreme Court began its deliberations in Jerusalem, while the state's provisional government, still temporarily headquartered in Tel Aviv, issued two official statements rejecting all plans to internationalize the city. Less than three months later a paved highway linking Jerusalem to the lowlands was dedicated, by-passing the Latrun salient, which remained in Jordanian control, and replacing the Burma Road. On that occasion, Ben Gurion described it as "a paved and permanent road...(that will connect) the centers of Jewish economy and power in the State of Israel with its eternal capital – Jerusalem."

Truce

During the autumn of 1948 violent exchanges still continued between the Israeli and Jordanian forces, even after the Arab Legion despaired of controlling the large areas of Jerusalem under Jewish control, or of enhancing its holdings in east Jerusalem. Then on November 30, 1948 a truce was signed which, despite some violations, held to the end of the war.

On November 8, 1948 Israel conducted its first census, in which the residents of the Jewish areas of Jerusalem were included. The Jordanians annexed the areas of east Jerusalem under their control to the other territories they had conquered. In so doing, they effectively eliminated the possibility of the creation of a separate Palestinian state envisioned in the UN partition plan of November 1947.

On February 14, 1949 Israel further demonstrated its assertion that Jerusalem was its capital by conducting the opening session of its legislature, the Knesset, in the city. Two days later in Jerusalem the Knesset elected Dr. Chaim Weizmann Israel's first president. The Knesset thereafter returned for a time to Tel Aviv, as the new State of Israel was seeking membership in the UN and did not wish to aggravate the atmosphere in that august body, which still maintained that Jerusalem should be internationalized.

Jerusalem's first Independence Day parade, 1949

fortified emplacements. This division left Mt. Scopus (with the Hebrew University and Hadassah Hospital) as an enclave in the Jordanian-held sector. This area received special status, becoming a demilitarized zone accessible to Israel, secured by a contingent of Israeli police rather than military personnel. In actual practice, Jordan would not permit the university or hospital to function. A similar de-militarized zone was created for the Government House area in the south of the city, where the United Nations Truce Supervision Organization (UNTSO) headquarters would be set up.

In the armistice agreement, Jordan agreed to allow Israeli citizens access to the Western (or Wailing) Wall in the Old City. In practice, the Jordanians allowed no access to any site in east Jerusalem by Israeli citizens; this ban applied to Moslem and Christian citizens of Israel as well as Jews. The State of Israel was unwilling to renew hostilities over this Jordanian failure to fulfill its commitments.

And so the fighting ended. Of the six thousand Israeli dead in Israel's War of Independence, two thousand fell in the battle for Jerusalem. This includes both civilian and military casualties. In 1949 the military struggle for Jerusalem ended; the diplomatic struggle continued.

Jerusalem is Declared the Capital

At UN headquarters in late November 1949, pressure was applied to implement the clause in the 1947 partition plan concerning the international status of Jerusalem, as recommended by the late Count Bernadotte. Countries of pronounced Roman Catholic heritage, especially those of Latin America, were forceful on the subject, with the clear backing of the Vatican. On December 5, 1949 a UN subcommittee approved an Australian draft resolution calling for the internationalization of Jerusalem. Israel's Prime Minister David Ben-Gurion reacted vehemently, convening his cabinet and declaring before the Knesset: "We will not countenance a UN effort to tear Jerusalem from the State of Israel – it is the eternal capital of the Jewish people... We declare that the Jewish people will never forsake Jerusalem, as it has never, in thousands of years, forsaken its faith, its distinctiveness as a nation, and its hope for a return to Jerusalem and Zion... We recognize

In early 1949 intensive meetings between Israelis and Jordanians took place, including secret meetings with King Abdullah and his senior advisors. Parallel negotiations were taking place on the Greek island of Rhodes, in the context of UN sponsored armistice talks between Israel and several Arab states. On April 3, 1949 an armistice agreement was signed with Jordan. The section covering Jerusalem determined that the city was to be divided between Israel and Jordan, with most of its area to be in Israeli hands. The Jordanians were to hold east Jerusalem, including all of the Old City. Between the two parts of the city a narrow no-man's land was to stretch, with the two sides facing each other from

no moral validity in the UN resolution of November 29, 1947 (the partition plan) considering that the UN never succeeded in implementing it. It is our view that the November 29th decision regarding Jerusalem is null and void."

On December 9, 1949 the UN General Assembly voted for the internationalization of Jerusalem, calling for the city to be transformed into a *corpus separatum*. The vote was 38 for, 14 against and 7 abstentions. Ben-Gurion's response was quick in coming: "Israel's position regarding Jerusalem was clearly and finally expressed in the Knesset on December 5, 1949 by all the factions of the Knesset. Jerusalem is an integral part of the State of Israel, and its eternal capital. No vote of the UN can change this historical fact."

In December 1949 the government of Israel decided to move its offices to Jerusalem. Almost all Israel's governing institutions were transferred there from their wartime headquarters in Tel Aviv. In the early days of 1950 the Knesset passed a law one sentence long: "With the re-establishment of the State of Israel, Jerusalem once again became its capital."

Along the City's Armistice Line

The final cease-fire agreement for Jerusalem between Jordan and Israel was signed on November 30, 1948 by the Israeli commander Moshe Dayan, and the Jordanian Abdullah al-Tel. A Mandate period map was attached to

Anti-sniper walls divided the two parts of Jerusalem. A peek at 'the other side' proved irresistible to this group of youths near the St. Louis Hospice

A portion of the barbed wire fence that formed the dividing line between east and west Jerusalem

Long after the battles were over, anti-sniper walls protected pedestrians on Jerusalem streets

the agreement on which Dayan, using a red marker, drew the line of Israeli positions, while al-Tel drew the Jordanian positions using a green marker. Their set of lines delineated an area seven kilometers long, running north to south in a jagged fashion, and leaving wide stretches of no-man's land in certain areas. Both sides regarded these markings as temporary, pending a precise delineation to be achieved during further negotiations. The negotiations never took place, and the crude markings on an overly small-scale map created an inaccessible area some 60-80 yards wide, that included many homes and entire streets. During the 1950s this became a frequent source of friction and mis-understanding.

So Close and Yet So Far

Each side, Israeli and Jordanian, became hyper-sensitive to anything that sounded like the firing of ammunition by the other side, and standard military operations had to be approved by the uppermost command echelons. At some points the no-man's land was less than fifty yards wide, a certain prescription for tension. Barbed wire, battle emplacements and anti-sniper walls became

permanent features of the city. Pious Jews gathered at certain points to stare across the rooftops of the Old City in the direction of the Western Wall, which was completely hidden from view, or the ancient Jewish cemetery on the Mount of Olives, where family graves were now unvisitable. Similarly, Arabs came to the walls and barricades to stare in the direction of homes they had lost or a Moslem cemetery located in west Jerusalem. The only route of passage between west and east Jerusalem was the Mandelbaum Gate, through which UNTSO personnel passed, as well as the rare tourist travelling from east to west Jerusalem, and the bi-weekly contingent of Israeli police assigned to guard the isolated enclave of buildings (the Hebrew University and Hadassah Medical School) on Mt. Scopus.

Jerusalem Recovers from War

Jewish Jerusalem, a large and sprawling area west of the Old City, suffered severe hardship during Israel's War of Independence. All its residents suffered long periods of hunger, thousands became casualties, many buildings were damage or destroyed, and the city's economic base was severely compromised. The pre-war population of

A transit camp for new immigrants outside Jerusalem's Talpiot neighborhood

100,000 was reduced by about one quarter, to seventy-five thousand. This figure began to grow as refugees returned and new immigrants settled in the city. In November 1948 west Jerusalem had 84,000 inhabitants; by the end of 1949 it had 103,000, and by 1950, 121,000.

During the early years of statehood, the main contributing factor to population increase in western, Jewish Jerusalem was the settlement of new immigrants who were part of an immense wave of immigration to Israel by Jews of Arab lands and by Holocaust survivors from Europe. At first the new arrivals to Jerusalem were settled in abandoned Arab housing and in neighborhoods at the city's outer limits. Then *ma'abarot*, hastily constructed transient housing tracts were built for them, as they were being built at that time all over Israel.

Jerusalem was in need of massive reconstruction and development, beginning with the steady provision of basic services such as electricity and water supply. As it received this attention, the commercial base revived, but the city could not thrive. Its landscape was marked by recent warfare, whose scars were on permanent display as residents and visitors looked eastward toward the line dividing west from east Jerusalem. From many street corners and windows in the commercial center, the ugly features of the no-man's land were easily in view. Jerusalem, Israel's capital, was at once an entity of great historical, religious, national and international

importance, and a city stranded at the end of a gradually narrowing land corridor. Merely a leftward glance toward the countryside at the city's entrance brought the traveller in eye contact with hostile Jordanian territory. The national institutions and the Knesset itself, stood not a thousand yards from the Jordanian border. An important factor limiting the city's development was the refusal of many countries to recognize Jerusalem as the capital of Israel, and their continuing support of the idea of internationalization. In this respect, the status of Jerusalem resembled that of the territory Jordan captured during 1948-49. Though Jordan declared the annexation of the territories known as the West Bank (of the Jordan River), only two countries recognized the annexation, Great Britain and Pakistan; only Pakistan recognized Jordan's claim to east Jerusalem.

Developments in East Jerusalem

In the early 1950s east Jerusalem endured a kind of paralysis, the outcome of the battles of 1947-49 and the city's partition, and also of Jordanian policy giving preference to Amman over Jerusalem. From 1949-1967 Amman underwent a ten-fold population increase, from 40,000 to 400,000, while the population of east Jerusalem grew by only five percent, from 65,000-68,000. Jerusalem, which during the Mandate period had been a seat of government and gateway to the eastern hinterland as far as and beyond the Jordan River, became, in the Jordanian sector, a small town, distant from centers of power and decision-making.

Taking this into consideration, change and modest development occurred in east Jerusalem. A new commercial center sprung up outside the Damascus Gate, to replace the ruined area of shops outside Jaffa Gate, which stood abandoned in no-man's land. A bus station was established in the same Damascus Gate area, from which bus and taxicab transport was available to the towns of the 'West Bank' and also to the 'East Bank,' where the capital, Amman was located. Tourism was minimal until a decision in the 1960s by Jordan's King Hussein to make Jerusalem a center for foreign visitors, caused a great increase in tourism.

The Hashemite royal house of Jordan, claiming to be descendants of the prophet Muhammed, were the official caretakers of the Muslim holy sites of Jerusalem.

The Hebrew University campus stood isolated on Mt. Scopus for nineteen years

Under Hashemite supervision, and financed by Jordan, Saudi Arabia and other Arab states, many schools, institutions and mosques were established in Jerusalem, and the golden dome of the Dome of the Rock shrine was re-gilted between 1958-1962. In the course of a 1951 visit to Jerusalem's revered al-Aksa mosque, the Hashemite King Abdullah of Jordan was assassinated by a Palestinian Arab extremist, ostensibly in punishment for the King's overly close relationship with Israel.

Under Hashemite rule, the status of Jerusalem's Christian Arabs deteriorated by comparison with their treatment during the British Mandate. Their number decreased, and there was a good deal of Christian inter-communal bickering, especially in connection with the Church of the Holy Sepulcher. While social conditions worsened for resident Christians, the Jordanian regime encouraged visits by Christian pilgrims and tourists. Christians wishing to pass through the Mandelbaum Gate from Jewish west Jerusalem to Arab east Jerusalem were permitted to do so, while the ban still remained in place on Israeli Christians. Likewise, Israeli Jews were not permitted to enter east Jerusalem. On very rare occasions an American or European Jewish tourist was permitted to visit the area of the Western Wall. They reported that the wall stood unvisited but unharmed, the area before it clean and manned by a Jordanian guard.

Other Jewish sacred sites under Jordanian control did not fare as well. While Christian shrines had Jordanian protection and care, all the synagogues in the Jewish Quarter of the Old City were destroyed, and during the 1960s a road was cut through the Jewish cemetery on the Mount of Olives. Graves were destroyed and headstones were used for building and paving purposes.

The Mount Scopus Enclave

Activities at Hadassah Hospital and Hebrew University on Mount Scopus were suspended with the outbreak of Israel's War of Independence. During the war Israeli forces used the sites as military emplacements, and struggled to keep control of the mount while the Jordanians took control of surrounding east Jerusalem. The institutions at the summit were indeed retained, however the approach was entirely in Jordanian hands. The cease-fire agreement permitted Israel to post 86

President Izhak Ben-Zvi, was first to establish the presidential residence in Jerusalem. Above, his swearing-in ceremony in the Knesset, December 1952

police and 35 civilians on Mount Scopus, to guard and maintain the buildings. Every two weeks a convoy would be sent up to Mount Scopus to relieve part of the previous contingent. This scenario brought about a bi-weekly urban drama of which Jerusalemites were only too aware. The buses carrying Jewish police, civil staff and supplies were a constant cause of concern. One way in which Jordan expressed diplomatic displeasure was to arrange for interminable delay in authorization for the passage of the buses. On the mount too, tension was always close to the surface. In 1958 Arab snipers killed four Jewish policemen patrolling the enclave's perimeter, as well as a UN observer, the Canadian Major Flint, who had rushed to the scene.

Jerusalem Takes on the Character of a Capital

From 1950 to 1955 western Jerusalem took on more and more of the character of a capital. It was the seat of the Knesset and the government, as well as most of the government bureaucracy. Israel's second president, Izhak Ben-Zvi, who assumed office in 1952 on the death of his predecessor, Dr. Chaim Weizmann, insisted that the presidential residence be maintained in his cabin in Jerusalem's Rehavia neighborhood. Ben-Zvi and his wife, Rahel, felt that the cabin, a modest wooden structure, gave symbolic expression to the austerity which characterized the struggling newborn state in the early 1950's.

An expanse of rolling hills on the western side of town was designated in 1951 to house government institutions, and over the years major offices were built there, from the treasury and Prime Minister's office, to the Knesset, Bank of Israel, and eventually, the Supreme Court. Nearby, a new campus was built for the Hebrew University, to replace the unusable campus on Mount Scopus. Not far from the new Hebrew University, Israel's national museum, the Israel Museum was erected. Its most visually distinguishable feature is the white-domed Shrine of the Book which houses ancient manuscripts and artifacts dating to the Second Temple period, including several of the Dead Sea scrolls.

Other monumental construction which lent the city the character of a capital included a central synagogue and seat of the chief rabbinate, and a major convention hall. Jerusalem's Mt. Herzl became the country's national cemetery. In 1949 Theodor Herzl, the visionary founder of political Zionism, was re-interred on the mount, and other Zionist leaders were buried there. The mount also became the country's central military cemetary. Not far from Mt. Herzl, land was consecrated to house a memorial to the six million Jews who perished in the Nazi Holocaust, and the Yad Vashem memorial rose there. A new Hadassah Hospital was built in Ein-Karem on the western outskirts of Jerusalem, to replace the facility standing unusable atop Mount Scopus.

A New Master Plan for Jerusalem

The last Jerusalem City Plan drawn up by the British was published in 1948. Since then events had completely changed the city's urban reality: Jerusalem became the capital of a new state and required a new long-range plan for housing Israel's national institutions; it also became a divided city, thus completely altering the field of

Capital city. In 1966 the Knesset, Israel's legislature, moved from temporary quarters on King George Street to its new location

endeavor of the urban planner and presenting new challenges. Senior urban planners of the Ministry of the Interior projected continued growth westward and southward, while the eastern and northern areas of the city were beyond Israel's border and thus outside the purview of the planners. During the Mandate period, government offices were located in the central commercial area of the city, and near the Old City. The new urban plan looked westward, foreseeing construction of government offices in an area of rolling hills and valleys as yet largely uninhabited on what was then the western edge of urban Jerusalem. Jerusalem's western extremities were to be a complex of residential areas, a government complex, public gardens and parks.

Many new neighborhoods were built in Jerusalem during its first years as the capital of Israel, and for the most part they broke the earlier pattern by which the location of neighborhoods was determined. The new neighborhoods were located at a considerable distance from the Old City and not clustered in concentric arcs around its walls. The great national priority of the time was the absorption of hundreds of thousands of new

*New immigrant housing in the Kiryat Hayovel
neighborhood, mid-1950s*

Jerusalem as a cultural and economic center paled by comparison with Tel Aviv. Jerusalem, Israel's capital from 1949-1967, was a semi-somnolent place; when government offices closed and the sun went down, it was said that city officials rolled up the sidewalks and went home to sleep, along with everyone else in the town.

Israeli Jerusalem's population stabilized at 150,000 after the great wave of immigration of the early 1950s. The city did not experience significant population growth until the 1960s, when the figure rose to 200,000, and projections indicated that steps ought to be taken to accomodate 300,000 residents. New public buildings were erected, and careful consideration was given to establishing 'green belts,' large public parks. During the 1960s Sacher Park, Bloomfield Park, the park around Mt. Herzl, and the Jerusalem Forest, were all established. In 1965, Teddy Kollek was elected mayor of Jerusalem. Kollek assumed the office after a respected line of mayors beginning with Daniel Auster, Rabbi Shlomo Zalman Shragai and Izhak Kariv, and including the publisher Gershon Agron, and Mordecai Ish-Shalom. It was soon obvious that Teddy Kollek was in a class by himself, combining in his character both vision and dynamism. Jerusalem entered a new era under Kollek's stewardship, which lasted twenty-eight years.

Events that Captured the World's Attention

In the 1960's Jerusalem captured the world's attention because of two events, one lengthy, the other brief. In 1961-1962 there took place in Jerusalem the trial of the infamous Nazi Adolf Eichmann, who had been the main organizer of the genocide of European Jewry. Televised around the world and covered extensively in the press, the proceedings in the Jerusalem courtroom brought forth horrendous eyewitness testimony which raised Israel's and the world's consciousness concerning the massive destruction of European Jewry.

In 1964 the brief visit to Jerusalem of Pope Paul VI aroused the world's attention and raised a number of controversial issues in Israel and abroad, one of which was the Vatican's troubling silence during the Nazi holocaust of European Jewry. Another was the Vatican's refusal to recognize the State of Israel. Furthermore, the

immigrants. The government frantically searched for a permanent housing solution for masses of people languishing in *ma'abarot* (transit camps). In Jerusalem, new neighborhoods such as Kiryat Hayovel and Gonen sprung up to absorb the residents of the *ma'abarot*, and the continuing influx of newcomers.

In certain well-established neighborhoods, prestigious areas such as Rehavia, Talbieh and Beit Hakerem, change also took place, as zoning regulations allowed for the construction of multi-storey residential units where once only one and two family homes stood. By contrast, other far less prosperous old neighborhoods such as Mea Shearim, Bet Yisrael and Nahlaot, continued to endure urban problems. To the list of economically depressed old neighborhoods were added several along the tense border between west and east Jerusalem.

Israeli Jerusalem's relatively small commercial center with its shops, offices and cafes was located on a triangle of thoroughfares: Jaffa Road, King George Street and Ben-Yehudah Street. When all was said and done, the

Pope Paul VI at the Mandelbaum Gate crossing point.
Beside him, Israel's President Zalman Shazar

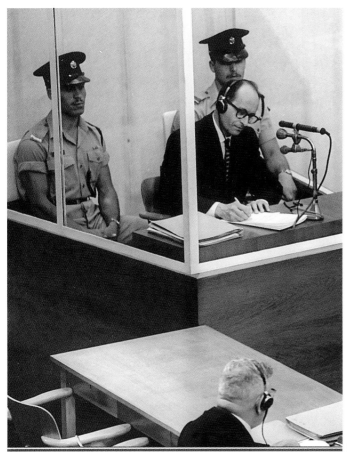

The Nazi Eichmann in bullet-proof booth at his trial
in Jerusalem

pope's visit again reminded the world of the tense armistice between Israel and its Arab neighbors. His pilgrimage involved several border crossings between Israel and Jordan, complex arrangements that would have been impossible for anyone else to achieve. The Israeli government exhibited a respectful attitude toward the pope's visit, and took special measures to assure its success. He entered Israel at a special crossing point created just for him, near Megiddo in the Samaria hills. After visiting Nazareth and Christian holy sites in the Galilee, he travelled to Jerusalem, where he spent a total of two hours in the western part of the city. His time there highlighted several features of Jerusalem's anomalous status as a city under divided sovereignty. He visited two sites on Mount Zion, the traditional Hall of the Last Supper, and the Cellar of the Holocaust, where he witnessed the lighting of memorial candles in memory of the six million Jews murdered by the Nazis in Europe during World War II. The pope arrived at Mount Zion via a route no one else could take, through the deserted no-man's land between the eastern and western sectors of Jerusalem. Part of his drive was on a stretch of road specially constructed for him by the Israelis, with Jordanian agreement. From Mount Zion Pope Paul VI travelled to the Mandelbaum Gate crossing point, where he was bid farewell in an official ceremony. After a short visit to Christian holy places in east Jerusalem he left the region as he had entered it, via Amman, Jordan.

Tension between Secular and Religious Jews

During the years 1948-1967 tensions continued to surface between secular and religious Jews in Jerusalem. A combative tone was set by the ultra orthodox Neturei Karta sect ('Guardian's of the City'). They attracted to their cause several groups of more moderate ultrareligious Jews. The Neturei Karta, zealous for the sake of Jerusalem's holy character and fiercely anti-Zionist and anti-secular, sought to halt public violation of the Sabbath by Jews in Jerusalem. They organized demonstrations in the religious Mea Shearim and Geula neighborhoods, grappled with police, and attacked cars passing through their neighborhoods on the Sabbath. Ultimately this resulted in the closure of

Rabbi Izhak Halevi Herzog, first Ashkenazi Chief Rabbi of the State of Israel

certain streets to vehicular traffic from sundown Friday to nightfall Saturday. These ultrareligious also protested the establishment of a Reform Jewish synagogue in Jerusalem, the opening of a swimming pool at which men and women used the facilities together, and railed against cultural performances and nightspots that were open for business on Friday nights.

The activism of the Neturei Karta sect coupled with their vehement opposition to 'the Zionist state,' including their flying of black flags on Israel Independence Day, was deeply offensive to a broad sector of Israelis. In the public mind, a false generalization was all too prevalent that all ultra-Orthodox Jews were Neturei Karta, and resentment against all ultraorthodox festered. For their part, the Neturei Karta lionized their members

the ultraorthodox was the creation of ultraorthodox neighborhood enclaves in Jerusalem, essentially, areas with their own culture and administrative autonomy. This development set a precedent for developments after June 1967.

Jerusalem's Intellectual Elite

The broad Israeli mainstream, religious and non-religious, looked upon Jerusalem as the center of the life of the mind in Israel. The city seemed unrivaled in this regard, notwithstanding the existence in the country of other centers of intellecual and cultural life. Professors of Jerusalem's Hebrew University were viewed as worthy authorities on an array of cultural and academic matters.

A number of prominent writers and intellectuals resided in Jerusalem, although Tel Aviv's literary scene often eclipsed that of Jerusalem. Among the Jerusalemites were writer and future Nobel laureate S.Y. Agnon, author Haim Hazaz, and philosopher Martin

'Heder' primary school in Jerusalem's ultraorthodox Mea Shearim neighborhood

University students contributed to Jerusalem's distinctive atmosphere during the 1950s and 60s. Here a light moment, parade of cars on Student's Day

who were aggressive at demonstrations and struggled with the police, and these individuals became heroes in ultra orthodox circles, despite, or perhaps because of, their limited numbers.

During the 1950s and 1960s, the sociological effect of the tense feelings between the general population and

Rabbi Ben Zion Hai Uziel, first Sephardi Chief Rabbi of the State of Israel

Amos Oz

Yitzhak Shalev

Uri Zvi Greenberg

Yehuda Amihai

Authors and poets of Jerusalem

Haim Guri

delayed educational opportunity, among them a good number of budding writers and poets who lived and studied in Jerusalem, took the measure of its streets, and socialized until late at night, filling the city's cafes with stimulating conversation and cigarette smoke.

The Allure of the Old City

The Old City of Jerusalem, the Western Wall and destroyed Jewish Quarter were in Jordanian hands and completely inaccessible to citizens of Israel. For Israelis there was subdued acceptance of this state of affairs, yet longing for the sites and sounds of the Old Ciy did not subside with the passage of time. Jerusalemites became familiar with a series of viewing sites from which the Jewish Quarter, and even a corner of the Western Wall, might be seen from the distance. Together with other Israelis and foreign visitors, Jerusalemites climbed to look-out points on the 'Hill of Evil Counsel,' the roof of the Histadrut building on Straus Street, the roof of the Notre Dame hospice, and most popularly, a parapet on Mt. Zion, which afforded viewers the closest view of the Old City at the Zion Gate area, the spot nearest the ruined Jewish Quarter.

Authors and poets picked up on the ephemeral longing that was part of Jerusalem's atmosphere. They captured it, some in sadness, others in resignation, still others in hope that one day it would be possible to go back again. The poet Yitzhak Shalev wrote: "Many a season has passed since I strode down the Street of the Jews, through alleys to the Western Wall... the common man of the city asks: 'Is anything missing in this town?' I respond, 'Joy is missing.' How shall the royal city look joyfully toward its future, when before its eyes its past lies murdered? The ninth of Av will come and go, and figures draped in prayer shawls will not walk in file 'round the circumfrence of the walls, Rosh Hashana will come and go, and the sound of the ram's horn will not set the air trembling before the Western Wall..."

The prevailing impression among Israelis was that the ruined Jewish Quarter of the Old City was a kind of inanimate prisoner of war. The Jordanians did nothing to rehabilitate the quarter, nor did they finish the process begun by angry mobs in 1948, of tearing it down. It simply waited.

Buber. In the religious world, Jerusalem reigned supreme as home to many yeshivot (high-level institutes for study of Torah and Jewish law), as well as home to the chief rabbinate and the Agudat Yisrael central institutions.

After the birth of the State of Israel, Jerusalem's status diminished somewhat, owing to the city's division and frontier aura. Still, a thriving intellectual life went on between 1948 and 1967. It featured literary ferment as well as the work of legal and medical personalities. The Hebrew University moved from Mt. Scopus to temporary quarters in the center of town, and from there to a new campus at Givat Ram, a hillside west of the city center. Many veterans of the War for Independence sought

Damaged Israeli tank near Mount of Olives, June 1967

The Six Day War of June 1967

May 15, 1967, Israel's nineteenth independence day, was marked in Jerusalem with a modest military parade. Care had to be taken not to bring in too many soldiers, and not to display heavy military equipment, lest the terms of the cease-fire with Jordan be violated. All explanations that the only intent was to stage a parade, fell on deaf ears.

Not long after Prime Minister Levi Eshkol and Chief of Staff Yitzhak Rabin saluted the modest Jerusalem parade, information reached them that Egypt was transferring arms and large military units into the Sinai peninsula. In various media, Egypt and other Arab states announced their intention to annihilate Israel. Israel began to take preparatory measures, and adopted a watchful stance. Over a three week period, verbal threats grew more intense in the Arab media, and tension mounted. The Israeli government seemed to be constantly in session, and reports were rife that it was seeking superpower help to re-open the Straits of Tiran at the mouth of the Gulf of Akaba, a shipping lane critical to Israel. The Egyptians had closed it to Israeli shipping, technically an act of war, but one which the

Israelis sought to deal with through diplomatic channels. Meanwhile, Prime Minister Eshkol broadened the government coalition because of the state of emergency. The loyal opposition assumed its place around the cabinet table, and respected war hero Moshe Dayan received the defense portfolio.

As the winds of war blew stronger, a wary calm prevailed concerning the city of Jerusalem, although its residents nevertheless busied themselves digging trenches. It seemed that if war came, it would come in the south, with Egypt. This perception changed on May 30, 1967 when King Hussein of Jordan flew to Cairo to sign a mutual defense agreement with his erstwhile rival, Gamal Abdel Nasser of Egypt. This occasioned a red alert in Israel's General Staff. Files were opened and hypothetical battle plans removed for inspection. Operation 'Pargol ('The Whip') was the plan for gaining control of the hills of Judea and Samaria (the West Bank) and east Jerusalem in the event of war with Jordan. The possibility of battle in and around Jerusalem still seemed unlikely, however the Egyptian threat grew from day to day.

On June 2 the Egyptian command issued its battle order proclaiming its war aim to destroy all Israel's military forces. An Egyptian general was dispatched to Jordan to command a combined Arab force. The next day two Egyptian commando battalions arrived in Jordan. On June 4, 1967 Iraq signed on to the Egyptian-Jordanian pact, and dispatched forces to Jordan. On that same day, Israel called upon Jordan not to enter into a war against Israel.

On the morning of June 5, 1967 Israel launched a pre-emptive strike against Egypt, the only strategy that could counter Egypt's vastly superior number of men under arms. Israel hoped that Jordan would not join the fray, however within hours west Jerusalem came under shellfire, as did a number of towns along the Israel-Jordan border. A Jordanian unit made its way to Armon Hanatziv, 'The Governor's Residence' enclave which was UN headquarters at Jerusalem's southern outskirts. Israel again contacted Jordan trying to dissuade it from further armed conflict. Jordan's King Hussein confirmed after the war that he had been contacted by Israeli premier Levi Eshkol, through the good offices of the chief of UNTSO, and had been asked to desist. "If you don't become involved," stated Eshkol, "you will not

Reserve soldier and his children walk among the ruins of the Old City

have to bear the consequences." The Jordanian attack continued. The Israelis counter-attacked at Armon Hanatziv and took nearby Jordanian emplacements as well. The battle for Jerusalem, a struggle the Israelis did not want, was in full swing.

On the evening of June 5 Israel mounted the second prong of its counter-attack on Jordan, an offensive to gain full dominance over east Jerusalem – the entire area outside the Old City. Three brigades were thrown into the effort: the 16th (the Jerusalem Brigade) the 55th (a reserve paratroop brigade) and the mechanized 10th (the Harel Brigade, whose veterans, including its commander, had opened the road to Jerusalem in 1948 and had participated in fighting in the city itself). The paratroops were to penetrate east Jerusalem and take control of it, while the Harel Brigade was to engage in a flanking operation against Jordanian forces arrayed in the northwest, and link up with the paratroops in the north.

In the early hours of June 6 the skies over Jerusalem glowed crimson as the Jordanian artillery barrage

Three whose entry into Jerusalem was immortalized in a commemorative poster: From left, Head of Central Command Uzi Narkiss, Defense Minister Moshe Dayan, Chief of Staff Yitzhak Rabin

Paratroopers with Israeli flag at the edge of the Temple Mount. Parapet on which four of them stand on the top of the Western Wall

continued. In the course of the night the paratroops advanced into east Jerusalem and reached the most difficult objective, Ammunition Hill, a heavily armed emplacement in the northeast corner of the urban perimeter. In one of the fiercest battles of the Six Day War the paratroops captured the hill, but the victory came at great cost in lives. Additional paratroops took other positions in east Jerusalem, while the Harel Brigade gained control of the northern approaches to the city. On June 6 Defense Minister Moshe Dayan and Head of Central Command Uzi Narkiss travelling in a command car could freely approach Mount Scopus in the northeast of the city.

On the second day of fighting in Jerusalem the Mount of Olives was taken, while the Jerusalem Brigade overran Jordanian positions south of the city. The Jordanian army in Jerusalem and in the West Bank was on the verge of collapse, and the Israel Air Force prevented its reinforcement. The Egyptian commander ordered the Jordanian forces to withdraw from the West Bank.

Mount Scopus - Jerusalem's unification under Israeli sovereignty was celebrated in a ceremony in the Hebrew University amphitheatre

The Temple Mount is in our Hands!

In essence, the battle for Jerusalem was decided by the morning of Wednesday June 7, but numerous deadly skirmishes occurred thereafter. Furthermore, the Old City stood untouched in the center of east Jerusalem, and, as a military objective it presented several problems. It held an incomparable collection of holy places sacred to three great religions. Damaging any of them was unthinkable, yet the commanders knew that battle situations do not foster conditions of total control. It was an architectural and historical gem; even the city walls, originally built for defense, were now a precious artifact. Finally, the interior of the Old City was a mass of twisting, narrow alleyways. They did not allow for the entry of armored vehicles, and were a sniper's paradise. In view of the heavy losses already suffered at Ammunition Hill, hesitation concerning the loss of lives in an assault on the Old City was understandable, especially since it was besieged and would eventually have to surrender. A persuasive factor in favor of an assault on the Old City was a pending resolution in the UN Security Council calling for an immediate cease-fire, which, once passed, would set the lines of conquest where they were at the

moment of its passage, thus perpetuating the ambiguous situation of who controlled the Old City. Within the national unity government hours of ponderous deliberations and passionate pleas preceded the ultimate decision to break into the Old City, with the clear provisos that the city walls were not to be subjected to artillery fire, the holy places were not to be targets, and the Temple Mount was to be taken without any gunfire whatsoever.

The battle was swift and not without painful cost, as sniper fire rang out from rooftops. Hundreds of paratroopers burst through the Lions' Gate. Their commander Motta Gur's voice soon transmitted a message fraught with emotion: "The Temple Mount is in our hands, I repeat, the Temple Mount is in our hands!" Moments later a human stream in khaki spilled into the narrow alleyway before the Western Wall. Many of the paratroopers wept, overcome by the immense significance of the moment, by exhaustion, and by thoughts of comrades who had fallen beside them in the previous few hours.

In looking back on the experience which put the Western Wall and the Temple Mount in Israeli hands,

Amphitheater of Hebrew University – Mount Scopus, June 1967. Chief of Staff of the Israel Defense Forces Yitzhak Rabin is congratulated upon receiving honorary doctorate. On dais, from left: President of Israel Zalman Shazar, President of Hebrew University Eliahu Eilat, and the University's Rector, Nathan Rotenstreich. Excerpt of Rabin's remarks p. 279

thousands of veterans of the fight, secular and religious alike, recall the battle as a surreal, mystical experience. When asked to comment on the most significant achievement of the Six Day War of 1967, soldiers who did not fight in Jerusalem nevertheless cite the taking of the Western Wall as the defining moment of victory.

UNITED JERUSALEM

Road

Post-1967 city limits

New Neighborhoods

To Ramallah

Atarot airport

Bir Naballah

Beit Hanina

Neve Yaakov

Hizme

Shu'afat

Pisgat Ze'ev

Beit Iksa

Ramot Allon

Mevasseret Zion

Ramot Eshkol

High-tech industries

Givat Shapira

Issawiyya

Hebrew University

To Tel Aviv

Har Nof

Mount Scopus

Moza

Supreme Court

Beit Hakerem

Mea She'arim

Heichal Shlomo

Old City

Mt. Herzl

Kiryat Ben-Gurion (Government offices)

City Center

Al-Azariya

Knesset (Parliament)

To Jericho

Givat Ram

Hadassah -Ein Karem Medical Center

Rehavia

Silwan (Siloam Village)

Abu Dis

Talbieh

Ora (moshav)

Kiryat Hayovel

Gonen (Katamon) Quarters

Abu Tor

Manahat

East Talpiot

Railway from Tel Aviv

Talpiot

Ramat Rahel (kibbutz)

Gilo

Sur Baher

To Bethlehem

Beit Jala

0 1 2 3

Kilometers

Map of United Jerusalem

After nineteen years as a city scarred down its middle by barbed wire, anti-sniper walls and no-man's land, Jerusalem was unified under Israeli sovereignty as a result of the Six Day War of June 1967. The guiding principles of Israeli policy regarding the city began to emerge a few hours after the Israeli flag was raised over

Inset: Jewish worshippers at the Western Wall immediately after its liberation. Below: The Shavuot holiday, June 1967. Masses of worshippers filled the plaza before the Western Wall on the first pilgrimage festival after the taking of the Old City

Bus route #9 renews regular service to Mount Scopus after nineteen years

Judaism's sacred Western Wall. Defense Minister Moshe Dayan declared, "Today the Israel Defense Forces liberated Jerusalem. We re-unified divided Jerusalem, the capital of Israel which was torn asunder. We have returned to our holy places, never again to leave them. To our Arab neighbors even in this hour – especially in this hour – we extend the hand of peace. To Christians and Moslems I solemnly promise that full religious freedom and religious rights will be protected. We have not come to Jerusalem to conquer the holy sites of others, nor to hinder the access of others, but to guarantee the wholeness of this city, and to live side by side in brotherhood." There was an immediate, wide consensus in the Israeli public that the city would remain united as Israel's capital, while the strong bonds of non-Jews would be respected and protected.

Israel's Prime Minister Levi Eshkol stood before the Western Wall and reflected on the enormity of the moment for the Jewish people, in Israel and around the world. "I view myself as the emissary of the entire Jewish people, the emissary of generations of Jews who yearned for Jerusalem and its holy places. To the residents of Jerusalem who suffered so much in 1948, who bravely and stoically endured the cruel shelling of the last few days I say, may the victory of the IDF, which has distanced the capital of Israel from danger, be a source of inspiration and comfort to you, and to all of us. May you be soothed by the comfort of Jerusalem. From Jerusalem the eternal capital of Israel I extend greetings of peace and security to all the citizens of Israel, and to our Jewish brethren around the world. Blessed be (the One) who has given us life and sustained us, and brought us to this time."

Gripped by an intense jubilation, Israelis descended upon the Jewish Quarter of the Old City and the Western Wall. The authorities, aware that the Jewish pilgrimage festival of Shavuot (the Feast of Weeks) would occur only a short time after the victory, cleared a dirt road from Mt. Zion to the Wall, and opened a dirt plaza before it. On Shavuot a massive throng of Jews arrived, and for the first time in many generations had open and unrestricted access to the Wall.

The reunification of Jerusalem and return to the Jewish holy places had a spiritual effect even on the most hardened of Israelis, the acerbic 'sabras.' Yitzhak Rabin, Commander in Chief of the IDF in 1967, observed in a speech delivered at the newly re-opened amphitheater of Hebrew University on Mt. Scopus: "The entire nation was awed, many even wept to hear the news of the taking of the Old City. Our Sabra youth, and even more so our soldiers, are not known for their sentimentality. They shun and are embarrassed by emotional public displays. But the efforts put forth in the war, the great fear that preceded it, the sense of salvation and of having been touched by the very essence of the Jewish historical experience, pierced their thick skins and their embarrassment. A wellspring of emotion burst forth, and a spiritual awakening. The paratroopers who took the Wall leaned against it and cried. Symbolically this was a very rare reaction; it is doubtful if there were many moments like that in the history of any nation."

Steps toward Unification of the City

Even in the midst of the Six Day War, Israel's Prime Minister Eshkol extended to the leaders of Jerusalem's various religious communities jurisdiction over their respective holy places. This decision was officially legalized some weeks later in the Protection of Holy Places Law: "Holy places shall be protected from desecration and any other violation and from anything likely to violate freedom of access of the members of the various religious groups to places sacred to them or their feelings with regard to those places... We, whose right of access to the remnant of our Holy Temple was guaranteed in the armistice agreement and yet never honored, understand the importance of our immediate declaration concerning religious rights of all the various

religious groups in Jerusalem. We hope this declaration will provide the foundation for a new set of relationships between the members of the monotheistic religions in Jerusalem."

On June 28, 1967 Jerusalem's unification was achieved through an administrative decision which set up an expanded area of jurisdiction for the Jerusalem municipality. Simultaneously the Knesset enacted a law empowering the Israeli government to extend its law, jurisdiction and administration to any area of the land of Israel that it saw fit. Within a month Jerusalem was declared an area affected by this law, and from then on it was a united city. Thirteen years later, in 1980, a Basic Law was passed regarding Jerusalem. (In Israel, the term Basic Law refers to a law with constitutional status.) Entitled 'Jerusalem, Capital of Israel,' the law emphasizes that the entire united Jerusalem is the capital of Israel. It directs the government of Israel to foster the city's development for the good of its inhabitants.

The city's municipal boundaries were drawn with three issues in mind: unification, development, and

The toppling of an anti-sniper wall, one of a series of barricades which had divided the city from 1949-1967

security requirements. In 1985 the city's area was tripled from 9,525 acres to 27,125 acres. In 1993 the area was increased to 30,750 acres. Within the municipal boundaries were included areas that dominate the city and its approaches from the point of view of security, including the Atarot airfield. There were areas set aside for industry, and areas necessary for securing the access routes to the city. At the same time, an effort was made to exclude nearby Arab villages from municipal jurisdiction.

Teddy Kollek, mayor of Jerusalem, 1965-1993

Putting these directives into action meant taking vigorous practical steps; border fences were torn down and minefields cleared along the former 'seamline' of divided Jerusalem. Bulldozers toppled concrete anti-sniper walls that had been erected across streets, backyards and various open spaces that afforded views from Arab east Jerusalem into the western part of the city. Within a short time it was impossible to tell where they had once stood. Teddy Kollek, the dynamic mayor of Jerusalem from 1965 to 1993, was in charge of clearing the scars of division. He recalled the first barrier-free day. "It was a great day... Jews and Arabs moved around freely, curiosity getting the better of caution. At first only a few people hesitantly crossed the former borderline; police and soldiers just stood around observing what was happening. Then, in the afternoon, a great stream of people came..."

Jews from the western part of the city descended upon the bazaars of the Old City while Arabs from the eastern sector turned westward, strolling the streets of the commercial and shopping areas, curiously examining store windows. They observed the traffic lights, a development which had not yet arrived in east Jerusalem. Acquaintances who had not seen each other in almost twenty years exchanged greetings and shared reminiscences. In a remarkably short period it seemed that the animosity and latent threat of violence that had loomed over the city for nineteen years simply disappeared.

Jerusalem, Ringed by Neighborhoods

Once everyday life resumed in Jerusalem, the differing attitudes of the city's Jewish and Palestinian populations became apparent. Jews almost without exception supported the unification of Jerusalem and rejected the notion of ever returning to a situation in which the city was divided. The city's Palestinian residents, along with the Jordanians who had ruled east Jerusalem, and all the Arab states, did not reconcile themselves with Israeli sovereignty over a united Jerusalem. They declared that east Jerusalem had to be returned to Arab sovereignty. King Hussein of Jordan declared his refusal to relinquish Jordan's claim of sovereignty over the city. On the less lofty level at which personal and trade relationships take place, a more pragmatic attitude prevailed. If a certain discomfort existed, nevertheless Jews and Arabs conducted everyday exchanges and went on side by side with one another.

In the city that had been joined together, steps were taken to make unification a tangible reality. The goal presented a challenge in many areas of endeavor. In the years 1948-67 duplicate municipal institutions came into being. In addition, the two halves of the city had developed at different rates and according to different guiding policies. East Jerusalem had a more stable economy than west Jerusalem, and had developed an economic hinterland while west Jerusalem largely did not. On the other hand, the average annual income per capita in west Jerusalem was four times that of east Jerusalem.

In 1968 a master plan was devised for Jerusalem's re-unification. The means were outlined in its introductory abstract. "The guiding principle of unifying the city has been understood until now to involve two areas of activity: First, repairing the damage to the urban fabric and municipal infrastructure which resulted from the city's division in the War of Independence. Second, re-building the city along lines that will prevent the congealing of two nationalist camps behind unmarked geographical boundaries that might one day be used to re-divide the city. The practical means (by which unification can be achieved) are the city's road system, its municipal infrastructure, parks and commercial centers."

The effort to unify Jerusalem gave rise to a great wave of urban development. New neighborhoods began to

Independence Day 1968. The parade passes before the Old City walls at a spot where the border once divided west from east Jerusalem. The choice of Jerusalem as the site of the parade was meant as a counterpoint to the nineteen year period during which any type of military or quasi-military movement prompted Jordanian objection and UN prohibition

pop up on hills north, south and east of the city. The densely packed building style of Jewish neighborhoods was intended to meet the burgeoning housing needs of the Jewish population and to prevent any future re-division of the city. There is no question that it changed the physical appearance, as the contours of undulating hills were hidden by housing tracts.

For the sake of urban expansion, large tracts of undeveloped land were expropriated from Jews and Arabs. Surrounding the kernel of what had been Jewish

Muslim peddler and ultraorthodox youth discuss the price of wares

Jerusalem new neighborhoods sprung up in concentric circles. The first ring of new neighborhoods arose in the north, where undeveloped lands lay between what had been Jewish west and Arab east Jerusalem. Between the Jewish neighborhoods on Jerusalem's northern edge and Mt. Scopus to their east, rose the Ramot Eshkol and Giv'at Hamivtar neighborhoods. Greater Sanhedria and Maalot Dafna sprung up nearby. At first the government took steps to encourage people to move to these areas, however the areas came to symbolize an idealistic spirit of renewal and had no trouble attracting a successful sociological mix of native-born Israelis and immigrants from western countries such as the U.S., Canada, Great Britain and others.

An innovative residential initiative undertaken at this time was later emulated elsewhere. People were offered the opportunity to build homes of their own design rather than purchasing tract housing. In Givat Hamivtar, adjacent to Ramot Eshkol, a neighborhood of private homes arose with a distinctly personal and suburban character.

A general trend in new residential design was the effort to echo the architectural lines and building styles of the Old City. Thus the Maalot Dafna neighborhood is composed of modern housing situated around a series of inner courtyards with lanes connecting them. Residents conduct their daily lives around courtyards closed to vehicular traffic. The architectural design aspires to encourage communal atmosphere, encourage social cohesion in the population of young families with small children, and achieve a happy partnership between traditional building styles and new building materials. A similar architectural approach was used in Greater Sanhedria, a neighborhood designed for an ultrareligious population.

Before long new neighborhoods ringed hilltops in the southeast (East Talpiot); northeast of Mt. Scopus (French Hill); and in the northwest (Ramot Allon). Further to the northeast Neve Yaakov arose on a formerly Jewish tract conquered by the Jordanian army in 1948.

Several obstacles were overcome in building the new neighborhoods, from challenges to Israel's right to build in these areas, to the appeals of environmentalists whose concern was preservation of the special panoramas surrounding Jerusalem. Today a third of Jerusalem's Jewish population lives in neighborhoods built after the Six Day War.

The new construction on the city's outskirts boasted features which appealed to growing families, and fostered an exodus of young families from centrally located, well-established neighborhoods to the new suburbs. Residents who remained in the established neighborhoods were typically an older population, and were joined by a growing number of professional and

The new Ramot Allon neighborhood on the city's northern outskirts

*Har Nof, a neighborhood on the western outskirts of Jerusalem
populated by ultrareligious and modern-religious Jews*

commercial offices. In some older neighborhoods the residential population has shrunk by half.

As the twentieth century draws to a close, there are few areas of Jerusalem available for new neighborhood construction. One new area, Har Nof, lies west of the city, while another, Massua lies to its south. Har Homa is planned for a site south of Kibbutz Ramat Rahel.

The Growth
of the Jerusalem Metropolis

Until its unification, west Jerusalem was a city on a dead end, with little suburban residential or commercial hinterland. It stood at the end of a land corridor which existed to meet political, not urban needs, and the flow of movement into the city ended abruptly at a hostile border. Consequently, the western part of the city did not grow in a normal manner. From 1967 on, Jerusalem's outskirts developed in all directions. As the largest city in Israel. Jerusalem became a focal point for small towns and suburbs that developed all around it. In the east Maale Adumim rose, in the west Givat Zev, and in the south Efrat and Upper Beitar.

Along the Tel Aviv–Jerusalem highway west of the city limits, communities which existed prior to Israeli statehood or which were established just after statehood, (e.g. Upper Motsa and Mevaseret Tsion) enjoyed a spurt in development, attracting families with financial means who sought a suburban environment.

*The Shaarei Hesed neighborhood which dates from the turn of the century, with the modern Wolfson Towers in the background.
This juxtaposition illustrates the change in residential construction styles in Jerusalem*

A Palestinian residential building in Beit Hanina, north of Jerusalem, in many ways typifies the Arab construction style in Jerusalem

Jerusalem's rapid development sparked growth in the Palestinian sector. The population grew, as did construction in the city and its environs. The Jerusalem municipality developed master plans for Palestinian areas to allow for construction for the general Arab population as well as set-asides to insure adequate modern municipal services, and to prevent random and substandard housing construction.

The development of Palestinian housing in Jerusalem and its environs has political implications which both Palestinians and Jews are aware of. Centers of Arab building are located north of Jerusalem between Shuafat and Ramallah, in A-Ram, Kalandia and Bir Nabala; in the east in Al-Aizariya, Abu Dis and Issawiya, and in the south in the area of Bet Sahur.

Renewal of the Jewish Quarter of the Old City

Early in the period of Jordanian control of the Old City, most of the Jewish Quarter was destroyed. Synagogues, yeshivot (houses of Torah study), community buildings and private dwellings were reduced to rubble. The goal of the vandalism seems to have been to eradicate evidence of the Jewish character of the quarter. After the Six Day War the Israeli government undertook the restoration of the Jewish Quarter. Soon serious differences of approach became apparent among the many people of good will –

public figures, architects and rabbis – who were eager to see the Jewish Quarter rebuilt. They differed over whether the area should be recreated to meet modern conventions of neighborhood design, or whether it ought to be rehabilitated according to the old layout. Also at issue were the conflicting goals of creating a vibrant neighborhood and preserving literally acres of antiquities – which could easily have entailed turning the entire Jewish Quarter into an open air museum in which no one could live.

After much deliberation it was decided to redevelop the Jewish Quarter along traditional lines. A number of pre-1948 structures were carefully restored, while others were rebuilt from the foundations in a style harmonious with surrounding structures. Arches and domes were incorporated into the new designs, and traditional construction techniques were employed. Certain open areas were designated for the display of antiquities, and elaborate plans were carried out to provide access to archeological treasures. (For more on this subject, see pp. 288-289).

Restoration of the Jewish Quarter took seventeen years and was completed in the mid-1980s. The Israeli government and the Jerusalem municipality created the Corporation for the Renewal and Redevelopment of the Jewish Quarter of the Old City of Jerusalem, which, with the help of government funds, restored six hundred housing units, synagogues, yeshivot and other communal institutions. Planners incorporated public squares and plazas in to the quarter's design to accomodate visitors.

The design challenges presented by the Jewish Quarter were not all successfully met. For example, renewed access to Judaism's holiest site, the Western Wall, demanded a public plaza which could accomodate thousands who prayed at the site daily, and hundreds of thousands who could be expected to descend upon it several times each year. A section of hovels near the Wall was evacuated and razed, its inhabitants compensated and enabled to settle elsewhere. Thereupon many interested parties took a hand in the design of the plaza, and the project was completed piecemeal, without fully taking into account the area's uniqueness and special needs. In 1987 the Jerusalem municipality and the Jerusalem Foundation undertook a series of improvements to the Wall area to guarantee easy access for all visitors.

The central square in the restored Jewish Quarter of the Old City of Jerusalem.
Restored arch of the destroyed Hurva synagogue rises at left

Another Jewish Quarter site whose treatment proved problematic was the ruin of the stately, domed Hurva synagogue, which had been a towering landmark until its destruction in 1948. Some called for its restoration to its former use and appearance, while others advocated its development as a display site or museum, presenting the theme of renewed Jewish settlement in the Old City. When it became clear that no design for the Hurva would satisfy all the parties, a compromise was accepted which provided for restoration of a single supporting arch. The

graceful stone arch, rising to the full height of the Hurva's original walls, (but not its dome) would be a visual reminder of the commanding presence of the original structure.

Another domed house of worship standing in ruin in the Jewish Quarter was the Tiferet Israel synagogue dedicated in 1865 and known by the name Nisan Bak. It was not reconstructed. In counterpoint to the Hurva and Tiferet Israel ruins, four interconnected Sephardi synagogues were completely restored and refurbished.

The ruins of the Tiferet Israel Synagogue, destroyed in 1948, stand unrestored in the Jewish Quarter of the Old City

They are the Johanan ben Zakkai, the Eliyahu Hanavi (Elijah the Prophet) the Istanbuli and Middle synagogues. The Johanan ben Zakkai had been the central Sephardi synagogue of Jerusalem until 1948.

The Old City as Open-Air Museum

Jerusalem is a city in which ancient history vies with the everyday. The poet Yehuda Amihai has observed: "Civilization is compelled to build, and to go on building. That is how it has been in Jerusalem... each king, each ruler built and built... out of a deep inner awareness that Jerusalem, inwardly focused, spiritual, is really not subject to change or expansion."

Construction anywhere in Jerusalem is likely to involve stumbling upon ancient ruins. This is particularly true in the Old City. During the renewal effort virtually every thrust of the shovel revealed ancient remains that aroused intense curiosity and a strong emotional response. The compelling question was how to create a successful coexistence between newly revealed ancient sites and modern residential buildings that were in the process of construction. The solution was to accomodate, wherever possible, both the past and the present.

Some new structures shelter archeological remains in their sub-basements, enabling occupants and visitors to take a peek at the ancient past. Among the significant remains in the basements of new buildings in the Jewish Quarter is the Israelite Tower, part of the northern defenses of First Temple period Jerusalem. Another basement houses the large area known as the Herodian Quarter, which contains remains of buildings of the Upper City of the Second Temple period, occupied in ancient times by wealthy priestly families. The building which stands over the Herodian Quarter houses Yeshivat Hakotel. Yet another subterranean site from the Second

Temple era is the Burnt House, a family dwelling which bears evidence of the conflict and fires which attended upon the destruction of Jerusalem in 70 C.E.

An area which exists partly in the open and partly under modern dwellings is the Cardo, a Jerusalem street of the late Roman and Byzantine periods. This column-lined thoroughfare once stretched from the Damascus Gate to Mount Zion. Today its archeological remains coexist comfortably with modern stores, galleries and restaurants.

The Return to Mount Scopus

For nineteen years Mount Scopus was an isolated Jewish enclave in Arab territory. The Jewish buildings on its crest, Hadassah Hospital and the Hebrew University, were maintained at minimum levels during the period of the city's division (see pp. 263-264). With the city's reunification it was decided to rehabilitate the buildings, initiate new construction, and restore the area to its former academic and medical purposes.

Students view scale model of First Temple period Jerusalem at the Ariel youth study center of Yad Ben-Zvi in the Old City

Campus scene, Hebrew University, Mount Scopus

The return to Mt. Scopus fulfilled the historic vision of Chaim Weizmann while also conforming to the plan for Jerusalem's urban growth, namely encircling the urban core with rings of development on the surrounding hills. The planners of the enlarged university complex on Mt. Scopus envisioned thousands of students and instructors coming up the mountain each day, with a portion living in student housing adjacent to the university. This housing would blend with the new neighborhoods in the city's northeast.

The expansion of Hebrew University on Mt. Scopus made possible the accomodation of a great many more students than would otherwise have been possible; the Givat Ram campus had reached its saturation point. The architectural design of the expanded campus expressed the national mood of Israel in the years after the Six Day War: pride in Israel's power and military might. Viewed from the distance the campus appears fortresslike, with a tower that can be seen for miles in all directions. The impact is powerful despite the fact that the buildings are only four storeys tall, and any additional gain in physical space was accomplished by building below ground level. Some observers detect in the university's design a modern echo of the Old City, encompassed by its fortress walls. Both sites are visible from one another, and could be seen as conducting a dialog between the new and the ancient. The complex has also attracted criticism due to its fortress-like appearance and labyrinthine nature. The move into the new university campus was made in stages and completed in 1982. The University Hospital-Hadassah Medical Center was repaired and refurbished as well, and reopened in 1975.

Jerusalem's Economic Development

Jerusalem never had a broad economic base. The most glorious moments in its long history occurred when the city was a major national and religious center which drew numerous visitors. In reunifying the city, potential economic effects had to be taken into account in addition to political and cultural issues. Just after the Six Day War, Jerusalem's population was estimated at a quarter of a million people. Of those, 200,000 were Jews and 68,000 were Palestinians. In the twenty five years after the war the city's population doubled; from the mid-1970's onward Jerusalem became the largest city in Israel. By the early 1990's Jerusaem had close to 600,000 residents. By comparison, the country's two other large cities, Tel Aviv and Haifa had just over 350,000, and 250,000 respectively. Three quarters of Jerusalem's

The varied consumer scene in Jerusalem. Above, dates for sale at the Mahaneh Yehuda market.
Below, the ultramodern mall at Malha

population was Jewish; the remaining population was Arab, mostly Moslem, with Eastern Orthodox and Latin Christians, and other small groups.

Beginning in the late 1980s Jerusalem absorbed a massive wave of Jewish immigration from the former Soviet Union. Thirty five thousand immigrants took up residence in Jerusalem between 1989-1992. Jerusalem nevertheless on balance lost more residents than it gained. In 1992 it had 10,000 new residents, while 16,000 left. Of those who left, many were young people with higher educations, and non-religious Jews; those who arrived were older, and religious. Among the things this testifies to is the city's limited ability to provide economic opportunity.

High-tech industrial park in Har Hotzvim

The occupational profile of Jerusalem's residents has not changed in the last several decades. Most of the work force is employed in service jobs; a relatively small number work in the productive sector. Production industries in Jerusalem receive government incentives and special support. One bright spot is the growth of a technology-based sector which exports electronic products, computer programs, pharmaceuticals and metal products. During the 1990s commercial and industrial parks were built in Talpiot, Givat Shaul and Har Hotzvim.

Tourism has always been important to Jerusalem's economy. The city's long history, its holiness to three religions, its unique atmosphere and alluring sites attract many visitors. Tourism to Israel reached a high point from 1967-1973, the years between the Six Day War and the Yom Kippur War. During that period many hotels were built in Jerusalem, and considerable resources were invested in tourism. After the October 1973 Yom Kippur War, and particularly after the outbreak of the Palestinian uprising known as the Intifada, tourism to Jerusalem decreased. In the aftermath of the signing of the Oslo Accords (1993) which seemed to bode well for peace in the region, there was an upsurge in tourism to Jerusalem.

The city's commercial life was invigorated by the construction of several shopping malls. The largest of them is the Manahat (Malha) Mall. The opening of the malls changed the patterns of shopping and leisure activities of the city's residents.

Capital City, National and Cultural Center

Jerusalem, the capital of the Jewish people in the days of David and Solomon three thousand years ago, resumed this role after the Six Day War, becoming Israel's largest and most centrally located city, imbued with rich cultural and administrative substance. Today most of Israel's central governing institutions are in Jerusalem: the President's House, the government complex in Givat Ram, the Knesset, the Bank of Israel, and a recent addition, the new home of Israel's Supreme Court – an edifice whose architectural distinction gives physical expression to the reverence accorded to the judicial system in Israel. In the wake of the city's unification, several government buildings were erected in east Jerusalem, among them the central headquarters of the Israeli police, the district court, and near Mount Scopus a cluster of buildings housing government offices.

Jerusalem is dotted with many national monuments. Mount Herzl is the burial place of Theodor Herzl, the national hero who foresaw Jewish statehood. There is also a burial section for the country's distinguished leaders, including the grave of Yitzhak Rabin, Israeli war hero and prime minister assassinated in November 1995. Adjacent to it is the national military cemetery whose reception area is the scene of annual national commemorations on Memorial Day for the IDF fallen, and on Independence Day. Not far from Mount Herzl is Yad Vashem, Israel's memorial for the victims of the Holocaust. This complex contains solemn historical displays, a chapel, commemorative art and sculpture, an archive and research and education facilities. Foreign heads of state and ranking diplomats officially pay their respects at Yad Vashem and acknowlege the Holocaust, the cataclysm of twentieth century history which is central to the Israeli national psyche and sense of purpose. For visitors, Israeli citizens and Jews from around the world, Yad Vashem is a place of somber encounter with the horrors of the catastrophe which befell the Jewish people in the years prior to the establishment of a Jewish state. Yad Vashem's large public plaza is the site for Israel's annual remembrance day ceremonies for victims of the Holocaust.

Jerusalem functions as a national cultural center, housing the spiritual and historical treasures of the

The home of Israel's Supreme Court

Jewish people. The National and University Library houses a myriad of manuscripts and documents which demonstrate the unique spirit of the Jewish people and their abundant cultural output. In its reading rooms gifted students study side by side with renowned scholars. Nearby, the Israel Museum and Bible Lands Museum house significant archeological collections. Among other things, they demonstrate the ancient Jewish connection with the land of Israel and identification of the Jewish people with it for more than three thousand years. These two museums and the nearby Science Museum also display finds and demonstrate discoveries illustrating the broad development of western civilization through the

"Holocaust and Resistance." Sculpture by Nathan Rappaport stands in the plaza of Yad Vashem, Israel's national Holocaust memorial, Jerusalem. The original casting stands in Warsaw, Poland

Jerusalem Day assembly in the Merkaz Harav Kook yeshiva

orthodox institutions; the Hebron and Mir Yeshivas, which study in the manner of the great Lithuanian yeshivot destroyed in the Holocaust; the Porat Yosef Yeshiva which studies in the Sephardi custom; the Gur and Belz Yeshivas, two of many institutions which study in the hasidic approach.

Present day Jerusalem is in many respects the fulfillment of the prophetic vision for the city: "For out of Zion the Teaching shall spread forth." With its burgeoning array of study institutes both secular and religious, the city has developed as a center of scholarly pursuits in a manner unparalleled in its long history. Most of its thousands of students are Israeli, however a large number arrive in Jerusalem each year from different parts of the world. Eventually they return to their Jewish communities of origin with a wealth of intellectual and spiritual riches. Their Jerusalem experience contributes to molding a young Jewish leadership for communities abroad. These students represent every facet of the ideological spectrum from ultra-orthodox and modern orthodox to a variety of religious approaches, and to secular scholars in various fields of study.

Jerusalem has another public face as a center for artistic and leisure activities. Theater, dance and musical performances are offered regularly at the Jerusalem Theater. An annual musical celebration, the Israel Festival, the Khan Theater, the Jerusalem Cinematheque and a Music Center all function in a central area along what was once the 'seamline' between east and west Jerusalem. Mishkenot Sha'ananim, the modest first Jewish neighborhood built outside the Old City Walls, has undergone a tasteful renovation and today provides accomodation for prominent artists and writers who have been invited to spend a period of time working in Jerusalem's incomparable atmosphere.

Attractive observation points have been constructed in Abu Tur and Armon Hanatziv from which it is possible to take in breathtaking views of Jerusalem's distinctive panorama and play of light and shadow. All across the cityscape the Jewish National Fund has created parks and picturesque sites so that Jerusalem is dotted with green oases. The new Jerusalem Municipality is a complex destined to become a popular tourist site. Its distincitive architecture employs modern materials in a design which harmonizes with century-old landmarks. The

ages. The Central Zionist Archive is also located in Jerusalem. It documents the history of the Zionist movement.

Jerusalem is home to numerous study and research institutes. Aside from the Hebrew University, it contains the Israel Academy of Sciences, the Academy of the Hebrew Language, Yad Ben-Zvi (The President Izhak Ben-Zvi Memorial Institutes) and more. Jerusalem is home to numerous yeshivot in which classical Jewish texts are studied by tens of thousands of students, including a large contingent who come from abroad to pore over texts in Jerusalem's rarefied spiritual atmosphere. Among the most prominent yeshivot are Merkaz Harav Kook, and Yeshivat Hakotel, modern

The Haas Promenade descends into the Peace Forest. This site which affords visitors a breathtaking view of Jerusalem, is located on the city's southern outskirts

The Jerusalem Theater for the Dramatic Arts

Municipality complex is a significant component of a painstaking architectural and urban renewal plan which will bring 'new' Jerusalem into close proximity with the Old City walls. Another component of this plan is the Mamilla Commercial Project with its adjacent 'David's Village,' a complex of luxury housing directly across from the Jaffa Gate.

The Political Debate surrounding Jerusalem

All Israeli governments since 1967 have vigorously supported the expansion of 'Jewish Jerusalem' in the context of buttressing the unification of the city and emphasizing its centrality to the Jewish people. From time to time the issue of Jerusalem's status rises to the fore in a number of forums: Israeli politics, Palestinian politics, the considerations of various Arab states, and the international community. Arabs in general press for a restriction of the Jewish presence and a limitation on Jewish building in Jerusalem and its environs. The issue of Jerusalem's expansion is a matter for debate in Israeli domestic politics, with some voices calling for limits on the city's expansion. There is, however, a broad consensus in Israel that the city must remain united under Israeli sovereignty.

The debate concerning sovereignty over Jerusalem pre-dates Israeli statehood, and has flared up several times since the city's unification. UN decisions called upon Israel to nullify steps it had taken to change the city's status, and to refrain from taking similar steps in the future. In 1969 the U.S. representative to the U.N. stated that areas not previously under Israeli control were regarded as conquered territory. The U.S. did not recognize Israel's right to build new neighborhoods on them nor did it officially recognize Israeli sovereignty over them. Israel has disregarded declarations made in a similar spirit in the UN General Assembly and Security Council. Over the years occasional alarming incidents brought the issue of Israeli sovereignty over east Jerusalem to the fore in the international media. Two of these were the 1969 attempt of a deranged Australian citizen to set fire to the mosque of al-Aqsa, and the 1990 riot of Arab worshippers on the Temple Mount which provoked an Israeli response in which dozens of Arabs were killed and wounded. These incidents occasioned a concerted effort in the UN on the part of Arab states to sway world opinion on the issue of Israeli sovereignty over east Jerusalem. At other associated forums, such as UNESCO, a UN body meant to deal with cultural and educational issues, representatives of Arab states pushed through virulent anti-Israel resolutions whose ostensible target was Israeli archeological excavations in Jerusalem. Extreme claims were made that the digging was causing harm to ancient sites and Arab neighborhoods and structures. A great number of censorious resolutions were passed by UNESCO although the extreme claims defied the actual findings of UNESCO experts who visited Jerusalem and were favorably impressed by the breadth and professionalism of the archeological work, and the care taken to preserve the sites.

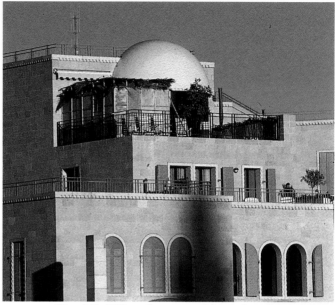

"David's Village," a new residential project near the Jaffa Gate of the Old City

In 1978 the issue of Jerusalem was raised in the deliberations leading to the Camp David Accords, on the eve of the signing of the peace between Israel and Egypt. The Egyptians demanded that east Jerusalem be placed under Arab sovereignty. Israel vigorously refused, and the two sides failed to find any compromise. It was decided that each would provide the American president with position papers. In the years thereafter, Arab pressure increased on the subject of Arab sovereignty over east Jerusalem. In 1980 the Basic Law entitled, "Jerusalem is the Capital of Israel" was passed by the Knesset. Its passage occasioned a diplomatic uproar; the UN Security Council condemned it and called upon all states with embassies in Jerusalem to remove them from the city. Thirteen states responded to that call, however, in time there was a gradual return of diplomatic facilities to Jerusalem.

The issue of sovereignty over Jerusalem remains on the world agenda. A factor of considerable influence is the U.S. position supporting the unification of Jerusalem, even while many of its leaders are not in favor of continued Israeli sovereignty over other areas conquered in the Six Day War. The U.S. approach, as well as that of many other countries, is that the final status of Jerusalem should be determined in the context of a peace process between Israel and the Arabs.

Together, Yet Apart

For twenty years after June 1967 Jerusalem's unification was to all appearances an accomplished fact. Jews and Arabs lived side by side reasonably harmoniously, albeit in separate neighborhoods. In a city which is in general a cluster of distinct neighborhoods, this was not an extraordinary situation. While daily life was marred by occasional murderous terrorist incidents, the overall situation fostered optimism. In 1988 the prominent Israeli historian Joshua Prawer could write:

"The two parts of the city, unified after twenty years of division behind concrete walls and barbed wire fences, did not immediately find avenues of communication. But even as the scars of battle healed, a rapid process of renewal and construction began, and a new style of daily life was established which allows us to live together, usually under peaceful conditions."

Just before Prawer penned these remarks, the Palestinian uprising known as the Intifada erupted, making matters considerably less clear than Prawer's assessment implied. The Palestinians had never recognized the legitimacy of Israel's moves in east Jerusalem, and had not responded to bids for active involvement in municipal life such as participation in the election process for the municipal council. The absence of Palestinian representation on that political body limited the likelihood that it would reach decisions for improvement of municipal services to predominantly Palestinian areas of the city. The Palestinian sector also refrained from making direct approaches to various city agencies to demand provision of municipal services. Because of this it took until the decade of the 1980s for the Jerusalem municipality to pay serious attention to upgrading services for east Jerusalem. By then the void had been partially filled by various Palestinian agencies which were financially supported by Jordan and other Arab sources. These Palestinian agencies function without accountability to any authority, and with virtually no Israeli supervision. In recent years the Palestinian leadership has been establishing its own social agencies and services with a mind to strengthening its standing among Jerusalem's Palestinian residents.

Israeli authorities had to modify original intentions to equalize the status of all the city's citizens through full imposition of Israeli law and administration on all areas of the city. Instead, schools in east Jerusalem function with Jordanian curricula, and Muslim courts work under the jurisdiction of the Supreme Muslim Council, which does not recognize Israeli authority. In east Jerusalem the Jordanian dinar is an accepted currency. These features of east Jerusalem life testify to an Israeli *laissez-faire* policy on practical domestic issues, which is paralleled by Palestinian pragmatism in areas of trade and commerce.

The *Intifada*, which erupted in autumn 1987, gave expression to Palestinian desires to arrest the trend of growing dependence on the Israeli sector. The prevailing conditions of mutual coexistence were disrupted. Israelis and tourists stopped thronging to the bazaars of the Old City in the wake of terrorist attacks, which occurred there and elsewhere. Periodic demonstrations took place. Clashes with the police occurred in east Jerusalem, particularly in the area of the Temple Mount, always a potential scene of unrest. Israeli cars parked in Arab neighborhoods or along the 'seamline' (the former border between the eastern and western sectors of the city) were randomly torched. 'Together, yet apart' was the phrase often used to characterize the new reality wrought by the *Intifada*: Palestinians and Jews living side by side, separately. Jews carried on their personal and business lives in Jerusalem's Jewish neighborhoods and its suburban ring of Jewish towns. Palestinians conducted themselves similarly, coming from outlying areas to east Jerusalem to shop, do business, visit with family and friends, and pray.

It would be innacurate to conclude that the two populations, Jewish and Palestinian, were totally cut off from one another. Palestinian workers from the eastern part of the city continued to work for Jewish employers, and many business relationships between Palestinians and Jews continued. In a number of instances the tense atmosphere fostered supportive relationships between Jews and Palestinians, as Palestinian merchants and importers whose businesses suffered because of *Intifada*-mandated strikes, entered into partnerships with Israelis. Some simply opened shop in the Jewish area of the city. The Jerusalem municipality continued to provide municipal services to east Jerusalem. One quarter of municipality workers were east Jerusalem Palestinians. Throughout the *Intifada* they continued to arrive at work regularly, although this often meant

*Muslims at prayer fill the plaza containing the Dome of the Rock and al-Aqsa mosque. Upper right,
plaza before the Western Wall*

overcoming great difficulties and pressures. The twenty years between Jerusalem's unification and the outbreak of the *Intifada* had brought about a certain amount of social and business interaction which was sustained through the period of unrest.

The Dilemmas of Modern Life in a Holy City

Jerusalem has highly distinctive sub-sets within the large Jewish majority of its population. The city's secular Jews display increasing evidence of prosperity. They want a beautiful, park-studded city boasting a thriving consumer marketplace, and vibrant cultural and night life including cinemas, theater, musical offerings, sports events and fine dining. The secular population co-exists, with an array of Jews of varying degrees of religious commitment, who share with them many of the above listed priorities. There is also a large and rapidly growing ultraorthodox element whose vision for the city differs sharply from the above.

The growth of Jerusalem's population has been affected by two main factors; migration to the city, and the high birth rate. Among immigrants to Jerusalem, a distinct subgroup are Jews from 'first world' countries.

These 'immigrants by choice' tend to be modern Orthodox or traditional in outlook, while some are ultraorthodox. They came to Jerusalem because of its sacredness, however they fall onto different sides of the cultural divide, the former groups largely open to cosmopolitan developments, the latter identified with the native ultraorthodox sector.

In the ultraorthodox sector, high birth and immigration rates have caused a pronounced growth in their representation within the total population of Jerusalem. In 1972 they numbred 52,000, or 22%. By the mid 1980s their number had grown to between 85,000 and 90,000, and they were 27% of the

total. In the mid 1990's they number 120,000. The ultraorthodox population strives to create frameworks in keeping with its religious needs. They view the lifestyle and priorities of 'secular' Jerusalemites as antithetical to Judaism, and tend to establish themselves in separate neighborhood enclaves. These have sprung up in Har Nof, Ramot Allon and Neve Yaakov, while older ultrareligious neighborhoods still thrive in Mea Shearim, Geula, Sanhedria and Bayit Vegan.

There is a separate ultrareligious education system in Jerusalem which, owing to the high birth rate, serves nearly 50% of the city's total student population (as of 1994). There is growing ultraorthodox participation in the city's political life, both as voters and as candidates for municipal office.

The city's demographic and social realities compel its leaders to deal with basic issues relating to its character. While many residents prefers a city of modern character, others want nothing less than a holy city, devoid of public manifestations of secularism. Dealing with these extremes demands tolerance and a wise weighing of options. Most of the city's residents understand that Jerusalem is loved by many, and that efforts must be made to find solutions that will allow co-existence based on mutual respect.

The Ben Yehudah Street "Midrahov", outdoor pedestrian mall in the center of Jerusalem. Inset: Examining myrtle branches prior to purchase, Mea Shearim neighborhood, eve of the Sukkot festival

The Jerusalem Covenant

On the twenty-fifth anniversary of Jerusalem's re-unification a pledge was signed in the residence of the President of Israel. Formulated in the manner of a covenant between the Jewish people and Jerusalem, it expresses the profound attachment of the Jews to the city, and the resolve to maintain Israel's sovereignty over Jerusalem. Among the signatories were Israel's President Chaim Herzog, Prime Minister Yitzhak Shamir, former Commander-in-Chief Yitzhak Rabin, Chief Rabbis Mordecai Eliahu and Avraham Shapira, Chief Justice Meir Shamgar, mayor of Jerusalem Teddy Kollek, and many more leaders.

In remarks after the signing ceremony, President Chaim Herzog alluded to the organic connection between the Jewish people and the city, and Prime Minister Yitzhak Shamir declared: "Jerusalem is our one and eternal capital. It will never again endure foreign rule. For us it is not a subject for negotiation, much as a man would not negotiate over his own heart."

The signing of the Oslo Accords in 1993 signalled a renewal of debate on the future of Jerusalem. Prime Minister Yitzhak Rabin asserted: "Shoulder to shoulder, in full cooperation, we will block efforts to deprive Israel of sovereignty over united Jerusalem, or to partition the city into two capitals."

The aim of the Palestinians concerning Jerusalem was stated by PLO Chairman Yasser Arafat in late 1994: "Jerusalem should be recognized as the capital of Palestine. The coming struggle will be the struggle over Jerusalem. They (the Jews) see it as a distant battle, but we see it as an upcoming one."

Israeli President Ezer Weizman is resolute concerning Jewish sovereignty over the city, but hopes for a compromise formula concerning municipal administration. During a visit to Egypt in December 1994 he suggested the establishment of a joint municipality to function on the basis of equality between Israelis and Arabs, so that Jerusalem could be at once under Israeli sovereignty and joint administration.

MK Ehud Olmert, who became mayor of Jerusalem in November 1993, promised: "Jerusalem is a city open to all religions, and will remain open to the faithful of all religions. We will not offer an opportunity to anyone who wishes to declare Jerusalem the capital of any other state. For three thousand years Jerusalem was the one capital of no nation other than ours, and it never will be."

In his October 1995 remarks in the Rotunda of the U.S. Capitol marking the beginning of 'Jerusalem 3,000' celebrations, Prime Minister Yitzhak Rabin observed: "Jerusalem is the heart of the Jewish people and a deep source of our pride. On this festive occasion, thousands of miles from home, we once again raise Jerusalem above our highest joy, just as our fathers and our fathers' fathers did... We differ in our opinion, left and right. We disagree on the means and the objective. In Israel we all agree on one issue: the wholeness of Jerusalem, the continuation of its existence as the capital of the State of Israel. There are no two Jerusalems. There is only one Jerusalem. For us, Jerusalem is not subject to compromise and there is no peace without Jerusalem."

Fireworks illuminate the night sky above the Israel Museum as 'Jerusalem 3,000' festivities are launched

Jerusalem Covenant

As of this day, Jerusalem Day, the twenty-eighth day of the month of Iyar in the year five thousand seven hundred fifty-two; one thousand nine hundred and twenty-two years after the destruction of the Second Temple; forty-four years since the founding of the State of Israel; twenty-five years since the Six Day War during which the Israel Defense Forces, in defense of our very existence, broke through the walls of the city and restored the Temple Mount and the unity of Jerusalem; twelve years since the Knesset of Israel reestablished that Jerusalem, 'unified and whole, is the Capital of Israel'; 'the State of Israel is the State of the Jewish People' and the Capital of Israel is the Capital of the People of Israel. We have gathered together in Zion, national leaders and heads of our communities everywhere, to enter into a covenant with Jerusalem, as was done by the leaders of our nation and all the people of Israel upon Israel's return to its Land from the Babylonian exile; and the people and their leaders vowed to 'dwell in Jerusalem, the Holy City.'

Once again, 'our feet stand within your gates, O Jerusalem · Jerusalem built as a city joined together' which 'unites the people of Israel to one another', and 'links heavenly Jerusalem with earthly Jerusalem.'

We have returned to the place that the Lord vowed to bestow upon the descendants of Abraham, Father of our Nation; to the City of David, King of Israel; where Solomon, son of David, built a Holy Temple; a Capital City which became the Mother of all Israel; a metropolis for justice and righteousness and for the wisdom and insights of the ancient world; where a Second Temple was erected in the days of Ezra and Nehemiah. In this city the prophets of the Lord prophesied; in this City the Sages taught Torah; in this City the Sanhedrin convened in session in its stone chamber. 'For there were the seats of Justice, the Throne of the House of David', 'for out of Zion shall go forth Torah, and the Word of the Lord from Jerusalem.'

Today, as of old, we hold fast to the truth of the words of the Prophets of Israel, that all the inhabitants of the world shall enter within the gates of Jerusalem: 'And it shall come to pass at the end of days, the mountain of the House of the Lord will be well established at the peak of the mountains and will tower above the hills, and all the nations shall stream towards it.' Each and every nation will live in it by its own faith: 'For all the nations will go forward, each with its own Divine Name; we shall go in the name of the Lord our God forever and ever.' And in this spirit the Knesset of the State of Israel has enacted a law: the places holy to the peoples of all religions shall be protected from any desecration and from any restriction of free access to them.

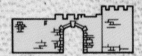

Jerusalem - peace and tranquility shall reign in the city: 'Pray for the peace of Jerusalem; may those who love you be tranquil. May there be peace within your walls, and tranquility within your palaces.' Out of Jerusalem, a message of peace went forth and shall yet go forth again to all the inhabitants of the earth: 'And they shall beat their swords into plowshares, and their spears into pruning-hooks; nation will not lift up sword against nation, nor shall they learn war any more.' Our sages, peace be upon them, said: In the future, The Holy One, the Blessed, will comfort Jerusalem only with peace.

From this place, we once again take this vow: 'If I forget thee, O Jerusalem, may my right hand lose its strength; may my tongue cleave to my palate if I do not remember you, if I do not raise up Jerusalem at the very height of my rejoicing.'

"And with all these understandings, we enter into this Covenant and write': We shall bind you to us forever; we shall bind you to us with faithfulness, with righteousness and justice, with steadfast love and compassion. We love you, O Jerusalem, with eternal love, with unbounded love, under siege and when liberated from the yoke of oppressors. We have been martyred for you; we have yearned for you, we have clung to you. Our faithfulness to you we shall bequeath to our children after us. Forevermore, our home shall be within you.

In certification of this covenant, we sign:

Speaker of the Knesset	Prime Minister	President State of Israel
Chief Rabbi (Sephardi)	Chief Rabbi (Ashkenazi)	President Supreme Court
Chairman Ministerial Committee for Ceremony	Deputy Prime Minister	Deputy Prime Minister
Mayor of Jerusalem	Deputy Minister for Jerusalem Affairs	Chairman World Zionist Organization
Representative of Bereaved Families for the Battles of Jerusalem	Chief of Staff Six Day War	Deputy President Supreme Court
	Minister for Education and Culture	

A CITY KNIT TOGETHER

THE HEAVENLY JERUSALEM AND THE EARTHLY JERUSALEM

EPILOGUE
by Prof. Menachem Elon
former Deputy President, Israel Supreme Court

Jerusalem is a reality, Jerusalem is a concept; Jerusalem is yearning, Jerusalem is history; Jerusalem is the earthly city, Jerusalem is the heavenly city; Jerusalem is the heart of the nation, Jerusalem is the body of Israel; Jerusalem is the city of the Holy One, blessed be He (*Leviticus Rabbah* 2:2, ed. Margolioth, p. 37). Jerusalem is the capital of Israel; Jerusalem is the center of the world, Jerusalem is the pupil in the iris of the eye (*Derekh Eretz Zuta* 9). Jerusalem is past, present, and future – a dream that has come to pass. There is no word of beauty, love, or praise that has not been lavished on Jerusalem, and countless books and articles have been written about it. *City of Hope: Jerusalem from Biblical to Modern Times* joins the distinguished body of literature about the city. Its author, Dr. Mordecai Naor, has admirably succeeded in encapsulating the three thousand years of the city's history.

When I was asked to write an epilogue to the book, I found myself at a loss. What can be said that has not already been spoken or written about Jerusalem? My remarks will merely give extra emphasis to a number of topics relating to the city. They were true when they were first expressed, and are just as relevant now, in the period marked by the independence of the Jewish state and the ingathering of the exiles, at a time for reflection on the past, the present, and the future.

There can be no more fitting beginning for my remarks than Psalm 122, a psalm unparalleled in its power and beauty. This Biblical passage provides the cornerstone and foundation for the spiritual, cultural, and political world of Jerusalem. Here is this Psalm, in its entirety:

> A song of ascents. Of David. I rejoiced when they said to me, "We are going to the house of the Lord." Our feet stood inside your gates, O Jerusalem, Jerusalem built up, a city knit together, to which tribes would make pilgrimage, the tribes of the Lord, – as was enjoined upon Israel – to praise the name of the Lord. There the thrones of judgment stood, thrones of the house of David. Pray for the well-being of Jerusalem: "May those who love you be at peace. May there be well-being within your ramparts, peace in your citadels." For the sake of my kin and friends, I pray for your well-being; for the sake of the house of the Lord our God, I will seek your good.[1]

When was this Psalm spoken, and by whom? What is the significance of details within it: pilgrimage to the Temple, standing in its gates, building Jerusalem and its

being knit together, the testimony of the tribes, the thrones of judgment and the thrones of the House of David, the prayer for the well-being, peace and welfare of the city, the walls, ramparts, and those who love it?

Commentators and philosophers have attempted to interpret all these concepts. The Temple had not been built in the time of David. According to one interpretation, King David declaimed this psalm "for the house he established in Zion"; according to another interpretation, King David composed it to be recited when the Temple would be built. The continuation of the psalm, which speaks of the "thrones of the house of David" that would stand in Jerusalem, indicates that it was uttered when kings of the Davidic line already ruled in the city. The wording "Jerusalem built up" implies the rebuilding of Jerusalem, and this may be one of the psalms of those returning to Zion in the Second Temple period, when Jerusalem was once again built. Yet another interpretation states that the Israelites will sing this psalm for the construction of the Third Temple.[2]

All of these are indeed legitimate interpretations, and the words of the psalmist are shared by all generations: that of King David; of the First and Second Temples; that of the rebuilding of the Third Commonwealth, for those who dwell in Zion and those who live in the Diaspora.

"Our Feet Stood Inside Your Gates, O Jerusalem"

The feet of the pilgrims to the House of the Lord stand inside your gates, O Jerusalem. Jerusalem has been a walled city since antiquity, and as the city expanded, additional walls were built around it to defend its new quarters and inhabitants. The ancient sources, including Josephus, a native and resident of Jerusalem, describe these early walls, remnants of which have been uncovered in archaeological excavations.[3] Jerusalem and the Temple Mount are still surrounded by a wall at present. Depictions of the seven gates in this wall illustrate the seven paragraphs of the Jerusalem Covenant which was proclaimed on the twenty-fifth anniversary of the reunification of Jerusalem.[4] It is said that in the future "Jerusalem will be encompassed by seven walls: of silver, of gold, of precious stones, of ruby, of sapphire, of carbuncle, and of fire, and its brilliance will shine from one end of the earth to the other."[5]

The Prophets and the Writings contain many passages about the walls and gates of Jerusalem and the walls and gates of the Temple of the Lord; the teachings of the Rabbis and the midrashic aggadot are replete with their praise. The words of the prophet Isaiah, "I will give them, in My House and within My walls, a monument and a name ... I will give them an everlasting name which shall not perish" (Isaiah 56:5), are explained by the aggadah: "'My House' is none other than the Temple ... and 'My walls' refers only to Jerusalem."[6] Isaiah further proclaims: "And you shall be called 'City of the Lord, Zion of the Holy One of Israel' ... And you shall name your walls 'Victory' and your gates 'Renown'" (Isaiah 60:14-18). The Psalmist requests: "May it please You to make Zion prosper; rebuild the walls of Jerusalem" (Psalms 51:20) for "the Lord loves the gates of Zion ... more than all the dwellings of Jacob" (Psalms 87:2) and the Holy One, blessed be He, replies to him: "I am beloved of the synagogues and the study halls, and what are even more beloved by me? The gates of Zion, which is My palace."[7]

"Jerusalem Built up, a City Knit Together"

The Psalmist is overwhelmed by a Jerusalem that is once again built up, and is wholly "knit together," with its buildings touching one another. The simple meaning of this phrase is that all the parts of the city: the City of David, the Ophel and the Temple Mount, the Upper City and the Lower City were united, each in their own time. The Sages and the halakhists, the philosophers and the masters of the midrash, however, regarded this verse as containing many laws and basic principles of Judaism, some of which we shall discuss below.

The Mishnah notes that on the three pilgrimage festivals (Passover, Shavuot, and Sukkot), everyone is regarded as strictly observant of the laws governing the ritual purity of food and drink, even the ignorant, who were not meticulous in their observance during the rest of the year (Hagiggah 3:6). The reason for this is provided by the Talmud: "Rabbi Joshua b. Levi said, This is because Scripture states, 'So all the men of Israel, united as one man, massed against the town' (Judges 20:11); Scripture unites them all as one man"

(Babylonian Talmud, Hagiggah 26a). When all of Israel assemble together, they are "united as one man." Consequently, when they are all gathered in Jerusalem, they must refrain from anything which will cause division, such as not eating of the food of the ignorant.[8] The Jerusalem Talmud derives this from the verse which provides our central theme: "Rabbi Joshua b. Levi said, 'Jerusalem built up, a city knit together' – the city which makes all Israelites as fellows. You would think, that this applies to all the days of the year? Rabbi Zeira said, Only at the time 'to which tribes would make pilgrimage'" (Jerusalem Talmud, Hagiggah 3:6). The Jerusalem Talmud propounds the same idea that is presented in the Babylonian Talmud, that the purpose of the pilgrimage is to unite all Israel, and that anything which is divisive is to be avoided. In another passage in the Jerusalem Talmud, Rabbi Zeira's dictum is formulated as follows: "'Jerusalem built up ...' – this is a city which joins Israelites one to another."[9]

The prayer of Solomon upon the completion of the Temple, also emphasizes that Jerusalem joins together and unites the prayers of all Israelites, wherever they happen to be:

> O Lord God of Israel ... May Your eyes be open day and night toward this House, toward the place of which You have said, "My name shall abide there"; may You hear the prayers ... When Your people take the field against their enemy ... and they pray to the Lord in the direction of the city which You have chosen, and of the House which I have built to Your name ... and they turn back to You with all their heart and soul, in the land of the enemies who have carried them off, and they pray to You in the direction of their land which You gave to their fathers, of the city which You have chosen, and of the House which I have built to Your name (I Kings 8:25-48).

The Talmud teaches that,

> If a person is standing [in prayer] outside the Land of Israel, he should direct his heart towards Eretz Israel, as it is said, "and they pray to You in the direction of their land"; if he is standing within Eretz Israel, he should direct his heart towards Jerusalem, as it is said, "and they pray to the Lord in the direction of the city which You have chosen, and of the House which I have built for Your name"; if he is standing within Jerusalem, he should direct his heart towards the Temple, as it is said, "if he comes to pray toward this House" (II Chronicles 6:32)... consequently, all Israel are directing their hearts to the same place (Babylonian Talmud, Berakhot 30a).

In addition to uniting all Israel, Jerusalem also belongs to the entire people, and no tribe or segment of the population possesses any special rights of ownership over it. This principle is expressed in an instructive manner in the disagreement among the Sages regarding the question whether Jerusalem, like all the other areas in Eretz Israel, is divided among the tribes. According to one opinion, just as each part of the territory of Eretz Israel was allotted to a specific tribe, so too Jerusalem was divided between the tribe of Judah and the tribe of Benjamin; while according to a second view, Jerusalem was not divided into tribal portions, but rather belongs to the people as a whole.[10] According to the latter opinion, a long list of laws which derive from ownership by a tribe, or by an individual from that tribe, do not apply to Jerusalem. Thus, the law states that houses may not be rented out in Jerusalem, because they do not belong to the residents,[11] i.e., householders may not rent lodgings to pilgrims, rather they must be let for free.[12] For the same reason, Jerusalem does not acquire impurity from *nega'im* (certain skin diseases);[13] it is exempt from bringing the heifer whose neck is broken (for an unsolved murder);[14] it cannot become "a city that has been subverted" (by idolatry, and which must be razed);[15] a house in it cannot be irredeemable.[16] Many other special practices apply solely to this city,[17] and they were included in the halakhic codes.[18] Jerusalem is the possession of the entire nation, and no concession or transfer of rights concerning the city tendered by individuals or groups can be either permitted or valid. "'[But look only to the site that the Lord your God will choose] amidst all your tribes [as His habitation, to establish His name there]' (Deuteronomy 12:5) – this is Jerusalem, in which all your tribes are partners."[19]

The significance of "Jerusalem built up," as "a city that is knit together," extends beyond the connection of the various parts of the earthly Jerusalem with the unity of all elements of the nation in it, and of its being the joint holding of the entire nation. The Sages in their teachings have linked the earthly Jerusalem with the heavenly Jerusalem. "Rabbi Johanan said: The Holy One, blessed be He, said, 'I will not come to the heavenly Jerusalem until I come to the earthly one.' Is there, in fact, a heavenly Jerusalem? There is, as it is said, 'Jerusalem built up, a city that is knit together'" (Babylonian Talmud, Taanit 5a).[20]

The midrash explains the reason for the existence of a heavenly Jerusalem which resembles its earthly counterpart. The Holy One, blessed be He, made the former out of His great love for the earthly Jerusalem, since Israel are beloved by Him. In order to ensure the complete building of the earthly Jerusalem, the Holy One, blessed be He, swears, as it were, that the heavenly city will not be built. This, then, is the true meaning of "a city knit together": the building of the heavenly Jerusalem is dependent upon the building up of the earthly city.[21]

How many laws, opinions, thoughts, and ideas have been read into and derived from, these words of the Psalmist: "Jerusalem built up, a city knit together!"

The Spiritual and Political Capital

The concept of the "heavenly Jerusalem," which was the subject of philosophy, poetry, and mystical teachings, had decisive meaning for the Jewish people in this world, in its down to earth daily life, especially after the Exile. Following the destruction of the Second Temple, the earthly Jerusalem ceased to serve as the political capital of the Jewish people, but remained, as it had always been, its spiritual capital, the heavenly Jerusalem. This is expressed in the daily routine of the Jew: in prayer and blessing, in commerce and labor, on joyous occasions and in times of mourning, in both individual and communal life. The vow taken by the exiles on the banks of the rivers in Babylon ("If I forget you, O Jerusalem, let my right hand wither; let my tongue stick to my palate if I cease to think of you, if I do not keep Jerusalem in memory even at my happiest hour" [Psalms 137:5-6]) was translated into action. Thanks to the heavenly Jerusalem, the earthly Jerusalem – even when its houses and palaces were destroyed – remained in the consciousness of the Jewish people their spiritual capital, living in their minds and to which they turned in every diaspora. This is expressed so fittingly in the words of the midrash:

"If I forget you, O Jerusalem" – when Israel were exiled, the Divine Presence was similarly exiled with them. The ministering angels said to Him, "Master of the Universe! It is to Your honor to be in Your place, do not disgrace Your Divine Presence." The Holy One, blessed be He, replied to them: "This is not something which is conditional." [For] thus I stipulated with their forefathers, when it is well for them, I am with them, and if otherwise – My glory is with them, as it is said, "I will be with him in distress" (Psalms 91:15) ... all the time that Israel are established in this world, the right hand of the Holy One blessed be He, is established with them ... therefore, when Zion said, "[The Holy One, blessed be He] has abandoned and forgotten me," the Holy One, blessed be He, said to it, "Am I capable of forgetting you? My right hand is established for you; will I forget you? If I will forget you, I will forget My right hand!"[22]

When Jerusalem was the political capital of the people of Israel, it was concurrently the spiritual center, both for those who dwelt in the land of Israel and for those who lived outside its boundaries. The reason for the obligation of pilgrimage to Jerusalem three times during the year, which was incumbent upon all the Israelites, wherever they resided, and the bringing of the festival offering (*Hagiggah*) is given by *Sefer ha-Hinukh*: "for it is not proper to come empty-handed before the Holy One, blessed be He" (Commandment 88). Especially instructive is the description of the obligation to bring to the Temple first fruits from the seven species with which Eretz Israel is blessed:

> How are the first fruits brought up? All the [people of the] cities ... assemble ... and they spend the night in the [main] street of the city ... and to the one arising early in the morning, the official would say: "Come, let us go up to Zion, to the [House of] the Lord our God!" (Jeremiah 31:6) ... and the ox goes before them, with its horns plated with gold and a crown of an olive [branch] on its head, the fluters preceding them playing, until they arrive close to Jerusalem. When they are close to Jerusalem, they sent before them, and they adorned their first fruits ... and all the tradesmen in Jerusalem would stand before them and greet them, "Our brothers, the inhabitants of such-and-such a place, you have come in peace." The fluters precede them playing, until they arrive at the Temple Mount ... when they arrived at the Temple Court, the Levites sang: "I extol You, O Lord, for You have lifted me up, and not let my enemies rejoice over me" (Psalms 30:2) (Mishnah Bikkurim 3:2-4).

The high courts of the people were located in Jerusalem, for "there the thrones of judgment stood" (Psalms 122:5). A Sanhedrin (court) of twenty-three members sat in judgment at the entrance to the Temple Mount, and an additional Sanhedrin of twenty-three sat in the *Hel* (at the entrance to the Temple Court); these were the lower Sanhedrins. The Court in the *Hel* was of greater importance than that at the Temple Mount, and the *Hel* also contained a study hall (Babylonian Talmud,

Sanhedrin 88b; Tosefta, Hagiggah 2:3). The Great Sanhedrin, which numbered seventy-one members, sat in the Chamber of Hewn Stone. This was the supreme Court of all Israel: its verdicts went forth to the entire nation, and it was the source of all legal decisions in Israel. "'The judge of that time' (Deuteronomy 17:9) – they are the fount of instruction, and from them issue judgments to all Israel" (Maimonides, *Mishneh Torah*, Laws of Rebels 1:1). The lower courts, which also were empowered to rule in capital cases (even outside Eretz Israel, if their members had been ordained in Eretz Israel), drew their authority from the Great Sanhedrin. Indeed, capital cases could be tried only while the Great Sanhedrin was convened in the Chamber of Hewn Stone, close to the Divine Presence (Babylonian Talmud, Sanhedrin 52b).

Another commandment which was fulfilled in Jerusalem, and which was intended to bring together all the people of Israel for the study of the Torah, was that of *Hakhel* ("Gathering" – Deuteronomy 31:10-12) which was to be performed on the Festival of Sukkot, following the end of the Sabbatical year:

> Trumpets are blown throughout Jerusalem. They bring a large platform, which was of wood, and they place it in the middle of the Women's Court [in the Temple], and the king ... sits upon it so that his reading will be heard, and all the Israelites who have made the pilgrimage for the Festival assemble around him ... and the king ... reads from the above Torah sections ... The reasons for the commandment: since the very essence of the people of Israel consists of the Torah ... accordingly ... it is proper that they all gather together ... to hear its words, men, women, and children ... for it [the Torah] is our essence, our splendor, and our magnificence ... this commandment applies when Israel [dwells] on their land ... this commandment is a strong pillar and great glory in [our] religion (*Sefer ha-Hinukh*, Commandment 612).[23]

Some of the commandments in practice during the time the Temple stood in Jerusalem, along with a long series of additional laws and customs instituted after the destruction of the Temple, were observed in the spiritual capital of the nation after the destruction as well.

Pilgrimage to Jerusalem continued to be a common practice even when the Temple no longer stood. Expounding on the verse, "Ah, you are fair. Your eyes are like doves" (Song of Songs 4:2), the midrash states: "Just as the dove, even though you take its young ones from under it, never leaves its dovecote, so too, Israel, even though the Temple has been destroyed, the three pilgrimage Festivals in the year were not canceled" (Song of Songs Rabbah on 4:2).

From this time on, the pilgrimage to Jerusalem entailed sadness and the tearing of one's garment [as a sign of mourning], unlike the pilgrimage when the Temple still stood. Lamentations Rabbah describes the latter-day pilgrimage:

> "When I think of this" (Psalms 42:5) – the congregation of Israel said, In the past I would make the pilgrimage at the time of the Festivals with the baskets of first fruits on my head ... those arising early would say: "Come, let us go up to Zion, to the [House of] the Lord our God!" (Jeremiah 31:6). On the roads they would say, "I rejoiced when they said to me, 'We are going to the house of the Lord'" (Psalms 122:1). In Jerusalem they would say, "Our feet stood inside your gates, O Jerusalem" (ibid., v. 2). On the Temple Mount they would say, "Praise God in His sanctuary" (Psalms 150:1). In the Temple Court they would say, "Let all that breathe praise the Lord" (ibid., v. 6). And now [they say]: "moved [silently] with them ... to the House of God" (Psalms 42:5). In silence they ascend, and in silence they come down ... In the past I would make the pilgrimage at the time of the Festivals and chant songs and melodies to the Holy One, blessed be He, as it is said, "the festive throng ... with joyous shouts of praise" (Psalms 42:5). Rabbi Levi said, This is like that spring of water which never ceases, neither by day nor by night, and [now only] small group[s] of five people ascend and descend (Lamentations Rabbah 1:16, ed. Buber, 40a-b).[24]

Pilgrimage after the destruction of the Temple did not resemble that during the time of the Temple, which was compared to a never-ending stream of water. After the destruction, however, only small groups arrived in the city, in a forbidding and bleak mood.[25]

A practice reminiscent of the *Hakhel* rite has been renewed in modern times at the initiative of Rabbi Eliyahu David Rabinovitch and carried out at the Western Wall since 1967.[26] This ceremony is held, at the end of each Sabbatical year with large numbers of people, the leaders of the State of Israel and the Chief Rabbis in attendance.[27]

After the destruction, Jerusalem remained at the center of the life of the Jew: in prayers and blessings, in rejoicing and holidays as in days of mourning, on weekday and Sabbath, and in the routine of everyday life. It is mentioned continually throughout the prayer book and in Grace after Meals. In some Jewish communities it was customary to recite the following passage every day, upon the conclusion of the morning prayer:

> I remember Jerusalem, as it is written: "If I forget you, O Jerusalem, let my right hand wither; let my tongue stick to my palate if I cease to think of you, if I do not keep Jerusalem in memory even at my happiest hour" (Psalms 137:5-6). May it be Your will, O Lord our God and the God of our fathers, that You have mercy upon the holy city Jerusalem, the city which You have chosen, and upon Your Temple in Your great compassion. Fulfill for us what You have promised, "The Lord rebuilds Jerusalem; He gathers in the exiles of Israel" (Psalms 147:2). "Upon your walls, O Jerusalem, I have set watchmen, who shall never be silent by day or by night. O you, that make mention of the Lord, take no rest and give no rest to Him, until He establish Jerusalem and make her renowned on earth" (Isaiah 62:6-7).[28]

On the anniversary of the destruction of the Temple, the Ninth of Av, the special *Nahem* ("Console") prayer is recited in the *Amidah* prayer. On New Moons and holidays, the worshiper requests of his Creator in the *ya'aleh ve-yavo* prayer: "May there arise and come ... be kept in mind, and recalled the remembrance and recollection of us and of our fathers, the remembrance of the Messiah son of David Your servant, and the remembrance of Jerusalem the city of Your holiness." When the Torah scroll is brought forth from the Ark before it is read, the congregation chants the verse from Isaiah (2:3): "For instruction shall come forth from Zion, the word of the Lord from Jerusalem." In the Sabbath eve service, a special prayer is recited for the well-being of Jerusalem: "Blessed are You, O Lord, who spreads the shelter of peace over all His people Israel and over Jerusalem. "The additional prayer recited on New Moons and Festivals contains the supplication: "And bring us to Zion Your city in joy, and to Jerusalem, to Your Temple, in eternal gladness," the purpose of which is stated in the Rosh Hashanah *Mussaf* prayer: to "worship the Lord on the holy mount, in Jerusalem" (Isaiah 27:13). The blessing "Next year in rebuilt Jerusalem" is proclaimed by Jews throughout the world at the conclusion of the Yom Kippur service, and at the conclusion of the Passover Seder. The recently instituted Prayer for the State of Israel contains the petition: "And remember our brethren, the entire House of Israel, in all the lands of their dispersion, and bring them speedily upright to Zion Your city and to Jerusalem the habitation of Your name, as it is written in the Torah of Moses Your servant...".

Just as Jerusalem is recalled in sacred matters and prayer, it is similarly mentioned in everyday life and on joyous occasions. Regarding the building of a house, "After the destruction of the Temple, the Sages in that generation instituted that a house plastered and painted as the palace of the kings was never to be built. Rather, a person plasters his house with plaster and coats it with lime, and leaves an unplastered place one cubit square by the door,"[29] because "every joyous thing must contain a remembrance of the destruction of the Temple, as it is written, 'if I do not keep Jerusalem in memory even at my happiest hour' (Psalms 137:5-6)."[30] A similar practice is observed when the establishment of a new Jewish family is celebrated: "When a groom marries a woman, he takes some burnt ashes and places them on his head, on the place of the *tefilin* [phylacteries]."[31] Rabbi Moses Isserles adds: "And there are places in which it is customary to break a cup during the wedding ceremony. All these things are meant to recall Jerusalem, as it is said, 'If I forget you, O Jerusalem, let my right hand wither ... if I do not keep Jerusalem in memory even at my happiest hour.'" The last of the Seven Blessings recited after a wedding and at the festive meals held during the following week is dedicated to Jerusalem: "Speedily, O Lord our God, may there be heard in the cities of Judah and in the streets of Jerusalem, the sound of joy and the sound of happiness, the voice of the groom and the voice of the bride, the sound of grooms rejoicing from their wedding canopies and youths from their melodious feasts."[32]

In this manner the Jewish people, both as individuals and as communities, in all its exiles and diasporas, maintained Jerusalem as its spiritual capital, in times of joy and mourning, on weekday and Sabbath. The holy city was never forgotten, and the longings of Israel for Jerusalem never ceased.

The Sages of the midrash spoke of the longing and expectation for the rebuilding of the Temple as an integral part of the daily life of the Jew:

> Every conversation of people is only about the Land: "Did the Land produce [its harvest]? Did the Land not produce?" ... All the prayers of Israel are only about the Temple: "Master of the Universe! Will the Temple be rebuilt? And when will the Temple be rebuilt?" (Genesis Rabbah 13:2, ed. Theodor-Albeck, p. 114).

Just as the farmer worries every day about his crops, so too do the Jewish people pray every day for the rebuilding of their Temple.

Jerusalem: The Mother of Israel

The relationship of the members of the Hebrew nation to Jerusalem is not only that of residents and citizens to their capital, it is also reflective of the bond between children and their mother. This moving expression recurs throughout the utterances of the prophets, midrashic literature, and in works of Jewish thought through the centuries. The prophet Isaiah declares: "Yet Zion travailed and at once bore her children ... that you may suck from her breast consolation to the full ... As a mother comforts her son so will I comfort you; you shall find comfort in Jerusalem" (Isaiah 66:8-13). The masters of the midrash expounded on the verse, "Let the mother go" (Deuteronomy 22:7, referring to the taking of birds from a nest): "This is Jerusalem, which is called the mother of Israel."[33] The Aramaic translation of the verse "It was there your mother conceived you" (Song of Songs 8:5) states: "At that time Zion, which is the mother of Israel, will give birth to her children, and Jerusalem will receive those in the exile." Indeed, the verse "Jerusalem built up, a city knit together" includes the meaning that it will be built up with children,[34] and this verse speaks of a Jerusalem that is connected with *Knesset Israel*, the entire congregation of Israel.

In addition to emphasizing the special relationship between the Jewish people and Jerusalem, the prophets of Israel also foresaw that all God's creatures would enter the gates of the city: "In the days to come, the Mount of the Lord's House shall stand firm above the mountains and tower above the hills; and all the nations shall stream to it" (Isaiah 2:2)[35] with each people retaining its own beliefs: "Though all the peoples walk each in the name of its gods, we will walk in the name of the Lord our God forever and ever" (Micah 4:5).[36]

Jerusalem in Responsa Literature

The halakhic literature is replete with laws concerning Jerusalem. Discussions of such laws are found in Tannaitic literature, in both Talmuds, and in post-Talmudic legal literature: commentaries and novellae, codificatory literature (*poskim*) collections of customs, collections of enactments, etc. The presence of the laws pertaining to Jerusalem in the responsa literature, which began in the time of the Geonim (from the eighth century on), is especially enlightening, because this literature deals with questions arising in everyday life. These queries were directed to the leading legal authorities of the time, whose responses provided guidance to those who asked the questions and defined the law. These laws dealing with the everyday reality of the Jew constitute compelling proof of the centrality of Jerusalem in the life of the people of Israel. Out of the plethora of responsa with Jerusalem as their subject, we shall cite seven examples:[37]

1. Maimonides (twelfth century, Spain-Egypt) was asked the following question:

> Concerning an Israelite who had a father and mother who yearned [many] times in their lifetimes, and also when they fell ill with the sicknesses from which they died, to be buried in Eretz Israel, or that their bones would be brought there after their death and reinterred [there]. God helped one of their sons, despite his great poverty and want. He was aided by a person, who led him to Jerusalem, and he brought with him the bones of his parents, and he buried them close to Jerusalem. Should he be censured in accordance with the law, and did he thereby fulfill a commandment or perform a transgression?

Maimonides replied, in his usual succinct and authoritative manner: "What he did was very good, and thus did the greatest Jewish sages. Written by Moses [ben Maimon]."[38]

2. A responsum by Rashba (Rabbi Solomon ben Abraham Adret, thirteenth-early fourteenth centuries, Spain) discusses the effective legal manner of granting power of attorney. In the Talmudic period, this was done by an act of acquisition by dint of immovable property. Since, however, the Jews were no longer landowners, this mode of acquisition was no longer possible for them.[39] In his responsum he cites Rashi (Rabbi Solomon ben Isaac, eleventh century, France), in the name of the Babylonian Geonim, that an act of acquisition may be effected by dint of the land (four cubits) that every Jew, no matter where he is, possesses in Jerusalem:

> Even the person who does not possess land at the present time, may write [a power of attorney by dint of land], for it is regarded as if he has [land]. For there is no individual in Israel who does not possess land in Jerusalem. The non-Jews who took possession of it and seized it do not have a legal claim of possession. For it is accepted by us that land may not be stolen, it is never taken by force, and Eretz Israel is in our possession eternally, even though we have no dominion over it at present.[40]

In addition to the intrinsic worth of this ingenious legal solution to a problem raised by the changing reality in the Diaspora, in which Jews no longer possessed real estate, the very establishment of the ownership by every Jew of four cubits in Jerusalem and the legal-halakhic use made of this determination are of profound significance, greatly exceeding that of the legal solution to the specific issue raised by the query.

3. A responsum by Rosh (Rabbi Asher ben Jehiel, thirteenth-early fourteenth centuries, Germany-Spain) contains the text of a vow taken by Rabbi Jacob ben Hananel and Rabbi Hezekiah, as follows:

> In honor of the God of Israel, who has chosen Jerusalem as the place where He dwells forever, and in honor of His perfect Torah which comes forth from Zion, for there the Lord ordained the blessing of eternal life, we the undersigned have accepted upon ourselves the commandment. We have taken a vow to the Mighty One of Jacob to ascend to Eretz Israel, "the land of the living," and to dwell in Jerusalem or in its vicinity. [This is] in accordance with what we shall agree, to do the will of God and to serve Him wholeheartedly, for there the observance of the commandments and the acceptance of the kingdom of Heaven and the [divine] service is pleasing [to the Lord], for that is the place of the House of our Lord and the gate of Heaven. The two of us have taken an oath to each other upon a Torah scroll with firm hand, in the name of the Omnipresent and in the name of many – that we shall be comrades, that from the day that we leave this land for seven years neither will part from the company of his fellow during this period. And if it will be the Creator's will that He grant us ample provision, for us and for the members of our households, the two of us will set fixed times for Torah [study]....And if, God forbid, the effort of one will not be sufficient to provide for the two households, both of us will labor in worldly matters to sustain ourselves and the souls of our households. Whatever we earn will be shared by both of us. If one [earns] more and the other less, one will not say: "I earn more and I will have a good livelihood," rather, both of us will be equal in all that we will earn. And from the time that we set out to depart together from Cordoba, for whatever profit the Creator will provide for us, in any manner that we will find sustenance, whether in a trade or in any other manner.[41]

The author of the query, Rabbi Jacob, lists in great detail a great number of difficult and distressing labors which led to the non-implementation of the vow in the specified period of time. He asks if he and the members of his household may immigrate to Eretz Israel by themselves, or whether this constitutes a violation of the vow, along with additional questions meant to prevent the disparagement of oaths and vows. Rabbi Asher concludes in his response that the vow is not in force, because it was based on erroneous assumptions, and for other reasons. He rules that Rabbi Jacob and his household are permitted to go to Eretz Israel by themselves. The formulation of the vow, and the details in the query, teach of the untiring efforts which were taken to fulfill the vow. We also learn of the difficult economic conditions which prevailed in Jerusalem during that period and of the economic measures which were taken to ensure livelihood, together with Torah study, after immigrating to Eretz Israel.

4. Rabbi Simeon ben Zemah Duran (the author of *Sefer ha-Tashbez*, a leading halakhist in Spain and Algeria, fifteenth century) discusses five detailed responsa concerning the sanctity of Eretz Israel and Jerusalem in his time, and the halakhic implications of the status of the Land.[42] He concludes that the authorities are unanimous that all the laws and practices pertaining to the sanctity of Jerusalem and the Temple are still in force,

> because of the Divine Presence, and the Divine Presence is not canceled ... and the sanctity of the Temple and of the city is not abrogated regarding the things which were stated regarding Jerusalem ... there is support and proof that the sanctity of the Temple and of the city still exists, because people still make pilgrimages from Egypt and from other lands ... for there still remain of the miracles which took place in Jerusalem, that no one said to his fellow, "The place is too cramped for me." The synagogues in Jerusalem are in need of the local inhabitants [to fill a quorum] the entire year. But they are filled to overflowing when people gather there, more than three hundred people, to celebrate the Festival of Shavuot, they all enter there and sit comfortably, for it [Jerusalem] still retains its sanctity. This is a sign of the third redemption.[43]

5. Radbaz (Rabbi David ibn Zimra, one of the leading writers of responsa in the sixteenth century, Egypt-Eretz Israel) was asked if it is permitted to enter certain upper stories which had been built around the Temple, since "people acted as if this were permitted, and no objections were raised." In his detailed response, ibn Zimra discusses the locations on the Temple Mount to which entry was either permitted or forbidden by Jewish law (based on the location of the Holy of Holies, to which entry was forbidden to all, with the sole exception of the High Priest). He also mentions various events which occurred in his time or previously, and gives a reason "for the universally observed practice of ascending to these upper stories, from which the entire Mount could be seen, and we neither heard nor saw anyone object to this."[44]

6. In the seventeenth century Maharit (Rabbi Joseph Mitrani, Constantinople) discussed the boundaries and different walls of Jerusalem and when they were built, in connection with the law which forbids delaying a burial overnight in Jerusalem. He devoted special attention to the question, how it was possible to state that the tomb of Huldah was located in Jerusalem. After a detailed discussion, he concludes:

> The tomb of Huldah initially was not within the city, rather the city was surrounded [by a wall] after she was buried. Similarly, the tombs of the house of David at first were outside the wall, for it was called "Zion, the City of David"; once again, it was encompassed and included within the wall. Due to their honor, they were not removed and no person even touched them, rather a tunnel removed the impurity [generated by the tombs] to the Kidron rivulet.[45]

7. In the early nineteenth century Rabbi Moses Sofer (Hungary) discussed the Kabbalists who preferred to live in Safed rather than in Jerusalem. In his detailed responsum, he rules that dwelling in Jerusalem is preferable: "Happy is the one who merits ... to dwell in Jerusalem itself, in proximity to the sanctity of the Mount of God,"[46] because dwelling in Jerusalem is more important than residing in any other place in Eretz Israel.[47] He consequently rules that "it is obligatory to prefer the residents of Jerusalem [in the giving of] a fine portion over those of the other cities of Eretz Israel," i.e., in the giving of charity. He states further on the subject of preference:

> If the two of them [the poor of Jerusalem and the poor of the other localities in Eretz Israel] are equivalent, in that they must subside on meager bread and scant water, we say that this [those in Jerusalem] take precedence. But if the people of Jerusalem have even meager bread, they no longer may make any claims until each of the other cities has this amount. Then, once again, from the remaining [funds], what is required for luxuries, [fine] clothing, etc., preference is to be given to [the inhabitants of Jerusalem] until all will be equivalent in this as well. And so in any matter, we do not say to reject but rather to give precedence, and no one will think this [to ignore the others] (idem.).

This responsum also incidentally illustrates the extreme

poverty suffered by many of the inhabitants of Jerusalem and of other cities in Eretz Israel in this period.[48]

The Status of the Temple Mount and Jerusalem in Israeli Law

The Temple Mount, the site of the Temple, is the heart of Jerusalem and the nerve center of the Jewish people. It traces its origins to the Binding of Isaac on Mount Moriah about 4,000 years ago. Its buildings – the First Temple built by Solomon and the Second Temple – were constructed, respectively, 3,000 and 2,500 years ago. It holds a central position throughout the Bible, in halakhah and midrash, in Jewish thought and poetry, and in both the revealed and mystical teachings of Judaism. The Temple Mount is perceived to be the center of the world and of the Hebrew nation, both in times of the latter's political independence and during periods of exile and suffering. The Supreme Court of the State of Israel (whose jurisdiction and control extend to the Temple Mount), sitting as the High Court of Justice, recently received a petition filed by the Temple Mount Faithful regarding the building projects conducted on the Mount by the Moslem Wakf (religious trust, to whom the administration of the Temple Mount is entrusted). A brief summary of the court's ruling, which reviews the history of the Temple Mount and includes comments on the status of the Temple Mount and Jerusalem in Israeli law, is in order here.[49]

The beginning of the ruling states:

We are called upon to consider a petition dealing with certain activities on the Temple Mount in Jerusalem, the capital of Israel. This subject, by its very nature, aroused intense feelings among the parties to the suit; and beyond them, it is part of a history of religious, spiritual, and political experience going back thousands of years. All this, by its very nature, leaves its mark on the arguments of the litigants, which combine both sensitivity and emotion, on the one hand, with "cold" [i.e., impassive] factual and legal arguments, on the other. We cannot do justice to a subject such as this on the basis of purely "legal" considerations. Rather, we are obligated to consider history as well, and that we will do (p. 226).

Due to the nature of the subject and the substance of the issues before us, the parties have raised arguments pertaining to the history of the Temple Mount. It is only proper that we too should first address this matter, albeit briefly, in order to place the Temple Mount in proper perspective and to correctly understand the historical and archaeological importance of the sites and antiquities it contains. This historical review is necessary before we turn to the factual and legal contentions presented to us.

The Temple Mount, on which the Temple was located (Isaiah 2:2 "The Mount of the Lord's House shall stand firm"; see also Jeremiah 26:18 and Micah 3:12 – "and the Temple Mount") symbolized the unique religious world and political independence of the Jewish people, from the beginning of its existence in the Land of Israel. In great measure, the history of the Temple Mount is the history of the Hebrew nation up to the time the nation's political independence ended. That this is true is attested to by the fact that historians and halakhists have labeled and identified the historical period of some thousand years during which the people of Israel dwelt in its own land with the Temple Mount. The first period of the history of the people in its land, up to the Babylonian exile (from the tenth to the sixth century BCE) is known as the "First Temple period"; and the second period, from the Return to Zion in the fifth century BCE to the destruction of the Temple in 70 CE, is called the "Second Temple period." The aggadists reiterated the centrality of the Temple Mount:

The Land of Israel is the umbilicus of the world, set in the center of the world,

And Jerusalem is the center of the Land of Israel,

And the Temple is in the middle of Jerusalem,

And the *Heikhal* [the Holy of Holies] is in the center of the Temple,

And the Ark is in the center of the *Heikhal*,

And the Foundation Rock, on which the world rests, faces the *Heikhal* (*Midrash Tanhuma* [ed. Buber], *Kedoshim* 10).

The people of this nation, both those in the Land of Israel and those in the diaspora, came to it as pilgrims throughout the year and on the three pilgrimage festivals, in times of distress as in periods of joy. They longed and yearned for it.

Just as the existence of the Temple on the Temple Mount was the highest expression of the political independence and religious singularity of the people of Israel, so was its destruction the most traumatic event in Jewish history, symbolizing the loss of Jewish political independence in its own land and its exile and dispersion among the nations of the world. Indeed, now that the Hebrew nation has returned to its land and has been restored to sovereignty after two thousand years by the establishment of the State of Israel, there are those who call our time the "Third Temple period. ..."

All the great attributes of Jerusalem – its beauty, splendor, and eternal nature, all the laws and legends which have adorned and lauded it stem from the Temple Mount. And just as the earthly Jerusalem mirrors the heavenly one, so too does the earthly Temple mirror the heavenly Temple (*Mekhilta Beshalah, Masekhta de-Shirata* 10, pp. 228-230).

Solomon's prayer upon the completion of the House (I Kings 8) expresses the uniqueness and purpose of the Temple:

But will God really dwell on earth? Even the heavens to their uttermost reaches cannot contain You, how much less this House that I have built! (v. 27).

The essence and mission of the Temple are that it is to be a place for the service of the Lord, for the manifestation of the Divine Presence, and for prayer, a place to which Jews individually and as a people direct their prayers and entreaties, whatever the time, place or circumstances:

And when You hear the supplications which Your servant and Your people Israel offer toward this place, give heed in Your heavenly abode – give heed and pardon (v. 30-p. 231).

The Second Temple occupied center stage in national events of major import in the history of the Jewish people. The Second Temple was the religious and national center also for the Jews of the Diaspora; and the teachings and law that went forth from it were accepted without challenge by Jews wherever they lived, in the Land of Israel and in the Diaspora. Herod's building projects on the Temple Mount rebuilt the Temple from its foundations.

As great as the religious and national significance of the building and existence of the Second Temple, so great were the mourning and tragedy that befell the Jewish people throughout the world, when the Second Temple was destroyed. The destruction of the Second Temple left an indelible mark on the laws and way of life of the Jewish people, in its days of joy as well as sadness; the expressions "In memory of the destruction," on the one hand, and "May the Temple speedily be rebuilt," on the other hand, are an integral part of every act or event, individual or communal, on joyous occasions as in times of trouble and mourning. The Ninth of Av, the day of the destruction of the Temple, has become [a day of] religious and national mourning, and every Jew, wherever he was, even if Jerusalem and the Temple were known to him only in his imagination, mourned the destruction of the Temple as if he himself had suffered a personal loss (p. 232).

The ruling contains a detailed survey of the building of the First and Second Temple, encompassing their plan, purpose, and description, the destruction of both Temples, and the laws and practices established since the destruction. Since the Second Temple was destroyed, the Temple Mount has passed from one conqueror to the next and each one has either built it or changed it according to his own agenda. The ruling describes the Mount under Romans, Byzantines, Muslims, Crusaders, Mamluks, Ottomans, the British and the Jordanians (pp. 230-244).

In consequence of and in light of this history and these events, the Temple Mount has been the most sacred site of the Jewish people, possessing unparalleled sanctity, for some three thousand years since Solomon built the First Temple on Mount Moriah (II Chronicles 3:1); and Mount Moriah had become holy for the people of Israel approximately a millennium earlier, ever since the Binding of Isaac by Abraham, the father of the Jewish people, [in] "the land of Moriah" (Genesis 22:2); "the Temple Mount is Mount Moriah... and our father Isaac was bound at [the site of] the Temple" (Maimonides, *op. cit.*, Laws of the Temple, 2:1-2; 5:1). This primal sanctity of the Temple Mount continues to the present day, even after the destruction of the First and Second Temples: "There is no Temple for future generations except in Jerusalem, and on Mount Moriah ... and it is said, 'This is my resting-place for all time' (Psalms 132:14)" (Maimonides, *op. cit.* 1:3). The western wall of the Temple which still remains, is the holiest site in Jewish tradition. For the members of the Islamic faith, the Temple Mount has been sacred for about 1,300 years, since the conquest of Jerusalem in 638 by the Muslims, who erected on it the Dome of the Rock and the Aqsa Mosque. For Muslims, the sanctity of the Temple Mount is less than that of al-Medina, which in turn is less than that of Mecca. The Christians also attribute religious importance to the Temple Mount.

Regarding the ties of the Jews to the Temple Mount after the destruction of the Second Temple, the ruling continues:

There is a great deal of evidence concerning prayers by Jews on the Temple Mount after the destruction of the Temple (on the portions of the Mount where Jewish law permits Jews to enter: see below). The halakhic sages as well as academic scholars have extensively discussed this matter (see: Prof. B. Z. Dinaburg [Dinur], "A House of Prayer and Study for Jews on the Temple Mount in the Period of the Arabs," *Me'asef Ziyyon,* Book Three [Jerusalem, 1929], pp. 54 ff. [Heb.]; Y. Y. Yahuda. "The Western Wall," idem., pp. 111 ff.; Rabbi S. Goren, *The Temple Mount* [Jerusalem, 1992], introduction: "At the Entrance to the Temple Mount" [no page numbers]; pp. 17-18; pp. 340 ff. [Heb.]; *Talmudic Encyclopedia,* "Temple Mount," pp. 575 ff.; the essays by Kimmelman, Koren, and Shilat mentioned below). We shall cite a number of examples.

In the first half of the fourth century, the pilgrim from

Bordeaux, who came to Jerusalem in the year 333, relates:

> And the Jews come to this place [the Temple Mount] once a year [on the Ninth of Av] and weep and lament by the one stone that has remained there from their Temple, and they anoint it with oil (see the essay by Yahuda, pp. 111-122).

The following description from the late eleventh – early twelfth centuries is provided by Rabbi Abraham ben R. Hiyya haNasi, in his book *Megillat haMegalleh* (ed. A. Posnaski and J. Guttman, [Mekize Nirdamim, Berlin, 1924], p. 99):

> At first, when the Romans had destroyed it, they did not prevent the Israelites from coming to it and praying in it; the Ishmaelite kings also were favorably disposed and permitted Jews to come to the Temple [Mount] and build there a prayer and study hall. Jews from all the diasporas near the Temple [Mount] would ascend to it on holidays and festivals, pray within it, and substitute their prayers for the daily and additional sacrifices. This practice continued during the entire Ishmaelite regime, until the wicked kingdom of Edom [the Crusaders] recently invaded the Temple Mount and displaced the Ishmaelites ... and they eliminated the daily offering, and prevented Israel from praying in the Temple [Mount] and from fulfilling the commandment of prayer in lieu of the daily offering; for from the time that those wicked ones attained power over the Temple [Mount], they did not permit Israel to enter it, and not even a single Jew is now to be found in Jerusalem.

In the twelfth century, in 1166, Maimonides described his visit to Jerusalem:

> And on the third day of the week, the fourth day of the month of Marheshvan, the [49]26th year of the Creation [= October 12, 1165], we departed from Acre to go up to Jerusalem, endangering ourselves in the process, and I entered the great and holy House [of the Lord] and I prayed in it on the fifth day [of the week], the sixth day of the month of Marheshvan (Rabbi Eleazar Azikri, *Sefer Haredim*, The Commandment of Repentance, chap. 3).

In his *Sefer ha-Massa'ot* [Book of Travels], Benjamin of Tudela, who came to Jerusalem in the twelfth century, describes the prayers of the Jews on the Temple Mount (for the text, see: Goren, *The Temple Mount*, introduction, pp. III, 18). Rabbi Menaham Meiri, one of the leading Talmudic commentators of the thirteenth century, states in regard to the Temple Mount: "There is a popular custom to enter there, as we have heard" (*Beit ha-Behirah*, Tractate Shevu'ot 16a, ed. Lange, p. 29).

There is additional evidence of the tolerant attitude of the Muslims toward Jewish prayer on the Temple Mount, as mentioned above by the statement of Rabbi Abraham ben R. Hiyya haNasi. The midrash Nistarot de-Rabbi Shimon ben Yohai [The Esoteric Teachings of Rabbi Simeon ben Yohai] states that

> the second king who arose to Ishmael was friendly to Israel, and he mended their breaches and the breaches of the Heikhal and dug up Mount Moriah ... and he built there a place for prayer [lit., a place for bowing down] on the Foundation Stone (A. Jellinek, *Beit Midrash*, 3, p. 79; for the date of the composition of this midrash, see Jellinek, p. xix).

The Tosafist Rabbi Petahiah of Regensburg (see: Dinur, p. 86; Yaari, *Journeys to Eretz Israel*, p. 53) is cited as saying:

> The [king of the] Ishmaelites built a fine chamber, and Jew-haters came and informed to the Ishmaelite king, telling him: "There is an old man among us who knows the location of the Heikhal and of the Temple Court," and the king pressed him until he showed him. This king was friendly to the Jews, and he said, "I wish to build a chamber there, and only the Jews shall pray there" (*Sivuv ha-Rav Petahiah mi-Regensburg* [The Tour of Rabbi Petahiah of Regensburg; Grünhut, 1905], pp. 32-33).[50]

After the Jordanian occupation in 1948, the Jewish inhabitants of the State of Israel were denied access to the Temple Mount and to the Western Wall...

In the Six Day War in June 1967, after the Kingdom of Jordan launched a military attack against the State of Israel and Jewish Jerusalem, the Temple Mount and the Western Wall were liberated from Jordanian control. In addition to the religious-cultural link between the Temple Mount and the people of Israel which had never been severed, Jewish political sovereignty over the Temple Mount, which had existed during a long period in the history of the Hebrew nation, beginning with the building of the First Temple by Solomon, ca. 3,000 years ago, was now restored. History had come full circle. While the Temple Mount was being liberated by the Israel Defense Forces, as the fighting was going on, IDF commanders gave orders not to harm the sites holy to other religions and to maintain a proper attitude towards them (see M. Gur, G. Rivlin, *The Temple Mount is in Our Hands* [Maarakhot], pp. 322-323; *The Jerusalem Covenant*, section 4 and bibliography). The Jewish fighters instinctively following the teaching of the Israelite prophet Micah: "Though all the peoples walk each in the names of its gods, we will walk in the name of the Lord our God forever and ever" (Micah 4:5). This legal, religious, and cultural stance was expressed on July 30, 1980 in Basic Law: Jerusalem, Capital of Israel, sections 1-3, as follows:

1. Jerusalem, complete and united, is the capital of Israel.
2. Jerusalem is the seat of the President of the State, the Knesset, the Government and the Supreme Court.

3. The holy places shall be protected from desecration and any other violation and from anything likely to violate the freedom of access of the members of the different religions to the places sacred to them or their feelings towards these places...

A few days after the liberation of the Temple Mount the government of Israel decided, for reasons of state, for security considerations, and in order to maintain public order, to order the paratroop company which had remained on the Temple Mount to evacuate their position; an observation post of the Border Guards was established there, and the site is under constant guard (Schiller, p. 40). The government also decided to allow Muslims to continue to maintain their presence and to pray on the Temple Mount. For these very reasons, and for other reasons which we shall discuss below, and in order to prevent friction with the Muslims, the government of Israel decided not to allow public prayer by Jews on the Temple Mount. From time to time petitions have been submitted to this court challenging the legality of prohibiting such prayer by Jews, but the court did not interfere with this decision of the Government of Israel (pp. 245-247).

The Court then discusses in great detail the arguments of the litigants concerning the works being implemented on the Temple Mount, in relation to the relevant laws – the Planning and Building Law and the Antiquities Law – and decides to conduct a tour of the site in order to gain first-hand knowledge of the nature of the arguments relating to the subject (pp. 247-259). To this end, the Court first discussed in detail the problem of entrance to the Temple Mount at present, as follows:

In order to understand clearly the nature and force of the arguments of the parties regarding the above-mentioned conduct on the Temple Mount, we decided to tour the site: the details of the tour will be set forth below. As previously stated, the government of Israel decided not to permit prayers by Jews on the Temple Mount. This decision was based, inter alia, (as will be seen below) on the halakhic prohibition against entering the Temple Mount. At the main entrance to the Temple Mount, above the Maghribi Gate, the Chief Rabbinate posted a sign with the following text:

According to Torah law, because of the sanctity of the Temple Mount, all persons are forbidden to enter the area (Schiller, p. 37).

Therefore, the first step in our analysis is to examine the relevant halakhot. According to the *Halakhah*, it is forbidden to enter the Temple, because its sanctity requires special purification as a condition for entry, and such a rite is not possible at present after the destruction of the Temple.

In *Halakhah* entry to the Temple Mount is the subject of many laws and disagreements (see *Talmudic Encyclopedia* "Temple," "Temple Mount"). This is not the place for a lengthy discussion, but we shall briefly examine a number of issues within this major topic that have been discussed in *Halakhah*, especially the disagreements pertaining to the scope of the prohibition against entry *at present* in various areas within the Temple Mount.

We have already discussed the special sanctity of the Temple Mount in *Halakhah*, in our review of Mishnah Kelim 1:6-8, which sets out the various degrees of sanctity of the Temple Mount as a whole and the special sites it contains, such as the Temple Courts, the area between the *Ulam* and the Altar, the *Heikhal*, and the Holy of Holies, which possesses the highest sanctity and which may be entered only by the High Priest on Yom Kippur. Even the individuals who were permitted to enter each of the above-mentioned places (after having purified themselves) could do so only to fulfill a religious obligation connected with the offering of the sacrifices or prayers, or for purposes of repair or construction (see, e.g., Maimonides, Laws of the Temple 7:23).

Maimonides and Rabad (Rabbi Abraham ben David, a contemporary of Maimonides and the author of a critique of Maimonides' *Mishneh Torah*) fundamentally disagree as to whether the sanctity of Jerusalem and of the Temple existed only while the Temple stood, or whether it exists for all time. Maimonides was of the opinion that this sanctity is for all time (Laws of the Temple 6:14), and explains:

Why do I say, regarding the Temple and Jerusalem, that its pristine sanctity continues for all time... Because the sanctity of the Temple and of Jerusalem is due to the Divine Presence, and the Divine Presence never loses its force" (idem, law 16).

According to this view, all the laws pertaining to the sanctity of the Temple remain in effect at present, and entry is strictly forbidden, because of the prerequisite of purification. Rabad, in contrast, maintains that the original sanctity of Jerusalem and the Temple does not remain in effect for all time (*Hagahot haRabad* on Laws of the Temple 6:14). Most halakhic authorities agree with Maimonides. According to some opinions, even Rabad does not permit entry to the Temple Mount at the present time, and his disagreement with Maimonides is limited merely to the nature and authoritative rank of the prohibition (see: Rabbi Abraham Isaac Hakohen Kook, *Mishpat Kohen* 96; for an extensive treatment of this topic, see: Rabbi Goren, *The Temple Mount*, chap.7 ff.).

This approach, which is unique to Judaism – that the more

sacred the place or matter, the greater the obligation to maintain one's distance from it and not to tread within its bounds – is not a reflection of a desire for distance, but rather an expression of affinity and esteem. Rabbi Kook, who dealt extensively with the subject of the Temple and the Temple Mount, wrote as follows:

Thus, the entire basis of reverence [for God] which is rooted in our heart is due to *distancing and not mentioning*. This teaches us that we cannot reach the sublime level necessary for mention of the holy Name. By our being careful regarding the holy place, since we are impure, we fulfill the obligation of veneration of the Temple, which is more precious than that veneration which comes from closeness for which we are not fit (Rabbi Kook, *Mishpat Kohen*, section 6).

Continuing this line of reasoning:

Our ownership and affiliation are manifest by our not touching this place. Our national genius is highlighted by our showing the entire world that there is a place which we do not enter ... the distance does not separate. On the contrary – it binds (Rabbi S. Aviner, *Shalhevetyah: Studies in the Holy and the Temple* [Jerusalem, 1980], p. 29).

Another question which has been discussed a great deal, especially recently, is that of permission to enter *certain areas* in the present Temple Mount plaza which were not part of the *original area* of the Mount. According to the Mishnah, "The Temple Mount was 500 cubits by 500 cubits" (Middot 2:1: a cubit was 48-60 cms.: see Ezekiel 42:20 and the Albeck edition of the Mishnah, Middot, Addenda, 2:1). The walled area of the Temple Mount at present is larger than the area specified in the Mishnah. The difference between the size of the Temple Mount as described in the Mishnah and its size in later periods is also indicated by the fact mentioned above, that for many generations following the destruction, Jews – including Maimonides himself (see above) – made pilgrimages to the Temple Mount and prayed there, despite the prohibition against entering the Temple Mount without the prescribed purification [although some interpret Maimonides to mean that he prayed in a building adjoining and overlooking the Temple Mount, but did not actually enter the Mount. See, e.g. *Responsa Yehaveh Da'at* by Chief Rabbi Ovadiah Yosef, second ed., 1:25 and n.). Contemporary halakhic literature extensively discusses what parts of the areas within the present-day Temple Mount correspond to the area of the Mishnaic Temple Mount, and what parts of the areas in the present-day Mount were not included in the Temple Mount of which the Mishnah speaks (see: Rabbi Y. M. Tykocinsky, *The Holy City and the Temple* 5, p. 80; Rabbi Z. Koren, *The Courtyards of the House of the Lord* [Jerusalem, 1977]; id,. "Proposed Prayer Areas on the Temple

Mount at the Present Time", *Tehumin* 3 [1984], p. 413, and esp. 417-422; Chief Rabbi M. Eliyahu, "An Opinion," *Tehumin* 3 [1984], p. 423; Rabbi Y. Shilat, "Building a Synagogue on the Temple Mount," *Tehumin* 7 [1986], p. 489, and esp. 497-511; Dr. A. Kimmelman, "The Boundaries of the Area of the Temple Mount and the Hel and Their Laws," *Hama'ayan* 8 [1986], pp. 3 ff.). This issue has recently been discussed at length by Rabbi Goren, in his above-cited book, which contains a detailed delineation of the areas within the present-day Temple Mount which clearly were not included in the original Mount (see chaps. 16-17, 27 ff.). These discussions particularly stress the importance of avoiding confrontations with the Muslims (see e.g. Shilat, *op. cit.*, p. 511). Some halakhic authorities oppose entry to any area of the Temple Mount, because of the difficulties in distinguishing precisely the area of the Temple from the area to which entry is permitted, and because of fear that granting such permission would lead to uncontrolled access to areas to which entry is forbidden, and that people would not strictly observe the conditions for entering the area...

We regarded our tour of the area as extremely important, in order to master the details of the issues under discussion and to understand fully the arguments of the parties. The Supreme Court, upon receipt of a petition relating to the Temple Mount, which is under the sovereignty of the State of Israel and subject to the jurisdiction of Israeli courts, is obligated to gain a proper understanding of the pertinent facts, which by their very nature require viewing as well as listening, so that the mind will understand how to deliberate and rule on the subject of the petition before us. In this manner we fulfilled the obligation of the judge who sits in judgment: "He can judge only what his eyes see, his ears hear, and his heart understands" (Meiri, *Beit haBehirah*, Ketubot 50b).

In order to observe the laws deriving from the sanctity of the Temple Mount and the Temple, I regarded myself, as an observant Jew, duty-bound to study the [works of the] *poskim* and their responsa, to ascertain the areas on the Temple Mount to which the prohibition against entry does not apply, i.e., the areas that are not included in the description of the Temple Mount appearing in Mishnah Kelim; and to understand what laws must be carefully observed when entering even the permitted areas. These laws are derived from the obligation of veneration of the Temple. Maimonides ruled:

It is a positive commandment to revere the Temple, as Scripture says, "and revere My sanctuary" (Leviticus 19:30). It is not the Temple that you must revere, rather the One who commanded its reverence (Laws of the Temple 7:1: see also:

Maimonides, *Sefer ha-Mitzvot* [The Book of the Commandments]. Positive Commandment 21).

Maimonides continued:

> Even though, due to our sins the Temple is destroyed, we are obligated to venerate it, as when it stood: who may enter only where entry is permitted, and may not sit in the Temple Court, or act frivolously ... as it is said, "You shall keep My Sabbaths and revere My sanctuary" (Leviticus, loc. cit.). Just as observance of the Sabbath is a commandment for all time, so too is veneration of the Temple, for even though it has been destroyed, its sanctity endures (Laws of the Temple 7:7, based on *Sifra, Kedoshim* 7:8, and T.B. Yevamot 6a).

The commandment to venerate the Temple applies always, at all times, even according to the opinion that its original sanctity applied only when it was standing (for recent interpretations, see Rabbi Kook, *op. cit.* and others).

The laws derived from [the commandment] to venerate the Temple are summarized by Maimonides as follows:

> And how is it to be venerated? One may not enter the Temple Mount with his staff, or while wearing shoes, or with his *afundah* [a garment not worn outdoors as outer wear – according to Maimonides' Commentary on the Mishnah, *loc. cit.*], or with dust on his feet, or with coins tied up in his cloak. Needless to say, it is prohibited to expectorate in the entire Temple Mount.... One may not make the Temple Mount a place which he enters by one entrance and leaves by the entrance opposite, as a shortcut; rather he must go around it on the outside. And one may enter it only for a religious purpose [*dvar mitzvah*] ... and anyone who enters the Temple Court must walk with measured pace, where one is permitted to enter ... with fear, reverence, and trembling, as it is said, "Sweet was our fellowship as we walked together in God's house" (Psalms 55:15) (Laws of the Temple 7:2, 5, based on *Sifra, loc. cit.* and T.B. Yevamot *loc. cit.*, Berakhot 54a).

Based on the above-cited sources, I examined for myself the sites in the area of the present-day Temple Mount which, according to all authorities (or at least according to the majority of those who have made rulings on this subject intended to be applied in practice), are not within the area of the Temple Mount specified in the above-mentioned mishnah, and therefore may be entered. I shall not detail here the exact location of these areas (as to which, see Kimmelman, "Boundaries," pp. 17-32; Rabbi Goren, *The Temple Mount*, chaps. 12, 27; id., the last two pages of the preface ["At the Entrance to the Temple Mount"]; id., introduction, pp. 23-24; Rabbi Koren, "The Temple Mount," pp. 413-423; Rabbi Shilat, "Building a Synagogue," pp. 489-512). I also

was guided by oral opinions of leading halakhists. When we ascended the Temple Mount through Maghribi Gate, we walked in the areas that are not part of the Mishnaic Temple Mount. We were especially careful not to walk in the area of the Temple Courts, the *Heikhal* and the Holy of Holies, entry to which is forbidden by Torah law, nor in the area of the *Hel*, entrance to which is prohibited by Rabbinical injunction (see: *Talmudic Encyclopedia*, vol. 15, "Ḥel," pp. 1 ff.). My fellow judges acted as I did during our tour.

Since our tour of the Temple Mount was part of the juridical responsibility of the Israeli Supreme Court, which is charged with preserving the rule of law in the State of Israel and the State's sovereignty, I regarded the entry to the Temple Mount as the performance of a religious duty and out of reverence for the Temple, I immersed myself in a ritual bath before ascending the Mount. I did not wear leather shoes as I usually do, nor did I take any money with me (see Rabbi Goren, *The Temple Mount*, end of the preface; introduction, p. xix: p. 373; Rabbi Koren, "The Temple Mount," p. 414; Rabbi Shilat, "Building a Synagogue," pp. 495, 511-512; Dr. Kimmelman, "Boundaries," pp. 13-17) (pp. 259-263).

Guided by these rules and directives, on June 16, 1991, the Court conducted its tour in the area of the Temple Mount. The visit is described in great detail in the ruling (pp. 263-268), and it guided the Court's deliberations on the factual and legal arguments of the litigants (pp. 268-280). Regarding the legal context, the Court said:

> As previously stated, and as the Attorney-General noted, "the area of the Temple Mount is part of the territory of the State of Israel" (section 1 of Appendix P/8 to the petition, quoted above in its entirety). Clear expression of this principle is to be found in the Basic Law: Jerusalem, Capital of Israel, section 1, which determines: *Jerusalem, complete and united, is the capital of Israel* [emphasis added – M. E.]. This has already been discussed in detail above...
>
> Obviously, it follows from the sovereignty of the State of Israel over united Jerusalem, and especially over the area of the Temple Mount, that all the laws of the State – including the Planning and Building Law and the Antiquities Law – are in effect in the area of the Temple Mount, and the right of every individual to freedom of religion, freedom of access to the holy places, and of protection against their desecration extends to the area of the Temple Mount. We have already discussed this above (sections 24, 35 of this opinion) in dealing with clause 3 of Basic Law: Jerusalem, Capital of Israel and with the Protection of Holy Places Law.
>
> It has also been ruled by this court that the power to give

practical effect of the right to worship resides in the executive authority, and not the judiciary, as has been established by the Palestine [Holy Places] Order in Council, 1924, sec. 2, as interpreted by H.C. 222/68, M.A. 15/69. It nevertheless should be emphasized that despite the absence of judicial review of the means by which the right of worship is made effective, this intrinsic right is eternal and inalienable. In the words of the late Supreme Court President Agranat:

> Needless to say... the right of the Jews to pray is their *natural right*, with deep roots in the long history of the Jewish people [emphasis added – M.E.] (idem, p. 221).

He continued (on p. 228):

> ...the right of the Jews to pray on the Temple Mount is *par excellence* the national and historical right of the Jewish people; they cherished it and longed to exercise it in every generation, and they exposed themselves to mortal danger to attain their desires regarding it; there were even those who boldly overcame the decrees [of hostile governments] and came to pray on the Temple Mount and established a house of prayer there... (p. 280-282).

As regards the essence of the petition, which was directed against the Attorney General, the mayor of Jerusalem, and the director of the Israel Antiquities Authority, who decided not to put the Waqf on trial for the activities which it conducted on the Temple Mount, the Court concluded not to intervene, on this occasion, in the decision of these authorities. The Court says as follows:

> We were faced with a difficult decision. On the one hand, the Petitioners correctly indicated – and we gained this same impression from our tour of the site – the many continuing violations *prima facie* committed by the Muslim Waqf in the Temple Mount region. On the other hand, Respondents argued that the nature of the construction does not justify prosecuting the Waqf or restoring the *status quo ante*, in view of the length of the time that has passed, the special political and religious sensitivity of the Temple Mount, and the need to maintain public security.
>
> It is difficult for us not to feel that Respondents did indeed, to a degree more than was proper, ignore the violations of the law by the Waqf. Nevertheless, but not without reservations, we have decided not to intervene, this time, with the Respondents' exercise of discretion (p. 283).

The Court included the following among other reasons for its non-intervention:

> The nature of the works done and the time which has elapsed since a substantial portion of the work was completed. As Respondents argued, and as we had occasion to learn during the course of our tour, much time has passed since the dirt cover was laid, paths were paved, and the prayer platforms were constructed; and as to some of the work, it is doubtful if a building permit was required. In any event, it is agreed that these works did not cause irreversible damage to antiquities. As to the construction and restoration work, these indisputably contributed to the preservation of the antiquities, thus supporting our conclusion not to interfere with the decisions of the Respondents, and, specifically with regard to construction already completed, not to require restoration of the *status quo ante*...
>
> The main reason why we concluded not to reverse the decision of the Respondents is their commitment to thoroughly and rigorously supervise activities on the Temple Mount, and to ensure that the law is observed and the value of all the antiquities on the site is not impaired...
>
> In contrast to the situation in the past (as was the case, e.g., at the time of the deliberations in H.C. 193/86) the Respondents maintain now, and will maintain from now on, meaningful supervision on the Temple Mount, and keep close watch to ensure that the law be enforced and observed. Respondents have stated their belief, and we assume that this supervision will ensure that from now on the letter and spirit of the law will be observed and enforced by all Respondents. We fully trust that this supervision will be a meaningful and "alert supervision," and not merely going through the motions.
>
> Accordingly, we add that the Respondents, in addition to the rigorous supervision in the future to uphold the law, must do everything in their power to preserve the antiquities in the Temple Mount, particularly in the situation that has now come to exist. Thus it would be desirable, e.g., for the Respondents to fence off and suitably mark the antiquities of the Temple Mount that have been covered (and certainly those which have not been covered) with earth, paths, or plantings. Respondents, and especially the Antiquities Authority, must undertake to ensure that no ancient or archaeological relic will be damaged or defaced, and take all steps necessary to preserve and maintain every such relic (pp. 285-287).

The Supreme Court concluded its ruling as follows:

> *Summary and Conclusion:* "The sanctity of the Temple Mount for the people of Israel, and all this implies, is not subject to question. Its holiness is eternal and is not dependent upon the government; the status of the sanctity of the Temple Mount is beyond any challenge, legal or otherwise" (H.C. 222/68, M.A. 15/69, at 219). The Temple Mount has been holy to the Jewish people for some 3,000 years since the construction of the First Temple, and for approximately 1,000 years prior to that, from the Binding of Isaac on Mount Moriah. Due to the centrality of the Temple Mount in

the spiritual, social, and political history of the Jewish people, entire historical eras have been named after it: the "First Temple period" (from the tenth to the fifth centuries BCE) and the "Second Temple period" (from the Return to Zion in the fifth century BCE to 70 CE). Even after the Temple was destroyed, it continued to occupy a central position in the religious and spiritual life of the Jewish people. The western rampart of the Temple Mount, the Western Wall, is the most sacred site in Jewish tradition. To members of the Islamic faith, the Temple Mount has been holy for approximately 1,300 years, and it is of lesser importance than Mecca and Medina; the members of the Christian religion also attribute religious importance to the Temple Mount. The legislation of the State of Israel and the rulings of this Court establish that Jerusalem, entire and united, is the capital of Israel, the area of the Temple Mount is part of the area of the State of Israel, and the law, jurisdiction, and administration of the State of Israel apply to it. These include, *inter alia*, the provisions of the Planning and Building Law and the Antiquities Law, and encompass the right of every member of the different religions to freedom of worship, freedom of access to the holy places, and protection against their desecration (Basic Law: Jerusalem, Capital of Israel). Respondents 1 to 5 determined not to prosecute Respondent 6, the Muslim Waqf, for its *prima facie* violations of the Planning and Building Law and the Antiquities Law in the Temple Mount area, and not to compel restoration of the *status quo ante*, for the reasons they have stated. We ourselves toured the Temple Mount, in the areas to which entry is permitted by Jewish law, we heard the arguments of the litigants who appeared before us, and we studied the material which was presented to us. We found it difficult to avoid the impression that Respondents 1 through 5 shut their eyes to these violations of the law more than they should have. We have decided, however, not without hesitation, that we shall not intervene on this occasion in the considerations of the Respondents, for the reasons which we have stated concerning what took place, and because of the conditions and provisions which we have prescribed for meaningful and strict supervision from now on, and for taking suitable measures to mark and preserve every ancient or archaeological relic. (p. 288).

The Supreme Court weighed a long series of rulings supporting the right of Jews, in theory and practice, to pray on the Temple Mount. As stated in the ruling cited above, the Chief Rabbinate decided, soon after the Six Day War, to prohibit entry to the entire Temple Mount, including those portions of the Mount to which entry is permitted in the opinion of many halakhic authorities.

The Government similarly forbade the conducting of prayer by Jews, even by individuals, in the entire area of the Temple Mount, in order to maintain public safety. The Supreme Court decided not to intervene in these considerations of the executive authority, for various reasons which shall not be listed here.[51] The Supreme Court has recently delivered a landmark ruling regarding the arrangements for prayer at the Western Wall,[52] which discusses the status of the Wall in Jewish law and thought, but this lies outside the purview of the present work.

Conclusion

"The Lord rebuilds Jerusalem; He gathers in the exiles of Israel" (Psalms 147:2). The Sages commented on this verse: "When will the Lord rebuild Jerusalem? When He gathers in the exiles of Israel" (Babylonian Talmud, Berakhot 49a). The Sages further stated, "Jerusalem will expand and grow on all sides, and the diasporas will come and are at rest in it, to fulfill what is said, 'For you shall spread out to the right and the left .... and shall people the desolate towns' (Isaiah 54:3)." Rashi, the premier commentator, adds: "The 'salvation of Israel' – this is the rebuilding of Jerusalem" (Berakhot, *loc. cit.*).

The rebuilding of Jerusalem, in all directions, including its suburbs and environs, is the salvation of Israel. Rebuilt Jerusalem, the city knit together, into which the exiles of Israel are gathered, is the salvation of the State of Israel. This was stated, written, and sworn by the heads of the State of Israel and its Defense Forces, the leaders of the people and their communities, during the signing of the Jerusalem Covenant on Jerusalem Reunification Day, Iyyar 28, 5752 (May 31, 1992), in the President's Residence, on the twenty-fifth anniversary of the defensive war waged by the Israel Defense Forces, namely, the Six Day War, in which the Temple Mount and Jerusalem were liberated:

> We shall bind you to us forever; we shall bind you to us with faithfulness, with righteousness and justice, with steadfast love and compassion. We love you, O Jerusalem, with eternal love, with unbounded love, under siege and when liberated from the yoke of oppressors. We have been martyred for you; we have yearned for you, we have clung to you. Our faithfulness to you we shall bequeath to our children after us. Forevermore, our home shall be within you.[53]

Notes

1 This Psalm served as the basis for the fundamental ideas expressed in the Jerusalem Covenant which was signed on Jerusalem Reunification Day, Iyyar 28, 5752 (May 31, 1992). See below, the end of the epilogue; and the text of the Covenant (above, pp. 302-303).

2 See the commentaries of Ibn Ezra and Rabbi David Kimhi (Radak) on Psalm 122.

3 See: Flavius Josephus, *The Wars of the Jews*, Book V, Chapter IV, London 1872, pp. 714-716.

4 See above, n. 1.

5 *Nistarot R[abbi] Shimon bar-Yohai* (ed. Jellenik, *Bet Midrash*, 3, p. 74).

6 *Otiyot de-Rabbi Akiva* (ed. Wertheimer, *Battei Midrashot* 2, p. 372).

7 *Yalkut Shimoni*, Psalms, sec. 836. Cf. *Midrash Shohar Tov* 87:4 (ed. Buber, 189b). When the Temple and Jerusalem were destroyed, the gates became the subject of mourning and lamentation. Rabbi Judah Halevi says in his poem-lament: "Zion, shall you not inquire about the peace of your prisoners Zion, perfect in beauty from the pit of enslavement they long for you and bow down opposite your gates."

8 See the commentary of Rabbeinu Hananel on Hagiggah loc. cit.

9 The version in the Jerusalem Talmud, Hagiggah, may possibly indicate that on the pilgrimage festivals each individual in Jerusalem had the status of *haver*, i.e., someone who was particular in matters of ritual purity and *terumah* [the heave-offerings], as opposed to the *am ha-aretz* [lit., the common person]. The term *haver* had diverse meanings in different periods. In the Talmudic period, it also meant one who observed the laws of ritual purity; in the Middle Ages in Ashkenaz (the Franco-German center), it implied a Torah scholar. See: M. Elon, *Jewish Law: History, Sources, Principles* (Philadelphia 1994), pp. 96, 725. In all periods, however, its primary meaning was "friend," based on Hillel's interpretation of the verse in the Torah, "'Love your neighbor [lit., friend] as yourself' (Leviticus 19:18): What is hateful to you, do not do to your *haver*," the same applies in the case under discussion. From all the other sources, the simple meaning is derived from *haverut*, friendship, in the sense of unity and being together.

10 Babylonian Talmud, Yoma 12a; Megillah 26a; Sotah 45b, etc.

11 Yoma and Megillah, loc. cit.

12 Rashi on Megillah, loc. cit.

13 Yoma and Megillah, loc. cit.

14 Sotah, loc. cit.

15 Babylonian Talmud, Bava Kamma 82b.

16 Bava Kamma, loc. cit.; Arkhin 32b. A house in a walled city irrevocably becomes the possession of the purchaser if the seller did not redeem the house within a year of its sale; the law of land redemption does not apply to it, and the Jubilee year does not cause it to return to its original owner. This law does not apply to the houses of Jerusalem, because "Jerusalem was not divided among the tribes, and who can impart to him [the purchaser, absolute rights to the house]" (Rashi, Arkhin, loc. cit.; see also Rashi, Bava Kamma, loc. cit.).

17 Bava Kamma and Arkhin, loc. cit.

18 Maimonides, *Mishneh Torah*, Laws of the Temple 7:14; Laws of the Uncleanness of Leprosy 14:11; Laws of Murder and the Preservation of Life 9:4; Maimonides explains the reasons for the laws. See: S. Bialoblocki, "Jerusalem in Halakhah," in *Alei Ayin: The Salman Schocken Jubilee Volume* (Jerusalem: 1952), pp. 27-42 [Heb.].

19 *Avot de-Rabbi Natan*, version A, 35 (ed. Schechter, 52b). Bialoblocki conjectures that the law that houses are not rented out in Jerusalem may have its source in the following practice: "The nobility of Jerusalem would open their homes to the pilgrims and did not take rent for this. This commendable custom, which was first practiced by individuals, later became a communal activity. Eventually, all the inhabitants of Jerusalem adopted this form of hospitality. When this practice had been followed for some time, it was established as the law. When a reason for this was sought in the halakhah, it was found that there is no absolute possession [of real estate] in Jerusalem, and individuals do not acquire in it on behalf of the tribes" (Bialoblocki, p. 42). Proof for his hypothesis is provided by the disagreement on the question of the apportionment of Jerusalem to the tribes, but the laws based on this principle are not the subject of a disagreement. It is possible that additional laws applying solely to Jerusalem developed in this or a similar manner.

20 As Rashi explains: "Until there is the holy in your midst below, i.e., Jerusalem, I will not come to the heavenly city until the earthly Jerusalem will be built up, a city knit together: that it shall be, [as] its joining and pattern, in accord with the established fact that there is another Jerusalem, and where is it, if not above?" See also: Rabbeinu Hananel, loc. cit.: "The Holy One, blessed be He, said to Israel that He will not come to the heavenly Jerusalem until they build the earthly Jerusalem and the holy Divine Presence will dwell among them." The Aramaic translation of Psalms 122:3 speaks in a similar vein: "Jerusalem which is built in heaven is the city which is knit together as the one on earth." This idea was further expanded in the *Zohar*: "Come and see, all of Eretz Israel is folded under Jerusalem, and it exists both above and below, in the same manner" (*Zohar, Hayyei Sarah*).

21 See *Tanhuma, Pekudei* 1. Regarding this midrash, see also: E. E. Urbach, "Heavenly and Earthly Jerusalem," in *Jerusalem through the Ages*, ed. J. Aviram (Jerusalem: 1969), pp. 156 ff. [Heb.].

22 *Pesikta Rabbati* 31 (ed. Ish Shalom, 144b-145a).

23 The inhabitants of Jerusalem engaged in special practices in many realms: education (Babylonian Talmud, Bava Batra 21a); marriage matches and wedding presents (Babylonian Talmud, Taanit 26b; Ketubot 66b; Lamentations Rabbah 4:2 [ed. Buber, 71a]); hospitality (Babylonian Talmud, Bava Batra 93b); commerce (Babylonian Talmud, Ketubot 94b); the return of lost articles (Babylonian Talmud, Bava Metzia 28b; Taanit 19a); and other matters (Babylonian Talmud, Sanhedrin 23a; some individuals were given honorific appellations, such as: "the precious ones of Jerusalem," "the pure-minded of Jerusalem," but this lies beyond the purview of this work). Special attention was paid to the cleanliness of Jerusalem: "The marketplaces of Jerusalem are to be cleaned every day," a rule which was of halakhic significance in various realms (Pesahim 7a).

24 See: Jeremiah 41:4-9 and the commentators, loc. cit. See also: S. Safrai, The Pilgrimages to Jerusalem after the Destruction of the Second Temple," *Jerusalem: From the Second Temple Period to the Present* (Jerusalem: 1981), pp. 11 ff. [Heb.].

25 See also below, in the section "Jerusalem in the Responsa Literature," the statement by the Tashbez which indicates that large numbers of pilgrims regularly came to the city.

26 See: Y. M. Tykocinsky, *The Holy City and the Temple*, vol. 4 (Jerusalem: 1970), chap. 15 [Heb.].

27 See the detailed description in the booklet "As a Reminder of the Commandment of *Hakhel*" [Heb.], pub. by the *Hakhel* Committee, 1952.

28 Rabbi Hayyim Joseph Azulai (Hida), *Avodat ha-Kodesh*.

29 *Shulhan Arukh*, *Orah Hayyim* 560:1, based on Babylonian Talmud, Bava Batra 60b.

30 *Mishnah Berurah*, loc. cit.

31 *Shulhan Arukh*, *Orah Hayyim* 560:2; Bava Batra 60b.

32 Babylonian Talmud, Ketubot 8a, based on Jeremiah 7:34.

33 *Yalkut ha-Makiri*; see: Septuagint on Psalms 87:5: "Indeed, it shall be said of Zion, 'Every man was born there'" –instead of "Zion," "the mother of Zion."

34 Cf.: "and that through her I too may have children [lit., that I may be built]" (Genesis 30:3).

35 With a textual change, see: Micah 4:1. See also: Isaiah 2:3-4; 56:7; Micah 4:2.

36 It was with this prophecy by Micah that Shneur Zalman Shazar, the third President of Israel, greeted Pope Paul III during his visit to Jerusalem on January 4, 1964; see Dr. Meir Mendes, *The Vatican and Israel* (Jerusalem: 1983), pp. 60-61 [Heb.]. See also below in the Supreme Court ruling regarding the Temple Mount, the text of section 3 of the Basic Law: Jerusalem, Capital of Israel.

37 Many responsa deal with those who immigrated to Eretz Israel and the laws relating to this immigration. See, e.g.: *She'elot u-Teshuvot ha-Ri Migash* [The responsa of Rabbi Joseph Migash] (eleventh century, Spain), in *Digest of the Responsa Literature of Spain and North Africa*, ed. M. Elon, vol. 1 (Jerusalem: 1981), p. 12 [Heb.]; *She'elot u-Teshuvot ha-Rambam* [The responsa of Maimonides], ibid., p. 61; *She'elot u-Teshuvot Rabbi Avraham ben ha-Rambam* [The responsa of Rabbi Abraham son of Maimonides], ibid.;*She'elot u-Teshuvot ha-Ran* [The responsa of Rabbeinu Nissim ben Reuben Gerondi] (fourteenth century, Spain), ibid., p. 173; *She'elot u-Teshuvot ha-Rashba* [The responsa of Rabbi Solomon ben Abraham Adret] (thirteenth century, Spain), *ibid.*, vol. 2, pp. 96-97. That is only to mention a few responsa dealing with Jerusalem.

38 R. Moses b. Maimon, *Responsa*, ed. Joshua Blau, vol. 1 (Jerusalem: 1958), p. 200, sec. 116 [Heb.].

39 *She'elot u-Teshuvot ha-Rashba* [Responsa of Rabbi Solomon ben Abraham Adret] 7, sec. 428.

40 For a detailed discussion of this regulation, see: Elon (n. 9, above), pp. 649-651 and loc. cit. the formulation of the Geonim "that you do not have a single individual in Israel who does not possess four cubits in Eretz Israel."

41 *She'elot u-Teshuvot ha-Rosh* [Responsa of Rabbi Asher ben Jehiel] 8:13.

42 *She'elot u-Teshuvot Tashbez* [Responsa of Rabbi Simeon ben Zemah Duran] 3:198-203.

43 Idem, 3:201. For the sanctity of Jerusalem at the present time, see also a court ruling concerning the Temple Mount, sections of which are cited below; and the discussion above.

44 *She'elot u-Teshuvot ha-Radbaz* [Responsa of Rabbi David ben Solomon ibn Zimra] 1:691. See also the court ruling regarding the Temple Mount.

45 *She'elot u-Teshuvot Maharit* [Responsa of Rabbi Joseph ben Moses Trani] 2:37.

46 *She'elot u-Teshuvot Hatam Sofer* [Responsa of Hatam Sofer (Moses Sofer)], *Yoreh Deah* 233.

47 Idem, 234.

48 Obviously, the larger the Jewish settlement in Eretz Israel, the more responsa which were issued regarding the laws and practices in force in Jerusalem. See, e.g.: *She'elot u-Teshuvot Mishnato shel R. Akiva* [Responsa from the Teachings of Rabbi Akiva] by Rabbi Akiva Joseph Schlesinger (nineteenth century; shortly after he wrote these responsa, he immigrated from Hungary to Eretz Israel), 10, 17; Rabbi Isaac Abraham Hakohen Kook (the first Chief Rabbi of Eretz Israel), *Iggerot ha-Re'ayah*, 1:39; Rabbi Eliezer Waldenberg, *She'elot u-Teshuvot Ziz Eliezer* 13:22, 52; the Hasidic leader Rabbi Abraham of Sochaczow, *She'elot u-Teshuvot Avnei Nezer, Yoreh Deah* 2:450; Rabbi Ovadiah Yosef, *She'elot u-Teshuvot Yehaveh Da'at* 1:25; 5, Yoreh Deah, 26. On the question of the offering of sacrifices, see those in favor: Rabbi Zevi Hirsch Kalischer, *Derishat Zion*, sec. 3; She'elot u-Teshuvot Hatam Sofer, *Yoreh Deah* 236; Rabbi Zevi Hirsch Hayyot, *She'elot u-Teshuvot Maharatz Hayyot* 2:76. For those opposing the reinstitution of sacrifices, see: Rabbi Akiva Eiger (cited in *Derishat Zion*); Rabbi Jacob Ettlinger, *She'elot u-Teshuvot Binyan Zion* 1; Rabbi David Freidmann, *She'elot u-Teshuvot She'eilat David, Kuntres Derishat Zion ve-Yerushalayim*; Rabbi Isaac Abraham Hakohen Kook, cited in Rabbi Hayyim Hirschensohn, *Malki Bakodesh* 4, fol. 3; *She'elot u-Teshuvot Ziz Eliezer* 10:7.

49 High Court of Justice 4185/90, 47(5), pp. 221-288. The ruling was written by the Deputy President Menachem Elon, with Justices Aharon Barak and Gavriel Bach concurring.

50 Also see the responsum of Radbaz cited above.

51 A study of these rulings lies outside the purview of this essay. Mention should be made of one of the major, and initial, relevant rulings: High Court of Justice 222/68, National Circles, registered society, and others vs. the Minister of Police, 24(2), p. 141.

52 High Court of Justice 257/89 and High Court of Justice 2410/90, Anat Hoffman and others and Susan Alter and others vs. the Supervisor of the Western Wall, the Minister of Police and others, 48(2), p. 265.

53 The seventh and last paragraph of the Jerusalem Covenant. The covenant was composed by Menachem Elon, Deputy President of the Israel Supreme Court. On the twenty-sixth anniversary of the Six Day War, all the senior officers who had participated in the war added their signatures to the Covenant. On this day a gathering of high-ranking IDF officers was held at Ammunition Hill in Jerusalem, the site of the decisive battle in the Six Day War, which removed the threat of an offensive by the Jordanian army and liberated the Old City of Jerusalem. The signed Covenant is on display in the museum at the official memorial site on Ammunition Hill.

Index

Photo Credits